St Petersburg and the British

St Petersburg
and the
British

The City through the Eyes
of British Visitors and Residents

Anthony Cross

FRANCES LINCOLN LIMITED
PUBLISHERS

For Serena, Mark and Freddie Misha

Frances Lincoln Ltd
4 Torriano Mews
Torriano Avenue
London NW5 2RZ
www.franceslincoln.com
St Petersburg and the British
Copyright © Frances Lincoln 2008
Text copyright © Anthony Cross 2008

First Frances Lincoln edition: 2008

A catalogue record for this book is available from
the British Library.

ISBN 13: 978-0-7112-2864-1

Printed and bound in Singapore

9 8 7 6 5 4 3 2 1

CONTENTS

INTRODUCTION

It was in mid-December 1959 that I first visited St Petersburg, then nearing the end of its fourth decade under the guise of Leningrad. I was at that time in my final undergraduate year at Cambridge and was fortunate to be selected to join one of the first student groups to visit the Soviet Union during the Thaw. After two weeks in Moscow, we had gone on to Leningrad. It was dark and very, very cold – my memories of all my winter visits during the 1960s and 1970s are of intense cold and thick ice on the Neva. I still have my diaries of that first visit, together with other ephemera, including theatre programmes, one with the autograph of the great Russian actor Innokentii Smoktunovskii, whom I saw in his role as Prince Myshkin in Tovtsonogov's stage version of Dostoevskii's *The Idiot* and was privileged to meet after the performance. Nearly fifty years on, I have read what I wrote about Leningrad, the city and its people. There is little that is worth quoting, but I see that I was immediately much more taken with its 'stern, harmonious appearance' than I had been with what I felt was Moscow's chaos and menace. A graduate year at Moscow University subsequently brought a different perception of Moscow, but my initial love for St Petersburg has never wavered. I have now visited the city on some forty occasions and I return each time with keen anticipation to see what is familiar and discover yet more of its delights. It is the city where the majority of my Russian friends live; it is a city where I have worked in many of its archives and libraries; it is a city which has formed the background to much that I have written over the years, but about which I wished to write in a way that reflected both its history and the particular angle from which it was perceived by the British over the first three centuries of its existence.

The British links with the city go back to the very year of its foundation and have continued unbroken to the present, except for the relatively few years from the late 1930s to the end of the Second World War, when Leningrad was closed to foreigners – by Stalin's diktat or German encirclement. Towards the end of Peter I's reign St Petersburg became home to merchants of the Russia Company, who formed the core of a steadily growing British community or colony that enjoyed its halcyon days in the reigns of Catherine the Great and Alexander I but remained numerically significant, if less conspicuously influential, until the October Revolution. In addition to the merchants and their families and their employees, factory owners, shopkeepers, naval officers attached to the Baltic fleet, physicians, craftsmen and tradesmen of all kinds, grooms and ostlers, tutors and governesses, gardeners and artists all figured prominently, as did diplomats and the English chaplain.

From the middle of the eighteenth century there were more and more visitors from Britain, firstly the Grand Tourists, adding an exotic variant to the customary southern-European routes, then, a century later, more of the simple tourists in the Thomas Cook mould. Many came to St Petersburg and went no further; others combined a visit to the capital with one to Moscow; others were more adventurous and St Petersburg formed but part, and sometimes a small part, of their itinerary. The last inevitably had the opportunity to form sounder opinions about Russia, but for many visitors St Petersburg was Russia and even then, for all its Western pretensions and surface, a strange and bewildering place that attracted and repulsed in equal measure.

From both former residents and visitors there came in increasing volume written accounts and impressions, some of which soon appeared in print, others only much later, while yet others, in the form of letters and diaries, remained known only to families and friends. Newspapers and journals carried reports of events in Russia and in its capital in particular and printed specially commissioned articles as well as excerpts from books. There were in addition many translations from accounts of other European travellers in book form and in journals. St Petersburg was given space in books of general history and geography and in encyclopedias; guidebooks to the city were published in English from the early nineteenth century. All are indicative of a sustained interest on the part of the British public in St Petersburg and in things Russian, if not of any degree of sophisticated knowledge.

The writers themselves varied greatly not only in their backgrounds but also in their ability to write, to record with any degree of freshness and vividness what they saw and experienced. As travel writers do, openly or covertly, many used and abused the works of their predecessors. Some, including of course the few who were termed 'armchair travellers', plagiarized quite shamelessly. There were others who, when faced with the task or tedium of recording the pictures in the Hermitage or the dimensions and locations of famous buildings, were content to refer their readers to already available accounts. For example, the Rev. William Coxe, whose weighty volumes of travels first appeared in 1784 and were many times reprinted, became the Baedeker of his day, the authority for all things Russian for his contemporaries and for a succeeding generation. Some author-travellers, however, literally abused their predecessors for their inaccuracies and myth-making, thus hoping to enhance their own reputations for telling things 'as they are'. For example, Dr Edward Morton's *Travels in Russia* (1830) pointedly subtitled 'intended to give some account of Russia as it is, and not as it is represented to be', had Dr A.B. Granville's massive two-volumed *St Petersburgh* (1828) squarely in its sights.

While the abundance of English writing on St Petersburg over three centuries is undoubted, its quality is not unexpectedly uneven and its value a matter of debate. A Scottish gardener, employed by the great Catherine to lay out an English landscape park at Peterhof in the 1780s, amusingly pointed out to his friend in England that 'As I know you have conversed with several Persons from this Country let me divide them into two Classes ie those who came to England & returned & others who came from here with the intention not to come back again. I must suppose their different accounts of Russia the Court &c &c are very curious. The former Class representing the Country little inferior to the Garden of Eden & the others execrating and making it as bad as the Regions under the North Pole. Please to draw the Line between their opposite accounts & you'll be about the Mark.' Some decades later, Leitch Ritchie, an author of one of the first 'guidebooks' in Heath's Picturesque Annual series, professing that he had considered 'the advantage of the public by making his book a work entirely of information, allowing whatever amusement it might contain to depend upon the nature of the facts communicated', later quoted the alleged observation of a Russian acquaintance that 'you English should travel in Russia for the avowed purpose of making yourself acquainted with the manners and character of the people, yet without comprehending a single word of their language. You come here with the greatest prejudices against us as a nation. You see everything different from what you have been accustomed to at home, except the manners of some dozen families whom you visit. You make no inquiries, no reflections, no allowances.' It was a cap that fitted many, perhaps the majority, of 'tourists', but the dismissive tone was typical of a nineteenth-century (and not only nineteenth-century) Russia, acutely sensitive to foreign criticism. The great nineteenth-century Russian historian Vasilii Kliuchevskii was ready to acknowledge the (limited) value of pre-Petrine and therefore pre-Petersburg foreign writing about Russia, given the absence of native Russian accounts, but was wholly dismissive of 'Russica' of what might be termed the early modern period, finding them shallow, repetitive, at best curious. In contrast, however, the leading contemporary historian of St Petersburg, Iurii Bespiatykh, a connoisseur and translator of foreign writings on the capital, suggests that 'there are few extant sources for the early history of Petersburg that so persistently attract the grateful attention of the reader as contemporary descriptions of Peter's reign and of those immediately following'. In the past few years he has presented his public with translations, in part but mainly in full, of foreign sources on eighteenth-century St Petersburg, among which British accounts are particularly prominent.

The Moscow art historian Viacheslav Shestakov recently made a valiant attempt to catch and define in the English character and English culture what he called "the English accent" (also the name of the book – *Angliiskii aktsent* (2000)), suggesting that 'in spoken English there is a particular 'English accent' by which an Englishman can be unfailingly distinguished from a representative of any other Anglophone nation, including the Americans. [. . .] The same accent is found also in English culture and gives to English art, literature, aesthetic traditions their original and unique character.' Even when we remember that the Russians have traditionally used 'England' and 'the English' as all-embracing terms and even Scots in Russia have had to go along with them (a petition from Scottish workmen to the Empress Catherine at the end of the eighteenth century began: 'We Englishmen of the Scottish Nation'), there is much here that is arbitrary and reductive. Nevertheless, it is interesting in the present context to speculate whether there exists an 'English accent' in writing on Russia? Bearing in mind such factors such as the historical moment, class, education, religion, profession, aim of journey, and what Kliuchevskii has called the 'arbitrary nature of a writer's subjective judgments', is it still possible to distinguish it from a more general foreign or European accent?

It is simpler, and perhaps more accurate, particularly in writings on Russia during the eighteenth century, to say that there is a general European language but that occasionally, and then in usually predictable contexts, an English or British accent may be detected. The European traveller or visitor generally arrived in Russia with his baggage full of prejudices and stereotypes, nurtured by earlier accounts of Muscovy, but also convinced by the imagery of the Enlightenment that the European sun was gradually unfreezing the North. Inevitably, it was the figure of Peter the Great and his creation St Petersburg that attracted his attention and provided evidence of Russia's transition from darkness to light. Even in the capital the traveller nevertheless always viewed from above, like a master at an apprentice, and although he might award six or seven points out of ten for progress and a good attempt, his sense of superiority was never shaken. In this respect, one might well see the accent: visitors, never tired of stating how glad they were to have been born British and revealing their learning by saying it in Latin – *o fortunatos nimium, sua si bona norint, Britannos*!

On the other hand, British travellers were no different from other travellers to Russia in seeking frequently to compare what they saw in St Petersburg with similar phenomena, events, buildings back home, thereby assisting their public, reading a private letter or a book, to visualize what was being described. Thus, for instance, William Coxe (and not only he) compares the Neva with the Thames as it flows through London; Sir Nathaniel Wraxall makes the interesting comparison of the architecture of the Winter Palace with the style of Sir John Vanburgh (the architect of Blenheim); while Ker Porter calls Nevskii Prospekt 'the Bond-street of St Petersburgh'; the young merchant James Brogden in a letter to his father praises the Peterhof Road and says the lamps are more frequent than on the Clapham Road in London; James Meader, the imperial gardener at Peterhof, writes disdainfully of Petersburg *traktiry* ('Tracters', as he calls them) as 'low stinking public houses worse than the worst in St Giles', but praises the magnificent houses of the nobility as 'superior to the houses of the

Great in Westminster, several more statly [*sic*] than Lord Shelburne's in Berkley Square'.

Much that they saw, of course, had no equivalent in England and the travellers strive to emphasize the strangeness of what was presented to their eyes. For many the Orthodox church was something they made little attempt to understand and they were happy to pour scorn on Russian veneration of icons which they continued to see as artless daubs. Many social customs were condemned out of a similar lack of comprehension. Inevitably, writers defied their readers to imagine the sinful behaviour in the *bania,* the bathhouse, as they watched in fascinated horror and with bated breath and described in great detail, until at least as late as 1820s. One tourist warned of the dangers of 'the violent use of the hot and cold baths' which made men and women old before their time and 'neither the one nor the other have that firmness of flesh, that florid colour, that belongs to the lower ranks of the English'. In other areas, forms of transport within the city were of perennial interest: the ferocious *izvozchik,* coachman, madly driving madly his *drozhki,* inevitably became a 'Petersburg city type', but interestingly in this case, an 'English accent' is not absent, in the sense that British travellers, one after the other, note the Russian aversion to *walking:* the British demonstratively walk here, there, and everywhere, commenting on the bad pavements and roads and on the Russians' reluctance to use their legs. Brogden suggested that 'the English are not afraid to use their legs if they think it will contribute to their health, & boldly make use of them even in spite of a little dirt [. . .] but you scarcely ever see a young Russian but he is lolling in his carriage'. Most of the examples which have been given are from eighteenth- and early nineteenth-century sources, but were often part of a continuum, a perpetuation of stereotypes and stereoscenes from even earlier centuries. And they often survived into the twentieth. The preference for inactivity, for instance, became a truism, repeated by countless British observers, and seemingly only challenged by the beneficient influence of English practice. A correspondent of *The Times* drew attention in 1910 to the 'great growth of interest in gymnastics and outdoor sport': 'St Petersburg has been inoculated with this interest chiefly by Englishmen and Swedes, and only persons intimately acquainted with Russian life can understand what it spells in the way of change of habits among the younger generation in such enervating conditions as those prevailing on St Petersburg' for 'the St Petersburg Russian has generally been averse to unnecessary exertion of any kind'.

It is not, of course, to Russian readers that this book is primarily addressed, although I would hope, in Bespiatykh's phrase, for their 'grateful attention' and trust that they will enjoy descriptions of well-known places and events purveyed from an unusual angle, complete with misrepresentations and distortions but also unexpected insights and illuminations. I would prefer not to subscribe to Hugh Walpole's ironical view of his own novel about the city that 'there is no Russian alive for whom this book can have any kind of value except as a happy example of the mistakes that the Englishman can make about the Russian'. The public it looks to, at least in the first instance, includes the thousands of British who have visited the city, as academics, students, businessmen, diplomats and, in their majority, as tourists on the increasingly popular city and art tours and cruises. It is designed to be an idiosyncratic variation on a straightforward anthology of extracts or a history of the city by offering a very personal selection of other people's flowers, arranged in chronological order and within a continuous narrative. I have not hesitated to quote often at length, not only because many of the sources are little known but also in order to give the reader a feeling of the writer's style. If the sources are often not always familiar, the names of many British visitors to the city are, if not in a Russian context. Apart from some of the most respected travel writers, journalists and diplomats from the eighteenth century to the present, there are such authors as Daniel Defoe, William Kinglake, Lewis Caroll, Hugh Walpole, Somerset Maugham, J.B. Priestley, Colin Wilson and Alan Sillitoe.

The attempt is made to give some sense of the development of the city and of important events and occurrences in its history and everyday life by selecting relevant passages from works by British visitors recording them not long afterwards. It is inevitable that certain scenes, such as the Neva panorama, general reactions to the city, are replayed down the decades, and that certain major buildings, such as the Winter Palace or the Admiralty, are revisited, not least because they undergo substantial changes: these are the red threads that help to hold the narrative. On the other hand, omissions of certain events, buildings, whole areas of the city are inevitable, not least for reasons of space.

There is, however, another red thread that gives the book its unique perspective and that is the attention paid to the British community itself within the Russian capital. British travellers were reproached, as we have seen, for spending much of their time with a very few members of the Russian aristocracy, with foreigners, and, most often, with their compatriots. Paradoxically, this gave rise to some of the most important descriptions and cameos in a historical sense, since we learn much about the way of life of the British colony and about many of its prominent representatives; we read of the English Embankment and the houses the British occupied and are taken inside the English Church. We are later witness to the break-up of that community at the time of the October Revolution and to the fate of the few survivors in Petrograd/Leningrad. It is hoped that today's visitors will be encouraged to seek the traces of the British in one of Europe's great cities.

The British eyes that looked upon St Petersburg were not only those of observers who committed to paper their impressions but also those of artists who sketched and drew and painted what they saw. It is impossible to say who was the first Briton to draw Russian scenes; it was not until Catherine's reign that views of Russia, including views of St Petersburg, drawn by British artists, were published for the first time, both separately and in books. There is a wealth of illustrative material that is scarcely known, even to scholars, and certainly not over such an extended period. A separate chapter is devoted to such painters as Joseph Hearn and John Augustus Atkinson, Sir Robert Ker Porter and John James, typical of authors illustrating their own travel accounts in the early nineteenth century, and many others, including the photographers of the post-Crimean War era, who specifically include St Petersburg among the many subjects and places for their brushes and cameras.

It is thus hoped that text and illustration will combine to provide evidence of the British fascination with Peter's great city by the banks of the Neva that began long before the tercentenary and will long continue.

Cambridge 2007

CHAPTER 1

FIRST REPORTS OF PETER'S CITY

In 1700 Peter I had declared war against Sweden and almost immediately suffered a humiliating defeat at the battle of Narva (in present-day Estonia). He soon reorganized his army and his tactics and gradually advanced towards the sea over lands that had been in dispute over centuries. In October 1702 he wrested from the Swedes the island fortress of Noteborg situated at the spot where the Neva leaves Lake Ladoga and renamed Schlüsselburg (the key town). In April 1703 the Swedish fortress of Nienschantz, where the River Okhta falls into the Neva, surrendered, and the route to the Gulf of Finland was open to Peter. A mile nearer the sea than Nienschantz, the small island chosen for the Peter and Paul Fortress was one of nineteen islands in the Neva delta and recommended itself precisely as an excellent site for a military installation, if not for the heart of a city. As work continued apace in creating a fortress, another island beyond the delta and out in the Gulf of Finland itself was also selected for its strategic importance. On a sand bank off the island of Kotlin was constructed a fort known as Kronslot, bristling with cannon and guarding the approaches to what was to become the city of St Petersburg. On Kotlin itself was soon to be built the fortress and harbour of Kronstadt, which would become the famous home of the Russian Baltic Fleet. The batteries of Kronslot and Kronstadt were able to ward off attacks by the Swedish fleet and leave Peter's city to survive, to grow and ultimately to prosper. The real turning point in the early history of the city, however, came in 1709 with Peter's crushing victory over Charles XII of Sweden at the battle of Poltava in Ukraine. Although the Great Northern War continued until 1721, the Swedish threat to St Petersburg was virtually at an end. On the day after the battle, Peter wrote, using the Dutch variant of the name he favoured: 'now are the foundations of Sankt Piterburkh truly laid'. The following year the royal family and court were summoned from Moscow and in 1712 St Petersburg became *de facto* capital of the Russian empire.

Legend has it that already in November 1703 the first merchant ship made its way from the Gulf of Finland up the River Neva to the Peter and Paul Fortress and was enthusiastically greeted by Peter. Peter, however, was absent on that occasion, as he had been on 16/27 May, when he was supposed to have cut the first turf on Yani-Saari, the Island of Hares, as the site for a fortress and a church within it. But legends about the founding of the city and its early days could hardly be formed without the presence, imagined or otherwise, of the legendary tsar. That first ship up the Neva was not British but Dutch; the second ship, arriving a few days later, however, was, and it might be said to mark the beginning of British commercial ties with Peter's city. It was only in 1723, when St Petersburg became the official trading centre of the Russian Empire, that the British Factory (the collective name under which British merchants of the Russia Company was known in Russia) was obliged to move there from Archangel on the White Sea, but British merchants had by then long been resident in the city. Vying with merchants as the first British representatives to stand on the banks of the Neva were, certainly, army officers (the first commandant of the fortress was Robert Bruce, who had been in Russian service since the 1680s) and, within months, shipbuilders and others engaged at the Admiralty wharf, which was established in 1704 on the left bank of the river and launched its first small craft two years later.

Peter the Great had visited England at the beginning of 1698 and British interest in who he was and what he did was enormous and so it remained during the remaining years of his reign. In 1698, however, the Great Northern War against Sweden had not yet begun and a capital city by the Baltic was not even the subject of dreams; indeed, if he had such dreams, then they were of the south and the Caspian. It is impossible to say with any certainty when the first reports of Peter's establishing a fortress, if not yet a city, on the Neva, reached London, but his progress in the war against Sweden was closely watched, not least by Daniel Defoe, who was not at all well disposed towards the Russians and Peter's presence on the Baltic. It was at the very beginning of 1705, in the introduction to his *Consolidator: Or, Memoirs of Sundry Transactions from the World in the Moon*, that Defoe first mentions Petersburg:

We see their Ships now compleatly fitted, built and furnish'd, by the English and Dutch Artists, and their Men of War Cruize in the Baltick. Their New City of Petersburgh built by the present Czar, begins now to look like our Portsmouth, fitted with Wet and Dry Docks, Storehouses, and Magazines of Naval Preparations, vast and incredible; which may serve to remind us, how we once taught the French to build Ships, till they are grown able to teach us how to use them.

He seems not to have become much more informed over the ensuing years, rather the contrary. Ten years later, in one of his typical mystifi-cations and transformations, in this case as 'a Scots Gentleman in the Sweedish [*sic*] Service', he produced the following highly confused account of the city's situation and foundation:

I must not omit to observe here, that this Schans-sterny, is a Fort near the Mouth of the River Narva, and of Lugna near Narva, it is esteemed, and that very rightly, to be capable of being made the best Port or Harbour in the whole Baltick, and is the same where the Czar has since built such fine Works, Docks, Yards, and Launches for the Building, repairing and laying up his Men of War; and has compassed it with such prodigious Works, such Numberless Forts, Batteries, and inaccessible Canals and Inlets of Water, by the help of his hired Engineers, that it is at the writing of this, said to be the most commodi-ous Port, and the most impregnable Fortress in all the Northern World. To this he has added fine Buildings, Streets, Churches, Market-places, &c. and has encouraged his People to come and live there, by giving them New-Houses ready built and finished, Privileges, and other Encouragements, that it is already become a Royal City; and if he must keep it, will be in a few Years the Metropolis of Muscovy, and perhaps the Terror of the North Parts of Europe: It is said that Prince Menzickof has built him a very fine Palace, and a large Church there; and that the Czar intends, and has laid out the ground, to build himself a Royal Court, and has called the city after his own Name Petersburgh.

Eight years later, in 1723, posing now as 'a British Officer in the Service of the Czar', he ventured only a few lines about the city in his *An Impartial History of the Life and Actions of Peter Alexowitz, the Present Czar of Muscovy*.

Here his Czarish Majesty contriv'd the Scheme, and actually laid the Foundation of a new Fortress at the Entrance of the Nye or Neva, the Inlet, which opens the Communication between the Lake Ladoga, and the Baltick; which Fortress he called Croonslot and farther up his Majesty has begun to build a Town, which he has call'd after his own Name Petersburgh, or according to some St Peterburgh. This was first but a small Place, but since is become a Royal City, and at present contains, besides publick Edifices, Churches, and a Magnificent Palace, not yet quite finish'd above Thirty Thousand Houses.

In the interim between the two accounts, Defoe, like the British public at large, had had the benefit of reading an account of Peter's Russia by a real British officer, who, along with dozens of fellow naval officers, shipbuilders, and other craftsmen and specialists, had been recruited by the tsar in 1698. Captain John Perry, a hydraulic engineer, had worked for Peter on building canals and similar projects mainly far away from St Petersburg up to 1713, when he managed to return to England and publish three years later his highly influential *Account of Russia, under the Present Czar*. It was only in 1710, when he was engaged to survey and supervise a Volga-Ladoga canal that Perry had seen St Petersburg for the first time. His description, however, could hardly have given his compatriots any clear idea of the tsar's new city; indeed, it was as confusing as Defoe's:

This intended Survey [of the Volga-Ladoga link] was in order to carry on a great and useful Design of the *Czar*'s, as beforemention'd; his Majesty having for a long time had Intentions to bring the Trade from *Archangel*, and all the other Parts of his Countrey, to his said new Favourite Town, situate at the Mouth of the *Neva*, which falls out of the *Lodiga* Lake into the *Baltick* Sea.

To which end, before I came from *Russia*, Storehouses were building for Merchants, and a great Number of Inhabitants already settled there; and though it be but a small part of what is designed in Variety of Undertakings, as particularly the Building of another Town on *Richard*'s Island, about 40 *Rus* Miles below the Mouth of the *Neva*, and 5 Miles from the Coast of *Ingermania*, which the *Czar* designs large enough for all his Nobility, Merchants, &c. with Canals through the

Streets, like that of *Amsterdam*, and an artificial Haven both for his Navy and Merchant Shipping that are intended to trade thither; yet notwithstanding these his Majesty's new Designs of increasing his Strength and Commerce there, it will be found very difficult and buthensome to his People, without a free Communication to be made to the more fertile Parts of his Countrey by Water; for by reason of the Tediousness of the Way, the being obliged to wait for Floods and Rains at several shallow Places, and the Vessels and Floats being often dash'd and staved to pieces against the Rocks and Falls that are by the way, and the Goods often lost and spoiled; and by reason also of the very great Scarcity and Dearness of Forage for Horses where Land Carriage is required.

What Perry does convey and reiterate is the isolation of the city and the strong opposition it evoked among the old Muscovite boyars and gentry:

[. . .] among some other Causes, one of the chief which makes the generality of the Nobility at present uneasy, is, that the *Czar* obliges them against their Will, to come and live at Petersburgh, with their Wives and their Families, where they are obliged to build new Houses for themselves, and where all manner of Provisions are usually three or four times as dear, and Forage for their Horses, &c. at least six times as dear as it is at *Mosco*, which happens from the great Expence of it at *Petersburgh*, and the small quantity which the Countrey thereabouts produces, being more than two thirds Woods and Bogs; and not only the Nobility, but Merchants and tradesmen of all sorts, are obliged to go and live there, and to trade with such things as they are order'd, which Crowd of People enhances the Price of Provisions, and makes a Scarcity for those Men who are absolutely necessary to live there, on account of the Land and Sea Service, and in carrying on those Buildings and Works which the *Czar* has already, and farther designs to make there. Whereas in *Mosco*, all the Lords and Men of distinction, have not only very large buildings within the City, but also their Countrey Seats and Villages, where they have their Fishponds, their Gardens, with plenty of several sorts of Fruit and Places of Pleasure; but *Petersburgh*, which lies in the Latitude of 60 Degrees and 15 Minutes North, is too

5

cold to produce these Things. Besides, *Mosco* is the Native Place which the *Russes* are fond of, and where they have their Friends and Acquaintances about them; their Villages are near, and their Provision comes easy and cheap to them, which is brought by their Slaves.

As for the *Czar*, he is a great Lover of the Water, and entirely delights in Ships and Boats, and in sailing, even to that degree, that in the Winter, when both the River *Neva*, and the Head of the east Sea is frozen over, that he can no more go upon the Water, then he has his Boats made on purpose, and ingeniously fix'd for sailing upon the Ice; and every Day there is a Gale of Wind, unless some very extraordinary Thing happen to prevent him, he sails and plies to Windward upon the Ice with his said Boats, with Jack-Ensign and Pennant flying in the same manner as upon the Water. But his Lords have no Relish nor Pleasure in those Things, and though they seemingly complement [*sic*] the *Czar* whenever he talks to them of the Beauties and Delights of *Petersburgh*; yet when they get together by themselves, they complain and say that there are Tears and Water enough at *Petersburgh*, but they pray God to send them to live again at *Mosco*.

In his attempts to leave Russian service Perry had sought protection from the ambassador extraordinary at St Petersburg, Charles Whitworth, who made his own contribution to early British awareness of Peter's city. In September 1704 Whitworth had been appointed British envoy extraordinary in Moscow and remained there until February 1710; in January 1712 he returned to Russia, but this time to St Petersburg, where as British ambassador he was to stay until the end of June 1713. It was, however, in the months between his two visits to Russia that Whitworth wrote a memorandum for the British government, which was eventually to be published in 1758 at the noted Strawberry Hill Press of Horace Walpole under the title *An Account of Russia as it was in the Year 1710*, and it contained only the following paragraph on St Petersburg:

At Petersburgh there is a little yard, where all sorts of boats and small craft are built, and some of the frigates are repaired. This is the Czar's favorite town and haven, built on two small islands in the river Nieva, which is there large and deep enough to recieve sixty gun ships close to the walls of the fortress. The foundation of this new town was laid soon after the taking of Nyenschantz, which the Czar demolished, in hopes it might one day prove a second Amsterdam or Venice; to people it the nobility were ordered to remove hither from the farthest part of the country, though with no small difficulty, since the climate is too cold, and the ground too marshy to furnish the conveniences of life, which are all brought from the neighbouring countries. However, the Czar is charmed with his new production, and would loose [*sic*] the best of his provinces sooner than this barren corner. The fortress is built on a seperate [*sic*] island with good stone bastions laid on piles but of much too narrow an extent to make any considerable defence, in case of an attack. The floods in autumn are very inconvenient, sometimes rising suddenly in the night to the first floors, so that the cattle are often swept away, and the inhabitants scarce saved by their upper stories; on which account they can have no magazines or cellars, nor is the ground practicable for digging, the water coming in at two foot depth. The river is seldom or never clear of the ice before the middle of May, and the ships can not hold the sea any longer than the end of September, without great danger.

Based on reports and rumours he had heard in Moscow, the passage is dismissive of the Admiralty and the Peter and Paul Fortress and underlines the ever-present threat of flooding, but emphasizes the tsar's devotion to his city or, as Whitworth would have it, his 'production'.

Once in St Petersburg, 'the most disagreable situation and climate I ever met with', Whitworth was able to see with his own eyes the progress that was being made. In one of his regular dispatches to the State Secretary in London, he wrote that 'the Czar set out a place for an exchange to be built, and laid himself the first foundation; it is now some years that the bastions of this fortress have been rebuilding of brick, a plan of a large arsenal is drawn, and two great churches are ordered, one of which is already begun; from whence you may please to see they are resolved to enlarge and beautify the place as much as possible'. He also gave details of:

[...] the orders which were signed by His Czarish Majesty the 18th of April [1712], and have been since sent to Moscow commanding a great part of the inhabitants to remove with their families from thence, and build them houses at Petersburgh.

They are to be of several classes viz:

1st a thousand of the best gentlemen, as stolnics, dwornins etc., who are to build on the river from above the Czar's palace on the same side, till they come over against Neyenschantz. Their houses are to be of lath work, timber and plaister after the old fashion in England;

2nd five hundred of the best merchants and five hundred more shopkeepers of meaner condition, who are to build wooden houses on the other side of the river over against the gentry, till the government can have prepared them houses of stone and warehouses on the island Ritzard, which is to be the great seat of trade. The plan of the future town is already drawn out, but I have not mentioned it, in expectation of getting a more particular information;

3rd two thousand mechanics of all sorts, as painters, tailors, joiners, smiths etc., who are to build on the same side up to Neyenschantz.

In all five thousand families, who are to be picked out by order of the senate, and to settle themselves here by next winter. As it is, provisions are extremely scarce and dear, the inhabitants and the houses increasing every day. There is above four thousand already, and when this new multitude comes upon them, they will have much ado to find subsistance, especially at so many hundred miles distance from their estates, which instead of money, that is not to be had, used to supply them with all sorts of provisions in nature.

The dispatch highlights not only Peter's draconian measures to populate his new city but also his indecision as to where precisely its heart or centre should be. Since Poltava the tsar had toyed with the idea of creating his city on the island which after 1723 became known as Kronstadt but which Whitworth calls 'the island Ritzard' and Perry, 'Richard's Island', corrupted from the Finnish Retusari, and equally known under Russian rule as Kotlin. Peter in 1712 was still prepared to see it as both a naval and commercial centre. Whitworth in a later dispatch provides a detailed description, which is no less important for drawing attention to the role played, and to be played over the next two decades, by Captain Edward Lane (d. 1729), a Welshman and an unsung hero in the history of Kronstadt:

I have often made mention of the island of Ritzard or Cotlin. It is about five english miles long and two or three broad in most places, and situated at the end of the Finish [*sic*] gulf, about thirty english miles from this place, and near three leagues from the land on each side. The opening between this isle and the finish coast is deep enough, but so full of rocks, that no vessel dares venture to pass that way; and from the ingrian shore a large sond with about seven or eight foot water in most places and fourteen in the deepest runs out to the point, where Cronschloss stands at a small english mile distance from the island, which narrow channel is deep enough for the largest men of war. The several points of the island are garnished with batteries to secure this passage, and a large mole is now run out near one third of the way to the depth of twenty four feet, which will be well provided with cannon, and be the head of the haven designed for their shipping. The direction of this work is under captain Lane, an englishman, who taught navigation on board the 'Woolwich', and was left in Russia some years ago, but what other knowledge he has in business of this nature must have been learned here. He makes use of great chests filled with stones, for the security of his piles, and tells me the whole will not be finished in seven years; but as they have very great trouble in carrying their men of war backwards and forwards every year over the bar at the mouth of this river, he is securing a little place for the present, behind the mole, where they may be laid up free from winds and ice, and the sudden attempt of an enemy, and this he hopes to have ready against the winter. On this place the Czar has fixed his point of view, and designs to raise a town for the residence of the merchants, which in a few years is to equal Amsterdam in its wealth and beauty, and to be the Venice of the north, in which the trade of all Russia is to center. The plan is already drawn for seven thousand brick houses, with a little yard to each, large warehouses and squares in the principal places, which are to take up the whole island, the chief streets being to cut through with canals as in Holland; and because the sea has often overflowed great part of it in the autumn, a digue is to be raised and carried quite around. The eight governments into which the dominions of Russia are divided, have undertaken to build each of them a share, and are to bring down people and materials for it this next winter. Prince Menshikoff has already begun a house for himself, as a model for the rest, the ground floor of which is designed for shops, and the cellars will be vaulted for warehouses, and these when ready are to be sold or hired to the merchants.

Kronstadt was to be the home of the Baltic fleet but not of the merchants, Russian and foreign, who were to settle in the areas or islands grouped around the Peter and Paul Fortress. The River Neva, bending westwards after it had passed the Okhta, was soon to split; to the north flowed the Big Nevka, which was to sub-divide further and form the additional Middle and Little Nevkas. The Neva itself was to flow past and round the Peter and Paul Fortress, before it itself divided again to form to the north-west the Little Neva, while the main channel, now known as the Big Neva, flowed on, past the Admiralty on its left bank and into the Gulf of Finland. The large island behind the fortress, formed by the Big Nevka to the east and the Little Neva to the west and known today as the Petrograd Side (*Petrogradskaia storona*), was originally known as Petersburg Island or Side or Town Side, but often referred to simply as Petersburg: this was the true heart of the city in the pre- and immediate post-Poltava years. The even larger island to the west was and is known as Vasil'evskii Island (*Vasil'evskii ostrov*), but was often referred to as the Prince's Island, for Peter gave it as a gift to his favourite Prince Menshikov, who was responsible for its initial development up to 1714, when the tsar took it back to be the new centre of his city. The left bank of the Neva, which is usually now regarded as the mainland, is, nevertheless, bisected by several rivers flowing from and returning to the Neva, principally the Moika and the Fontanka, and the territory from the left bank to the Moika was called the Admiralty Island (*Admiralteiskii ostrov*) and essentially confined for a number of years the city's development to the south.

It was in mid-February 1714 that there arrived in St Petersburg Friedrich Christian Weber as a member of a mission from the Elector of Hanover and he was to remain there for the next five years as Resident. In August 1714 his master became King George I of England and it is likely that Weber's dispatches were a source of information also for the British during a period when Anglo-Russian relations deteriorated and finally ruptured. He was to serve the British public in a much more open way when the book which he published in Germany after his return from Russia became available in English translation in 1722–3 under the title *The Present State of Russia*. Weber presented his work essentially as a diary, sometimes re-worked with hindsight. Thus he presents his first and later impressions of the city:

> When I arrived there [February 1714], I was surprized to find instead of a regular City, as I expected, a Heap of Villages linked together, like some Plantation in the West Indies. However at present [1720] Petersbourg may with Reason be looked upon as a Wonder of the World, considering its magnificent Palaces, sixty odd thousand Houses, and the short time that was employed in the building of it.

Later, he adds that:

> I once heard the Prince Menzikoff say, that Petersbourg should become another Venice, to see which Foreigners would travel thither purely out of Curiosity. Setting aside the perpetual Objection of the raw Climate of the Place, it is possible his Saying might prove true in time, if the Russians would be less refractory to the Czar's Intentions, and use Strangers better than they do at present, as likewise if Passengers were allowed more Liberty than hitherto, in going thither, and returning from thence, and if Care was taken to provide against the excessive Dearness of all Necessaries of Life at Petersbourg.

Weber provides interesting glimpses of the former Swedish fortresses of Nienschantz and Noteborg, the former simply destroyed and the latter rebuilt as Schlüsselburg:

> In November [1714] I went to view the ruins of Nienschantz, a Town demolished by the Russians the beginning of the present War, lying two short Leagues from Petersbourg up the river near its Banks. I only found there some Ruins, the deep Ditch, Wells, and Cellars, all the Materials of the Houses having been removed to Petersbourg, and employed in the building of that City. The inhabitants, who carried on a good Trade in the Baltick, are for the greater Part Prisoners, and the single Women were taken into the Service of the Czarina, Princess Menzicoff, and other Ladies of Quality, and afterwards married.

A year later:

On the 20th of October [1715] we went with the Czar to Sleutelbourg, to solemnize there upon the Spot the Anniversary of the taking of that important Fortress. It lies just at that End of the Lake Ladoga, which is nearest to Petersbourg, in the midst of the Neva, both sides of which River it commands with its Cannon. It has high and thick Walls, and six Bastions, and seeing the Place is surrounded on all Sides with the Water of a rapid Stream, it was Matter of Wonder, that the Russians took it with scaling Ladders. It was formerly called Notebourg; but the Czar changed its Names into that of Sleutelbourg, because it opened the Door to the Russian Conquests, Sleutel signifying a Key in the Low-Dutch. It was built four hundred Years ago by a Princess of Novogrod, whose Name was Marfa. The Czar has provided it with Necessaries for ten Years, and caused it to be strengthened with Out-works, and with Cazerns within, of very durable Work, which may hold above four thousand Men. In the midst of the Fortress stands a Church, to which the Russians have added a Steeple; next to it stands a small wooden House, in which Count Piper [a Swedish prisoner] was confined.

He also offers informative insights into what was happening within the city itself, remarking at the end of 1714, for instance, that 'Strict Orders were issued to all the Inhabitants of Petersbourg, who had Houses but one Story high, to put another Story upon them. As for the rest, a late Mandate was confirmed, by Virtue of which the great number of Wooden Houses were permitted to stand, but it was forbid to build any more, otherwise than with Roofs of Tiles and Walls of Stone-work'; and in 1718, highlighting the new fire regulations, 'the like of which are hardly to be met with any where else in the World':

The building of Petersbourg having cost the Czar such immense Sums, and his Heart being so set on the Preservation of that Place, and yet the greater part of the Houses being at present built only of Wood, his Majesty takes all imaginable Care to prevent Dangers arising from Fire, and with this View has assigned to all his Officers Military and Civil of all Degrees, certain Employments and Functions in case of Fire, to which is annexed a small monthly Salary. The Czar not only has taken upon himself such a function for which he receives his monthly Pay, but even goes to work in Person on such Emergencies, climbing with the most eminent danger of Life on the Tops of the Houses which are on Fire, to encourage his Russians by his Example to follow and assist him. It is owing to these good Regulations that all the Fires that have hitherto happened, how dangerous soever, were always extinguished before four or five Houses could be burnt down.

Among the events that Weber records is his diary are several that are of particular Anglo-Russian interest and are also linked with important buildings in the young city. Within days at the beginning of 1719 there took place the funerals of two prominent 'Englishmen', although the first was a Scot and Jacobite sympathizer, the erudite Dr Robert Erskine, who had been in Russia since 1706:

Doctor Areskin the Czar's first Physician and titulary Councellor, being lately dead at Alonitz, his Corpse was sent for to Petersbourg, from whence it was carried in Procession with great funeral Pomp on the 4th of January 1719 to the new Monastery Alexander Nefsky, seven Wersts from Petersbourg. The Czar himself assisted at the Funeral; in the House where the Corpse lay in State the Minister of the Reformed Church made a funeral Speech in Low-Dutch in Praise of the deceased: His Majesty hereupon gave some Marks of the Esteem he had had for the deceased, and at the same time shewed particular Favour towards his Relation Sir Harry Stirling, who was come to Russia under the Czar's Protection to see the Doctor's last Will put in Execution. The Corpse was carried on the Shoulders of the Physicians and the principal Surgeons who wore long Mourning Cloaks, and was followed by a numerous Procession and two hundred Flambeaux, as far as the Bridge of the German Slabada. From thence the Funeral proceeded upon Sledges to the aforesaid Monastery, Soldiers being ranged on both Sides of the Way leading from the Gate to the Chapel, with lighted flam-beaux in their Hands. The Czar himself followed the Corpse carrying a burning Taper in his Hand according to the Russian Custom, as far as the Vault, which was built between two others in which the Corpses of the late Princess Natalia, and a certain Dutch Rear-Admiral were deposited. All the Company among whom were both the Lutheran and the Reformed Ministers, were presented with Pieces of Crape and a golden Mourning Ring on which was ingraven the Name of the Deceased and the Day of his Death, and afterwards they were all splendidly entertained. The Deceased by his last Will had bequeathed to his Mother, Brothers and Sisters all his ready Money; to the Czar's eldest Princess his Estate in Land and his Boors; to the Hospital at Edinburg the Money arising from his Moveables that were to be sold. The Czar made a Present of his Library to Dr. Blumentrost the younger, who is now first Physician to his Majesty, as the elder is to the Czarina.

Erskine was buried at the Alexander Nevskii Monastery, which had been founded by Peter in 1710 at the junction of the Neva and Chernaia Rivers in honour of the Novgorod Prince Aleksandr Iaroslavich's victory over the Swedes in 1240. George Paddon, dismissed from the Royal Navy in 1714 and entering Peter's service as a Rear-Admiral, was, however, buried near the wooden Church of St Sampson, which was on the Vyborg Side by the Big Nevka; it also had been founded in 1710 to mark the first anniversary of the victory over the Swedes at Poltava (27 June 1709). Near the church was the first official graveyard for non-Orthodox foreigners:

Mr Paddon, an Englishman, and Rear-Admiral in the Czar's Service, died suddenly, and was most honourably interred, the Czar, all the foreign Ministers, all the Sea-Officers, &c. attending the Funeral. The Esteem which the Czar had had for this Gentleman, may be collected among other things from this Circumstance, that his Majesty followed his Corpse a-foot from the House where it had lain in State to the new Church on the other side of the River Neva, which lies a good league off. That new Church was consecrated on the Anniversary of the Battel of Pultava, and dedicated to St. Samson, which Saint is in great Repute in the Russian Legends on account of his Affection and Hospitality towards Strangers, for which Reason the said Church has been assigned for a Burying-place to the Foreigners. The deceased's Widow received a Gratification of one thousand Rubles to defray the Expenses of the Funeral, and was allowed for her Subsistence half her late Husband's Salary during Life.

Weber had not intended initially to include 'an exact description' of St Petersburg, but was prevailed upon to do so. It is this fifty-page appendix, entitled 'A Description of the City of St. Petersbourg with Several Observations Relating to It', and itself a updated and revised version of a German original appearing a few years earlier, that was to prove the most reliable and accessible source on Peter's city for the contemporary British reading public. No less significant was the accompanying detailed plan of the city 'as it stood in the Year 1716', the first ever to published in England. It was now possible to trace, from a further small inset sketch in the top left-hand corner, the route of the Neva from Lake Ladoga through the delta as far as Kotlin Island (and the fortress of Kronslot itself was depicted in a further small drawing to the right of the main plan), but more importantly, to identify on the large plan the location of the sixty-one numbered buildings and areas listed in the accompanying key and described elsewhere in the text. The reader could not but be struck by the impressive development of the city, particularly on Vasil'evskii Island, where the grid of the streets and squares appeared a model of rational town planning. The problem, however, was that it was not the city 'as it stood in the year 1716', but as it was planned to be, and as it would never be.

Following his decision to make Vasil'evskii Island the centre of his capital, the tsar had accepted the scheme of his Italian Swiss architect Domenico Trezzini and the plan published by Weber merged what existed with what was only projected. This is nowhere made explicit, but becomes obvious from his subsequent detailed description of the island:

Wasili-Ostrow is a large and fine Island, of which the Czar has made a Present to the Prince Menzicoff, who lives upon it with his Family and Servants. But as the Czar afterwards took a particular Fancy in the Situation of it, which it seemed he had not minded at first; he resolved, that the true City of Peterbourg should be built upon it in a regular Order. Accordingly he caused several Draughts to be made of a new City, to be raised on the Compass of that Island, and having met with one to his liking, he approved of it, by putting his Sign-manual to it, so that the new City is to built after that Model. Pursuant to this Resolution the Streets and Canals were laid out and marked with Poles in the Year

1716, proper Palaces were also shared out for the Houses to be built, and an Order issued, enjoyning the Czar's Subjects to build and settle there. This Order has had so much Effect, that many Persons have made a Beginning: The Street is actually built on both Sides, and other Streets laid out, the Houses of which, though only of Wood, yet are for the greater Part covered with Pan-tiles, and of better Condition than those that stand in the other Parts of the Town. Many Persons of Quality have already built their Stone-Palaces there, and others have sent the Materials for theirs thither, pursuant to the Czar's Orders. They have for the greater Part pitched upon the Corner of the said Island, where they have got Places measured out, on which they intend to build, for which Reason several Saw-Mills, that stood there before, have been taken down, and removed to other Places. To judge by the Draught, it may become a considerable Town in Time, and render Petersbourg one of the largest Cities in Europe, the rather because all that is already built, is to remain so as it is. And though the greater Part of the said Island is still covered with a thick Wood and Bushes, except a small Spot of Ground cut out and laid open, this will prove no Obstacle to the Czar's Will and Intention, at whose simple Command so many thousands of People must be ready to put his Designs in Execution. The whole Island is to be taken in, and fortified with a Line of Breast-Works.

When Weber saw Vasil'evskii Island for the last time in 1719 there were still very few buildings except along the bank of the Neva towards its eastern end, known as the Spit or *Strelka*. Not unexpectedly, it was Menshikov who alone had had the time and the resources to make his mark. Since 1710 there had risen on what is today known as the University Embankment an imposing four-storey stone palace, bigger by far than the modest winter palaces of the tsar on the left bank and begun initially by the architect Giovanni Fontana and later continued by Gottfried Schädel. Weber provides a detailed and historically important description of the palace, its adjoining Church of the Resurrection (built in 1714 and dismantled in 1730), extensive gardens, and other mansions near by:

The first remarkable Thing on the said Island is the Prince's House. [. . .] The same is built of Stone after the Italian Manner, three Stories high, and covered with large Iron Plates painted red. It has Wings behind and before, is all Vaulted underneath, and as for the rest, provided with every thing that is requisite in a fine House. It has a great Number of Apartments furnished with rich Household Goods, particularly of Silver and Plate. In the middlemost Story is a spacious Hall, in which are usually kept all great Entertainments, and the Weddings of Kneeses and Boyars. Against the House, over a small Canal, is the Prince's Church, built of Stone, with a pretty Steeple, which has a sort of a Chime that is but indifferent. About twenty two Years ago, when there was no Thought of Petersbourg the Prince caused a sumptuous Church and Steeple to be built in the city of Moskow [the non-extant Menshikov Tower], and to be provided with a Chime, which is still subsisting there. His said Church at Petersbourg is neatly contrived, and has a Gallery going round on the Out-side. Within are some Figures carved of Wood, and another sort of a Gallery, both which things are not very customary in Russia. There is, besides, in this Church a Pulpit, in which Sermons are preached now and then in Russian, a thing very extraordinary, and entirely new in this Country; for the Russian Priests never preached before, but contented themselves with performing Mass. [. . .] The next large House by the Church was built by the Prince's Master of the Horse, Fedor Salavioff; it is of Stone, and covered with large iron Plates, the finest House in Petersbourg, excepting the Prince's Palace, and that of the Admiral. The two foremost Rows of Houses joyning to it, are to be pulled down, to make Room for the Boyars, and other Persons of Distinction, to whom Places have been assigned here, as was mentioned above. But the two hindmost Rows, where the Houses are built after the manner of Holland, though but of Wood, are to remain, and a Canal is to be dug in the middle of the Street, which will be the more easily done, because the Ground there is very low and marshy. Next comes the Prince's Garden and Pleasure-House. The Gardens are very large, as appears by the Plan; however, there is but little in them, except that the Arbour-work of the Walks on both Sides is finished, and Hedges and Trees planted along them. The House in it is but of Wood, two Stories high, yet built after the Italian Manner, and has noble Apartments. Side-ways of the Garden the Prince has caused a Lane to be cut out, extending to the Shore, which they call

Perspectiva. At the end of it stands a wooden House with a Steeple, that can be seen from the opposite Continent, and very far at Sea, and serves the Seamen for a Mark to steer their Course by in sailing up and down the River, the Channel of which runs close by the said Steeple. [. . .] Behind the Garden, along the Water, [on the Malaia Neva] there live at present the Prince's Architects, Gardiners, and Mechanicks: But Time will shew whether they will be left in the Possession of so convenient Places. Further North-west is the Prince's Farm, which is stocked with all sorts of tame Fowl for his Kitchen. [. . .] The said Prince's Island is covered all over with a Forest of Fir, Birch, and Alder Trees, and the Ground of it is very marshy, which Inconveniency they are in Hopes may be remedied, by the great Quantity of Earth which is to be dug out of the many Canals that are to be cut into the Island.

Vasil'evskii Island was essentially a place for future development, Menshikov's palace apart, and it was on Petersburg Island and across the Neva on the left bank, on Admiralty Island, that the most significant building had taken place from the very beginning. Weber's description of the buildings around Trinity Square on Petersburg Island underlines the importance of an area which was thereafter increasingly to lose out to the left bank and to Vasil'evskii Island and which today, with the exception of the tsar's 'little house', gives little indication of the role it played in Peter's time. The wide Trinity Square, the first of the great squares that would give the city its special cachet in the first decades of the nineteenth century, received its name from the Church of the Holy Trinity, originally built in 1703 and reconstructed in 1710 and vying with the nearby Peter and Paul Cathedral for the first steeple to grace the city's skyline. Nearby around the square were located the main administrative and commercial buildings, such as the huge trading rows or *gostinyi dvor*, the Colleges and Senate, the printing-house, 'a great Curiosity in these Parts, for there are few or no Russian Books, of what sort soever, to be had for Money', the chancery (which, unbeknown to Weber, had burnt down in 1720), as well as 'the principal *Kabak*, or Tap-House, where they sell Wine, Beer, Brandy, Tobacco, and Cards, for his Czarish Majesty's Account, for that sort of Trade belongs solely to him throughout his dominions'. Several of these buildings were built in a method much favoured by the tsar as cheap, rapid and relatively fire-resistant, referred to by Weber as 'Carpenters Work', known in Russian as *mazankovyi*, and described by Whitworth in a dispatch quoted earlier as 'of lath work, timber and plaister after the old fashion in England'.

The inside of a frame of vertical posts and horizontal planks was filled with clay and the exterior walls were also daubed with clay and then plastered, frequently to resemble brick, and roofed with pantiles. None of these structures has survived. Stone became the recommended material, although brick came to be most widely used, plastered and coloured washed in characteristic Petersburg yellow, green, blue, and occasionally red.

The Admiralty Island was essentially divided into two in Weber's time. From the Admiralty itself to the west as far as the Galley Wharf it was an area dominated by the needs of shipbuilding: storehouses, workshops, a great rope-walk, furnaces, and accommodation for ship-builders and other craftsmen, beginning with 'Prince Menzikoff's Inn, a long Building of Carpenters-work, covered with Pantiles'. It was to the east of the Admiralty along what eventually was to become Palace Embankment to the Summer Gardens and beyond, where a rare area of higher and therefore drier land was to be found, that the palaces and mansions of Peter and his family and other influential members of the Court were being built. Nearest to the Admiralty on the site of the present-day Winter Palace was the house of the Grand Admiral Apraksin, 'the most splendid, and contains above thirty rooms', which together with its neighbours 'give a fine Aspect from the Water-side'. Weber notes, however, that as a consequence of the feverish building and the widening and strengthening of the embankment, the tsar's own 'Winter Habitation and his usual Residence, a Stone Building two Stories high' had lost out!:

It had formerly the Prospect over the greater part of the City, the fortress and the Prince's House, and even towards the open Sea by one Arm of the River; but since they have made a Wharf or Key along the Banks, and built houses upon it, the Street in which the Czar's Residence stands, has lost all that Prospect, and they have built another house for the Czar on the said Wharf.

The building in question was the second Winter Palace which stood at the junction of the Winter Canal (*Zimniaia kanavka*) and the Neva. Work had begun in 1715 to plans by the architect Mattarnovy and was virtually finished three years later.

Original British sources on St Petersburg during the last years of Peter's reign were few and none was published at the time. On 1/12 April 1714, a few weeks after Weber, there arrived in the city Peter Henry Bruce, a Scot, albeit one born in Westphalia and speaking German as his mother tongue, but a kinsman of Robert and James Bruce, who were close associates of the tsar, and like them, serving in the Russian army (since 1704). Only much later in retirement in Scotland did he produce an English version of his memoirs which were posthumously published by his widow in 1782, and although they were in the main presented in diary form, they had obviously benefitted from his reading of Weber and other sources in the interim. Nevertheless, there are passages which retain a freshness and immediacy, as in this evocation of St Petersburg as building site:

> The great stir there was at this time in all parts of the city is past description, nothing was to be seen or heard all day long but tradesmen and labourers at work in building ships and galleys, or houses either of brick or timber, digging canals and paving streets. The river was continually full of large vessels bringing all sorts of materials, as bricks, tiles, and stone for the streets. Large floats of timber came daily down the river for building ships and houses. Every body being employed in one shape or other, there was not an idle person to be seen.

He repeats, or at least, writes inevitably about, much that is described in Weber. Unlike Weber, however, he mentions Peter's small wooden house on the Petersburg Island and that to preserve it, it had been enclosed with a wooden pavilion with a gallery (designed by Domenico Trezzini and completed in September 1723):

> He found only four fishermen's huts, to which he added a house for himself on an island in the north side of the river, and called it Petersburgh. This house was only a shelter from the weather and to rest in; it is a low hall built of wood, inclosed in a wooden gallery, and the

year 1704, in figures, carved over the door; but in memory of this great undertaking it has been preserved ever since. Lieutenant-general Robert Bruce, commandant of the city, has the charge and use of this original hall, and has built a very good house adjoining to it for himself, which was one of the first that made a shew in this place.

He is particularly informative about Peter's Summer Palace and adjoining gardens on the Admiralty Island and provided one of the first 'day in the life of the tsar' descriptions for the British reader:

The czar has both his winter and summer-palace on this island; the former is next the river, and the latter at the east, or upper end of the island, where his yachts and pleasure-boats are ranged close up before the door; here are exceedingly fine gardens and a large park, inclosed by a large and deep canal; the gardens are full of water-works, Italian statues, covered walks and arbors. A fine avenue of large trees, which stand by the side of the river, were dug out of the ground in the winter, with large quantities of frozen earth sticking to their roots, and brought in that condition and planted here, and flourished to the surprize of all who saw them. In the park was built a house which contains all sorts of mathematical instruments; also the famous globe of Gothorp, contrived by Tycho Brahe, in which twelve people can sit round a table and observe the celestial constellations as it turns on its axis. In the garden was a long gallery, or hall, where the czar attended every day from eleven to twelve o'clock at noon, when every body had free access, and he then received petitions from all ranks of his subjects; after that hour none was permitted to address him except upon affairs of consequence. He dined commonly at twelve o'clock, and only with his own family; one dish only was served up at a time, and to have it hot he dined in a room contiguous to the kitchen, from whence the dish is received through a window from the cook; at one o'clock he lies down and sleeps an hour; he spent the afternoon and evening in some diversions or other till ten o'clock, when he went to bed, and got up again at four in the morning, summer and winter.

In the holidays, he invented all manner of diversions, and frequently entertained company in his long hall in the garden, which being surrounded by water, the guests come in their boats, which, as the

21

company disembark, are all secured under a guard in the harbour, that no body may give him the slip before the company depart altogether, which seldom happened before the next morning.

There are many lively descriptions of 'all manner of diversions', including the carnival that followed the birth of the tsar's son Petr Petrovich on 28 October/8 November 1715 and of the assemblies and feasts Peter organized in the specially built *mazankovyi* Post House on Trinity Square on Petersburg Island:

> The czar now gave frequent balls and entertainments at his own winter and summer palaces, and not at prince Menzikoff's as formerly; but finding this inconvenient, ordered a large house to be built mid-way between them, for a general Post-Office, with spacious rooms above stairs for public balls and entertainments; but on grand festivals, and extraordinary occasions, the entertainments were given at the senate-house; between which and the fort was a spacious open place where they played off the fire-works. Upon these public meetings, a great many tables were covered for all degrees of persons; one for the czar and the grandees; one for the clergy, one for the officers of the army, one for those of the navy; one for the merchants, ship-builders, foreign skippers, &c. all in different rooms; the czarina, and the ladies, had their rooms above stairs; all these tables were served with cold meat, and sweet meats, wet and dry, interspersed with some dishes of hot meat: these entertainments commonly ended with very hard drinking. After dinner, the czar went from one room and table to another, conversing with every set according to their different professions or employments; especially with the masters of foreign trading vessels, inquiring very particularly into the several branches of their trade. At these times I have seen Dutch skippers treat him with familiarity, calling him by no other name but *Skipper Peter*, with which the czar was highly delighted. In the mean time, he made good use of the information he got from them, always marking it down in his pocket-book.

Bruce remained in Russian service until 1724 and was last in the capital some two years earlier. With the rupture in Anglo-Russian relations and on the instructions of George I, Weber was to leave St

Petersburg on 14/25 September 1719, in the company of James Jefferyes, the British resident who had arrived earlier that year but was never officially received by Peter. Jefferyes left little of note about the city in his dispatches, apart from an arresting passage underlining continued Russian opposition to Peter's city and Peter's prescience of what would happen after his death:

> I cannot omit taking notice of a remarkable discourse the Czar had on this occasion [his forty-eighth birthday celebrations] with some of the old gentlemen here who do not like all the innovations he has introduced into this country, viz: that he was not ignorant how great an aversion they have to St. Petersburgh, that he knew well enough they will set fire to it and to the fleet too as soon as he dies, that then they design to return again to their beloved Moscow, but that as long as he lives, he will keep them here, and make them sensible that he is Czar Peter Alexeiewitz.

They also had little appreciation for the tsar's irrepressible love of jokes, as illustrated in the following cameo:

> Wednesday last being the first of April [1719] His Majesty invited most of the nobility and gentry in and about this town to a comedy; some of his own domestics were ordered to go from house to house to the ministers of state to make the invitation, and the drums went several times about the streets to give notice to the rest. The time appointed being come, a great company, consisting of the ministers of state, the officers of the crown, and a multitude of ladies and other people, met together at the play-house, where everything seemed to be in readiness, the candles in order, and the actors dressed. After two hours expectation the company was not a little surprised to see a curtain drawn aside, and a machine let down on the theatre from a cloud on which was writ in capital letters, and in russian and german characters the word 'April', the merry Andrew at the same time advancing on the stage, and with a profound reverence and an impudent face, telling the company that they were all a parcel of fools. The trick being then perceived, the people began to gaze on one another, and by little and little sneaked out of the play-house, some ashamed of having been imposed on, and

others grumbling for the loss of their money; but they were all obliged to go away without other satisfaction or comfort than that of solamen miseris socios habuisse doloris.

Jefferyes was the first English observer to describe, albeit with obvious distaste and affected superiority, the traditional ceremony of the 'blessing of the waters' in the new Russian capital:

His Majesty has been present at the solemnity here which is ordinarily celebrated here on the 12 day. As this solemnity gives some idea of the genius of this people, I would not omit sending your lordship a short account of it: It is on the river Neva that this farce is acted; the ice is opened in a certain place on that river, where the chief ecclesiastics present themselves to bless the water. This ceremony being performed, all those amongst the people who have either a mind to wash away their sins or to be cured of some distemper, approach the sanctified place. People of distinction content themselves with washing their faces, but the common undress and plunge themselves overhead and heels with so great an assurance of relief either to soul or body, as their necessity requires, that I could not but admire both the zeal and the robust constitutions of those who, in spite of the terrible frost we have, acted in this farce. The devote parents bring their little infants, just born, to be here baptized, and they do not fail at their leaving the place to fill their vessels with this holy water and to carry the same to their houses, which they keep by way of preservative against any evil that may befall them for the year to come. This is one of the ancientest customs among the muscovites, to which His Czarish Majesty likewise submits to shew that in matters of religion he will not separate himself from the meanest of his people.

A final excerpt reveals Jefferyes's concern about the British ship-builders in St Petersburg in whose company Peter delighted and whose expertise was helping Russia to create a fleet that might threaten British interests:

I now beg leave to entertain your lordship with another set of people, who because the Czar greatly favours them, have got here the nickname of chips by those that envy them, but by others are called ship-builders; these in my humble opinion (if continued long in this service) will not fail of setting the Czar on such a footing as will enable him to bid fair for the mastery in the East-sea. One of them assured me lately that if the Czar lives three years longer, he will have at sea a fleet of forty ships of the line from seventy to ninety guns each, as good as any the world can afford, besides twenty frigats from thirty to forty cannon each, all built at this place; these people the Czar flatters and caresses as much as possible: their salaries are large and punctually paid, they eat in private with him, they sit at his table in the greatest assemblies, and he hardly goes anywhere or takes any diversion but some of them accompany him. By these caresses the Czar means to captivate their affections so as to engage them not to quit him; but whether it will be for the interest of Great-Britain to be a spectator of so growing a power as this, especially at sea, and brought about by her own subjects, I humbly submit to your lord-ship's consideration. Might I presume to give my opinion, it is high time they be called out of the service. Here are five master-builders besides worklings, all british subjects; three of the masters are reck-oned as good carpenters as any we have in Great-Britain.

The presence of the British in the Russian capital, in this case, of a British merchant well known to the tsar, was also noted in another contemporary account:

I stopt at the house of Mr. Evans, an English Merchant, of whom I received a great many civilities. His House stands upon this Road [Nevskii] about a Werst from the City, near the great Canal. It is well built, and has a garden belonging to it, which renders it very agreeable. There were found in digging it a great Number of the Heads of those poor People, who died in working at the Canal, and were buried upon the Spot wherever they fell down

The author was a Frenchman, Aubry de La Motraye, who spoke fluent English and who was to spent much of the later years in London, where he published in 1732 in not identical English and French versions his account of a month's visit to Russia over a year after the death of

Peter the Great. It provided the British public with a unique description of the city from a period when Anglo-Russian relations were at a low ebb and was in every sense an important update on Weber's work which had appeared a decade earlier. La Motraye arrived in St Petersburg towards the end of September 1726, just past the mid-point in Catherine I's brief reign, and virtually surveyed the city, literally pacing out the length and breadth of various buildings. Weber had stressed in his descriptions of certain buildings that work was still in progress and La Motraye did likewise, although things had moved on – or in several cases, had not. Here is La Motraye's description of one of St Petersburg's key landmarks, the Cathedral of Saints Peter and Paul within the fortress, subject of only a brief paragraph in Weber, although it is interesting that both mention Domenico Trezzini, unusually for a period in which architects were rarely named:

> There is a magnificent Church, dedicated to S. Peter, which was not then quite finished for Want of Money; and this was the Case of divers other Works begun before the Death of Peter the Great [. . .] This Church was built upon the Designs, and by the Direction of that excellent Architect, Signor Tressini. The whole is worthy of his exquisite Genius. The Body of the Building is of Brick, except the Pillars, the Corners, and Shoulderings. All the Ornaments of Architecture and Sculpture appear throughout the whole, disposed with the greatest Judgment and Elegance. The Steple is all of Stone, except the Spire, which is of Timber, covered with Copper, gilt towards the top of it. It is raised upon four Rows of Pillars, one above the other; two of the Ionian, and two of the Corinthian Order. There is a very good Chime in it; the Portico of the Church is noble; the Pillars are of hard free Stone, very high, and of the Tuscan Order. The Catafalco of the late Emperour is still to be seen there; it is covered with Cloth of Gold, raised upon a Floor of five Degrees, spread with purple Sattin, under a Canopy of the same Silk and Colour, laced with Gold; with his own Name, and that of his Infant-Daughter, who died a few Days before [after] him, embroidered in Cyphers with proper Devices. This Catafalco was attended with four Statues of Wood, painted white; two at the Feet, and two at the Head, with four large Candlesticks, in which were white Wax-Tapers as big as one's Thigh. The statues,

which were at the Head, represented Hercules and Alexander; and those at the Feet Religion and Russia. Besides the two Guards at the door of the Church, by each Taper was placed a Soldier in a black Cloak, with a Halbard in his Hand: on the left Hand of this Catafalco hung a branched Candlestick, with only one little Taper, burning Night and Day. All this, they told me, was to continue in this Manner, till the Parts or Ornaments of a magnificent Monument of Marble were brought from Italy.

The original church in the fortress had been of wood and Trezzini began to build his stone cathedral around it in 1712. By the time La Motraye visited the site, the wooden church had been dismantled and rebuilt on Petersburg Island where it remained until 1806. Trezzini's cathedral was only finished in 1733, but the gilded sheets had been added to the top of the spire in 1723; and Peter's coffin was to remain in the church until May 1731.

La Motraye was obviously and rightly much taken with Trezzini's work and mentions him again as responsible for drawing up the plan in 1717 for the development of the Alexander Nevskii Monastery, where the remains of another famous Russian were to be brought on 30 August 1724 (the third anniversary of the victorious conclusion of the Great Northern War). Although Weber and Bruce both mention the monastery, La Motraye is the first to provide a detailed description in English:

The Monastery, if it is finished, will be the largest, the best built, and the most magnificent in all Russia. It is sufficient to give a grand idea of it, to say that Signor Fresini [sic] formed the Plan of it; and several other good Architects have been employed upon it. There is yet but half of it finished as far as No. 1 in Plate III, where there was a noble Church begun: That Church was designed to be in the Center of the whole Building, and the Building to be as it is represented in that Plate. But if there are no more Workmen put upon it, than were then, it will not be finished these 20 Years. Divine Service however was performed in the mean Time in another Church, No. 2 on the West of the Monastery. It is for the most part of Timber, but very elegantly. There is also a Chappel in the Body of the Building, which is a Master-Piece of Architecture, and beautifully adorned. In this Chappel are deposited the Ashes of S. Alexander Newsky. They are inclosed in a little Coffin covered with crimson Velvet, adorned with Embroidery of Gold, with Laces and Fringes of the same in the Corners. This Coffin is Placed on the right Hand, or the epistle-Side, of the Altar. A little lower on the same Side stands the Throne, upon which Peter the Great sat, when he canonized him. [...]

The Monastery is built of Stone and Brick; what is finished of it is well contrived and executed, it is above 50 Paces long and 26 broad: There is an Hall, or Gallery, above of the same Form, and almost of the same Extent, and high in Proportion. The Cells are very neat; there were 65 Monks besides the Abbot.

The plate to which La Motraye refers was printed at the end of his account and although he expressed his understandable annoyance with his engraver for reversing the plan and making west east, it was nonetheless the first representation of a Petersburg building published in England. It was also like the Trezzini plan of Vasil'evskii Island which was reproduced in Weber, not what was, but what was projected. The main cathedral church had been begun in 1720 by the German architect Theodor Schwertfeger; unfinished when La Motraye saw it, it was to be dismantled in 1755, still incomplete.

La Motraye was much taken with 'the Beauty of the Situation [of the monastery] with the Pleasantness of the Road thither' and it is his description of 'the high Road of S. Alexander Newsky' towards what might be called the city end that is also a notable first. In his systematic pedestrian tour of the city La Motraye had come from the banks of the Neva from the foundries (*liteinyi dvor*, founded in 1711), which gave their name to the present Liteinyi Prospekt, as far as the Great Perspective Road (*Bol'shaia pershpektivaia doroga*). This is the road that was called the Nevskaia perspektiva from 1738 and would receive only in 1783, in the reign of Catherine the Great, the name by which it would universal recognition – Nevskii Prospekt (*Nevskaia preshpekt* or *prospekt*). It was at the junction of the Fontanka River and this main thoroughfare, which was for a long time the true city limit to the south, that Mortraye had rested at the house of Mr Hill Evans before proceeding towards the Admiralty:

You cross this Canal [the Fontanka] by a Drawbridge, in the Place
where it cuts the high Road of S. Alexander Newsky. This Bridge is
above 50 Steps long, including the two Parts between which it is fixed.
It is made in the Dutch Manner, as are all the others upon the several
Canals. There is a little Ditch on each Side of this Road, with
Lanthorns after the English Manner upon Posts, from 45, to 50 and
60 Steps from each other. The little Canal [the River Moika], which
forms Admiralty-Island, cuts this Road about the middle of this
Suburb, and you cross it by a Drawbridge almost as long as the other.
This Road, which is every where equally broad and well-paved, ends
at the Admiralty.

La Motraye is describing early variants of the bridges across the
Fontanka and Moika, known as the Anichkov and the Narodnyi (the
latter originally called the Green (*Zelenyi*) and, later, the Police
(*Politseiskii*)), as well as the first (hempseed) oil lamps, very probably
designed by the English mechanic John Pateling (d. 1750) who had
arrived in the city in 1718 to install the steam pump to raise the water
for the fountains in Peter's Summer Garden (from the river that
became known thereafter as the Fontanka).

Virtually everywhere La Motraye looked there were buildings
under construction: the Cathedral in the Fortress, the Alexander
Nevskii Monastery, the Isaac Church ('a fine Church built of Brick, or
which seemed to promise so when I saw it, for it was not then finished'),
the Winter Palace ('a vast Building, which they were repairing and
enlarging slowly, as they did every Thing else'), the new 'magnificent
Edifice' on the Neva embankment of Vasil'evskii Island that was to
accommodate the Imperial Academy of Sciences, Peter's famous collection of rarities, and the Gottorp Globe (seemingly perpetually on the
move since its arrival in St Petersburg in 1713). At the same time, there
is the frequent note of delay, of bad building materials ('the Badness of
the Bricks'), of the assaults of rain and flood ('defaced by the Rain and
other Injuries of the Weather'), and the suspicion that 'the Court seems
to be much more pleased with residing at Moscow, than Petersbourg'.
In the very year of publication of La Motraye's book, however, the
Court of the Empress Anna Ivanovna returned to St Petersburg.

CHAPTER 2

THE CITY OF THE FIRST
EMPRESSES, 1725–61

T he death of Peter was to bring to Russia and to St Petersburg years
of uncertainty as the succession was fought out among opposing
factions. Initially, the Petrine legacy seemed secure with the installation
in January 1725 of Peter's widow as the Empress Catherine I. This was
largely orchestrated by Prince Menshikov, who, after the empress's
sudden death in May 1727, seemed to have cemented his own power
with the accession of Peter's grandson, Petr Alekseevich, as Peter II and
his betrothal to Menshikov's daughter. Within months, however,
Menshikov was overthrown and exiled with his family to Siberia.
Under the influence of members of the old aristocracy, Peter II
returned the Russian court to Moscow, where it would undoubtedly
have remained, had not smallpox struck him down in January 1730 and
led to another constitutional crisis. This was eventually resolved in
favour of Anna Ivanovna, Peter the Great's niece and daughter of his
half brother Ivan, who was to reign for the next decade. Prior to her
marriage and residence in Courland, Anna had spent many of her early
years in St Petersburg and seemingly was not scarred by the experience.
Following her coronation in Moscow, the court eventually moved back
to St Petersburg in January 1732 and a new and important chapter in the
city's history was opened.

Anglo-Russian diplomatic relations, which had been officially
broken off in 1719, had begun to warm after the deaths of Peter the
Great and his consort and in August 1728 Thomas Ward arrived in St
Petersburg as the British consul-general to discover that Peter II had
abandoned a place 'where there is nothing to be seen but marshes and
water' for Moscow. It was to the old capital that he then set out, accompanied by his wife Jane. Jane in her only letter describing St Petersburg
before their departure finds it 'pleasantly situated on a fine river called
the Neva', the houses and streets on Vasil'evskii Island, 'very handsome' and 'mostly uninhabited, for the Admiralty-island is by much the

most populous', and dismisses the second Winter Palace, designed by
Mattarnovy and rebuilt by Trezzini in the early 1720s and in which
Peter the Great had died, as 'small, built round a court, [it] is far from
handsome, has a great number of little rooms ill-contrived, and nothing
remarkable either in architecture, painting, or furniture. The summer-
palace is still smaller, and in all respects mean, except the gardens,
which are pretty (for this country, fine) with a good deal of shade and
water. The best idea I can give you of it is Boughton [seat of Duke of
Montagu in Northamptonshire]'.

Jane was soon to lose her husband and to marry in Moscow his
secretary Claudius Rondeau, who became the British Resident in St
Petersburg virtually to the end of Anna's reign. (Newly widowed
women in the English community were, incidentally, in great demand
and soon remarried.) The Rondeaus hastened back to St Petersburg to
welcome the arrival of the empress and her court:

> [. . .] her majesty was met two miles from the city by all the members of
> the courts of justice, the land and sea officers, the foreign merchants,
> the members of the academy, and foreign ministers. She passed under
> five triumphal arches built on this occasion. She then went to church,
> and after being some time at her devotions, she got again into her
> coach, and went in the same pomp to the palace, where several
> speeches were made to congratulate her arrival. When this was over,
> she went to dinner, and there dined at the table with her the ministers
> of the first rank of her own court and their wives, and the foreign
> ministers and their wives, about eighty people in all. There were tables
> in other rooms for the rest of the company and in the evening a ball.

Mrs Rondeau then launched into characterizations of the empress and
members of her court far more flattering than they deserved. Her
husband, on the other hand, in his dispatch to London of 22 January
O.S. revealed other aspects which were of less interest to his wife:

> The 16th instant in the morning Her Majesty made her public entry
> into this city, which was very fine. As soon as she was come to the
> palace, everybody went to congratulate her upon her safe arrival, as did
> also the foreign merchants; but I never was more surprised, than when

I saw the english advance to see that m-r James Gardiner [Gardner], one of the treasurers of the factory, was so imprudent as to offer to make a speech to Her Majesty; but before he had repeated three lines, he stopped short, not being able to go on with his harangue, so that he exposed himself and all the british factory to be laughed at.

I am very sorry to inform your lordship, that, I believe, there never was an english factory so disunited as this; but I shall do all it is possible to be done to persuade them to live in friendship, and as countrymen ought to do; but by all I can hear since my arrival at this place they do their utmost to ruin one another.

Rondeau did much to heal wounds, preparing the ground for the long-desired Anglo-Russian Commercial Agreement that was signed in 1734 and brought the British the status of 'the most favoured nation' and the merchants many of the privileges they had craved since the first negotiations in Peter I's reign. The British Factory, as the association of British merchants in Russia was known, was able to secure its head-quarters in and dominate the new trading centre and warehouses (*gostinyi dvor*), which were eventually completed in 1735 after a design by the ubiquitous Trezzini on Vasil'evskii Island, facing the Little Neva. Its predecessor had been on Trinity Square on the adjacent Petersburg Side and continued, according to Rondeau, to be used by Russian merchants:

Whereas all foreigners in obedience to an especial order from the college of commerce did in 1731 remove all their foreign merchandise to the new gasthof on Vasily Ostroff, and whereas the russes do yet continue to lodge all their light goods as hides, wax, linens, and linen yarn etc. at the old gasthof, which from the distance between both places causes great delays and inconveniencies to trade, – the english merchants desire, that the russ merchants may be obliged to lodge all their light goods as hides, wax, linen, and linen yard etc. at the new gasthof on Vasily Ostroff and that the remaining part of the said new gasthof on Vasily Ostroff may be built and copled, and that the same be covered with iron, as well as the new customhouse or portorio adjacent thereto, to prevent the danger of fire and the damage the merchants are liable to suffer from leakage etc. And for the future security of their merchandise in the said new gasthof on Vasily Ostroff from fire they desire the powder magazine lying near the said new gasthof may be removed.

We have another, complementary, description from the same year from the Scots doctor John Cook, recently arrived in the capital:

On the west [east] end of the same island is the custom-house, and the exchange, where, as in London, the merchants meet. The exchange is nothing else than a very great timber stage, built one half of it on that branch of the Neva which washeth the east side of the island. It is about 300 paces long, and proportionally broad. Near to it is a most noble magazine for preserving merchandize; it is a square built with brick and has only one great port or entry. An hundred soldiers keep watch here day and night, that no harm may happen to the merchants goods. A merchant may have a very large room for paying ten shillings per month. The side of the stage next the river is well lined with ships of a smaller burthen, during the summer season, for the readier dispatch of business.

Trezzini's new building was depicted in the album of prints which was prepared to celebrate the city's first fifty years in 1753 and enjoyed particular popularity among the merchants back in London, where it was produced, with some amendments, as a separate coloured engraving in 1755.

Rondeau's dispatches were first published only in 1889, but his wife's gossipy *Letters from a Lady, Who Resided Some Years in Russia*, stronger on personalities than on places, appeared towards the end of her life in 1775, and John Cook's *Voyages and Travels through the Russian Empire, Tartary, and Part of the Kingdom of Persia*, a few years earlier, in 1770, and both therefore during the reign of the great Catherine. These three important sources were, however, preceded by an account that appeared, at least in its first edition, when Anna was still on the throne. Elizabeth Justice's *Voyage to Russia* was published in 1739 and appeared in a second augmented edition in 1746. Mrs Justice, who travelled to St Petersburg in 1733 and spent three years as governess to the family of a prosperous

English merchant, Hill Evans (whose home, as was mentioned in the preceding chapter, was visited by La Motraye), thus became the first Englishwoman to publish an account of Russia and the first known representative of a form of employment that Englishwomen were to enjoy or endure with British and Russian families right up to the October Revolution. Hers is a view of Russia and Russian society from a comparatively lowly position. Very conscious of social status, she speaks with due respect of Mrs Rondeau and with awe of the empress, who was 'tall, and very lusty; and has an Aspect becoming a crown'd Head: She has both Majesty and Sweetness in her Countenance; she lives up to the Rules of her Religion; she has Courage unusual to be found in her Sex; and she has in Her all the good Qualities that a Princess can be wish'd for; and tho' absolute, yet she is always merciful'. On the other hand, she is quick to berate Russian servants as 'the most ignorant Creatures living, and have everything which attends Ignorance, that is, Ingratitude, Dirt and Sauciness; and are, in my opinion, far inferior to a well-taught Bear'. There is much detail about Russian customs and ceremonies, food and dress, but comparatively little about the city itself, which simply strikes her as 'very large'.

In contrast, there is much about the city in an account that was only published in 1959 but was written in 1733 by a young aristocrat, whose visit might well qualify him as the first British tourist to St Petersburg. It was Weber who quoted Menshikov's alleged prediction or hopes that St Petersburg 'should become another Venice, to see which Foreigners would travel thither purely out of Curiosity' and La Mortraye was certainly among the very first whose curiosity, rather than need, duty, or profession, drew him to the new Russian capital. A year after the publication of La Motraye's book in London, the twenty-five-year old Sir Francis Dashwood, already a seasoned traveller on the Grand Tour, took the opportunity to sail to Russia with Lord Forbes, who had been sent from London to further negotiations for the commercial agreement. There seems little doubt that Dashwood intended his diary if not for publication, then for circulation among interested members of the Prince of Wales's circle, to whose household he belonged. His conclusion that 'people make great mistakes in their conjectures

...ew across the Neva towards Thomas de Thomon's new Exchange (begun 1805). Coloured aquatint by J. Clark ...m a drawing by Mornay. Published in *Picture of St. Petersburg* (1815).

The Police Bridge (designed by William Hastie, 1811) across the River Moika on Nevskii Prospekt. Engraved by J. Clark from a drawing by Mornay. Published in *Picture of St. Petersburg* (1815).

The Bronze Horseman and Rinaldi's St Isaac's Cathedral, as finished by Vincenzo Brenna. Engraved by J. Clark fr[om] a drawing by J.T. James. Published 1816.

View across the Neva towards the Strelka of Vasil'evskii Island and Thomas de Thomon's Stock Exchange from t[he] Boulevard between the Admiralty and the Winter Palace. Lithograph by J.T. James. Published 1826.

ST. PETERSBURGH.

A JOURNAL OF

TRAVELS TO AND FROM THAT CAPITAL;

THROUGH FLANDERS,

THE RHENISH PROVINCES, PRUSSIA, RUSSIA,

POLAND, SILESIA, SAXONY,

THE FEDERATED STATES OF GERMANY, AND FRANCE.

BY A. B. GRANVILLE,

M.D.; F.R.S.; F.L.S.; M.R.I.; F.G.S.; & M.R.A.S.

Physician in Ordinary to H.R.H. the Duke of Clarence, Physician-Accoucheur to the Westminster General Dispensary, and to the Benevolent Lying-in Institution; Principal Physician to the Royal Metropolitan Infirmary for Sick Children; Hon. Member of the Royal Academy of Medicine of Madrid; Corresp. Member of the Imperial Academy of Sciences of St. Petersburgh, and Hon. Member of the Imperial Medico-Chirurgical Academy of the same town; Foreign Associate of the Royal Academy of Sciences of Naples; Member of the Physico-Mathematical Class of the Royal Academy of Sciences of Turin; Corresp. Member of the Medico-Chirurgical Society of Berlin; and Ordinary Member of the Natural History Society of Halle; Corresp. Member of the Provincial Physical Society of Bonn; of the Philosophical and Phrenological Societies, and the Senior Medical Foundation of Paris; of the Philosophical and Literary Society of Manchester; of the Georgofili of Florence; of the Medical and Scientific Societies of Marseilles, Florence, Philipi, Val d'Arno, Padua, Venice, &c.; and Member of the Royal College of Physicians in London.

IN TWO VOLUMES.

VOL. I.

LONDON:

HENRY COLBURN, NEW BURLINGTON STREET.

1828.

LEFT: Title page of A.B. Granville, *St. Petersburgh* (1828).

BELOW: Plan of St Petersburg. Engraved by Sydney Hall from Russian map of 1827, published by Henry Colburn in August 1828. From A.B. Granville's *St. Petersburgh*.

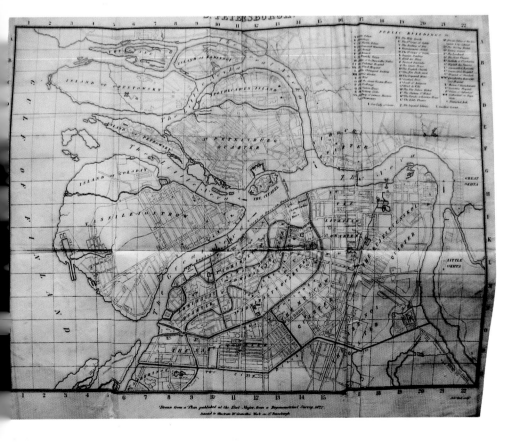

The Hermitage Theatre on Palace Embankment (designed by Giacomo Quarenghi, 1783). Engraving from a drawing by unknown artist in Granville's *St. Petersburgh* (1828).

View of the Winter Palace through the arch of the General Staff Building (architect K.I. Rossi, 1819–29). Engraving by Bonner from a drawing in Granville's *St. Petersburgh* (1828).

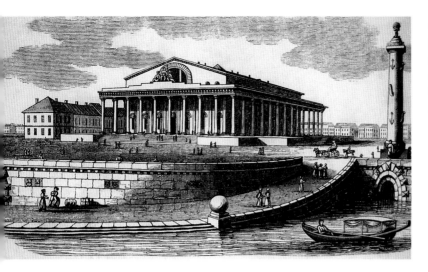

The Exchange. Engraving from a drawing by an unknown artist in Granville's *St. Petersburgh* (1828).

The English Quay, or Embankment. Engraving by Mary Byfield from a drawing by an unknown artist in Granville's *St. Petersburgh* (1828)

The Imperial Academy of Sciences and the Observatory on Vasil'evskii Island. Engraving by Lee from a drawing by an unknown artist in Granville's *St. Petersburgh* (1828).

| Admiralty. | Bridge. | Labanoff. | Peter's Statue. | New Cathedral. |

View of the Admiralty, the Bronze Horseman and Monferrand's new St Isaac's Cathedral. Engraving from a drawin by an unknonw artist in Granville's *St. Petersburgh* (1828). (The dome was only erected in 1853.)

The St Michael Castle (designed by Bazhenov and Brenna on the site of Elizabeth's Summer Palace). Engraving fro a drawing by an unknown artist in Granville's *St. Petersburgh* (1828).

he Aleksandrovskii Park at Tsarskoe Selo. Watercolour by Adam Menelaws, *c*.1830.

nsecration of the Alexander Column, 1834. Original watercolour by A.G. Vickers. Previously unpublished.

The 'Jordan', being prepared for the Blessing of the Waters by the bell-tower of the St Nicholas Cathedral on the Fontanka, 1834. Original pencil and watercolour by A.G. Vickers, previously unpublished. (Engraved in somewhat different form as the frontispiece for *Heath's Picturesque Annual for 1836*.)

he Haymarket. Engraving by W. Chevalier from a watercolour by A.G. Vickers. Published 1 October 1835.

e Admiralty and Palace Square with the Alexander Column, seen from the Manège. Engraving by E. Radclyffe
m a drawing by A.G. Vickers. Published 1 October 1835.

The Isaac (pontoon) Bridge seen from Vasil'evskii Island, looking towards the Admiralty. Engraving by T. Higham from a drawing by A.G. Vickers. Published 1 October 1835.

The Smol'nyi Convent, seen from the Neva. Engraving by T. Higham from a drawing by A.G. Vickers. Published October 1835.

iew down Nevskii Prospekt near Vallin de la Mothe's Grand Bazaar towards the City Duma Building. Engraving by
Appleton from a drawing by A.G. Vickers. Published 1 October 1835.

e Trinity Cathedral (designed by V.P. Stasov, 1828–35), on the River Fontanka. Engraving by J. Appleton from a
wing by A.G. Vickers. Published 1 October 1835.

Russian types. *Cartes-de-visite*. Photographs by William
Carrick, 1860s.

Petersburg cabbie. Photograph by William Carrick, no date (1870s).

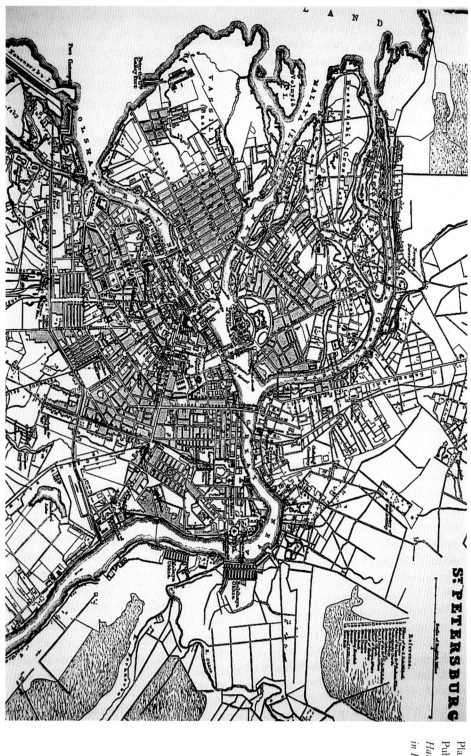

Plan of St Petersburg.
Published in Murray's
*Handbook for Travellers
in Russia* (1869).

ew of the British Embassy, decorated for the occasion of the marriage of the Duke of Edinburgh and the Grand
ıchess Mariia Aleksandrovna. Drawing by F.W. for *The Illustrated London News*, 7 February 1874.

Drawing water from the River Neva. Drawn by 'our special artist' for *The Illustrated London News*, 7 February 1874.

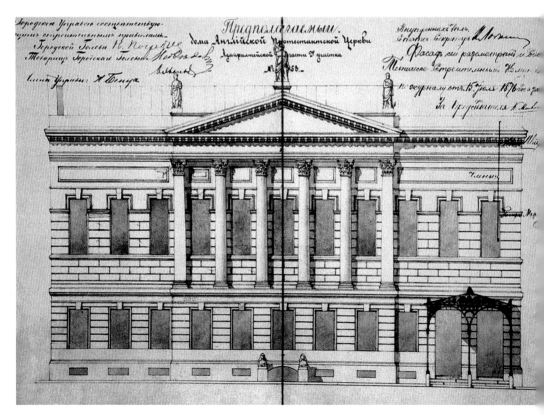

Projected reconstruction of the English Church by D. Boltenhagen, 1876.

concerning this Court, though I am very well contented with my journey, and think it very much, worth any curious man's while, going to See, and to Stay there three weeks or a month, but after once curiosity is Satisfied, I think one could amuse oneself better, in more Southern Climates' to some extent sets the tone for generations of future British tourists.

Twenty years on from Whitworth, Dashwood begins with a detailed description of Kronstadt, where he enjoyed the company and experience of two former officers in the British navy and Jacobite sympathizers, Admirals Thomas Gordon and Thomas Saunders:

Saturday June the 9th. I went over, and viewed the Isle of Crownstad which is about five miles in length, the plan of this prodigious work is very regularly laid out, it is built upon a Marsh and Bog, in the Sea, the entrance into the Haven is excessive Strong there being seven hundred peices of Cannon. there are large Canals, well lined with stone, for to bring Ships or large Vessels, into the town, there is an exceeding large fine Windmill, by the force and invention of which Severall Machines, are Sett a going, for the lading the water out of the Canals, which by drains is conveyed into the Sea, the same Mill Saws, several Planks at the same time, this same invention, was Made and built by a Dutchman, the side of the Isle facing the Haven is built with large brick houses, and a very large Quadrangle under Arches all which from want of proper repair, and through the violence of the cold, are gone very much to decay there are two Chapels, or Churches in the Isle with hansome altar pieces in the Greek way, upon the Island are four thousand Soldiers and ten thousand Sailors (or people destined to the Sea, as admirall Saunders told me), upon the South East is a Haven, called the Merchants Haven, within the Outer Works. the fort stands distinct by itself, on the South, and all boats and Ships pass, betwixt that and Crownstad, Admirall Gordon at present Commands, both the Isle and the Fort. the Isle was designed by Peter the Great, for the residence of all Merchants, and his own Navy, but his plans have been faintly put into execution, since his decease, nevertheless they continually, keep doing, there being actually five hundred people at work, under the inspection and direction of Vice Admirall Saunders, who has been in this country and in this fleet these 18 years. [. . .] there are Severall large fine houses, going pretty much to decay, in Crownstad, amongst which, there are two or three, particularised by the name of the Monarchs own, and one of Prince Mempsicoffs building, that are most to be distinguished besides about a hundred, the rest are built of wood after the Russian fashion. (there is a fine forge at Crownstad, for anchors and other Iron worked for Shipping where there are about a hundred men continually employed.)

The particular buildings on Kronstadt to which he refers in the closing lines were the three-storey brick palace with a high steeple, built for Peter in 1720–2, and an earlier small wooden house, built soon after the tsar's similar 'little house' in St Petersburg, as well as Menshikov's so-called Italian Palace.

Dashwood's first impressions of the capital itself were generally positive. He highlights Peter's never-fulfilled plans to have a system of canals on Vasil'evskii Island and, more interestingly, he mentions something that the tsar himself would hardly have countenanced, the first pontoon bridge across the Neva, which was first erected in 1727 on the instructions of Menshikov, linking his palace on Vasil'evskii Island with Admiralty Island, at a spot where the church of St Isaac of Dalmatia stood to the west of the Admiralty. After a gap of five years the bridge was built again after the ice had disappeared in 1732 and was thereafter rebuilt every year.

[. . .] the streets are pretty well paved, streight, and of a good breadth, in Severall there are canals, they say, the Czar designed cutting Canals through most of the Streets, especially opposite to the Palace which is now inhabited by her Majesty, called the Summer Palace, that being the reall town of St. Petersburgh, where the exchange is, where the Merchants dayly resort, though not reside, as also the greatest part of the Shops, for retail commoditys. Petersburg is situatd between 7 and 8 leagues up the river Nerva (and built on very marshy low ground), which runs with a pritty strong current, through, and divides, the town, its from ten to twelve feet deep, and more than half the Breadth of the Thames, about below bridge, most of the Merchant men, come up as high as the town, there is a good hansome bridge upon boats, that goes from the Suburbs, of Vasiliostoff. where her Majesty and the best part of the court inhabit, and the Suburbs, all the foreign Ministers likewise inhabit the former, as well as all the English Merchants, and I believe most other foreign merchants, it is called the Isle of the admiralty, the Admiralty house being built there, the Rope walk also there, the foundery for Cannon, and the Docks, for Ships and Camels &c there is now a ship upon the stocks, of a hundred and twelve guns, but probably it may be rotten before it is launched. – The Summer Palace where the Czarina lives at present, is a long building, of wood, one Story high, there are large apartments, and it looks very well for the season, it was entirely built from the ground, when she came from Moscow, in six weeks' time, but they make nothing here, of employing two thousand men at work upon the same building [...]

The one-storey wooden Summer Palace, located in a corner of the Summer Garden and facing the Neva, was built for Anna in 1732 and was used by her throughout her reign. It was one of the first buildings by Bartolomeo Rastrelli and was dismantled in 1747, when it was moved to Ekaterinhof, west of the Galley Wharf. It was Rastrelli who also in 1732 began work on the new (third) Winter Palace. Dashwood noted in his diary that 'the High Admirall Aprakin dying, he left a fine house upon the waterside, a legacy to her Majesty, therefore they are building two monstruous great wings, to this, and it is called the Winter Palace, it will be very large when finished, but not a peice of much Architecture'. Admiral Fedor Apraksin's large and impressive three-storey wooden mansion stood at the western end of what would become known as Palace Embankment, next to the Admiralty of which he was the commandant; it occupied the territory that is nowadays associated with the State Hermitage and was the site for the final Winter Palace that Rastrelli was to build for Elizabeth. Rastrelli's palace for Anna with its various additions and alterations probably deserved Dashwood's verdict as 'not a piece of much Architecture', but Mrs Justice managed to get inside and was suitably impressed:

It is very large, and lofty. The Ceiling is finely painted: The throne is very spacious: The Canopy is richly embroidered with Gold, and a deep Gold Fringe: the Chair, she sits in, is Velvet; the Frame is Gold:

And there are two other Chairs, which are for the Princesses. One side of the Room is fine gilt Leather, in different beautiful Representations; and the other Side, being Looking-Glass (with all Manner of Birds near it) afford a very pleasant scene. From the Window you have a fair Prospect of the river, and Shipping. The other Rooms are all hung; some with Velvet, some with Gold and Silver Stuffs. I saw Three Beds. One of which was Velvet; the other Two were Damask: the former of a Blue, and the latter of a Yellow Colour.

Much was happening on Vasil'evskii Island in the early years of Anna's reign, although, as Dashwood notes, there were 'long rows of large houses, that look well on the outside, but allmost all unfurnished, and most uninhabited'. Menshikov's palace, which Mrs Justice thought 'for Largeness is remarkable: it has as many rooms in it as there are Days in the Year', had been confiscated after his fall and, as Dashwood noted, 'it is now an Academy, for about 400 Cadets Sons of the Chief Noblemen in the Country, where they are all taught the use of arms, and all other Academicall accomplishments; they exercise, after the Prussian manner, I saw fourscore file four deep go through their Manall exercise marching, and firings, with great dexterity, the Parents of these young Gentlemen are oblidged [sic] to send them before they are sixteen, to this Academy, or they are liable afterwards to be pressed for common soldiers, at this Palace they are Lodged and Nourished, and are kept under strict discipline'. The First Cadet Corps had been established by Anna in July 1731 (as the Corps of Cadets) and opened the following year; it was to be an important educational and social institution in the life of the city and it was there, during the reign of Elizabeth, that cadets formed the first amateur theatre group in Russia that was to produce the first tragedies of a former cadet Alexander Sumarokov, the 'Northern Racine', whom a British ambassador was soon to call 'a very extraordinary genius'.

To the east of the former Menshikov Palace, to which he was adding new teaching buildings, Trezzini had virtually completed the great stone building of the Twelve Colleges he had begun in the last years of Peter I's reign and to which, at the time of Dashwood's visit, the various colleges, or ministries, were finally transferring. Further along the embankment the new Kunstkamera, housing Peter's collection of rarities and monstrosities, as well as the Gottorp Globe, was at last finished (without the help of Trezzini) and was part of the Russian Academy of Sciences, which also occupied the adjacent former palace of the Tsaritsa Praskov'ia Fedorovna for its press and other needs. La Motraye provided the English public with its first information on the Academy, its members, and some of its earlier locations, but Dashwood was the first Englishman to describe a visit to the Academy's new home and, indeed, to mention the Newtonian telescope, through which, incidentally, only weeks previously, the empress herself had gazed on the rings of Saturn.

> In Vasiliostoff, besides the Colleges and the Cadets Academy before
> mentioned, there is the rarity Chamber, the printing house as also for
> stamps, and Catts, Mathematicall instruments, for Physicall demon-
> strations, a Vast Globe of nine feet Diameter and on the inner side, a
> Seat round a table where severall of us got in, and the back of the bench,
> is the Horizon and all round the superferies on the inner side is the
> Celestail globe with the twelve signs of the Zodiack, and above that is
> an Observatory. – in the rarity Chamber there are severall curiositys all
> collected by Peter the first, and some that I never Saw before, all Parts
> of the Human System, entire and distinctly preserved in spirits, with
> the graduall growth of a Child in the womb from a week, to nine
> months, a mummy of a Child made at St. Petersburgh, the upper skin of
> a hand entirely separated and taken off preserved also in spirits, there
> are adjacent two or three little Chambers where the Czar Peter the first
> used to Study, where are severall curious things in Ivory of his turning.
> in one of these chambers is kept, his Hat, Boots, Coat, and Sword that
> he wore at the Battle of Pultava. in the observatory there is a very fine
> reflecting Telescope, of Sir Isaac Newtons.

In addition to his tour of the city, Dashwood visited some of the nearby estates, especially along what became known as the Peterhof Road which ran by the Gulf of Finland past Peter's palaces at Strel'na and Peterhof as far as Menshikov's Oranienbaum. The well-travelled Dashwood was much taken with the pavilions of Monplaisir and Marly at Peterhof, finding them 'both the prittiest things I have seen in these parts, and both, worthy of place in any Garden in Italy', but like Mrs

Rondeau, he was sorry to see the condition of many of the fine paintings they held. The waterworks were a constant source of wonder for visitors (Elizabeth Justice included) and John Cook provides the best early description in English of the great cascade that descended from the original palace, built by Braunshtein, Le Blond and Michetti in the last decade of Peter's reign, and of various ingenious waterworks:

> The garden on the north is betwixt the palace and the gulf of Finland: It contains many acres of ground, and has in it many pleasure-houses, cascades, jetts, and waterworks. A large cascade 30 or 40 feet broad, runs from under the pavement of the palace, and, in its egress, falls down large steps made of hewn stone, sloping about 20 or 30 feet: Then it flies over the entry of a large grotto, 16 or 18 feet perpendicular, upon a pavement of hewn stone, and, at last, loses itself in a very large circular bason, of at least 40 feet in diameter, ever full, but never overflowing: From the middle of which, springs up a splendid spout or jett of water, which rises to a great height; and is, I was told, larger than the famous one in France. Out of the water, much to my agreeable surprise, arose a dog and three ducks, made of copper or iron, and in appearance all alive: The ducks flutter through the water quacking, the dog follows after them barking. There is, in a subterraneous place, a charming chime of chrystal bells, which play by water. The grotto, of which I spoke, covered before with the cascade, has two entries, one at each side of it. The entries are guarded by statues, which, when you are in, prevent any getting out, till the keeper, by turning a handle, puts a stop to them. These statues evacuate so much water, by vomiting and shooting out of stone pistols and guns, that, the keeper said, it would founder any man. The bottom is of channel, interspersed with a very great number of small pipes, imperceptible to the unwary stranger. The keeper placed us in certain niches, where we could see every thing, and not a drop of water touch us. He then turned a handle, upon which these pipes played with very great force, so that the perpendicular jetts rose near as high as the roof. The roof and walls were all covered with rock, and different sorts of moss.

It was along the Peterhof Road that British merchants were quick to acquire houses and small estates: Dashwood stayed at one such owned by Hermann Meyer and the Rondeaus soon had their idyllic country cottage near to the unfinished palace of Strel'na (the site of Vladimir Putin's recently completed presidential residence):

> I have now got a little cot in the country, which is a vast delight to me, for here we are free from that constraint which always attends a court, and the company, or more properly the people, that we cannot avoid seeing in town. We have one English family with whom Mr. R_ has contracted a great friendship; I say, he has, for they are two brothers, whose conversation and understanding would make their acquaintance courted in England. They often go down with us. The house is built of wood, and has only a little hall, with two parlours on one side of it, and a kitchen and offices on the other, with four bed-chambers, and closets above. It stands on a rising ground, that leads with a natural green slope to a fine meadow, which is terminated by the sea; behind it is a wood, of many miles, of birch and fir. There is no art or cultivation about it, for the uncertainty of this country would make that expence ridiculous, and as it is rural without, it is rustic within; the tables furnished with delft, and the beds with white callico, rush chairs, and the rest in proportion. One parlour is furnished with books and maps; those, and my frame for embroidery, are the only things that make it differ from a farm. Here we spend three days in a week very agreeably. Mr. R_ reads to me, and I work, while our cows, sheep, and poultry feed around us, and are so tame they come close to the windows.

For all her delight in the simplicity of the country, Mrs Rondeau was pleased to attend and describe some of the entertainments at court. Particularly striking is her description of the celebrations that were held in the Summer Garden for the fall of Danzig during the War of the Polish Succession in 1734 and her dismay at the parading of captured French officers:

> [. . .] the entertainments then were in the garden of the summer-palace. The ladies were dressed in stiffened bodied gowns of white gauze with silver flowers; their quilted petticoats were of different colours, as every one fancied. I was pleased with a gentleman's description of a lady; on my not knowing which he meant, he said 'Celle-là avec le cotillon rouge.'

('That in the red petticoat.') On their heads was only their own hair, cut short, and curled in large natural curls and chaplets of flowers. The empress and the imperial family dined in a grotto that faced a long walk terminated by a fountain, and inclosed on each side by a high hedge of Dutch elms. There was a table the whole length of the walk, which joined at one end to her's in the grotto. Over this long table was a tent of green silk, supported by voluted pillars, which had wreaths of natural flowers twisted round them; between these pillars, in the niches of the hedges, were the side-boards, the whole length of the table, on each side; one furnished with plate, the other with china; the gentlemen drew tickets for their partners, and every man sat by his partner at table; so that a man and a woman sat all the way. There were three hundred people at table, and six hundred dishes in a course; two courses and a dessert. After dinner the company separated into parties, and amused themselves in the garden 'till the cool of the evening, when the garden was finely illuminated, and the ball began under the same tent where we dined. The voluted pillars being illuminated had a very pretty effect. The music was placed behind the high hedge, so that it appeared as if the deity of the place supplied that part of the entertainment. When the ball was begun, the French officers taken at Dantzick, were introduced. I own, I thought this so cruel, that I got near enough to observe their behaviour on so delicate an occasion. Their leader, count de la Motte, was a fine person of a man, about fifty-five, grave and manly in his whole deportment. He looked as if he had a soul that felt his disgrace, and despised the insult.

The Russians had a particular predilection for fireworks and illuminations. Peter during his stay in London in 1698 had specifically sought out books on pyrotechnics, and anniversaries, victories, festivals throughout his reign were celebrated in fire and light. Anna not only continued the tradition but welcomed several illustrated publications with appropriate firework verses by her academicians. Mrs Justice was much impressed by the 'very fine Illuminations, such as, I believe, there is not the like in any Place'. Russian victories over the Turks provided an obvious excuse for a grand firework display, centred on the 'Theatrum', the specially constructed platform off the very eastern end of the Strelka of Vasil'evskii Island and opposite the Winter Palace, and described with gusto by Cook:

Many very entertaining and magnificent fireworks were exhibited on the river Neva, and grand illuminations for the success of the Russian arms against the Turks, so expensive and grand that many people skilled in such works, said that they did not believe the like had ever been seen in any part of Europe: The rockets were terrible. The charge of each large one was said to weigh an extraordinary weight, and when they had risen to an immense height in the air, they burst with an explosion equal to that of a large cannon, and exhibited many fire balls, of various colours, falling down to the earth: A great variety of wheels, and many other things whose names I am unacquainted with, were played off, so that in midnight, one might have seen as clearly as in mid-day. The grand illuminations were placed on a large timber building of two stories high, and a great length, erected on the north side of the river opposite the winter palace. The lamps exhibited flames of different colours, representing the last city or fortification taked from the Turks, such as Azoph, Perecop, Kinburn, Kinbam, &c. Before the fireworks were played off, there was erected upon the river a large tall mast, on which was hung a white sheet of cloath, as broad as the sail of the largest ship of war, but longer, fire was put to this as a signal for beginning: The flame ran up the sheet instantly like a flash of lightening, but left upon it the figure of the city, for the honour of which the works were to be played off, in a deep and glossy fire which continued ten or twelve minutes, before the sheet was destroyed. Whilst the spectators were observing this figure, all the lamps were expeditiously lighted, which, as was said, exhibited the same figure, but in much more extensive space, and these continued burning the whole time, and even longer than fireworks lasted. As the timber galleries were upwards of two hundred foot long, the regularity and dispatch in performing these wonderful works no doubt surprised me, and they had much the same effect upon people more acquainted with them.

Cook is a mine of information about all manner of events and customs in St Petersburg. As befits a doctor, he took particular interest in medical matters and questions of hygiene, noting that 'that the common people may have no pretext for leaving nastiness in any part of the streets, convenient places are built upon the banks of the river and its canals: Besides, all houses which are built two stories high, and in straight lines, are well supplied with every conveniency to keep the city sweet and clean'. This was still a time when the Neva was a river to admire – 'the beautiful Neva, than which no chrystal is more pervious or transparent'. Cook also provides short descriptions of some of the main buildings built or altered during Anna's reign and which are not found in other contemporary British accounts. He begins with the two hospitals which Peter founded in 1716–17 on the Vyborg Side:

> One is for the army, the other for the fleet. They are joined together, compleating three sides of a very large square, in the middle of the side facing the river Neva, is a fine church for the use of both hospitals; the wards are very well contrived; the building is two stories high, and covered galleries go quite round both hospitals, so as any person may walk without being exposed to the injuries of the weather. At each corner of each hospital is a noble theatre, and dissecting chamber.

The stone church, possibly designed by Trezzini's son, that Cook mentions was not in fact finished until 1741.

In 1732 Anna decided that the original Admiralty tower of 1711 should be replaced and over the next few years the Russian architect Ivan Korobov erected the new tower and spire described by Cook:

> The Admiralty is on the south side of the river, opposite the Academy: It is almost a square; one of the sides facing the river is fortified only with *chevaux de frize*; the other three sides are surrounded by a high rampart of earth, upon a wall of stone eight or ten feet high, above the water of a very deep and broad fossee; the rampart is flanked with good bastions, and the whole well stored with many brass cannon. There are three entries into the admiralty over draw-bridges; on each side is one. Within this fortification are noble buildings, containing offices for every thing belonging to the royal navy. Many ships, sloops, and boats are built here. I saw the Royal Anne launched, a ship which carried 120 pieces of brass cannon. There is a tower, and on the top of it an high spear, covered with copper, double gilt, with a ship on the top of all, of the same metal, and also double gilt.

The man-of-war he saw launched on 13 June 1737 was built by the great British shipbuilder Richard Brown (who is buried in the Alexander Nevskii Monastery). Francis Dashwood had seen it on the stocks in 1733 and wrongly predicted that 'it may be rotten before it is launched'. Mrs Justice, who mentions the launch of ships at the Admiralty as great public events, also witnessed the launch of the *Empress Anna* a few weeks before she left Russia.

Cook, incidentally, gives a very good impression of the way spires dominated the city, describing the belfry of the Peter and Paul Cathedral in the fortress with 'a high spear like that in the admiralty, terminating at the top with a cross richly gilt' and the cannon foundry, which was located, opposite the hospitals, on the left side, where the present Foundry Prospect (*Liteinyi prospekt*) ends by the Foundry Bridge across the Neva, 'a very noble building, with a spear topped with a burning bomb, all gilt'. The original *mazankovyi* buildings of the foundry (1711–13) were replaced in the mid-1730s by the stone structure Cook describes. It was during Cook's sojourn that the road that linked the foundry with the Neva Perspective Road (later, Nevksii Prospekt) received its name. Along Nevskii itself, at its junction with Great Garden Street (*Bol'shaia sadovaia*), another important landmark, the new wooden market (*Gostinyi dvor*),was completed in 1737:

> Near the southernmost part of the city is the market-place, where all sorts of goods, both home and foreign, are kept to be sold. It is a very large square with four entries; on each side whereof is a range of shops, both within and without. There are covered galleries built quite round the square, both on the out and inside, that people may be defended from rain. A stranger need not, as in other places, hunt through this great city for what he wants to buy: A pleasant walk in these galleries will give him the opportunity of seeing many of the best people in St Petersburgh, and all sorts of commodities in the world. The younger merchants and their servants guard it during the night, and in it great order and decency are always observed.

Cook, Elizabeth Justice and Jane Rondeau were in the city when great fires once again devastated parts of the Admiralty district in 1736 and 1737, but Mrs Rondeau makes no mention of them. Although Cook is confused about the sequence – the first fire occurred on 11/22 August 1736 in Malaia Morskaia; and the second on 24 June 1737 by the Palace Embankment and along Millionnaia – he describes in graphic detail the first of them of which he was an eye-witness:

[...] two very terrible conflagrations in the city of Petersburgh.

The first happened in May or June, and burnt down many fine palaces, besides her Majesty's great Dispensary, and the Medicine Chancery in that street called the Milion. The other burnt down some hundreds of houses, mostly indeed of timber, in that part of the city called the Little Morskoy.

Here I was present, and happened to stand by the side of a canal near a great brick house belonging to a prince, all in flames. The roof was fallen in, and few of the bystanders were taking any notice of it, when it suddenly blew up with such a shock as made the earth tremble where we stood.

The day was serene, little wind, but very hot, but in an instant we were all covered in so thick a smoke, that the sun could not be seen for some time: In a minute however, after the blast, or less time, many chairs, tables, and other pieces of furniture, some of them half burnt, fell from the air into the canal adjoining, without hurting anyone person. It was indeed fortunate that none of them fell on the other side of the canal where were very large and costly magazines of hemp, ropes, cables, pitch, tar, &c. belonging to the Empress, for had the fire reached that magazine, all the English merchants houses and the Admiralty would have been destroyed.

It was found out that the fire was set to the houses in different streets at once, so that the poor inhabitants could scarcely save any thing, and before any help could come, the whole Morskoy was in flames. Three incendiaries were taken, two men and a woman, these I saw executed a few days thereafter, in the ruins of the Morskoy. The men were each chained to the top of a large mast fixed in the ground; they stood upon small scaffolds and many thousand billets of wood were built from the ground, so as to form a pyramid round each mast. These pyramids were so high as to reach within two or three fathoms of the little stages on which the men stood in their shirts, and their drawers. They were condemned in this manner to be burnt to powder: But before the pyramids were set on fire, the woman was brought betwixt these masts, and a declaration of their villany, and the order for their execution, read. The men called out loudly, that, though they were guilty, yet the woman was innocent, however the woman's head was chopped off, for they never expose the persons of women, either by hanging or burning, let their crime be what it will. Possibly had the Empress Anne been at Petersburgh, the woman would have been pardoned; it was said however, that the proof was very clear, and the woman knew, that the villains were determined to commit this horrid crime, some days before it happened.

No sooner was the woman's head chopped off, than a link was put to the wooden pyramids, and as the timber was very dry, it formed in an instant a very terrible fire: The men would soon have died had not the wind frequently blown the flames from them; however, they both expired in less than three quarters of an hour, in great torment.

It was as a result of these particularly devastating fires on Admiralty Island and in the vicinity of the Winter Palace that the Commission for the Orderly Development of St Petersburg was established: it introduced new building regulations and also elaborated a plan for the city that incorporated the so-called 'three prongs' as the major design principle. The outer prongs were Nevskii Prospekt to the east and and the future Voznesenskii Prospekt to the west with the narrower Pea Street (*Gorokhovaia*) in the middle. They were not, however, the subject of comment by a visitor who arrived in the summer of 1739 or, indeed, of any visitor before the reign of Catherine. Although Italian, Francesco Algarotti was almost an honorary Englishman: his *Letters*, first published in his native tongue but appearing in English in 1769, was dedicated to John Hervey, Lord Hervey of Ickworth and he travelled from London on the yacht of Charles Calvert, 5th Lord Baltimore, to attend a royal wedding in St Petersburg. Hervey and Baltimore were, incidentally, members of the Prince of Wales's circle to which Dashwood belonged and into which Algarotti had been introduced. It is in his 'letter' dated 30 June 1739, that Algarotti began his account of the Russian capital with words which have become among the most famous in travel literature on St Petersburg, not least because Alexander Pushkin took a version of them as the epigraph to his poem *The Bronze*

Horseman: 'I am at length going to give you some account of this new city, of this great window lately opened in the north, thro' which Russia looks into Europe'. It was a view shared by his companion Lord Baltimore, who, although leaving no account of his own, voiced his more pessimistic opinion in a later conversation with the Crown Prince of Prussia, the future Frederick the Great, to the effect that 'Petersburg is the eye of Russia through which she looks upon the civilized countries; if that eye were put out, it would inevitably relapse into the barbarism from which it had only just emerged'.

Algarotti gives a striking picture of the approach from Kronstadt up the main course of the Neva, past 'the most wretched generation of trees that ever the sun shone upon', until:

> After having sailed some hours in the midst of this hideous and silent wood, behold, the river turns at once, and the scene changing in an instant, as at an opera, we see before us the imperial city. On either side, sumptuous edifices grouped together; turrets with gilded spires rising every here and there like pyramids; ships, which, by their masts and floating streamers, mark the separation of the streets, and distinguish the several quarters; such was the brilliant sight which struck our eyes: we were told, here is the Admiralty, there is the Arsenal, here the Citadel, yonder is the Academy, on that side the Czarina's winter palace.

Distance, however, had indeed led enchantment to the view, for:

> when we were in Petersburg, we no longer found it so superb as it had seemed to us from a distance; whether it be the gloominess of the forest had ceased to embellish the perspective, or that travellers resemble sportsmen or lovers, I will not pretend to determine.

Recognizing what had been achieved on the most unpromising of sites, he nevertheless found that 'the materials of which it is built are not worth much, and the plans of the buildings are not those of an Inigo Jones, or a Palladio'.

In December 1739 Anna Ivanovna ordered the architect P.M. Eropkin and the Academician G.V. Kraft to design a palace made of ice for a wedding of quite a different order from the one attended a few months earlier by Algarotti and Baltimore, the mock wedding of the unfortunate Prince Mikhail Golitsyn and his Kalmyk bride Anna Buzheninova. Engravings of the palace, in which everything down to playing cards and flowers were fashioned from ice, were published to accompany Kraft's scientific composition on the subject, copies of which made their way to Britain. The palace is generally assumed to have disappeared by April 1740, but Cook says he saw parts of it as late as July, when he returned to the capital after an absence since September 1737. His description is also a damning epitaph on an empress whom, ten years earlier, Mrs Rondeau had flattered to excess:

> I saw yet remaining betwixt the palace and the admiralty part of the ice-house, which the late Empress Anne had caused build with a view to ridicule one of the most antient and respectable families in Russia, by causing marry one of that family disordered in mind, to a woman troubled with the same infirmity. Few great personages have ever appeared in the world, who have not one time or other discovered some weakness, which could scarcely have been suspected, till detected. The Empress Anne was said to have been a sensible, humane, judicious lady, but she could not check her childish levities; and it is not easy to imagine what was her policy or pleasure in this improper display of her power. The walls were of ice; the bed-stead, and all pieces of household furniture were made of ice; they fired out of ice cannons: But for what? to do honour, or, which is the truth, to ridicule the Russ nobility in the person of a poor foolish pair, taken from the best family in Russia. The same sum of money, which was expended upon this dream, might have made many honest good families in Russia very happy. I could not help thinking, that it looked as if heaven had designed to let us see, what a poor end the greatest earthly grandeur frequently comes to; for no sooner was this farce of mock magnificence ended, than that great Empress was taken ill and died; and although the succeeding summer was extremely hot, yet part of the walls of that ice-house stood, to expose the last action of the great Empress Anne, till the month of August, as it were to let people, living at the distance of thousands of miles, have time to witness the last whim of one of the greatest personages upon earth, to have been only fit to amuse children.

At virtually the same time as Cook returned to St Petersburg, two young aristocrats, Charles Cottrell and Robert Carteret, arrived with their tutor Johann Caspar Wetstein at an early stage of a tour that would take them to Austria, Prussia, Switzerland and France. Their extant letters offer little more than society gossip, but they were forced by inclement weather to delay their departure until January 1741 and were thus in the capital when the empress died on 17/28 October 1740. On 12/23 December, they witnessed the funeral procession taking the body to the Peter and Paul Cathedral, noting that 'she had lain in state for a month but not having been rightly embalmed was almost fallen to pieces before her burial'. It was only in a letter written months later in August 1741 from Basel that Cottrell essayed any comment on the Russian capital, but it is a striking one:

> [. . .] the Country about Petersbourg has full as wild and desert a look as any in all the Indies; you need not go above 200 paces out of the town to find yourself in a wild wood of firs, and such a low Marshy boggy country that you would think God when he created the rest of the world for the use of Mankind had created this for an inaccessible retreat for all sorts of wild beasts. One must have had as great a genius and firm resolution as Peter the first had, to make such a country habitable. The Dutch may brag that Amsterdam is built out of the water, but I insist that Petersbourg is built in spite of all the four elements, Earth, air, water, and fire; the Earth is all a bog, the air commonly foggy, the Water sometimes fills half the Houses, and the fire burns down half the Town at a time, the Houses being for the most part built of wood.

And the British diplomatic representative, Edward Finch, whom Cottrell and his companion found friendly and welcoming, continued to purvey his masters in London with the same doom-laden analysis of the city's future:

> [. . .] after all the pains which have been taken for these last forty years to bring this country out of its ancient state, it is only violence and superior force which prevents it falling back into it immediately, as it will do one day or other, sooner or later, for there is not one of them who would not wish St. Petersburgh at the bottom of the sea, and all the

conquered provinces at the devil, so that they could but remove to Moscow, where by being in the neighbourhood of their estates, they could all live in greater splendor and with less expence.

The opening years of the new decade were, indeed, turbulent times for Russia and St Petersburg. Following Anna's death, the throne was to be occupied by the infant Ivan VI (b. 12/23 August 1740), under the regency of the late empress's favourite Ernst Bühren. Bühren was overthrown and exiled to Siberia in November and replaced as regent by Ivan's mother, Anna Leopol'dovna, the late empress's niece. A year later, on 25 November/6 December 1741, Ivan and his mother were in turn deposed and Peter's daughter, the Empress Elizabeth, was brought to the throne to reign for some twenty years. For her there was no question of deserting his father's creation.

British chroniclers of the city under Elizabeth are remarkably and regrettably few and in most cases laconic. It is only in the great tomes that the merchant Jonas Hanway devoted to his *Historical Account of the British Trade over the Caspian* (1753) that the briefest account of the capital is to be found, although as the author disarmingly admits 'nothing is more common than to be ignorant of that which we have had a good opportunity of learning, but particularly in the instance of an accurate inquiry into things relating to a place which a man considers as his home':

St. Petersburg, which was founded by Peter the Great in the beginning of this century, may at present be considered as the modern and polite metropolis, and the chief residence of the Russian empire; and though so lately a morass, it is now an elegant and superb city, very healthful and abounding in all the necessaries, and many of the pleasures of life. It was formerly built of wood, but now the use of this material is permitted only in the suburbs.

This city is ranged on both sides of the Neva, extending from east to west near two English miles; at the upper end of the north side is the citadel, which is more famous for the number of lives it cost in building than for either its strength or great importance, though it has several uses. It contains a stately church, in which the remains of its founder Peter the Great, and his empress Catherine, are deposited. It also serves to beautify the town, and as a prison for offenders against the state. This city has neither gates nor walls, but the marshy land near it, both in Ingria to the south, and Finland and Carelia to the north, and the gulph of Finland to the east, render the access to it extremely difficult for an army. It is divided by several canals, Peter the Great intending to take Amsterdam as his model in building it; but from the reluctance, with which it was originally begun by his subjects, who were compelled to build, and likewise from errors in the plan, some part of the city remains intirely unexecuted, and in other the houses are too near the canals. This does not hinder, but there are some regular, broad, and well-built streets, and several very noble structures, particularly the great chancellor's, the vice-chancellor's, the marshal Shepeloff's, the senator Shevaloff's, count Cheremoteff's, count Gallowin's, and some others of less note.

The encouragement which the Empress has given to building, for which she seems to have a passion, contributes to the beauty of the city. Besides the two royal palaces already mentioned [the Winter Palace, which he had simply termed 'magnificent', and the Summer Palace, although only its garden received praise for its 'choice statues and delicious walks'], this lady has built a noble palace, said to be intended for the great duke, in case he had been so happy as to have children. There is also a nunnery lately built; and about fifteen English miles distant from the city at CZARSKO ZELO, is a royal palace. These edifices are for the most part of brick, and plaistered over so as to make an elegant appearance; but the work is generally done in a hurry, and the materials not very durable. An ITALIAN architect having been some years since established in RUSSIA, the taste of ITALY is adopted in almost all their houses; and though the severity of the climate is so great, they abound in windows much beyond our houses in ENGLAND. As a further additional beauty to this city, the Empress has caused a large equestrian statue of Peter the Great in metal, to be made under the care of the ingenious and much esteemed count Rostrelli [sic], intending to erect it on a pedestal in the area before the palace, in pious memory of her father.

This first great equestrian statue of Peter by Carlo Rastrelli was, however, never erected where Elizabeth intended and was simply kept out of sight during the reign of Catherine II, who was to commission her own 'Bronze Horseman'; it was, however, to be rescued by the Emperor Paul, who placed it in 1800 before his Michael Castle with the inscription 'To Great-Grandfather from Great-Grandson'.

It is ironic that Hanway fails to mention that the Italian architect of most of the buildings to which he refers was none other than Bartolomeo Rastrelli, the son of his 'much esteemed' sculptor Carlo Rastrelli and the great architect of Elizabeth's reign, although, as we have seen, he had begun his illustrious career under Anna. It was Rastrelli who strove to fulfill the empress's 'passion' for building, creating a series of palaces and churches in the heavily ornate style of the high Baroque which she adored. The Winter Palace to which Hanway referred was, however, still the one built for Anna and incorporating the Apraksin mansion: the present, fifth, palace was begun by Rastrelli only in the year of the publication of Hanway's book. Although the palace which would seem to be the Anichkov, situated at the junction of Nevskii Prospekt and the Fontanka, and destined not for for the Grand Duke Peter but for the empress's favourite A.K. Razumovskii, was built by Zemtsov and Dmitriev and only completed in 1754 by Rastrelli, Rastrelli had by then built a new wooden Summer Palace for Elizabeth (at the junction of the Fontanka and the Moika) and a temporary wooden Winter Palace (at the corner of Nevskii Prospekt and the Moika); he had also virtually finished his graceful Smol'nyi Cathedral (but without its planned independent belltower) and completed his famous Catherinian Palace at Tsarskoe Selo, to both of which Hanway refers, but he was also engaged in rebuilding the Grand Palace at Peterhof and, within the city itself, the Stroganov and Vorontsov Palaces. Rastrelli is perhaps today the best-known name among all the architects to have worked in St Petersburg, but he had to wait decades, more than a century, before he received any sort of recognition in Britain. In the reign of Catherine the Great, the British, who were to come in far greater numbers, would have no time for him nor for his architectural style – neither would the new empress.

A mansion, built in the 1730s and described as 'a regular structure of Italian architecture', when an engraving of it appeared on the pages of the London *Gentleman's Magazine* in the 1790s, did, however, command a place of affection in British hearts after it was acquired by the Russia Company in 1753. Formerly the house of Count B.P.

Sheremetev, it had stood empty and neglected for many years but, after much reparation, the English Church opened for divine service in March 1754 and became the centre and symbol of the British community in St Petersburg until the October Revolution. The chaplain at the time wrote that

> we intend, please God, to fit up a large and lofty Room or Salle, in the middle Story, for a Place of Divine Worship. The Summer being the only Season proper to build or repair Houses here, we are making the best use of it we can, and hope we shall be able, towards the end of next Autumn, to remove our old Pulpit and Pews, from a ruinous Salle into one half-finished. But as to the full Completion of the Work, our funds are not yet sufficient for it.

The church was located on the left bank on the Neva, west of the Admiralty and along the embankment known as Galley (*Galernaia*). It was already a place where prominent members of the British community were living, as both Cook and Mrs Justice testify: shipbuilders, already in the reign of Peter I, then merchants, then others — the Rondeaus lived there in the 1730s. In the remaining decades of the eighteenth century, it became known, as yet unofficially, as the English Line or Embankment.

CHAPTER 3

CATHERINE THE GREAT'S CITY
AND THE NORTHERN TOUR

If Elizabeth's St Petersburg attracted few British tourists and fewer accounts, Catherine's city was to prove a magnet for all manner of visitors, including those who were to be employed as naval officers, gardeners, doctors, specialists and craftsmen, an inevitable clutch of adventurers and fortune-seekers, and an increasing stream of tourists, a number of whom travelled, pen in hand and with an eye on possible publication. One of the publishing variety noted towards the end of the 1780s that 'Russia begins now to make a part of the grand tour, and not the least curious or useful part of it', and events in France soon made a trip to the north an attractive alternative to the more common European routes. Already in the early years of Catherine's reign, however, the concept of a 'northern tour' had gained currency; as a title, it seems to have been used for the first time in 1777 for the travel letters of John Henniker, later 2nd Lord Henniker, prepared for publication but never seeing the light of day. The travelogue in general was also enjoying great popularity in the last decades of the eighteenth century; Russian 'tours' began to feature with some regularity and included contributions from 'armchair travellers', who considered Russia distant enough but interesting enough as a suitable case for treatment. Accounts from earlier reigns (Mrs Rondeau and John Cook) were also published for the first time, although the St Petersburg they described was already 'historical'.

From a wealth of sources available from Catherine's reign (1762–96), eight have been chosen, spanning the years 1774 to 1792, to register the initial impact that St Petersburg had on visitors. They vary from published contemporary accounts to letters and diaries, which have remained in archives or were published at a much later date. The authors were young aristocrats and gentry on the Grand Tour; travelling tutors, themselves still in their thirties; sons of merchants; and the wife of an English physician, accompanying her husband.

The twenty-three-year-old Sir Nathaniel Wraxall may be considered the first British tourist to publish an account of a visit to the Russian capital and his book, describing his visit in 1774, enjoyed considerable popularity and five editions:

[. . .] you must not expect any description of this great capital, which though only a creation of the present century, has already grown to a vast size, and contains infinitely higher matter of entertainment and instruction than either of those from whence I am lately come [Copenhagen and Stockholm]. I am struck with a pleasing astonishment, while I wander among havens, streets, and public buildings, which have arisen, as by inchantment, within the memory of men still alive, and have converted the marshy islands of the Neva into one of the most magnificent cities of the earth. The imagination, aided by so many visible objects, rises to the wondrous founder, and beholds in idea the tutelary genius of Peter, yet hovering over the child of his own production, and viewing with a parent's fondness it's [sic] rising palaces and temples. [. . .] This city is as yet only an immense outline, which will require future empresses, and almost future ages, to complete. It stands at present on a prodigious extent of land; but as the houses in many parts are not contiguous, and great spaces are left unbuilt, it is hard to ascertain it's real size and magnitude.

The Rev. William Coxe, Cambridge don and travelling tutor to George, Lord Herbert, describes in a book published in 1784 the impressions of his first visit to St Petersburg six years previously:

The views upon the banks of the Neva exhibit the most grand and lively scenes I ever beheld. That river is in many places as broad as the Thames at London: it is also deep, rapid, and as transparent as crystal; and the banks are lined with handsome buildings. On the north side the fortress, the Academy of Sciences, and Academy of Arts, are the most striking objects; on the opposite side are the Imperial palace, the admiralty, the mansions of many Russian nobles, and the English line, so called because the whole row is principally occupied by the English merchants. In the front of these buildings, on the south side, is the Quay, which stretches for three miles, except where it is interrupted by the Admiralty; and the Neva, during the whole of that space has been lately embanked by a wall, parapet, and pavement of hewn granite; a magnificent and durable monument of imperial munificence.

Dr Thomas Dimsdale first visited Russia in 1768 to inoculate Catherine and her son Paul and returned thirteen years later to repeat the operation on Paul's sons, the future Alexander I and Constantine. Just months earlier, the sixty-eight-year-old had married as his third wife the forty-eight-year-old Elizabeth, whose record of their visit in 1781 remained within the family until its publication in 1989:

> St Petersburg is a much finer Place than I expected. On my entering it appeared very grand, as all the Steeples and Spires are covered with Tin and Brass, and some of them gilt, the Sun shining full upon them made a very gay appearance. The Palace is a prodigious fine Building, and a great many elegant Houses are dispersed about the City. The Streets in general are very good, and particularly that which leads to the Admiralty, which I think was near two Miles in length; in general they are paved, but a few remain in the old state. The View upon the Banks of the River Neva exhibited the grandest lively Scenes I ever beheld.

The young George Norman's unpublished letter to his stepmother in 1784 conveys quite a different reaction:

> this City is large, contg. near 200th people, & has some Streets very magnificent, but there are stately palaces & miserable ruins mingled throughout. [...] the marble palace of prince Orloff which the Empress has bought of his heirs, the royal palace, & the museum are the only things in the town worth attention. I have walked almost every morning, & pried into every place; & by that means perfectly acquainted with ye town. To give you a discription of it would be tedious & incomprehensible. you find a mixture of grandeur & filth, in & out of their Houses, in every Street. [...] the chief pleasure I have in traversing this City, is in contemplating the State of this place the beginning of this Age, & in knowing a little of the History of the great man who began it, & brought it to great perfection.

In 1787 the twenty-two-year-old James Brogden was sent by his father, a prominent merchant of the Russia Company, to see something of the city and country he had known decades earlier:

The first appearance to a foreigner has a very striking effect, as I suppose there is hardly any Town in Europe that has so many magnificent public Buildings. Many of these & some of the Palaces of the Nobility are built upon a much more magnificent Scale than any buildings I am acquainted with in London. The Empresses Palace is a great pondrous mass of Building and does not please me so much as some of the former. [. . .] The appearance of the Town, considering there are no shops, is very gay.

The Scot Andrew Swinton, a sentimental traveller in the Sternian mould, was much given to evocative pen-pictures in describing his stay by the banks of the Neva in 1788:

Petersburg, with all its stately palaces and gilded domes, is situated in the midst of a wood, as wild and barren as any in the north. It presents a wonderful picture of what power and genius can accomplish. Independent of art, the Neva is its only ornament: a dead, sandy, flat country, covered with brush-wood, surrounds it upon every side; a few miserable huts scattered about, complete the scene. The great Peter did not look to the most beautiful, but to the most useful spot, for the site of his capital: his object was commerce solely. Petersburg is the emporium for naval – Moscow for rural affairs.

Lionel Colmore, a young Oxford graduate on the Grand Tour, visited St Petersburg in 1790 and his lively and irreverent letters were published in 1812, a few years after his death:

Petersburg is in some respects a finer place than I expected to find it, in others it is not so fine: all the buildings are of coarse brick, and very badly constructed; they are stuccoed, but the white falls off, or grows green and dirty, which gives the town the look of a decayed place, rather than of a rising one. The houses too are most of them low, some with two stories, many with only one; and, as the streets are very broad, the effect is but indifferent. Besides, as the houses are so low, they are consequently very long, which gives a straggling appearance to the whole, and extends the streets out of all proportion: the one which I inhabit is full two English miles long, yet it does not contain so many inhabitants as a street of moderate length in London.

Finally, the much-suffering Oxford don and 'bear-leader' John Parkinson, kept memorable diaries of his visit in 1792, published only in 1971:

I cannot describe the impressions which were made this morning on my mind by the first sight of this magnificent town, which in grandeur very far exceeds every other that I have seen. But I am particularly struck in all the private as well as public edifices with such an uncommon display of Grecian Architecture, which might lead us to fancy ourselves under the genial atmosphere of Athens, instead of so northern a latitude. [. . .] In walking through this fine Town one cannot help forseeing that if ever it comes to be neglected it must necessarily become very forlorn and ragged, from the stucco dropping off, which will expose the shabby brickwork behind.

Inevitably, given their backgrounds, ages and tastes, there is no unanimity among the writers in what they highlight, what they praise or condemn, but the majority were clearly impressed by what they saw, particularly by the views by the Neva, by many of the buildings and the streets. Superlatives trip off the tongue, but there are many words of caution about the quality of the building and the feeling that all could rapidly deteriorate. They were aware of how much had been accomplished in so short a time and of how much had still to be done to match the dreams of the great Peter.

Coxe did not exaggerate when he suggested that, following Peter, 'succeeding sovereigns have continued to embellish Petersburgh, but none more than the present empress, who may be called its second founder'. Hanway had pointed to Elizabeth's 'passion' for building, but Catherine was a self-confessed 'maniac' – for plants and gardens, for England, indeed, and for building, not only throughout the city but also on her many estates, including, most notably, Tsarskoe Selo, where her

British architect Charles Cameron was reveal his versatility in the years following his arrival in 1779. It was perhaps the decision 'to dress the Neva in granite' that led to one of the most remarkable and lasting achievement of her reign. Shortly after her accession, she established a Commission for the Stone Construction of St Petersburg and Moscow and, within a year, work had begun on the reconstruction of Palace Embankment. This was soon followed by the embankments west of the Admiralty – the Galley Embankment – and to the east, past the Summer Garden. Later in Catherine's reign it was the turn of the Catherine Canal and the River Fontanka. Work proceeded over many decades and the turn of the Moika and of the embankment on Vasil'evskii Island lay in succeeding reigns, but Coxe was more than justified in hailing 'a magnificent and durable monument of imperial munificence' and all but the most begrudging of visitors failed to be impressed. Behind the embankments houses and palaces were being built, led by the empress's own additions to the Winter Palace.

British reactions to the Winter Palace continued to be mixed, with the majority impressed by the size but not by the taste. Wraxall was among the first to offer his opinion:

> The public buildings of different kinds are so prodigiously numerous in this city, that I am inclined to believe they constitute a fifth or sixth part of the whole capital. Some are of stone, but the larger part are only brick, or wood plaistered. The winter-palace is composed of the former materials, and was erected by the late Empress Elizabeth: it is very large and very heavy: one would have supposed Sir John Vanbrugh was invoked to lend his aid in the plan of it, since nothing can more strikingly resemble his style. It is not yet quite finished, like almost every thing else in Russia. The situation is very lovely, on the banks of the Neva, and in the center of the town.

He was obsessed by the feeling of the city as a vast building site with so much not yet finished and so much that would never be – sentiments shared a decade later by Baroness Dimsdale, commenting about the embankment that it would 'certainly when finished make a very grand and elegant appearance; but the Russians are with great truth remarked to begin things with great spirit and for a little time go on very rapidly, then leave for some other Object'. Far from enamoured of the Winter Palace and soon dismissing Rastrelli, the empress was indeed intent on creating additions that would conform more to her own preferences for the classical and for the small and intimate. In 1764 she commissioned J.B. Vallin de la Mothe to build the Small Hermitage to the east of Elizabeth's palace; this was followed within a few years by Iurii Fel'ten's Old Hermitage; and a decade later, this was connected by a covered bridge above the Winter Canal to Giacomo Quarenghi's elegant Hermitage Theatre, built on the site of Peter I's Winter Palace.

It was to the Small Hermitage in February 1769 that the British ambassador, Lord Cathcart, and his wife Jane were invited to an intimate *soirée*, hosted by Catherine's favourite Grigorii Orlov. In a letter to a friend back in Scotland Lady Cathcart, the most sympathetic, attractive and self-effacing of ambassadorial wives, captures the intimacy of the evening and provides a memorable pen-picture of Catherine in her prime, but also describes the way the meal was served without the presence of servants and the enchantment of the Hanging Garden which adjourned the apartments:

We were in haste to get back to Petersburgh, having received an invitation to sup at Count Orloffs and to be there at six o'clock. This, in other words, was to spend the evening and sup with the Empress, a most distinguished honor which has been payed to no other of the Diplomatique since we have been here, nor before, as I am told. At six we went to the Count Orloff's house, who received us at the head of the stair and stayed with us and some three or four others that are most frequently of the Empress' parties, his brother and his wife, Countess Bruce, Count Lochar Chemicheff [Zakhar Chernyshev], his wife, and one other lady was all the company, besides Count Panin and the Vice-Chancellor and three others, of which the Hetman Rasomorsky [Razumovskii] was one of those that we found playing at cribbidge with the Empress when we were conducted to her appartment. It looks upon the river on the one side and on the other side of a very large high room, I would call a Gallery, but for the breadth, there are arched windows that look into a greenhouse which was all lit up and is one of the most elegant and perfect things in its kind that ever was executed perhaps anywhere. We were immediately carried into it, and found ourselves in a Garden full of all the fragrant odours of the Spring. In the upper story there is a charming aviary of which you have none of the dirt and trouble – I suppose you see the birds by daylight, some of which are nightingales of which they have great numbers at Moscow, and in many parts of the Empire. Some of the Canary birds sang even then upon hearing people speak.

There were two or three parties of cards added to the Empress's table. My Lord was understood not to be a card player, so a chair was set for him near the Empress, who conversed with him the whole evening, minding her cards very little.

The arrival of supper was a new sight of entertainment; it was to be served without the intervention of servants present; all was prepared below and two squares of the size of the two tables at each end of the room opened in the floor, which run off in a groove, and up mounted the table with everything of the first course and candles lighted on it. Three courses were charged in like manner.

Her Majesty sat down at one end and made my Lord and his wife sit down on each side of her. One lady of the household, the Grand Echaneson Nanschkin's wife [le grand veneur Naryshkin] sat by my Lord, Mareschal Rasomorski by me, and Count Panin opposite the Empress, Count Orloff by the lady. The rest of the compny at the other table, with jokes and merriment throughout th whole supper, the Empress and Count Orloff among the merriest. The foundation of it arose chiefly from the novelty of this way of being served, for when the plates are changed you pull a string by the side of everybody's right hand which goes underneath the table and rings a bell. Your plate goes down, as all around it is composed of so many divisions like stove holes. You write down upon a slate and pencil which is fixed ready, and what you want immediately comes up. A great diversion was from one table to the other to send something or other that served to laugh. To the Empress from one of her Ministers at the other table came up two papers, the sight of which made her laugh, but she said she hoped to be excused from reading them at that time, and put them in her pocket with the greatest good humour of which I saw many instances that evening.

For example, when she took a walk with me in her garden after supper she found many of her flowers in glasses overturned, and some thrown quite out, which she immediately understood by those that had walked in it while she was at cards; she took them up herself and replaced them without the least discomposure, said the walk was narrow and she would infringe on the border to widen it.

Her dress was remarkably becoming to her that evening, it was all of a thin crimson velvet, a gown down to the ground without plaits behind and up as high as a man's coat with a little cape of the same, a petticoat and waistcoat of the same velvet all plain, and her blue ribband across, and star which was not of jewels as I have always seen her wear before, but I suppose this was understood to be in the Surtout stile. The sleeves were like a sack cuff sleeve with quite short lace, ruffles, and a frill round the neck like a riding dress. She had a small hoop and her gown long and graceful on the ground, her headdress is French without affectation, very easily dressed as her hair is very fine and in great quantity. She has here and there an immense single diamond stuck like pins and vast large diamond tops of earrings all of the first water. Her face is very handsome on the whole, and her figure also, suitable each to the other, and all to her station in which she contrives to keep up everything that is proper, at the same time that she puts it all out of her own thoughts, and is really mindful of nothing but the amusement, pleasure, and profit in some shape or other of every other being about her.

Baroness Dimsdale, benefitting from the empress's benevolence towards her husband, was allowed to wander through the palace, complementing Lady Cathcart's description of the Little Hermitage and the Winter Garden, but also describing other rooms in the palace, temporarily housing Catherine's already considerable collections of paintings, recently augmented by the Walpole Collection from Houghton, while the new gallery in the Old Hermitage was completed. She also draws attention to one of the few canvases painted during his short sojourn in Russia by Richard Brompton, the former President of the Society of Artists, who had been appointed painter to the imperial court in July 1780:

The Apartments in the Palace are very magnificently furnished, many large elegant Rooms, one is 180 feet high, 90 feet long, and 90 feet wide.

I was admitted into one as a great favour, passed by some Guards of Soldiers at each Door, in this Room the Jewels, Imperial Crown and Sceptre are kept; the Brilliant which forms the top of the Sceptre, is the largest in the known World. Prince Orloff gave more than ninety thousand Pounds for it, and presented it to the Empress; the weight of it is one hundred and ninety four and three quarters Carats, and the Crown is almost covered with large Diamonds and precious Stones, on the top is a prodigious fine Ruby, the Value of it never known 'tis quite perfect, and the weight of it is three Ounces and one quarter English weight. They are on a crimson Velvet Stool, covered with a large Glass like a Bell in the middle of the Room, a Gentleman gave me a Model of the Ruby and Diamond and a great many Cases are round the room like the shew Cases in our Jewellers Shops all full of Jewels to an immense Value.

From several of the Windows there is a most beautiful Prospect of the River Neva, and in one of the rooms a very fine Picture of the two young Princes Alexander and Constantine as large as life done by Brumpton. Alexander is drawn cutting the Gordian Knot in two. I likewise saw the Empress's Collection of Pictures, which are numerous and of the best Masters, among them were the whole of the Orford Collection, they are at present placed in a Gallery in the uppermost Story of the Palace, and in good Preservation. But a magnificent Gallery is building for them to which when finished they will be removed. On the upper part of the Palace there is also a spacious Apartment covered entirely with Glass and warmed by Stoves when necessary, in which there are a variety of Flowers and Shrubs, with some Birds of different kinds flying about. The Empress as I was informed takes great pleasure in frequently visiting this delightful place when she is there in the Winter.

It is to John Parkinson that we turn for a description of the Hermitage Theatre, which was completed only in 1787:

Our carriages not arriving in time we borrowed Dr. Rogerson's and instead of the Theatre were set down at the Grand Duke's apartments; from whence we were obliged to walk a long way to the Hermitage. In our way to the theatre we passed through a Suite of twelve apartments all crowded with paintings. Before we entered the theatre we were required to deliver our Swords. The Theatre resembles the ancient theatres in the arrangement of the Seats, which are of a semicircular form and rise one above the other. This has a very agreable effect and it must particularly from the stage.

The Grand Duke, the Grand Dutchess, and the young Princesses of Baden who arrived on Sunday Night, entered before the Empress and took their seats on one of the Benches. On their entering the company all stood up. The Grand Duke makes rather an insignificant appearance. The Grand Dutchess [Maria Fedorovna] is a large woman and seemed to behave with great decorum and good humour. [. . .] The Company all stood when the Empress came in and continued standing till she sat down. The Grand Duke set the example by doing the same. As everybody was very much dressed, particularly the men, the appearance was very brilliant. The play was Partie de chasse d'Henri IV, and it was followed by a ballet in which le Pique danced. It is the fashion to cry up very much the Scenes and the decorations, but I own that I was not particularly struck with them.

Catherine not only allocated apartments to her successive favourites but built palaces for them within the city and in its environs. In 1768 she commissioned Antonio Rinaldi to build for Orlov what became known as the Marble Palace on account of the twenty-eight varieties of marble used on both its interiors and exteriors, and which effectively closed the impressive sweep of Palace Embankment at its eastern end. It was one of the few buildings to interest George Norman and was praised by Coxe:

The brick houses are ornamented with a white stucco, which has led several travellers to assert that they are built with stone; whereas, unless I am mistaken, there are only two stone structures in all Petersburgh; the one the church of St. Isaac, of hewn granite, and marble columns, not yet finished; the other the marble palace constructed at the expence of the empress, on the banks of the Neva. Her imperial majesty gave this superb edifice to prince Orlof; and, at his death [in 1783], purchased it from his executor for 2,000,000 of roubles. The style of architecture is magnificent but heavy: the front is composed of polished granite and marble, and finished with such nicety, and in a style so superior to the contiguous buildings, that it seems to have been transported to the present spot, like a palace in the Arabian tales, raised by the enchantment of Aladdin's lamp. It contains forty rooms upon each floor, and is fitted up in a style of such splendor, that the expence of the furniture amounted to 1,500,000 roubles.

The other 'stone' building mentioned in this passage by Coxe, St Isaac's Cathedral, was also designed by Rinaldi, although continued by Vicenzo Brenna, and was indeed begun in the same year as his Marble Palace. The church was the third to bear the name of St Isaac of Dalmatia, (whose day, 30 May O.S. was also the birthday of Peter I). The original wooden church in front of the Admiralty had been replaced by one in brick by Mattarnovy in 1717 on a site a little nearer to the river than that chosen in 1766 for Falconet's Bronze Horseman. Rinaldi was given a new location behind the statue on the Peter Square (now Decembrists' Square) and nearer to the present St Isaac's Cathedral, for which, still uncompleted, it was eventually to be demolished at the beginning of the next century. It is, however, the ceremony of laying its foundation stone in August 1768 that is recalled by William Richardson, tutor to the Cathcart children, who published his letters in 1784:

I am just returned from witnessing the ceremony of the Empress's laying the foundation of a church dedicated to St. Isaac; and which is intended to be the largest in St. Petersburgh. St. Isaac is held in esteem by the Russians, not so much for any distinguished character of his own, as that the day consecrated to him was the birth-day of Peter the Great. [. . .] As the ceremony I shall now describe to you was reckoned of great importance, it was performed with great pomp and magnificence. All the space to be occupied by the church had been previously railed in; and into this place, only persons of high rank, and those who had a particular permission, were admitted. An immense multitude of people were assembled without. An arch, supported upon eight pillars of the Corinthian order, and adorned with garlands, was raised immediately over the place intended for the altar. Beneath this arch was a table covered with crimson velvet, fringed with gold; upon which was placed a small marble chest, fixed to a pully directly above the table. On a side-table, fixed to one of the pillars, was a large gold plate, with medals and coins, to be deposited at the foundation, and a gold box to contain them. On another side-table was another gold plate, containing two pieces of marble in the form of bricks, a gold plate with mortar, and other two plates of the same metal, in which were two hammers and two trowels of gold.

Twenty years later, when the building was at roof level, a young twenty-four-year old British naval captain took it into his head to impress with his funambulism the daughters of Lev Naryshkin, who lived in an adjacent mansion:

> The church looked immediately into Narishkin's windows, and because the girls happened to be looking at us when we were on the ridge, Bentinck [Count William Bentinck] took it into his head to walk along it from one end to the other for no one reason that could possibly be given, for he did not better his view in the least by it, and the way was much worse than that we had come up. If he had slipped his foot in the least nothing could have prevented his fall to the ground, which from the ridge of the roof is as near as I can guess nearly two hundred feet. When I [Captain James Hawkins] attributed to vanity his having performed this exploit, he was quite angry.

More famous than the Marble Palace but more melancholy in its fate was the Taurida Palace that Catherine built for Prince Potemkin. Designed by the Russian architect Ivan Starov, who was also responsible for the Trinity Cathedral that rose with its St Peter's- rather than St Basil's-style dome over the Alexander Nevskii Monastery, the palace was an impressive essay in severe classicism, light years away from Rastrellian baroque. It was begun in 1783 and finished a year or so before it was seen by Colmore in 1790:

> The finest *skeleton* of a house (for there is nothing but bare walls) is Prince Potemkin's; it is but one story, but there is no end to the rooms, and they are all as immense as himself. there is one gallery two hundred feet long, with a double row of fifty pillars on each side; one of the sides opening into a winter garden, so large, that there are several walks in it, with a temple in the middle, in which is a statue of the Empress. In

summer the window-frames are taken out, and the whole thrown open to a large English garden, where there are a piece of water, shrubberies, temples, ruins, &c. All this is in the town; most probably, however, it will never be finished, as he has sent for his gardener and architect, and is building a palace and laying out gardens at Jassy.

When it was visited by Parkinson two years later, Potemkin was dead and Catherine had taken the palace back as an imperial residence. It was a place she loved and which still held memories of the famous celebrations that Potemkin, after his triumphant return from the Crimea, had orchestrated in her honour on 28 April 1791 and to which Parkinson alludes:

At twelve o'clock we had appointed to go with Gould to the Taurida Palace, which was built by the late Prince Potemkin and is now the autumn residence of her Imperial Majesty. We were met there by Paget [a member of British Embassy] with three Poles and a Polish lady. Unfortunately the young Grand Duke happened to visit the palace this morning; which obliged us to hide ourselves for half an hour in a gallery.

This noble edifice was created in twelve months about seven or eight years ago after a design of the Prince himself. The most remarkable thing in it, however, is the great hall. This room is 60 feet broad and 250 long, terminating at each end in a bow raised a step above the floor and separated from the winter garden on one side and the salle du dome on the other by a double colonnade of eighteen Ionic Columns. Simplicity, grandeur and good taste reigns throughout, especially in the architectural decorations. In the bow at one End the Prince used to dine and has often entertained the Empress. In the bow at the other a band of Music was stationed which always played during dinner. The Empress dines in the middle of the room. The Galleries in the Colonnade were intended for Spectators. The Empress resided here about a week only this year, but she intends to make a longer residence the next.

The dome in the room I call the 'Salle du dome' is a decagon, which as well as some other is exceedingly well managed. A temple stands in the middle of the winter garden wherein is placed a marble statue of the Empress by Shubin with this very chaste and elegant inscription in

Russian, 'To the Mother of her Country and more than Mother to me'. There are two vases one at each end of the great hall, copies from the antique at Rome, adorned with bas reliefs representing a Bacchanalian procession and the sacrifice of Iphigenia, the price of which was ten thousand ducats. The garden, which consists of a number of walks winding among groves of winter plants, is embellished with marble Statues, Urns and vases. Artificial palms support the roof the festoon and various decorations of that kind which were put up three or four years ago on occasion of a great illumination made here by the Prince still remain. On that occasion the wax alone was an expense to him of fourteen thousand roubles, [which] equals near eighteen hundred pounds. He had given orders, which orders I suppose were counter-manded, for an organ to cost fifty thousand roubles.

Parkinson's guide was William Gould, the eminent English gardener from Ormskirk in Lancashire, who was responsible for the care of the magical Winter Garden and also for transforming the land around the palace into an English landscape garden. When, in February 1794, after an interval of fifteen months, Parkinson again visited the palace, he records that

> [Gould] walked with me once more through the saloon and Winter Garden, with which I was again as much struck as I had been at the first sight. The Model for a bridge of one arch over the Neva which we went to see in the Vasili Ostrof is now removed hither and placed over a piece of water. Potemkin meant to have embellished the Ground in front of the palace with Colonnades. The work at present going on is an Ah Ah and iron railing to encompass the whole garden.

The model of a bridge to which Parkinson was referring is of consid-erable historical interest. He had earlier met its inventor, the self-taught and ingenious Ivan Kulibin, and seen the model in its original home in the Academy of Sciences, where Kulibin, who was for many years head of the workshops, had built it in 1776. It was there that William Coxe had also gone to inspect this revolutionary single-arch bridge, designed to cross the Neva but destined instead, as a wooden model, to straddle a small canal in the grounds of the Taurida Palace:

The divisions of Petersburgh, on each side of the Neva, are connected by a bridge on pontoons, which was usually removed when the large masses of ice driven down the stream from the Lake Ladoga, first made their appearance, and for a few days, until the river was frozen sufficiently hard to bear carriages, there was no communication between the opposite parts of the town. the depth of the river renders it extremely difficult to build a stone bridge; and if one should be constructed, it would probably be destroyed by these vast shoals of ice. To remedy this inconvenience, a Russian peasant projected the sublime plan of throwing a wooden bridge of a single arch across the river, which in its narrowest part is 980 feet in breadth. the artist has executed a model 98 feet in length, which I examined with great attention, as he explained the proportion and mechanism.

The bridge is constructed on the same principle as that of Schaffhausen, excepting that the mechanism is more complicated, and the road not so level. I shall attempt to describe it by supposing it finished, as that will convey the best idea of the plan. The bridge is roofed at the top, and enclosed at the sides: it is formed by four frames of timber, two on each side, composed of beams or trusses, which support the whole fabric. The road is not carried over the top of the arch, but suspended in the middle. There is a difference of 35 feet between the road at the spring of the arch, and the road at the center; in other words, as acent of 35 feet in 490, which is little more than eight-tenths of an inch to a foot. The bridge is broadest towards the sides, and diminishes towards the center.

The artist informed me, that to construct the bridge would require 49,650 nails, 12,908 large trees, 5,500 beams, and that it would cost 300,000 roubles, or £60,000. He speaks of this bold project with the warmth of genius, and is convinced that it is practicable. I must own, I am of the same opinion, though I hazard it with great diffidence. What a noble effect would be produced by a bridge springing across the Neva, with an arch 980 feet wide, and towering 168 feet from the surface of the water! The description of such a bridge seems almost chimerical; and yet, on inspecting the model, we are reconciled to the idea. But whether the execution of this stupendous work may be deemed possible or not, the model itself is worthy of attention, and reflects high honour on the inventive faculties of untutored genius: it is so compact, that it supported 3,540 pood, or 127,440 pounds, without swerving from its direction, which is far more, in proportion to its size, than the bridge, if completed, would have occasion to sustain from the pressure of the carriages added to its weight.

The projector of this plan was apprentice to a shop-keeper at Nishnei Novogorod; and, like the Swiss carpenter who built the bridge of Schaffhausen, unacquainted with the theory of mechanics. Opposite to his dwelling was a wooden clock, which excited his curiosity; by repeated examination he comprehended the internal structure, and, without assistance, formed one exactly similar. His success in this essay urged him to undertake the construction of metal clocks and watches. The empress, acquainted with these wonderful exertions of native genius, took him under her protection, and sent him to England; from whence, on account of his ignorance of the language, he soon returned to Russia. I saw a repeating watch of his workmanship at the Academy of Sciences: it is about the bigness of an egg; in the middle is represented the tomb of our Saviour, with the stone at the entrance, and the centinels upon duty; suddenly the stone is removed, the centinels fall down, the angels appear, the women enter the sepulchre, and the chant performed on Easter eve is heard. These are trifling, although curious performances; but the plan of the bridge was a sublime conception. This person, whose name is Kulibin, bears the appearance of a Russian peasant; he has a long beard, and wears the common dress of the country; he receives a pension from the empress, and is encouraged to follow the bent of his mechanical genius.

There is no evidence that Kulibin ever went to England, but English inventions certainly made their way to Catherine's Russia. It was Kulibin, indeed, who had repaired and demonstrated to Parkinson and his companions the workings of the great Peacock Clock, invented by the London watchmaker James Coxe and bought by Potemkin from the notorious Duchess of Kingston for his palace (but now a highlight of the Hermitage): 'a curious piece of Mechanism made by Cox in which a tune is played with balls; a golden peacock unfolds his plumage and a golden Cock crows. A tree with gilded leaves embellishes the work'.

Examples of British expertise and workmanship and of less obvious British influences were to be found in another palace that was built in the middle years of Catherine's reign and was situated at the other end of town from Potemkin's Taurida Palace. On the Petersburg–Tsarskoe Selo road (not far from the present-day Victory Square (*Park pobedy*) and the Moscow Prospekt) the Russian architect Iurii Fel'ten began in 1774 a palace for the empress which originally bore the name of Kekerekeksinskii, as Baroness Dimsdale valiantly attempted to convey in the following excerpt:

> A few days before I left St Petersburg a Gentleman took me to Hickeri-Kickeri which in English is called Frog-Hall, distant four or five Miles from Petersburg on the Road to Sarsko-Sello. It is a small elegant House, with only one large Room on a floor, the first Room had not any thing extraordinary in it, it was furnished very handsomly [*sic*] and had a compleat Set of Wedgewood ware, with a green Frog painted on every Piece by the particular Orders of the Empress, as there are a very large quantity of Frogs on the ground, it being a deep Swamp. In the Room on the second floor, were Pictures of all the crowned Heads in Europe, the Empress Grand Duke and his first Dutchess were placed at the upper end of the Room, and I was pleased to observe that our King and Queen were hung next to them, very near was a fine Picture of the Prince of Wales and the Duke of York, at the Age of eleven or twelve with their hands placed on each others shoulder. This was painted by Brompton, and esteemed a very fine Picture.

Catherine liked to call her palace 'La Grenouillère' and it was the emblem of a green frog that was to adorn the 952-piece table and dessert service she was to commission from Wedgwood in 1773. The service bore views of British houses, castles, gardens etc., among which was Longford Abbey in Wiltshire. It was on a drawing of Longford Castle that Fel'ten had based the triangular shape of his palace, which, along with the recently finished adjacent church in the fashionable 'Moorish' style, was renamed the Chesmenskii in 1780 to celebrate the stunning Russian victory over the Turkish fleet a decade earlier. The 'Frog' service, like the portraits of King George III and his consort, painted by George Dance, and the painting of the royal princes (by Benjamin West and not by Brompton), which the king had given Catherine in 1778, are now in the Hermitage.

All things connected with Peter were an inevitable attraction for British visitors and the empress did much to foster links between her reign and her predecessor's, symbolized not least in the inscription 'Petro Primo Catharina Secunda' on the rock of the Bronze Horseman. The boat known as 'the Grandfather of the Russian Fleet' and the wooden 'Little House of Peter the Great' were part of the cult and the empress sought to preserve both within specially built brick structures, as William Coxe records:

> Within the fortress is a four-oared boat, secured with great veneration, in a brick building, and preserved as a memorial to future ages of its being the origin of the Russian fleet. Peter I used to call it the *Little Grandsire*, and, in the latter part of his reign, ordered it to be trans-ported to Petersburgh: it was conducted in solemn procession, to excite the admiration of the people, and exposed to view that they might compare the former condition of the marine, with the improved state in which he left it. [. . .]
>
> From the fortress we took water, and landed at an adjacent spot in the island of Petersburgh, near a wooden hovel, remarkable as the habi-tation of Peter the Great, while the fortress was constructing. It still remains in its original state, and stands under a brick building, erected to preserve it from destruction. the house is a ground floor, with only three rooms, which I had the curiosity to measure. They are but eight feet in height: the apartment for the reception of company is 15 feet square; the dining-room 15 by 12, and the bed-chamber ten. Near this house is another four-oared boat, the work of Peter's own hands, which has been erroneously called the *Little Grandsire*.

Elizabeth Dimsdale made the same pilgrimage and then proceeded to view Peter's collections of curiosities gathered in the Kunstkamera on Vasil'evskii Island, to the description of which she brought her own inimitable style:

> The Library belonging to the Academy is a large Building containing several Rooms and Galleries, it is furnished with many thousand Volumes. In the first Chamber of Rarities is the Empress's and Grand Duke's Profile in Plaister of Paris, with many others of considerable

Note. I was very much pleased to see the Baron's Profile, but I cannot say it was like him, for I should not have discovered it if in large black Letters there had not been wrote over it Dimsdale, in this room were many more things too tedious to mention. The next Apartment was full of all kinds of Animals stuffed, a Skeleton of an Elephant, and one stuffed with the figure of a Turk riding as they do in Turkey, there were a great many bones of Elephants found in Siberia, and what was very singular the oldest Person living in those Parts cannot from any Tradition remember ever to have heard of an Elephant being in any part of that Country. The Horse that Peter the great usually rode and was upon at the Battle of Pultona and a Spaniel Dog both stuffed (the Dog always went with him) and the Saddle and Stirrups he used to ride on, are covered over with a large Glass Case, and are preserved extremely well. We saw the Cabinet where they informed me were many Eastern Coins, this room has several very antient Manuscripts, and valuable Books, one Manuscript although of very modern date is yet highly valued and curious on account of the August Person by whom it was written, and is preserved in an elegant Vase of Bronze gilt, it contains the Empress's Instructions drawn up by herself and written with her own hand, and in one part of it she says, the young Women are sufficiently inclined to marry, it is the young men we must encourage; this MSS is always placed on the Table whenever the Members of the Academy hold a solemn Meeting.

In a small room adjoining I was very much entertained with a wax figure of Peter the Great as large as Life sitting in an armed Chair, the Features bear the most perfect resemblence to the Original because they were taken from a Mould applied to his Face when dead and coloured in imitation of his real Complexion. The Eyebrows and Hair are black, the Eyes dark and Complexion swarthy, the Aspect has a fierce look, and the Head inclined to one side according to his usual Custom, the figure measures about six feet, it is clothed in the only full Dress which that Emperor ever wore; and is the same he had on when with his one hand he placed the Crown upon the Head of his beloved Catherine, it was worked by her, it is a Suit of blue Silk richly embroidered with Silver, the Stockings are of flesh-coloured Silk with Silver Clocks. This Apartment contained also the brass hilted Sword which he wore at the Battle of Pultona [Poltava], and the hat used on the same

Occasion, which was pierced near the Crown by a Musket Ball, his Trowsers, a pair of worsted Stockings mended by himself, Shoes and Cap which he wore at Sardan in Holland when he worked in the Dock Yard in the Character of Master Peter, a piece of Leather which he bought of a Cobler when he was in England and it is said of him that as soon as he had taken it in his hand and felt of it he turned to the person with him his Countryman, and said when shall I see such a piece of Leather made in Russia.

We next went up Stairs into a Gallery where we saw many Kamschatkadale Curiosities, amongst them were Kamschatkadale Sorcerers, they were accoutered as in the Exercise of their Profession, and had hanging round them a number of Iron rings, they had in their hands a musical Instrument resembling a Drum, were as large as Life, and many more figures of the same size drest in their different Country Dresses in the Empress's Dominons in Siberia, Tartars, Finns, and Laplanders etc: and several of their Idols which they worship are the strangest I ever saw.

It was, however, the Falconet statue of Peter, the Bronze Horseman, that became an inescapable subject for description and comment in letters and diaries and published books, especially following its official unveiling on 7/18 August 1782. Especially, but not initially, for the first published description dates from 1768 and was based by its anonymous author on viewing the so-called 'small model' of the statue that Falconet had produced soon after his arrival in St Petersburg in February of the same year:

The sculptor, who is at present employed in making an equestrian statue of Peter the Great, gives us simply the figure of his heroe [*sic*] on horse-back. Yet simple as this image is, the countenance, the air, the right-hand which is extended express, in characters legible by every poetic eye, the thought and deep reflection of the founder of an empire: the astonishing rapidity with which he produced those revolutions in the manners and customs of his people, is clearly signified by the galloping of his horse: the difficulties he had to encounter in his enter-prizes are most aptly designed by his ascending a rifted rock, which serves as the pedestal of his piece: nay, he has even found the means to mark the period of his heroe's life, by shewing that he never reached the decline. If, instead of this poetry, which is so naturally in his subject, the sculptor had described him driving the allegorical figures of barbarism, ignorance, and superstition before him, I much doubt but this benefactor of his country had appeared like a tyrant, who in wantonness trampled his subjects under his horses houghs [*sic*]. It is quite from my point here to speak of the execution of this work, and therefore I say nothing of the beauties of the drapery, which is so happily pictoresque, or of the difficulty of representing the courser in the attitude I have just mentioned. As yet the artist has only finished his small model, the large one is but just begun.

The large model was seen in 1774 by Wraxall, who had long conversations with the sculptor and offered an interpretation that affords a valuable complement and variation to the earlier reaction:

In this production he has united the greatest simplicity with the truest sublimity of conception. No other statue, whether antient or modern, gave him the design, which is singular in it's kind, and is admirably adapted to express the character of the man, and the nation over which he reigned. Instead of a pedestal adorned with inscriptions, or surrounded by slaves, he appears mounted on a rock or stone of a prodigious size, up the ascent of which the horse labors, and appears to have nearly reached it's summit. This attitude has given him room to exert great anatomical beauty and skill in the muscles of the horse's hind thighs and hams, on which the whole weight of his body is necessarily sustained. The Czar's figure is full of fire and spirit: he sits on a bear skin, and is clad in a simple habit not characteristic of any particular country, but such as may be worn, without violation of propriety, by an inhabitant of any. His eye is directed to some apparently distant object, designed to be the citadel, and on his features are most strongly impressed the sentiment of 'deliberation and public care:' his left hand holds the bridle, and his right is extended, as the artist himself expressed it, en pere & en maitre.

The unveiling of the monument was recorded in the British newspapers and journals and numerous eye-witness accounts appeared over the following decades. A similar reaction on seeing the finished monument, or at least, 'the Thunder-Stone', on which the statue was placed, was shared in 1784 by George Norman, who found that 'the famous Statue of Peter Ist does not answer my expectation. the rock, once 1200 tons, is chipped away to one Quarter; & a small part only appears above ground: not enough in proportion to the Size of the figure which certainly is fine', and by William Coxe, who, on his second visit to St Petersburg, suggested that Falconet had been 'too lavish of the chisel' in reducing the great rock.

A visitor who had little time for monarchs, living or dead, was the philanthropist John Howard who visited St Petersburg in 1781 and again in 1789, driven by his obsession with the state of prisons and hospitals in various parts of the world. Although Howard, according to Elizabeth Dimsdale, on gazing at the Neva panorama, 'turned to me and observed that it put him in mind of a Story he had heard of a Person who was so delighted with a fine Prospect that he said this and Heaven is too much', his attention was generally fixed on institutions that would benefit people, educate them, alleviate their sufferings – or cause them to suffer. Here is his account of Petersburg prisons, including the Peter and Paul Fortress, in 1781:

The governor of the police at Petersburg was so kind as to fix a time for showing me all the instruments commonly used for punishment – the axe and the block – the machine (now out of use) for breaking the arms and legs – the instrument for slitting or lacerating the nostrils – and that for marking criminals (which is done by punctuation, and then rubbing a black powder on the wounds) – the knoot whip – and another called the cat, which consistes of a number of thongs from two to ten. The knoot whip is fixed to a long handle a foot long, and consists of several thongs about two feet in length twisted together, to the end of which is fastened a single tough thong of a foot and a half, tapering towards a point, and capable of being changed by the executioner, when too much softened by the blood of the criminal.

10 August, 1781, I saw two criminals, a man and a woman, suffer the punishment of the knoot. They were conducted from prison by about fifteen hussars and ten soldiers. When they arrived at the place of punishment, the hussars formed themselves into a ring round the

whipping-post, the drum beat a minute or two, and then some prayers were repeated, the populace taking off their hats. The woman was taken first; and after being roughly stripped to the waist, her hands and feet were bound with cords to a post made for the purpose, a man standing before the post to keep the cords tight. A servant attended the executioner, and both were stout men. The servant first marked his ground, and struck the woman five times on the back. Every stroke seemed to penetrate deep into her flesh. But his master thinking him too gentle, pushed him aside, took his place, and gave all the remaining strokes himself, which were evidently more severe. The woman received twenty-five, and the man sixty: I pressed through the hussars, and counted the number as they were chalked on a board. Both seemed but just alive, especially the man, who yet had strength enough to receive a small donation with some signs of gratitude. They were conducted back to prison in a little wagon. I saw the woman in a very weak condition some days after, but could not find the man any more.

In the fortress there were many vaulted rooms, some of which are now used for the confinement of deserters, and criminals of various sorts, who work on the fortifications. Some were glad of the privilege of being employed in the governor's garden, for the sake of the flour which he gave them for their labour. Others, with logs to their legs, were drawing wood out of the Neva. Thirty-five were crowded into one of the rooms, which therefore was excessively hot, having only two small apertures (ten inches by nine) for the admission of air. In another part of this building, seventy-five slaves with logs fastened to both their legs, were lodged in four rooms, which were still more close and offensive. In a few rooms (used as barracks) some officers were confined. Every room was furnished with an oven or stove, and most of them with barrack-beds.

In the police-station there were in one room nine women, and in two other rooms forty-four men. In two small and low arched cellars (very hot and offensive) I saw fifteen men, most of them in irons. In a room called the infirmary, detached from the rest of the prison, there were seven persons sick. All the prisoners subsist on voluntary contributions, collected in boxes before their grates, and at church. This is all the advantage they derive from the church near the prison, for they are never permitted to enter it, or to go out of their rooms; except on particular occasions with guards of soldiers.

The prison for debtors consists of four vaulted rooms communicating with one another, and furnished with stoves and barrack-beds. The prisoners are never permitted to go out of their rooms. They subsist by alms received from passengers in little boxes placed before the windows; but government supplies them with wood for fuel. One told me, he had been confined for five years, for a debt of fifteen roubles; and another, four years for twenty-five roubles.

These impressions may be counterbalanced by his positive account of improvements that he observed in Petersburg hospitals on his return in 1789:

At St. Petersburg I took partly the same round of the prisons and hospitals that I had done just eight years before. As to the former there has been little alteration; and the new house of correction, which was then nearly finished, has never been inhabited, and is going to ruin, as many of the upper floors are fallen in; so that I now shall pass over the prisons, and with pleasure mention some of the improvements in the hospitals of this city.

The marine and military hospitals nearly join, and make a large square with a morass in the middle; which if formed into a bason with a canal into the river Neva, would be salutary and sightly. The rooms are all empty, and lately white-washed, except three, in which were venereal patients, and 36 slaves who had their irons on. All the other sick were in the summer lazaretto, which I formerly mentioned with great approbation. These are rooms made of wood in an enclosed area or garden, the size 40 feet by 26: most of them have nine windows on each of two sides, and two opposite doors at the ends, with apertures over them. these rooms have chimnies, are floored, and are about nine inches from the (sandy) ground. They are 20 feet asunder; each room contains about 42 patients, who have separate beds. the rooms were in general clean and quiet; but some much more so than others, according to the disposition of the two (women) nurses that were alloted to each room. In the centre is the bathing house. The number given me of all the sick at one of my visits, namely, Aug. 31, 1789, was 534.

A new and splendid hospital has been erected just out of the city, and opposite a fine canal: the rooms are spacious, lofty and clean, and had been lately white-washed. The patients were of both sexes, in separate summer lazaretts in the adjoining court; the rooms and beds were clean and neat. Men and women prisoners come here every day; the latter to wash and clean the rooms, the former to remove what is offensive from the outside sewers of every room.

An institution which elicited his admiration and praise on both visits was the Smol'nyi Institute for Young Noblewomen, situated in the buildings adjacent to Rastrelli's Smol'nyi Cathedral:

On a rising ground at a little distance from Petersburg, and on the south side of the river Neva, there is a stately pile of buildings, originally designed for a convent, but ever since 1764 converted by the Empress Catherine the Second, into a public establishment for educating the female nobility of Russia, and a limited number of the children of commoners. The sleeping room and dining-halls in these buildings are remarkably lofty and airy, having large galleries round them; and adjoining to the buildings there are spacious gardens and lawns, which extend to the banks of the river. The number of children of nobility on this establishment is two hundred; and the number of the children of commoners, or peasants was, till 1770, limited to two hundred and forty: but since this year it has been increased to two hundred and eighty, by a fund provided by the munificence of General de Betskoi, the enlightened and liberal head and director-general of this, and all the other institutions of the same kind established by her Imperial Majesty.

Howard then launches into a most detailed description of the education provided for the girls, their uniform, their dress, their health, their amusements, games and entertainments, noting that nobles and commoners receive equal treatment, except the latter are dressed in coarser cloth and their educational programme 'is confined to needle-work, reading, housekeeping and such other occupations and improvements as are suitable to the humbler walks of life, for which they are intended'. A visit to see the 'monastery girls' (*monastyrki*) became an essential part of every visitor's itinerary and similiar descriptions are found in Coxe, Dimsdale and others.

It was the Scot Andrew Swinton who professed that, rather than the description of buildings, 'wherever I travel, my first enquiries relate to the customs, manners, and amusements of the people, by which alone their real characters are to be estimated', but not only his account but many others are full of descriptions that evoke the daily life, traditions, festivals and festivities of the capital's population, high and low. What follows is merely a sample from the riches on offer in both published and unpublished accounts.

Swinton had an eye for the picturesque and delighted in movement and song. Here are two characteristic passages:

In the Summer evenings, when the weather is calm, the citizens of Petersburg delight in sailing upon the Neva in their pleasure boats. The boats of the Nobility are very elegantly ornamented. The company are seated in the stern, under a canopy of silk, or other stuff, and have with them musicians or frequently the party themselves perform upon different instruments. The rowers are all chosen among such of their servants as have the best voices, and either sing in concert with the instruments, or without them. When they have rowed the boat against the stream, beating time to their songs with their oars, they allow her to drive with the current, fixing their oars in a horizontal position from the boat's sides; and the rowers collect in a circle. It is at this period they exert their vocal powers, and make such exquisite harmony, as to draw the inhabitants to the galleries of their houses upon the river's banks, and the foot passengers to the water's edge, to listen to the music; and many follow the boat, to enjoy their native tunes. The vocal and instrumental parts are generally performed alternately, and among the former is always one, who, with a whistle, or, by blowing upon his fingers, makes a very shrill noise, accompanying the music at intervals. When the concert is ended, the audience upon the streets go away, repeating the songs, and echoing them into every quarter of the city. Perhaps another boat, conveying another concert, approaches, and arrests the auditors of the first melodies.

These concerts often continue to ten and eleven o'clock at night, and when still silence reigns upon the face of the waters, it is beyond the power of description to convey any idea of the pleasing effect they have upon the mind.

A companion winter scene describes the pleasures and dangers of sleigh riding and the skills and wiles of the *izvozchiki*, or drivers, who are as constant a presence in tourists' accounts as the Neva itself:

It is now desperately cold weather, no less than 25 degrees of Reaumur. I shall be frozen to a statue. We drive about the streets and upon the Neva in sledges, of a different construction from those used for travelling; some resembling a small boat, and others the body of an open chaise. The higher ranks in general, however, use their coaches, placed upon a sledge frame: and it is merely for an hour's amusement when they drive in sledges.

Every gentleman and lady of the lower order, *as long* as they have a copic [copeck] to spend, lay it chearfully in hiring the street-sledges, ranged at all the corners, *pro bono publico*. They look like so many phaetons by the speed of their horses; only their carriages have no wheels.

The ishwhoshics [*sic*], or sledge-drivers, make it a point of honour to pass every other brother of the reins; they use no whips: there is a continual struggle for such preeminence. Their horses are excellent; few of them worth less than twenty or thirty guineas. The ishwhoshics, by a peculiar management of the reins, make them answer the double purpose of a whip, and indeed they have but to speak to their geldings if they wish them to run; they cannot stop them so easily. I have never seen horses with more spirit. [. . .] The Russian beau attends his mistress in a sledge, sitting with her or standing behind. The grand field, where they parade, is the Neva. It is the race ground where the gentlemen display their expertness at driving, and the fleetness of their nags; a part of the frozen river is railed for the purpose. But, in ordinary, there is racing every where, and it is well if one escapes being rode down. This gives constant exercise to the eyes in watching, as well as to the feet in getting clear off. And this, I presume, may be the cause of the quick step and look of the Peterburghers. There is a perpetual flight in the streets, to preserve legs and arms, and the word pady, or get out of the way, resounds from morning to night. Street travelling is much cheaper here in Winter than in Summer. The sledges are very numerous: many of the Russians in the country, whose work is put to an end by the frost, come into town with their horses, and commence

stood in the Year 1716'.
Published in [F.C. Weber],
The Present State of Russia
(London, 1723). (The plan
shows the city not as it ever
stood but rather as it was
projected to be.)

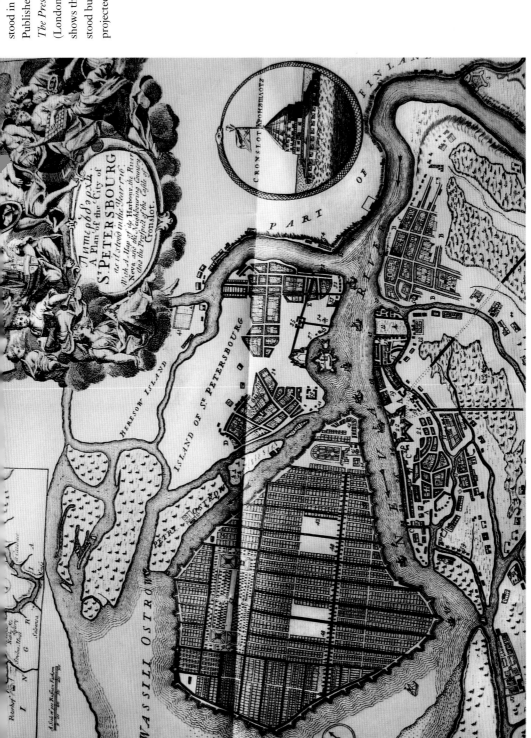

Плант столичнаго
A Plan of the City of
St. PETERSBOURG
as it stood in the Year 1716.
With A Map of the Harbour, the River
Neva, and the Neighbouring Country
and the Prospect of the Castle of
Cronslot.

CRONSLOT КРОНШЛОТ

PART OF FINLAND

RIVE

BERESOF ISLAND

ISLAND OF St PETERSBOURG

PETR OSTROW

WASSILI OSTROW

The exchange and warehouses on Vasil'evskii Island (built after a design by Domenico Trezzini in 1723–35 and dismantled in Catherine's reign), seen from the Little Neva. Unsigned copy of an engraving by I.P. Eliakov from an original drawing by M. Makhaev, 1749. Published in London in 1755.

The Empress Elizabeth's Summer Palace (built after a design by Bartolomeo Rastrelli in 1741–4 and dismantled in 1790s). Unsigned copy of an engraving by A.A. Grekov from an original drawing by M. Makhaev, 1750. Published London in Bankes' *New System of Geography* (1770s).

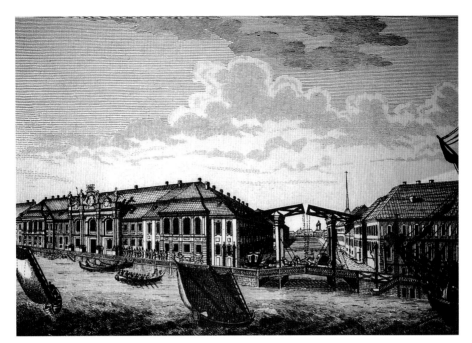

he Old (Second) Winter Palace (designed by Mattarnovy for Peter I and dismantled in the early 1780s) and the scule bridge over the Winter Canal. Unsigned copy of an engraving by E.G. Vinogradov from an original drawing M. Makhaev, 1750. Published in London, 1770s.

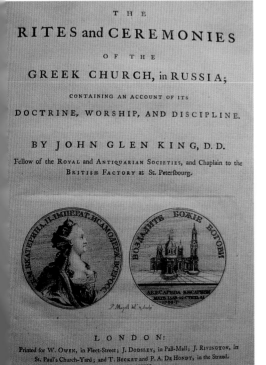

le page of John Glen King, *Rites and Ceremonies of the eek Church, in Russia* (1772). Engraving by P. Mazell the medal by Timofei Ivanov, commemorating the ing of the foundation stone of Antonio Rinaldi's St ac's Cathedral, 1768.

The Smol'nyi Cathedral (begun in 1748 after a design by Bartolomeo Rastrelli). Unsigned engraving from King, *Rites and Ceremonies* (1772).

The Bronze Horseman. Statue of Peter the Great by Etienne Falconet. Engraved by James Basire from a drawing by Pierre Falconet. Published in 1777.

View of the English Park at Peterhof, showing the Birch Cottage, bridge and cascade. Watercolour (1782) by James Meader, imperial gardener responsible for creating the park.

View of the English Park at Peterhof, showing a pavilion and the bridge to the deer park. Watercolour (1782) by James Meader, imperial gardener responsible for creating the park.

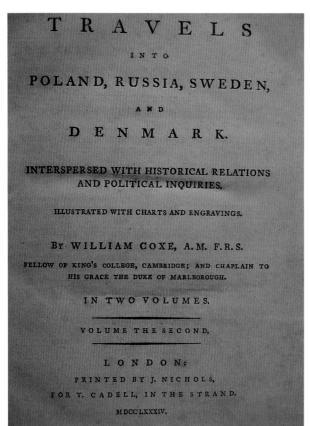

TRAVELS

INTO

POLAND, RUSSIA, SWEDEN,

AND

DENMARK.

INTERSPERSED WITH HISTORICAL RELATIONS AND POLITICAL INQUIRIES.

ILLUSTRATED WITH CHARTS AND ENGRAVINGS.

By WILLIAM COXE, A.M. F.R.S.

FELLOW OF KING'S COLLEGE, CAMBRIDGE; AND CHAPLAIN TO
HIS GRACE THE DUKE OF MARLBOROUGH.

IN TWO VOLUMES.

VOLUME THE SECOND.

LONDON:

PRINTED BY J. NICHOLS,

FOR T. CADELL, IN THE STRAND.

MDCCLXXXIV.

LEFT: Title page of William Coxe, *Travels into Poland, Russia, Sweden, and Denmark* (1784).

BELOW: Plan of St Petersburg. Published by Thomas Cadell in The Strand on 26 March 1784. From William Coxe, *Travels into Poland, Russia, Sweden, and Denmark*.

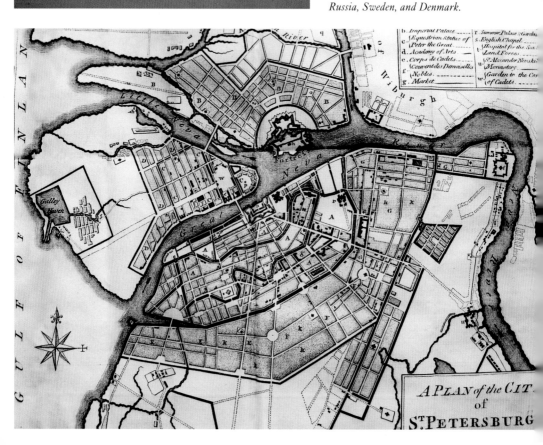

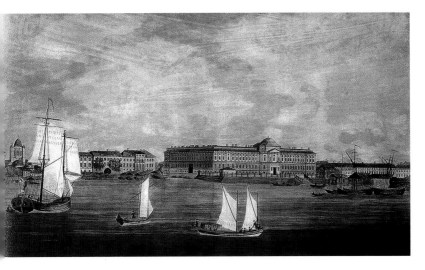

The Academy of Arts on Vasil'evskii Island (built after design by Vallin de la Mothe, 1764–88). Drawn by Joseph Hearn, engraved by Thomas Malton. Published in 1789.

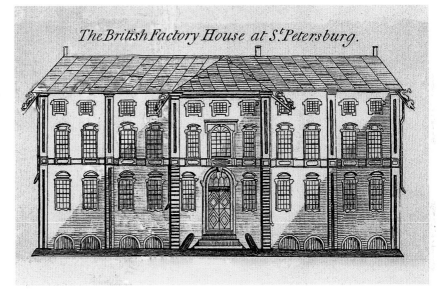

The English Church : British Factory House (former ieremetev mansion) n Galley (later nglish) Embankment. ngraving from entlemen's Magazine 793).

The English Church, as redesigned by Giacomo Quarenghi in 1815.

Public Festival on Palace Square. Drawn and etched by J.A. Atkinson. Published 1 February 1804.

Consecration of the Waters by the Winter Palace. Drawn and etched by J.A. Atkinson. Published 12 May 1804.

rdman (*Dvornik*) and Policemen (*Budochniki*). Drawn and etched by J.A. Atkinson. Published 1 February and 1 July 1804.

bathhouse or *bania*. Drawn and etched by J.A. Atkinson. Published 1 July 1804.

noramic views of St Petersburg. LEFT, ABOVE: The Admiralty from Vasil'evskii Island. LEFT, BELOW: The Strelka of sil'evskii Island and the Peter and Paul Fortress. ABOVE: The Twelve Colleges (architect D. Trezzini) on Vasil'evskii nd. Drawn on the spot from the observatory of the Academy of Sciences on Vasil'evskii Island and etched by J.A. kinson. Published 1802–3.

The Little House of
Peter the Great on the
Petrograd Side.
Engraving by
T. Medland from
an original drawing
by Sir John Carr.
Published 1805.
(The house was
protected by a brick
pavilion during
Catherine II's reign.)

Palace Embankment and Neva panorama from the Peter and Paul Cathedral. Engraving by T. Medland from an original drawing by Sir John Carr. Published 1805.

The Isaac Square, seen from the Neva, and showing the Bronze Horseman, Rinaldi's St Isaac's Cathedral and the Pontoon Bridge. Engraving by J.O. Stadler from a drawing by Robert Ker Porter. Published 1809.

Stone, or Big, Theatre, seen from the Catherine Canal. Engraving by J.O. Stadler from a drawing by Robert Ker ...ter. Published 1809. (Original theatre designed by Antonio Rinaldi in 1777, opened in 1783; rebuilt by Thomas de ...mon in 1802 but destroyed by fire in 1811.)

A Russian Nurse

Pub.d Jan.y 2, 1809, by R. PHILLIPS, Bridge Street, London

ABOVE: The Academy of Arts and the embankment on Vasil'evskii Island towards the Peter and Paul Fortress. Engraving by J.O. Stadler from a drawing by Robert Ker Porter. Published 1809.

LEFT: A wet nurse. Engraving by J.O. Stadler from a drawing by Robert Ker Porter. Published 1809.

e Winter Palace. Engraving from a drawing by Robert Johnston. Published 1815.

Kazan Cathedral (after design by A.N. Voronikhin, 1801–11), by the Catherine Canal, facing Nevskii Prospekt.
raving from fanciful drawing by Robert Johnston. Published 1815.

Kronstadt boatmen. Engraving from a drawing by Robert Johnston. Published 1815.

A 'flying mountain'. Engraving by C. Williams from a drawing by Robert Johnston. Published 1815.

hackney sledgemen. When Summer returns, the gentlemen and ladies are turned out of their carriages, and again press the pavement with their feet. The wheel carriages are double and triple the expence of the Winter equipage. There are no regulations for the hire; a circumstance which very frequently calls forth the most violent exertions of oratory. The ishwhoshic knows by a glance of your countenance how much to ask – If you are a foreigner, he demands five times his fare; if a Russian, he only asks double. Calculating upon receiving a half of his demand from each. The hirer makes an offer *en passant*; it is refused, and he walks away: the ishwhoshic endeavours to persuade him to give more, until the gentleman is out of hearing, when, being convinced that argument is fruitless, he drives after him, and receives the passenger without exchanging another word. Those sledges actually add to the severity of the Russian climate. The quickness of their motion, if the wind is in your face, occasions, besides the increased coldness, a sensation as if your brow was cut with a razor. Against this you must defend yourself as you can by the aid of a muff, which covering the whole of your face, you sit very comfortably while taking an airing in the dark. The ladies have the advantage of their male relations: they paint inch thick; which, if it does not add to their beauty, at least prevents them from being frost bitten; I see fair damsels gallopping in 20 degrees of *Reaumur*, without even a bonnet; while the sons of Mars, swords, bucklers, *and all*, are rolled up in sable. Vanity in our sex has the same effect as paint in the other. A Russian beau of the first magnitude despises a warm dress, as it spoils his shapes – he struts in silk stockings, a hat and cockade; and as often as the cold will permit, he throws his fur cloak aside, to display his silk breeches, and satin vest.

The ice-hills, or *montagnes russes,* as they were often termed, were equally the subject of frequent description. They were to be found not only on the Neva but also on imperial estates such as Tsarskoe Selo and Oranienbaum and elsewhere. The hills at Tsarskoe Selo were described in detail in a pamphlet written by one of the English chaplains, the Rev. John Glen King, and, moreover, illustrated with a yard-long engraving, but Coxe's account was among the best known and oft quoted. Parkinson, as concerned as any traveller to the frozen North with the cold of a Petersburg winter, ventured to try the dangerous pastime on more modest hills constructed at the Stroganov villa outside the city:

Baron Stroganoff having caused two ice-hills to be erected at a Villa six Versts from Petersburg on the way to Peterhoff [. . .] When we arrived at the place of our destination, though the wind was high and the ground at the foot of the hills very slippy, it did not prevent the company from going down. Even Madame Somoilov ventured before dinner, as several of the ladies did after. I went once under the escort of Golofkin. The other English, Lord Dalkeith, Bootle and Garshore did repeatedly. You ascend by a stair to a platform; from whence an inclined plane floored with long oblong masses of ice descends to the ground. The adventurer places himself either alone or with another person before him on a little low sledge, and slides down the inclined plane with a degree of force which causes him to continue his course for a considerable time after he reaches the level. He then takes up his sledge and ascends with it by a stair to another hill of the same kind which is situated in such a manner, as to enable him to slide back to the stair of the other, in a line parallel to his former flight but at the suffi-cient distance not to interfere with it. They have also besides sledges a large mat couve, for it is in the form of a couve [tub?], on which they go down without the slightest danger; four or five Persons one behind the other descend in this.

These hills were not more than two *toises* [12 feet] high, but they are sometimes, and particularly on the Neva when the strength of the ice allowed it, of three times that height, with a declivity most alarm-ingly rapid. There is no Comparison we were assured between the Velocity of the Motion down one of these and that which we experi-enced. Yet these Russians make a practice of skating down these frightful descents, and that not infrequently with a child in their arms or on their head. We had a very cheerful and excellent dinner: after which the company, ladies as well as gentlemen, returned to the Amusement of the day.

An even more engrossing spectacle was the *bania*, or bathhouse, which, as Coxe noted, had been 'described by every [male!] traveller who has given to the public any relation of this country' – and he follows suit, relating, of course, only 'what fell under my immediate notice'. Young Wraxall writes that 'I am only just returned from being a spectator of one of their customs, [. . .] a sight rather excitive of disgust than desire, and to which only curiosity could ever have led me'. Curiosity had a lot to answer for, and the sensitive natures of the two British naval officers, both of whom were to become admirals in the British navy, William Bentinck and James Hawkins, were assailed by what they saw: 'such a monstruous Scene of beastly Women and indecent men mix'd together naked as our first parents without the least appearance of Shame, as to shock our feelings'. Parkinson recorded that 'we went to the public baths this morning out of curiosity' – to the women's bath, of course, and his verdict that 'nothing could be more disgusting than most of the figures, their breasts hanging down in the most hideous manner' is proffered as if to excuse his – and others' – voyeurism. Parkinson, however, later sought to alleviate his rheumatism in the bathhouse and 'found the sensation exceedingly agreeable. I felt like a River God: or like the statue of Moses with water flowing down a long beard and long locks'. He regretted only that he had missed out on being whipped with birch twigs, for 'the sensation from it I am told is very acute and singular'.

Far less agreeable was the smell from the 'necessary', when Parkinson and his companions paid a visit to Count Osterman's: 'In entering we were almost poisined with the Stench of the necessary. Though in fact there is no such thing in any Russian house; in the whole Palace there is said to be not one. They have however I suppose some common receptacle, from which the odours in question issued. In winter, from being froze, the inconvenience is not conceived: but in Spring, particularly when it begins to thaw, the Nuisance is insufferable.'

A more 'legitimate' venue for the voyeur than the women's bathhouse was, of course, the theatre, particularly the ballet. Play-going was as much a part of the social round as balls, card-playing, and visits to salons. By preference the British visitors would go to performances by the permanent French and German troupes, or attend the private amateur performances of French plays in aristocratic houses or in institutions like the Smol'nyi Institute. They were also present at performances by Russian companies, particularly when these were of ballets, operas, or comic opera, where dance, song, and music made knowledge of the language less relevant.

In the 1780s and 1790s the Empress Catherine herself provided the libretti for no less than five comic operas, the music for which was composed by some of the foremost Russian and foreign composers of the day, as well as a great historical pageant entitled *The Beginning of Oleg's Reign*, which a Scots doctor in Russian service called 'a curious and uncommon treat to Strangers visiting her capital, as well as to the true Russian Patriot and *antiquarian*'. Colmore, Parkinson and Brogden were among those 'strangers' who saw the various imperial offerings. Brogden saw one of the first public performances of *The Brave and Bold Knight Akhrideich* (October 1787) and left his impressions of the new Stone (*Kamennyi*) Theatre, which was only opened in 1783 on a spot not far from where the Mariinskii Theatre now stands: he found it

> very large, much larger than the Hay Market, but it does not by any means present so grand a spectacle. It is fitted up in a much plainer manner, the company in general are not well dressed, & the house is kept so dark that it is almost impossible to distinguish those who are there [. . .] the Scenery was very fine, the music and dancing excellent; at the head of the dancers are lePicq & Rosi, but as the dancing was comic it was not well calculated to display their Talents.

Early in Catherine's reign, a spectacular 'theatrical' event had been the Grand Carousel, which was performed in a wooden amphitheatre constructed on Palace Square for the event by the architect Rinaldi. It was witnessed on its second performance on 11/22 July 1766 by Thomas Newberry, who had been Professor of Mathematics at the Naval Noble Cadet Corps in Cronstadt during the last years of Elizabeth's reign and the first years of Catherine's, and described by him in a private letter to a friend in London:

> About the middle of the Month, Her Majesty entertaind the whole City with a Grand Carousal, which was held in a place built on purpose before the New Palace. It was a Square, the longest side being about 200 yards, and the lesser 180. There were six Rows of Seats on each side, the lowest of which was eight feet from the Ground. all round the Square, there was a path of about 5 yards in breadth and the rest was inclosd in a handsome manner breast high, and turn'd into the form of an Oval, in

the Centre of which sat the Famous old Count Munich, who with his officers, was to judge of the performances and distribute the Prizes. The Knights, Sir, were sixteen, and the Ladies eight, besides an innumerable train of Squires, who carried their Arms, Shields &c. They were divided into four Parties call'd Quadrills, and supposd to be of four different Nations, namely, the Roman, the Sclavonian, the Turkish, and the Indian, and were all properly and most magnificently Cloath'd in the Habits of their several Countrys but more especially the Ladies who armd as they were, seemd each a Pallas moveing in a blaze of Jewels, which gave additional lustre to the Sun's beams. The Knights, or you please Cavaliers were all mounted on very fine Horses richly caparison'd, and each Lady sat simply in a Superb Gilt Carr, which were each drawn by two Horses and drove by Noblemen, who were proud of being their Squires.

At about 5 o'clock, Sir, the Grand Duke came with his attendants and soon after Her Majesty gladen'd the whole Company with her presence. She sat on the East side opposite his Highness, who was in the West.

A Gun was now fird to notify Her arrival, and a second commanded the procession to begin, which was from the several places they were stationed at in different and opposite parts of the City, and all equally different from the Carousal, which they all enter'd nearly at the same time by two opposite doors, namely the North and South. Each Company was preceeded by a Noble Band of Music peculiar to their Country, and their Colours were all display'd. The Eagles, some borne upon Staves [?] and other flying in Standards, shew'd the Romans, and Sclavonians, while the Crescent and Horsetails, shew'd the Turks, and the bows and quivers filld with arrows, pointed out the Indians. They all mov'd once round the Square in solemn procession, all the music playing at the same time, they paid their Obeisance to Her Majesty, after which they divided, and took posts in the four Angles. Now all was silent, and a Herald was sent to demand their intentions, they each beg'd leave of their Sovereign to Enter the Lists, which was readily granted, and directly the Trumpets sounded to the charge, and now, Sir, the hearts of the Combattants seem'd to be agitated between hopes and fears, so great in generous Minds, is the desire of Conquest and the dread of being vanquishd, even in things almost indifferent, the disgrace and honour of which is only momentary – Let me now tell you

Sir, that they were not to attack each other, but Beasts only, who appeared in the formidable shapes of Bears, Lyons, Tygers and Dragons, who had no sense of fear, and were extremely harmful in their rage. The Arms they attackd with, were Swords, Spears, Darts and Pistols: Four Knights and two Ladies chargd at the same time, going on in a full Gallop, and in a Serpentine manner, so as not to interfere with each other, and they were deem'd the greatest Victors, who cut off most heads, broke most Spears, threw most effectually their darts, and whose fire was directed nearest to the mark.

This attack, Sir, was repeated untill all the four Orders had try'd their abilities and dexterity, after which the prizes were impartially distributed according to their several merits, and then the whole concluded with the Admiration, and unanimous Applause of all the Spectators [...]

By way of a companion piece is a lively description of a sumptuous entertainment mounted by students of the Noble Cadet Corps on Vasil'evskii Island to mark the signing of the peace treaty between the Russians and the Turks in July 1775. It is found in the unpublished diary of John Henniker, later 2nd Lord Henniker, visiting St Petersburg soon after coming down from Cambridge:

I have just been Spectator of Russian ingenuity, and magnificence. An Entertainment, for which we are obliged to Mr Betskoi, Director of the *Corps de cadets*, began at eight o'Clock in the Evening. We were placed in an Amphitheatre nearly semicircular, containing about seven hundred Persons; which turned upon an Axis. Near the Summit of this Axis was a Gallery of Music; and on the Top stood Peace with an olive branch in her Hand. The first performance was a Play in French; of which *l'amour de la patrie* was the subject. The Young Gentlemen of this Establishment were the only persons who exhibited throughout, and I must add, much to their own Credit, and our Satisfaction. At the conclusion of this Piece, a Ship was drawn on the Stage; from which the chief Characters descended; Waves were represented around it by Canvas; and Neptune with his subaltern deities attended: Cars also of different kinds brought their respective Companies. Branches of Lamps on pedestals, as by Inchantment moved in, and placed themselves under Piazzas, illuminated with different Colours, forming the Borders of the Stage. There were more in the Pedestals than we saw, to make them move: they were each the Prison of its bearer, leaving him only the use of his Legs. We now come to the most astonishing part. It was not Harlequin, who drove to Lilliput with his magic Wand; but in good Truth some strong capsterns that turned the whole Amphitheatre round with its Company: first to a Scene of Sculpture, and then a second Time, to present us before a Carousel, richly illuminated. The young Gentlemen performed their evolutions, with great dexterity; and their different degrees of Merit were immediately rewarded, by a present of a Sword, a pair of Pistols, and a Whip. We were again moved round our common Centre and saw a Comedy on a different Stage. When this was finished we walked through an Avenue, to a terrestrial Elysian Fields. Bowers with Fountains in them playing over Pedestals, adorned with coloured Lamps, Music, Illuminations of various Kinds, transparent Paintings, a path of Light, effected by Lamps at equal distances, through an Avenue terminated by an enlightened Star, together with a glow of Satisfaction that shined on every Face, formed one of the most beautiful scenes imaginable which the four Elements fortunately assisted to render more luxurious. All this was executed in the open Air, which was extremely soft, and the Night very fine: the Fire and Water laid aside their natural Enmity, and united in each Bower to please: and the Earth strewed with Roses offered a delicious Softness to the Step. I am going to bed, and shall perhaps enjoy the fairy Visions a second time in Dreams.

There was considerable interest in the Orthodox Church, not least, of course, among travellers in orders such as Coxe and Parkinson, and its ceremonies were also perceived as a form of theatre. The Rev. John Glen King, already mentioned for his interest in ice-hills, published during his Petersburg chaplaincy, a substantial book on *The Rites and Ceremonials of the Greek Church, in Russia; Containing an Account of Its Doctrine, Worship, and Discipline* (1772), which became a standard work of reference, although the great Russian theologian Metropolitan Platon suggested that it 'was not to be depended on'. It was to witness Platon perform divine service that Coxe and Lord Herbert accompanied Prince Potemkin and the British ambassador Sir James Harris:

This learned prelate, whose name is Plato, received us with great politeness, and, at the close of a short conversation, conducted us into the church. On his entrance the choristers began a short hymn, which they finished as he approached the shrine: having then said a short prayer, he placed himself upon a raised seat in the middle of the church; and taking off his mandyas, or common garment, the attendant priests kissed his hand, while they delivered to him the different parts of the costly pontifical vestments, which, in receiving, he raised to his lips, before he invested himself with them. He also placed on his head a crown richly ornamented with pearls and precious stones. We were informed, that this dress is similar to the imperial robe, formerly worn by the Greek emperors of Constantinople, which they permitted the supreme dignataries of the church to put on at the time of divine service; and the same attire still continues to distinguish the hierarchy of the Greek church established in Russia from the lower orders.

The archbishop being robed, repaired to the shrine within the great folding-doors, and soon afterwards began the celebration of divine worship. Part of the service was performed in the Sclavonian tongue by the different priests, and part by the archbishop in the Greek language, which he pronounced according to the accent of the modern Greeks. In conformity to he rules of the church, no organ, or any other musical instrument, was introduced; but the vocal harmony, which consisted in hymns, was exceedingly pleasing. Lighted tapers and incense seemed no less essential parts of their worship than among the Roman Catholics.

Towards the conclusion of the prayers, the archbishop and clergy retired into the shrine, to receive the communion. The folding-doors were immediately shut, and none of the laity at that time partook of this rite; but we, as strangers, were allowed to view what passed through a side-door that was left open for that purpose. The communicants stood during the ceremony; and the wine was, according to usual custom, mixed with warm water; the bread, which was cut into small pieces, was put into the wine; and the elements of both kinds were given at the same time in a spoon.

The whole service lasted about an hour: the archbishop, having pronounced the final benediction, again seated himself in the middle of the church, divested himself of his pontifical garments, and clothed himself in his common robe. We then followed him to his house; where we found a collation, consisting of an eel-pye, a sterlet, red and pickled herrings, and various sorts of *liqueurs* and wines. After enjoying for some time the intelligent and entertaining conversation of the archbishop, who spoke fluently the French tongue, we made our acknowledgements and retired.

In sharp contrast to the ironic view of the ceremony of the Blessing of the Waters, quoted earlier from a dispatch by the British resident Jefferyes in 1719, are the several detailed descriptions from Catherine's time, by such as Coxe and Parkinson. The principal ceremony in the capital which during Peter's time had taken place by the Winter Canal was under Catherine by the canal which separated the Admiralty from Rastrelli's Winter Palace: the empress preferred to watch from a window in the palace, rather than participate directly, as her predecessors had done, and some of her nineteenth-century successors would also do:

We were present this morning [6/17 January 1793] at the blessing of the waters, a ceremony held in great veneration all over Russia, and performed on this day in every part of the Empire professing the Greek religion. Mass being first said in the Chapel Royal, a numerous procession consisting of several Bishops and priests intermixed with a variety of other persons and brought up by little parties of soldiers conveying the colours of their respective regiments, set off from the Chapel, passed through the palace, and advanced along a scaffolding erected for the purpose to an octagon pavilion erected on the Canal which encompasses the Admiralty. The Archbishop, after the proper service had been performed descended by a ladder, dipped a cross into the water down to which a hole had been cut through the ice, baptised a child, and sprinkled with holy water the colours which had been carried in procession. A number of canons were fired to announce either the commencement or the completion of the ceremony, during which I observed that the people by crossing themselves expressed a great deal of devotion. they did the same particularly as the cross passed by and indeed kept their heads uncovered almost the whole time of the procession, both as it went and as it returned. For after the ceremony they returned in the same order. The Crowd of people was immense; the area before the Canal was almost entirely filled; there were likewise a great many spectators on the top of the palace as well as on a low building adjoining to Count Bruce's. In general they make a point of conscience not to be absent on this occasion. The soldiers who had been on duty near the Pavilion made almost the circuit of the Area after this and passed in review under the Empress's windows.

To day the weather was not very severe; when it happens to be so it is exceeding hard service to those poor fellows, who remain on their posts from eight in the morning without any extraordinary cloathing. There have been instances of a great many lives being lost. For which reason, if the cold is very severe, the Empress now defers the ceremony. I had the curiosity to go up to the Pavilion about half an hour after the water had been blessed and was much amused to see the anxiety with which the people were procuring it in Jugs and bottles; some were drinking, others washing their faces, and one man had dipped his whole head in and drenched his locks almost completely. As the procession returned several persons were employed in sprinkling the holy water over the crowd on each side. Sir Watkin [Williams Wynne] as a stranger by his account was particularly favoured.

It was as a sort of perpetual procession or masquerade that Andrew Swinton interpreted the multi-ethnic mix he observed in the capital's population:

Besides the variety of nations which compose the Russian Empire, in my daily walk through the city I meet with English, Danes, French, Swedes, Italians, Spaniards, Portuguese, Venetians, Poles, Germans, Persians, and Turks; the latter are arrived here prisoners from Oczakow. This assembly is a natural masquerade, and no city upon earth presents any amusement of this kind in such perfection as Petersburg. In other great cities the variety of strangers are not so distinguishable as here, owing to their accommodating themselves to the dress of the country in which they reside, or sojourn, in order to prevent the mob from staring at them.

In Petersburg there is no need of this compliance: let foreigners be dressed ever so oddly, they will find, in every lane, subjects of the

Russian Empire to keep them in countenance. She brings into this ball her various swarms, from the snowy mountains of Kamschatka, to the fertile plains of the Ukraine – a space of 4,000 miles! Siberians, Tongusians, Calmucs, and an endless train of Tartar nations, the Fins, the Cossacs, &c. Petersburg is a strange city, even to the Russians: it increases daily, with new recruits from every corner of the empire.

British visitors were not unexpectedly attentive to the particular place, both physically and socially, enjoyed by their resident fellow-countrymen. Catherine's was the reign when not only did the British visit St Petersburg in increasing numbers but the resident British community achieved its pinnacle of eminence and influence, following the successful re-negotiation of the Commercial Agreement in 1766. It was in 1770 that both the famous English Club, which was to flourish until the October Revolution, was founded and the comparatively short-lived English Masonic Lodge, 'Perfect Union', was erected. The church, the acquisition of which was described in the preceding chapter, was, however, at the heart of the community and its most prominent members were to buy or rent houses in its immediate vicinity. Coxe, looking across the river from Vasil'evskii Island, wrote that 'on the opposite side are the Imperial palace, the admiralty, the mansions of many Russian nobles, and the English line, so called because the whole row is principally occupied by the English merchants' and it was young Brogden who informed his father that 'you have some idea of the English Line, but by all accounts this as well as every other part of the Town is very much altered since you were here. The banks of the Neva, the whole length of the Line, which is exactly a Verst, is lined with granite & ornamented with a small parapet & a foot path of the same materials, which makes a delightful promenade'. The granite facing of the English Line or Quay, or as it was still officially called, the Galley Embankment, was begun in 1767 and completed during Brogden's stay in the capital. Also completed in 1788 was Ivan Starov's elegant high bascule bridge with stone columns that replaced the existing wooden bridge over the Kriukov Canal, joining the Moika to the Neva and situated at about mid-point along the embankment. Many leading merchants, and not only merchants, acquired impressive three-storey houses with balconies 'large enough to drink Tea in', as Baroness

Dimsdale quaintly observed, and almost every house to the west of the Kriukov Bridge to the end of the embankment by the Galley Wharf was at some time or other British-owned during Catherine's reign.

The Englishness of the English/Galley Embankment was parallelled, indeed, given depth by the Englishness of Galley (*Galernaia*) Street, which in Soviet times was given the name Red Street to match the Embankment of the Red Fleet into which the English Embankment was similarly transformed. Not only did the embankment houses have entrances into their courtyards from Galley Street, but frequently had independent buildings. James Brodgen, a guest of the Cayleys in 1787–8, describes the house as 'situated in the English Line, which is joined to a Lane they call the *back line* by a long yard, at the bottom of which is a small house over the gateway', in which he was to stay. Galley Street was a very animated, narrow thoroughfare, with shops and tradesmen, a coffee house, an English Inn, and access to the church and to its Subscription Library (founded in the 1760s). It was at the English Inn that the subscription balls, notable highlights in the social season, were held and one such was the subject of a delightful cameo in one of Brogden's letters to his father:

> This Ball is held at the English Inn, which is one of the best houses in theLine & belongs to a Russian Nobleman. The Card & Supper rooms are very fine, being hung with goblin [Gobelin] tapestry, the Chairs of the same with gilt frames. The Ball room is abt the size of the one at the London Tavern & fitted up much in the same stile. A whole Suit of Rooms, 6 in number, are opened on the ball nights, but only the Card & spper rooms are fitted up in the expensive manner I have described. There are 172 Subscribers, among whom are the Chief of the Russian Nobility: Pce Potemkin & Pce Besbaratki [Bezborodko] at the head, who are Ministers of State; all the foreign Embassadors, most of the English Merchants, the Neopolitan, French, Polish, Spanish, Sardinian & Danish, were all at the last, all ornamented with their different orders; & as most of the Secretaries are officers, the variety of uniforms are very entertaining. The Russ uniforms are very brilliant, the footguards Green with broad gold lace & the Horse gds blue & gold. You wd think I exagerate were I to describe the number of Stars & Ribbands of all the colours of the Rainbow which glitter on every side, but they are

so very common in this Country that they loose their Effect. The Ladies do not dress by any means so fine as the Gentlemen: they come, as they call it, à l'Angloise, which word many of them seem to think means *dirty & shabby*. But this is not the case with the generality. The Russian ladies are many of them very handsom; they come very much without Caps. We change partners every dance. There are 2 long sets which are divided by a rope as at the Citty Assembly; the Gentlemen draw the Tickets, which we wear all the Evening at the button hole. Country Boamkin, as they call Country Bumkin, is a very favorite dance, tho' they make it quite different from the dance so called in England. The supper is very elegant, but so much in fashion is everything English that Beefstakes, Welsh Rabits & Porter is the most fashionable meal. I myself saw the Duke of Capriola, the Neopolitan Embassador, in his red heeled shoes, very busy at a great Beef Stake, a dish I dare say he had never tasted in Italy. These dishes are as fashionable among the ladies as the Gentlemen; the former, tho' they do not eat many sweetmeats at Supper, pocket them & apples without Scruple. There were 3 Greek ladies at the last Ball & one of them was very pritty. The English ladies do not shine. French is the universal language at the ball.

It was on a landing-stage by the embankment itself and in front of the house he was renting that the British ambassador, Sir James Harris, hosted in June 1778 a celebration of the King's birthday, which was described by his sister Katherine, for whom 'Living in Russia [was] like living in the time of ones Great grandfather to all other civilised European Nations':

In the evening he gave a Ball to all the english in honor of the Kings birth day & which he kept according to the old stile for the sake of the Weather. We danced on the Platform as you land; it was cover'd with an Awning & near 60 feet long wide enough for two setts, there were near 80 much dancing and cards in four rooms in the House. at ten there was supper in 3 rooms & covers for 72 people, besides side boards, every body seem'd easy & pleased after supper they sung God save the King & then we return'd to dancing till two a fine calm morning

The 'English style' of living elicited a great deal of comment from British visitors. Brogden wrote:

> I need not be particular in describing the entertainments I meet with at each separate house. I have found at all I have hitherto been (except old Mr Coole, who lives more retired) a stile of living, in regard to variety of eating & drinking, far superior to the common mode of living in England. I was obliged here, as the Company consisted mainly of Foreigners, to talk French, & I find I shall frequently be forced to use this language, which I hope will enable to acquire some proficiency in it. [...]
>
> The houses of the English & the other civilized Europeans are fitted up with every convenience, even at the expence of appearance, by which as in all other things we are so peculiarly distinguished from the Russians, whose prevailing passion seems to be the desire of shew.
>
> Fire places are become much more common than they were by your account when you were in this part of the World. I have hardly been in a house yet that has not an English fire Place where they burn new Castle and Scotch coal, both which being brought as ballast is cheaper here than in London.

Similar pictures were painted by Lady Elizabeth Craven, a rare female traveller, who noted during her brief sojourn in 1786 that 'I find English grates, English coats, English coal, and English hospitality, to make me welcome, and the fire-side chearful', and by the English chaplain William Tooke, who suggested that 'in the houses of the Britons settled here a competent idea may be formed of the english manner of living. Furniture, meals, establishments; everything is english – even to the chimney fire. Here where wood is in such plenty, the Englishman fetches his coals from home'.

The size and prosperity of the English colony was undoubtedly the reason that induced a travelling troupe of players to try their luck in the Russian capital towards the end of 1770. Amateur theatricals had inevitably found a place in the life of the Petersburg British, but the arrival of a professional company was an unparalleled event and as such, worthy of inclusion in a diplomatic dispatch from the British ambassador at the time, Lord Cathcart. It was, however, his secretary and children's tutor, William Richardson, who wrote the account that soon appeared in the *Scot's Magazine* and was repeated in his book of 1784:

You will be surprised to hear, that we have got at St. Petersburg an English Playhouse. A Company of Players arrived here in the end of autumn. They were advised, you may be sure, to return home without loss of time; they chuse, however, to make their home, at least for one winter, in Russia, and trust to the well known humanity of their countrymen in the Gallerinhoff. Accordingly, with great diligence, and much tinsel, they furbished up an old barn into the likeness of a theatre; and that every thing might be as complete as possible, they had in it, not only a seat for the British Ambassador, but boxes for the Great Duke and her Imperial Majesty of all the Russias. So, on the first night that the theatre was opened, all their countrymen came to them, to give them charity, and to laugh, as might have been expected, at the Tragedy of Douglas [by John Home]. But instead of laughing, they cried. The part of Douglas was performed by a female player with inimitable pathos. The audience were surprised into the warmest applauses. The fame of this excellent performance was spread through the city; and for two or three successive evenings the theatre was crowded with Russians and Germans as well as English. On the fourth night of the representation, just as the play began, the door of the Empress's box was unexpectedly opened; and her Majesty, without giving any previous warning, took possession of her seat. You may easily imagine how much we were pleased and flattered with this mark of her Majesty's confidence and condescension. This was still more the case, when, in answer to some apology that had been conveyed to her, about the badness of the accommodation, she replied, 'that, among the English, she was quite at ease'. In order, however, to remedy the real inconveniences of the situation and to testify still farther her present partiality to our nation, she ordered a better theatre to be prepared; and on occasion of opening it, the player who had drawn so much attention, delivered the following Prologue:

> Without the aid of ornament or art,
> To speak the language of a grateful heart,
> I come respectful. [etc etc]

The barn in which the actors initially performed was in the grounds of a house owned by an British merchant on the Moika near the Summer Garden, but in February 1771 they were able to move to the 'new English theatre', a converted wooden stable on the Tsaritsa's Meadow (*Tsaritsyn lug*), now the Field of Mars, also by the Summer Garden, and they performed there until the spring of the following year.

The British travellers, although much diverted during their stay in the capital, were anxious also to make outings to nearby, mainly imperial, estates, as they had done at least since the reign of the Empress Anna. Peterhof was from the beginning the most popular destination, but had an increasingly strong competitor in Tsarskoe Selo. Visits were also made to Oranienbaum, beyond Peterhof, and, occasionally to Gatchina, Orlov's palace beyond Tsarskoe. It is striking, however, that we have no contemporary British account of Pavlovsk, the estate given by Catherine to his son Paul and his wife Mariia Fedorovna in 1780, where Charles Cameron began to build his 'Palladian villa' on the hill above the Slavianka River.

It is Coxe who detailed the changes at Oranienbaum, both to the original Menshikov Palace and by way of new buildings in the extensive grounds, introduced by Grand Duke Peter and his wife, the future Peter III and Catherine II. He was much taken with the 'toy' fortress, Peterstadt, which had been constructed in the late 1750, so that Peter could play at soldiers. It was the architect Rinaldi who added two curving wings to the Menshikov Palace as well as the grand staircase leading to the formal lower gardens and the canal that linked a small harbour with the Gulf of Finland. He was also responsible for a new palace for Peter and the Chinese Palace, for Catherine:

> In the garden is an elegant pavilion, constructed by order of the empress when great-duchess; it contains eighteen apartments, each furnished in the style of different countries, and is situated in the midst of a thick plantation. The approaches being circular, we had not the least glimpse of the building until we arrived; and as it generally causes an emotion of surprise, it has, for that reason, received the appelation of *Ha!*

Gatchina, the estate most closely associated with Paul I, who gained possession in 1783, when still Grand Duke, originally belonged to Grigorii Orlov, for whom the industrious Rinaldi began to build the palace in 1766. It was still far from finished when Wraxall arrived in July 1774, although the gardens had already been laid out by yet another British gardener, Charles Sparrow:

> I have made one or two excursions into the country, particularly to Gatchina, a palace of Prince Orloff's, about forty miles off. It is situtate in the most eligible spot within a great distance of the metropolis, and will when finished be a superb seat. The gardens are laid out in the English taste by a man of great merit, who was sent for by the prince on that account. The nature of the ground, and a fine piece of water near the house, gave him scope for his genius.

Peterhof had undergone considerable rebuilding since Dashwood and Cook had visited: the Grand Palace, for instance, had been reconstructed by Rastrelli in the late 1740s, but the formal gardens and waterworks remained much as Cook described them. Wraxall's and Coxe's descriptions added little, but Wraxall is worth quoting for his evocation of a magical masquerade he subsequently attended in the grounds during the white nights:

> I went down to Peterhoff yesterday again, when there was a masquerade and illuminations in the gardens. The former of these is rather a *bal paré en domino*, as there are very few or no fancy dress, nor is any character supported. Every person, without distinction, is admitted on this occasion, and there were not less than 4 or 5,000 persons present. Her majesty was dressed in a blue domino, and played cards most of the night. The illuminations in the gardens far surpassed any I ever saw in my life. In these, as also in fire-works of every kind, I am assured the Russians excel any nation of Europe. Two prodigious arcades of fire extended in front of the palace: the canal, which reaches to the gulf of Finland, was illuminated on both sides, and the view terminated by a rock, lighted in the inside, and which had a beautiful effect. From either side of the canal went off long arched walks illuminated; and beyond these, in the woods, were hung festoons of lamps differently coloured. All the jets d'eaux [*sic*] played. Artifical cascades, where the water tumbled from one declivity to another, and under each of which lights were very artfully disposed, amused and surprised the spectator

at the same time. Besides these, there were summer-houses, pyramids, and temples of flame; and beyond all appeared the imperial yachts on the water, in the same brilliant and dazzling ornaments. Nothing could be better calculated to produce that giddy and tumultuous feeling of mingled wonder and delight, which, though it arises neither from the understanding or the heart, has yet a most powerful influence over both. The senses alone are captivated, and leave neither time nor capacity to reason on the nature of the entertainment they proffer, but whirl us away in an impetuosity which is not to be resisted. If we add to all this the powers of music, dancing, and wanton hours, together with the presence of a multitude of both sexes, habited in a dress which levels all distinction, and is designed for that purpose, a heart must be uncommonly misanthropical or unfeeling, which does not catch some spark of mirth and gallantry at such an altar. This impression, however, as it is violent, and produced from temporary causes, soon subsides, and expires with the oil and taper which gave it birth. It is a kind of short intoxication, the delirium of a few hours, when reason resigns her sceptre, and leaves us to the guidance of any sense which happens to predominate; nor, on a retrospect, does it appear any other than a gay vision, which is passed before we had well contemplated it. there is so little obscurity at this season of the year (for there is no darkness) that if the night had not been very cloudy, the illuminations could not have produced their full effect. This favorable circumstance however, super-added to the black vapor which rose from such a multitude of lamps, and hung over the gardens, caused a degree of gloom, which, under the shelter of the woods, approached nearly to darkness for about two hours, from eleven to one in the morning; but before three the envious day-light burst in upon the splendor of this dazzling scene, which required the canopy of night to give it any lustre. That lassitude and bodily fatigue which I had not felt before, now reminded me of the necessity of repose. The lamps were expiring on every side; the company began to disperse, and quit the place; each moment dimin-ished the magic which had charmed erewhile, and the fugitive enchantment was passed. I was glad to leave it before it totally left me; and between four and five I got into my carriage, and in a few minutes fell fast asleep. It was eight o'clock when I arrived in town, and the sun began to grow already very warm. I threw myself on the bed, quite spent with the pursuit of pleasure, and glad to retire to silence and requiescence. – As magnificent and princely as was this illumination, they assure me it is not to be compared with those which the empress made about two years ago, when the royal prince of Prussia was here

A unique perspective on what Catherine herself planned for Peterhof is found in the letter book of a British gardener. She turned her attention not to the existing lower gardens but to the heavily wooded territory above and inland from the Grand Palace and proposed the laying-out of a large landscape park in which a new palace was to be located. The gardener was the Scot James Meader, who had entered her employ in 1779, the same momentous year as Giacomo Quarenghi, who was to design the palace, and Cameron. Meader was impressed by the site he was given:

The spot allotted for me is a park though great part thereof is full of fine Trees. Here are fine pieces of Water which want but little help to make them elegant, with a vale where I propose to form a magnificent Cascade, the water being above & in these affairs I am under no restraint either to extent of land or water; the bounds are only limited by the Gulf of Finland.

He was soon complaining about Russian gardeners' lack of expertise and outlining his plans:

[. . .] they never use the Hoe nor have they any of these tools except Dutch Hoes for scuffling the sand walks, which in this Country are general, for they had no idea of Gravel Walks till those of England were so much extolled & Bush & Sparrow came to this Country & set the example by introducing them; the beauty firmness & superior lustre of gravel being visibly to every eye has made the great one [the Empress Catherine] gravel mad. The old Gardens at Peterhoff had all sand walks, some about a mile long when I first came, & disagreable to walk on. I soon found a Pit of Gravel which (without mixture of loam) is as good both for colour & firmness as any I ever saw in England, of which I directed the walks heretofore sand to be made, as also the new Gardens I am making, which has given general satisfaction.

A year later, he wrote:

I have finished a piece of Water admired by everybody, built a bridge of my own designing which is much noticed, chose a spot for a grand Palace in the Garden and workmen are employed on the foundation under the direction of a very ingenious Italian Architect [Quarenghi], the whole to be completed in 3 Years.

By 1782 he was reporting that

I have built this summer a most remarkable Bridge with petrified Moss & roots; numbers of People come to see it; also four curious wooden Bridges of an Original construction (I detest copying). I still continue employing 33 Men on new work & am going to extend our works much further than at first proposed. I hope I shall have time this Summer to make a Grand Cascade & Grotto.

It is not known whether he ever finished his grotto, which he wished to excel that constructed by Joseph Lane at Painshill and for which the empress agreed he should import large quantities of Derbyshire spar. It is not shown on the four watercolours he painted of the English Park, which convey something of its charm at a relatively early stage of its development, nor mentioned by Swinton, who visited the park in 1788:

Near Peterhoff, and in the midst of a forest, is a garden executed in the modern English taste – a very delightful spot; and when the natural flatness of the ground is considered, it is amazing what art and taste have been exerted in finishing it. – Here are winding rivulets, cascades dashing over moss-clad rocks, antique bridges, temples, ruins, and cottages. In one of the huts I found a collection of prints, from the subject of Sterne's Sentimental Journey: La Fleur's dapple seemed to be running off with the jack boots, to the Pole. In the garden is building a new Palace for the Grand Duke.

The English Park and its English Palace, built on the west bank of the main lake, survived until the Second World War when they were caught between German and Russian artillery fire and obliterated: there are no plans for restoration.

Restored or, rather, re-created, in time for the tercentenary in 2003, however, was the famous Amber Room at Tsarskoe Selo, the original of which was spirited away by the Germans. It was Tsarskoe Selo, rather than Peterhof, where she stayed only when her duties demanded, that was Catherine's favourite residence. She took delight not in Rastrelli's great baroque palace but in the new suites of rooms and further exterior additions that Cameron was to build for her in the 1780s and in the gardens, dominated by the Great Pond, which were shaped into her idea of an English landscape garden by her naturalized English gardener and former owner of a nursery in Hackney, John Bush. Tsarskoe Selo was where Catherine liked to relax during the summer and enjoy the company of her grandsons and chosen friends. It was to Tsarskoe Selo to inoculate the grand dukes that Baron Dimsdale repaired in the summer of 1781, giving his wife Elizabeth an unequalled opportunity to inspect at leisure both palace and grounds at an important time in their development:

I accompanied the Baron to Sarsko-Sello: the Palace is a magnificent Building of a prodigious length, and was built by the Empress Elizabeth, it is a brick Edifice stuccoed white: the Capitals of the outside Pillars, many other exterior Ornaments, and the wooden Statues which support the Cornice, and adorn the roof are all gilded, and some part painted green that when the Sun shines on them, it makes a very gay appearance. We were situated in exceeding good Apartments on the first floor near the centre of the Palace, and directly under the Royal Apartments, I believe the best in the Palace, except the Empress's and Grand Dukes. [. . .]

The Apartments of the Palace are large and magnificent, some are filled up in a very sumptuous manner, one room is very much admired, being richly inlaid with Amber, a present from the late King of Prussia. Some Rooms are building which will be amazingly superb, only three of them were finished before I came away, which I saw, one in the Chinese Taste, with prodigious fine China Jarrs, the other in the Turkish manner very grand, but at the end of the two fine large Rooms is a small one, which I believe I shall never forget. It was grand beyond any thing I can described, I thought it appeared like an enchanted place, the sides of it inlaid with Foil red and green so that it dazzled ones Eyes to look at it. I have had sent me the particulars of another of these fine Rooms, which was near finished when I was there, and what it cost, which is as follows, and is called the Lyons Room, as the Tapestry was made at Lyons in France, from which place the Room takes it name. [. . .] The Dimensions of the Room are 36 feet by 32, height of the Room 28 feet. There are likewise in this fine Room, twelve Plate Glasses 13 feet long by 4 wide, the Windows are formed of two Plates of Glass each 7 feet in length, these open upon hinges like Folding-doors.

The Gardens are laid out in the English Taste and are very prettily diversified with Lawns, Gravel Walks and Wood, A very fine large piece of Water is near the centre with an Island which has a Building on it, which was very much frequented when the flying Mountains were in fashion, but they are all destroyed except one, which was showed me, and the manner of a Carriage, being fixt, and how it was conducted, which gave me as clear an Idea how it was, as if I had really seen one go off. [. . .]

In another part of the Garden is a pretty Building called the Hermitage and the first Floor contained only a very large Sopha with wheels attached to it. The young Princes and the English Women were with me, and we all sat down on the Sopha, and in an instant we were drawn up into a very large elegant Apartment, at the four corners of the Room were large bow Windows which made four little Rooms; after I had admired the elegance of them, and returned into the great Room to my surprize a Table was in the middle which would dine ten People and four small Tables round the great one, and four dumb Waiters, Plates with silver rims, and something of the slate kind in the middle of them, and a Pencil with a string fixt to the Table under each Plate, if anything the Person seated near it wrote on the bottom, and pulled another string, which was under the Plate which was connected with a bell below, the Plate immediately sunk down and returned up again with what was ordered; the Dishes are changed in the same manner. This Place is now neglected by the Empress as she very seldom dines there, without it is to entertain a Foreigner once or twice in the Summer. The Empress Elizabeth took great delight in going and dining here with a select Party, and not an Attendant or Servant was admitted, for pulling the string of the bell and writing on the Plate answered every purpose.

There is a fine Building near the large piece of Water called the Admiralty the first Floor only contains all the Boats, and places for the water Fowls to live in the Winter. The second Story is one large Room hung round with English Prints of Houses, and Views of different places in England, in it is a bow Window which looks full upon the Water, and opposite in the Water is placed a lofty Pillar to the memory of Count Alexey Orloff who gained a great naval Victory at Tchesme. There are several Buildings scattered about the Garden, many of which were raised in honour of those Persons who at different times distinguished themselves in the Imperial Service. There is also Triumphal Arch to the Memory of Prince Orloff for his repairing to Moscow in order to quell the Insurrections of the People at the time the Plague raged with great violence in that City, in the Year 1775. [...]

There are several Bridges in the Garden and two remarkably fine, one in the Turkish, the other in the Chinese Taste. The Turkish Bridge is built of fine dark Marble, and had a very magnificent appearance. The use of one of the Bridges amused me, it was about the size of a small Boat and had a Chinese rail on each side, a rope was tied on one side and was fixed over the Water on the opposite side, and fastened to another Bridge, therefore upon stepping upon one of the Bridges, they being exactly alike, and pulling the rope I gently crossed over, and this motion brought the other Bridge from the opposite side, so that there is always on each side a Bridge ready to convey you. I was surprised to see in a retired part of the Garden a fine Pyramid, which I was informed could not have been built for less than two thousand Pounds, and under it was a large hollow dome with a door, which the Baron one day opened when he and I were walking in the Garden, and crept in to see the size of it, and said it was large enough to hold him, this Mausoleum is to deposit the Bodies of two Italian Greyhounds, which the Baron had presented to the Empress, they had become very great favourites, and it was now the fashion for all the Court to keep one.

When the Dimsdales were at Tsarskoe Selo, Cameron had virtually finished the so-called Fourth Apartment, which comprised the official

reception rooms, where his versatility in adapting styles other than the
Graeco-Roman is revealed in the Arabesque Room, the Lyons Drawing
Room and the Chinese Hall, and was engaged on the Fifth Apartment, a
suite of six small rooms for the empress's private use and including a
bedroom decorated with twenty-two Wedgwood plaques. He was soon to
start on the new wing which would include the Agate Pavilion and the
Colonnade, which would be known to posterity as the Cameron Gallery.
A description of these later additions is provided by Parkinson following
his visit in January 1793:

> The baths consist of two floors on the upper level of which there are
> three apartments, and on the lower the baths. In the largest room there is
> a large bath lined with tin. I believe, into which either hot or cold water
> can be let in: in the next a large tub with two cisterns above it by means of
> which the water can be made of any temperature; there is also a Russian
> Bath. The Empress's dressing room is adjoining to the second. The apart-
> ment in the middle is of a considerable size, but those at either end rather
> small. One of these is cased with Jasper and the other with Agate. That
> which is lined with Jasper is ornamented with columns of agate. I think
> we were told that this building cost 500,000 roubles: not including the
> Agate and the Jasper, which comes from the mines of Kolgwan
> [Kolyvan]. When it was finished the Empress walked over it holding
> Cameron by the Arm and said, It is indeed very handsome 'mais ça
> coûte'. She frequently dines in the Baths when her party is small. She aslo
> sits there a great deal in hot weather on account of their great coolness.
>
> But her usual dining room is in the Gallery. This is a long room
> encompassed by a broad walk, on one side protected from the South by
> the building in the middle and on the other from the North. She walks on
> one side or the other according to the circumstances of the weather. On
> the Balustrade round this walk she has placed a great number of Bronze
> busts: and here we saw that of Fox between the busts of Cicero and
> Demosthenes. In order to arrive at the Gallery we descended from the
> hanging Garden I think by a stair, on which I remarked the statue of
> Junius Brutus.

The bronze bust of the statesman Charles James Fox was a copy of
the marble original Catherine had bought in 1791 from the sculptor

Joseph Nollekens as an expression of her admiration for Fox's opposition to the British Government's anti-Russian stance during the so-called 'Ochakov Crisis' during the Russo-Turkish War (an action which, incidentally, provoked in Britain a series of savage caricatures by James Gillray and others). As Parkinson had noted earlier, however, by 1793 she was prepared to 'throw a veil over his bust', for the sympathy Fox was then expressing for Poland and the French revolutionaries.

* * * *

By the end of Catherine's reign St Petersburg had firmly etched itself into the British consciousness. An indication of this would seem to be the article, 'A Description of the City of Petersburgh' that *The Times*, founded only the previous year, ran in three consecutive issues on 15–17 November 1786. It was a sort of synthesis of geographical, historical, social and architectural information available in a variety of sources, often unreliable and mainly concentrating on the early years of the city, but giving most detail to the organization of the Academy of Sciences, the Winter Palace and the Bronze Horseman. Generally favourably inclined towards the city's magnificence, it nevertheless concluded with advice to travellers, including the warning that 'the morals of the people, as in all large cities are much depraved: and the suspicious vigilance of the Russian Government renders it necessary for a stranger to be very circumspect in his words and behaviour'.

CHAPTER 4

ALEXANDER I'S IMPERIAL CAPITAL

Between the two long and 'glorious' reigns of Catherine II and Alexander I was the short and violently truncated reign of Paul I that straddled the centuries, from November 1796 to March 1801. Anglo-Russian relations were initially cordial, and had naturally improved with the extension of the Commercial Treaty in 1797 and Paul's eventual commitment to the Coalition against Napoleon. They rapidly deteriorated, however, from the end of 1799 and relations were broken off in May 1800. Paul introduced an embargo against British goods and seized British ships, re-activated in December the Armed Neutrality of 1780, and moved towards an alliance with Napoleon, envisaging the invasion of India. 'Crazy Paul' became, like his mother a decade earlier, the target for the ferocious satires of the British caricaturists. British travellers in Paul's Russia left damning accounts of his tyranny and included almost every other aspect of Russian life and culture for good measure. None was more caustic than Edward Daniel Clarke, another Cambridge don accompanying a young pupil on a grand tour. He deigned to ignore St Petersburg entirely in his influential account, first published in 1810, but left a devastating account of the Catherinian Palace at Tsarskoe Selo (and its celebrated Amber Room):

> The palace of *Tsarskoselo* is twenty-two versts from *Petersburg*, and the only object worth notice between that city and *Novogorod*. It is built of brick, plastered over. Before the edifice is a large court, surrounded by low buildings for the kitchens and other out-houses. The front of the palace occupies an extent of near eight hundred feet; and it is entirely covered, in a most barbarous taste, with columns, and pilasters, and cariatides, stuck between the windows. All of these, in the true style of Dutch gingerbread, are gilded. The whole of the building is a compound of what an architect ought to avoid, rather than to imitate. Yet so much money has been spent upon it, and particularly upon the interior, that it cannot be passed without notice. [...]

The gardens of *Tsarskoselo* are laid out in the English taste; and therefore the only novelty belonging to them is their situation, so far removed from the nation whose customs they pretend to represent.

The interior of the building presents a number of spacious and gaudy rooms, fitted up in a style combining a mixture of barbarism and magnificence hardly to be credited. The walls of one of the rooms are entirely covered with fine pictures, by the best of the *Flemish,* and by other masters. These are fitted together, without frames, so as to cover, on each side, the whole of the wall, without the smallest attention to disposition or general effect. But, to consummate the *Vandalism* of those who directed the work, when they found a place they could not conveniently fill, the pictures were cut, in order to adapt them to the accidental spaces left vacant. [. . .] But the most extraordinary apartment, and that which usually attracts the notice of strangers more than any other, is a room, about thirty feet square, entirely covered, on all sides, from top to bottom, with *amber;* a lamentable waste of innumerable specimens of a substance which could nowhere have been so ill employed. The effect produces neither beauty nor magnificence. It would have been better expended even in ornamenting the heads of Turkish pipes; a custom which consumes the greatest quantity of this beautiful mineral. The appearance made by it on the walls is dull and heavy. It was a present from the king of Prussia. In an apartment prepared for *Prince Potemkin,* the floor was covered with different sorts of *exotic wood,* interlaid; the expense of which amounted to a hundred *roubles* for every squared *archine.* A profusion of gilding appears in many of the other rooms. The ball-room is an hundred and forty feet long by fifty-two feet wide, and two stories high. The walls and pilasters of another apartment were ornamented with *lapis-lazuli,* as well as the tables it contained. *The Cabinet of Mirrors* is a small room lined with large pier-glasses, looking upon a terrace, near which is a covered gallery above two hundred and sixty feet long. There are various statues about the house and gardens, in marble and in bronze, all without merit. The chapel is entirely of gilded wood, and very richly ornamented.

Paul's St Petersburg was remarkable for the buildings he ordered to be dismantled or leave unfinished rather than for those he built.

Committed to undoing much that his mother had done, he saw no reason to finish the Stock Exchange on the Spit of Vasil'evskii Island, commissioned by Catherine from Quarenghi and more or less abandoned for reasons of finance after the outbreak of the Russo-Swedish War in 1787. He was even more peremptory with the wooden Summer Palace built by Rastrelli for the Empress Elizabeth at the junction of the Fontanka and Moika rivers and fortunately caught for posterity in one of the engravings prepared for the fifty-year celebrations of 1753. It was in that palace that he had been born, a good Freudian reason, it has been suggested, for his pulling it down. He also recognized an excellent site for a new palace of his own, one that would be a fortress, with two sides of his proposed moat already there. Recent research suggests that he himself took a hand in designing the Michael Castle (*Mikhailovskii zamok*), but otherwise it is to Vasilii Bazhenov (who had suffered greatly at Catherine's hands by her rejection of the remarkable palace complex he was building for her at Tsaritsyno outside Moscow) that the work was initially entrusted, although finished by Paul's favourite architect Vincenzo Brenna. A strange palace, offering four different façades in a mixture of classical and gothic architecture with hints of masonic or Maltese-knight symbolism, it was still not finished, when from impregnable castle it turned into the place of the tsar's assassination. When British travellers again began to appear in the Russian capital, the castle, known popularly as the Red Castle for the brick from which it was constructed, became a site of morbid fascination. Among the first to describe it was Sir John Carr, visiting St Petersburg in 1804 and within months producing the large tome that contained the first widely accessible account of Paul's end:

> we went to the palace of Saint Michael, where, as I have related, the last Emperor perished. As Paul had expressed so much aversion to the imperial mansions in which his mother delighted, I felt a curiosity minutely to examine a palace of his own creation. In addition to what has been before observed, the whole of this enormous pile was built by an Italian, of red Dutch brick, which at a distance has an animating appearance, upon a basement of hewn granite, that resembles a foundation of rock. The grand entrance from the great perspective through the riding-room and offices, is very handsome. Upon the architrave is

written in Russ characters, as it was translated to me, the following singular motto: 'May my house endure like the Lord's.' The Russians observe, with their accustomed superstition, that the number of letters of this inscription correspond with the number of Paul's years, and that out of them an anagram may be composed, denoting that he who raised the building would perish by a violent death. The interior is vast, but very gloomy. The chambers which were shewn were stripped of their furniture and all their moveable decorations, which are lodged in the cabinet of jewels, but the ornaments which remained exhibited a style of costly magnificence; the doors, some of which were of various-coloured glass, and richly gilded, were uncommonly superb. We saw the room in which the unfortunate Sovereign perished, and his private stair-case before mentioned.

The painter Robert Ker Porter, arriving in St Petersburg in the summer of 1805 and already familiar with Carr's work, adds colourful anecdotes of his own:

This huge pile of windows, friezes, pediments, and chimneys, a sort of architectural *melange* of military and domestic ornaments, was built on the site of the old Summer Palace; the residence of Peter the Great [not so – Porter confuses the Summer Palaces]. It is surrounded by a wet ditch, defended by draw-bridges; and during the time of the late Emperor, was his favourite abode. He considered it the child of his creation; and a most dear one it proved: for here, in the apartment which look into the plain for exercising the imperial troops, he met with that fate so well known to all [Porter here refers us to Carr's account of the murder].

Amongst the many absurd whims which infected the brain of this monarch, was one for painting with various discordant colours, the bridges, the watch-houses, and imperial gates throughout the empire. These harlequin jackets were put on every thing that answered to this description, from one end of Russia to the other, by a special ukase, all in one day. The Red Palace was indebted for its present fiery hue to a very simple circumstance. A lady of high rank, of whom His Majesty was a great admirer, happened to appear one night at a ball where he was present, with a pair of gloves of this colour on her arms. The fancy of Paul was so struck, that the next day it became his favourite tint; and he gave instant orders that his new residence should be painted accordingly. Hence it is called the Red Palace: and a most frightful, glaring appearance it makes. Another caprice of the Emperor tended to fill up the ridiculous of this unfortunate abode. He must needs have his cypher of P. 1st surmounted with a crown, affixed in every part of the building; for what reason, he never declared, only it was his will: and now over every corner, frieze, door window, or latticed-hole, are these imperial letters multiplied without end. A person once attempted to count them, and left off perfectly weary and in despair, after he had numbered eight thousand.

Another building which did not escape Paul's fury was the Taurida Palace (*Tavricheskii dvorets*), associated not merely with hated mother but with detested favourite. Captain Thomas Freemantle, serving with Nelson's fleet on its way to besiege Kronstadt, when Paul's assassination took place, arrived in the city, 'beautiful beyond description', on 8 May 1801 and two days later 'went in the morning to see the palace of Prince Potemkin, which is now converted into a barrack and the flooring &c. totally destroyed, the Garden which is quite in the English stile is very pretty and laid out with much taste, but now much neglected'. So much neglected in fact that William Gould was brought back from Lancashire to restore it and, according to the fulsome testimony of Ker Porter, soon succeeded:

During the short summer of this country, the pleasure-grounds which surround the palace, wear a very charming appearance. They are laid out in the English style; having extensive shrubberies, romantic walks, rustic retreats, hot-houses, and conservatories, as well as every other feature in a British garden. For these beauties, the imperial family are indebted to the taste and exertions of Mr. Gould, an Englishman, who has long resided in St. Petersburgh; and who plans and superintends all its most distinguished works of this nature. He is the Repton of Russia. His true English honesty, excellent heart, and hospitality, claim the esteem of all ranks; and add a still firmer decision to that respect for the British character already awarded to it by the generous admiration of the Russian empire.

By the end of Alexander's reign, the palace had been fully restored and had become, somewhat ironically, one of the homes of Paul's widow, the dowager Empress. It was visited by Benjamin, Lord Bloomfield, who was 'never was more struck with any entrance':

It is Oriental, and resembles in large our little pavilion at Brighton. One enters a spacious hall, then a beautiful round hall of immense dimensions, lighted from above. Then a room as large as the riding-house at Brighton, perhaps larger, and an extensive garden, under cover, connecting with the larger room. I never beheld such a fairy scene, and these apartments had been prepared for a grand fête, which did not take place, owing to the Emperor's illness. The arrangement for lighting was in very good taste, and would have made a wonderful effect. The theatre was boarded over and tables placed for the suppers. The garden was beautified with fine trees and a piece of artificial water with boats; the walks admirably kept. The living rooms were in two wings, and the old Empress inhabits this Palace in the autumn. Her bed-room was very large, but the walls were simply coloured upon plastering with coloured borders, very simple, but clean and livable. I was charmed with the Palace; indeed, nothing could exceed the effect on first entering.

Rinaldi's St Isaac's Church, still unfinished decades after William Richardson described the laying of its foundation stone, had, however, been completed by Paul, but in a way that still showed his contempt, while allowing him to divert the marble for his own Michael Castle. Carr

stopped at the marble church of St. Isaac, which was erected, but not finished, by the late Empress: it is entirely built of Siberian marble, porphyry, and jasper, at an immense cost, has a vast copper dome gilded, and is the most magnificent place of worship in Petersburg; yet, after all, it has a very *sombre* appearance without.

The late Emperor, disgusted, as I have already explained, with every thing which had engaged the care and regard of his Imperial mother, raised in ridicule a little tower of brick, covered with a small dome, on the west side of this temple.

Porter agreed – and one of his possible alternatives was to be fulfilled before the end of Alexander's reign:

> The foundation of the church was laid by the Empress Catherine, and finished wretchedly with brick by the Emperor Paul. For the honour of the empire, I hope that it will either be altered to the Empress's original design, or pulled down altogether. It stands in one of the finest squares in Europe, called Isaac's Place, and particularly celebrated for containing the admirable equestrian statue of Peter the Great.

Porter was not alone in expressing his admiration for Falconet's statue and no account – or letter home – was complete without some description, although opinion was as divided as ever over the rock on which it stood. Two nicely contrasting views come from letters sent home to Ireland by Martha Wilmot, the companion of Princess Ekaterina Dashkova, and Eleanor Cavanagh, maid to Martha's sister Catherine. Martha wrote in August 1803:

> I am just return'd from Walking to examine the celebrated Statue of Peter the Great. It is undoubtedly noble beyond what one could almost suppose possible in imitative art, for the Horse actually cheats you after some time into a belief that the swelling veins, the strong sinews, and ardent impatient air with which he grandly endeavours to bound over all difficulties, and the ease dignity and commanding air of the Hero who holds the reins in one hand while he seems to command worlds by the expression of the other, could only be convey'd by *life itself.* It really is the finest Statue I ever beheld – but with grief I add, the beautiful allegory is nearly lost by the barbarous use which has been made of the Chisel reducing the rock on which it stands till 'tis almost too small for proportion, and plaining its ruggedness which was one of its best qualitys. However it is a glorious Monument and the Russians value it as such.

Two years later, Eleanor's reaction was of a somewhat different order:

> I thought the Screech wou'd have Choak'd me when turning round my head what wou'd I see leaping over a *rail* Rock but a Giant of a Man on the back of a *Dragin* of a Horse. 'Stop him' (sais I), for I declare to God,

Miss Henrietta, but I thought the Life wou'd have left me to see a live Christian making such a Fool of himself, when what did I hear but that he was a *Marble Emperor*! Some old snake of a Man that they call Peter, or *Peter the Great*, or something like that!

Other monuments of Catherine's age which had gone unremarked in earlier accounts now received their first description from British travellers to Alexander's city. One such was the famous railings of the Summer Garden by the Neva, designed by Fel'ten and erected by Eropkin in 1784, which enthused Sir John Carr:

> In the evening I visited the summer gardens that face the Neva, the palisade of which, unquestionably the grandest in Europe, is composed of thirty-six massy Doric columns of solid granite, surmounted by alternate vases and urns, the whole of which, from the ground, are about twenty feet high, connected by a magnificent railing, formed of spears of wrought iron tipped with ducat gold. The decorations over the three grand entrances are also exquisitely wrought and covered with gold of the same superior quality. As near as I could ascertain by my own paces, the length of this magnificent balustrade must be about seven hundred feet. The pillars would certainly be improved were they thinner or fluted.

It was probably these words that gave rise to an anecdote appearing in a Russian work about the beauties of St Petersburg and Moscow that was translated into English in 1814:

> Rumours of the extraordinary beauty of the iron railings of the Summer Palace persuaded a certain Englishman, a great connoisseur of the arts, to travel to St Petersburg in order to verify this claim with his own eyes. Having inspected the railings and confirmed that he had not been deceived about their fine qualities, he immediately returned to his homeland.

Even Pavlovsk, Cameron's masterpiece beyond Tsarskoe Selo, and usually neglected in visitors' accounts, received a belated tribute from Lord Bloomfield:

We drove to Pavloffsky, the Empress dowager's favourite residence. The gardens were wilder, and therefore more beautiful to my eye; the ground varied and very pretty. We stopped at a rustic temple in a charming situation, where the Empress sometimes has tea; within view of a pretty cascade. We then passed on to a beautiful ball-room, where there reunions every Sunday. It is surrounded by a flower-garden, and fitted up inside and out with a profusion of flowers. The candelabra were already prepared. The room itself was very fine and several other rooms besides. It is near a considerable piece of water covered with boats. Thence we reached the Palace, which is considerably raised above the garden, and the fall from the front of the house is striking and pretty: the water flowing below has a most agreeable effect.

There had been published in the early months of Alexander's reign a work, albeit of foreign origin, that was the first reliable and comprehensive guide to St Petersburg to appear in English. Henry Storch's *Picture of Petersburgh* (1801), which had originally appeared in German, then Russian, was, with its good map and a detailed key, a nineteenth-century equivalent to Weber's work at the end of Peter I's reign, but went much further with chapters covering not only the buildings but institutions, entertainments, customs – and the arts, including the first metric translation of a Russian poem, which evoked the city at night:

> My train of servants sunk in sleep,
> And all the town in silence deep.
> Neva's full stream was heard no more,
> Nor Balta foamed along her shore,
> But dark repose, encamp'd around,
> Had banished every ruder sound.

The translator was the indefatigable William Tooke, who had resigned his position as British chaplain in the Russian capital in 1792 and had devoted himself in London to providing the British public with much-needed information on Russia. Storch's work was nonetheless a guide to Catherine's St Petersburg at the beginning of the 1790s and thus justifying Tooke's comment that 'it is natural that many changes must have happened in the living scenes of this picture during the delays necessarily attending the compiling, printing, translating and reprinting of a work of this nature'. Alexander I's reign was to bring Peter's city to its imperial climax with a flurry of mighty buildings that fixed the classical image on the heart of the city. Two years after Alexander's accession, the city celebrated its centenary; at his death, nearly a quarter of a century later, the city was, indeed, Pushkin's 'beauty and wonder of the northern lands' and one the British travellers, among others, flocked to see.

The enthusiasm of Ker Porter is hard to match, but his first impressions, dating from 1805, convey better than most the impetus given by Alexander to grandiose new building schemes.

I am at a loss, my dear friend, where to commence a description of this splendid city. Every object excites admiration; and those objects are so numerous, that I find it difficult to select what you might deem most interesting, from an assemblage of such, to me, equally prominent beauties. I, who have come direct from London, may perhaps view St. Petersburgh with peculiar impressions. The plainness of our metropolis, the almost total neglect of all architectural graces in the structure of even the best houses, and the absolute deformity of many of the inferior sort; all these things strike the eye as forcibly, though in an opposite direction, as mine was with the magnificence of St. Petersburgh. Such grandeur and symmetry in building, I never before beheld in any of the different capitals to which my fondness for travel has conducted me. Every house seems a palace, and every palace a city.

On every side are long and wide streets of highly decorated stone edifices; interspersed with the still more stately mansions of the nobility, the roofs of which are curiously painted in rich colours, harmoniously blending with the gilded domes and spires of the neighbouring churches. Although this city abounds in public buildings, in a style of gigantic architecture no where else to be found, yet the taste of the Emperor and the industry of his subjects are daily undertaking new works; which, when completed, will still more strongly call forth the admiration of the traveller. Amongst the most beautiful of these growing structures are the Kazan church, the new Exchange, the Manege for the chevalier guards, and the Façade of the Admiralty. I suppose no country can boast so long and uninterrupted a street as the *Great* and *English*

Quay; the granite front and pavement of which are unparalleled. The canals are worthy of the same august hand; and the superb bridges which clasp them from side to side, rear their colossal pillars in all the majesty of imperial magnificence. The dingy hue of bricks, or the frippery of plaister, seldom offends the eye in this noble city. Turn where you will, rise immense fabricks of granite: and did you not know the history of the place, you might suppose that it had been founded on a vast plain of that rocky production; whence had been derived the stones of the buildings; and in the bosom of which had been dug the river and canals that intersect its surface. But it is from the quarries of Finland that the Russians dig these bodies of granite, and transport and place then here in lasting monuments of their own unwearied industry. That mass on which is erected the immortal statue of Peter the First, is one huge instance of their indefatigable labour; and the forest of columns in the new Metropolitan church, is not a less worthy proof of the vigour with which they pursue so meritorious a toil.

Before we follow progress on these great monuments of Alexander's reign, it should be said that the more sober critical note about building materials, reminiscent of many British travellers of the previous reign, continued to be struck. Here is Reginald Heber, recently elected Fellow of All Souls, Oxford, and future Bishop of Calcutta, who arrived in the capital at approximately the same time as Porter:

In my last letter I promised you an account of Petersburg; and I know nothing to which it can be better compared than some parts of the new streets in London, without their causeways and railed areas. There is every where displayed the same activity in beginning, the same slightness in the materials, and the same want of accurate finishing or perseverance. There is indeed nothing more striking than the apparent instability of the splendour of this great town; houses, Churches, and public buildings are all of plaistered brick; and a portico worthy of a Grecian temple is often disfigured by the falling of the stucco, and the bad rotten bricks peeping through. The external ornaments and structure even of their great Casan Church, which, when finished, will be a noble building, are of the like materials. But whatever may be their durability, their general appearance, with their gaudy ornaments, their gilt spires and domes, and the gold-leaf which is lavished on the capitals and bases of their pillars, produces altogether a very glorious and novel effect.

It is a theme to which Heber returns more than once, playing variations on the fragility of beauty, 'the instability of the splendour', which forms a potent ingredient in the Petersburg myth:

The only obstacle to St. Petersburg's becoming the noblest city in the world is its want of good materials. Its quays of granite are all that are likely to go down to a very distant posterity; and if the court were removed, a hundred years would almost destroy every vestige of its present grandeur. Even the new Cathedral of Casan, which is magnificent specimen of genius, is of so perishable a stone (excepting the granite pillars within that they intend to cover it with stucco and white-wash. The only square in the town is that before the winter palace; the Isaac's place is a vast irregular area, containing the marble Church of St. Isaac, and the famous statue of Peter the Great; it is formed on one side by the boulevard, a gravel-walk, planted with lime-trees, carried along the glacis of the admiralty, which the present emperor has levelled for the purpose.

The city Heber viewed was yet scarcely Alexander's, although he raised a question mark over the Kazan Cathedral, the first great monument of his reign that would replace (and for a few years yet, live alongside) the Kazan Church that had welcomed Catherine at the time of her coup. It occupies a strategic position along Nevskii Prospekt, where the latter bisects the Catherine Canal (another creation of Catherine's reign from the swamp of the River Krivusha) and formed a large open space with the curve of its great colonnade (which was to be matched by a never built colonnade on the south side). The colonnade fronting the Nevskii appears to be the cathedral's main entrance, although that was in fact from the east. Heber and Porter had both seen the model and the church some years into its construction, and Porter, while not mentioning the colonnade, refers to another feature which was not built – 'And at some distance, in front of the building, is to be erected a single column of granite of two hundred feet in length; a piece of that size, sufficient to form it, having lately been discovered. Its magnitude will be so immense as to exceed the height of Pompey's pillar by many feet. It is expected that in the course of four or five years the whole work will be completed. At that period the old church is to be pulled down; and thus an area will be left that must considerably improve the situation of the new'.

Visitors over the next few years gave their work-in-progress reports, but the first to describe it after its completion was the young Oxford scholar and amateur artist J.T. James, publishing his account two years after his 1814 visit; he was also the first to mention that Charles Cameron (whom, incidentally, Carr had portrayed living comfortably in retirement in rooms in the Michael Castle allocated to him by Alexander) had submitted plans 'more correct in taste' than those accepted; and, whereas earlier writers had been content to call the architect a talented 'slave' of Count Stroganov, he was the first at least to attempt to give him a name, noting that 'Woronitchki' (Andrei Voronikhin) had 'just lived to see it opened to the public at the beginning of the present year'

James found the new cathedral 'one of the most splendid structures that modern art has realised':

The plan is laid in the form of a cross, terminating each arm with a Corinthian portico: a lofty cupola rises from the centre, and the front is received into a grand semi-circular colonnade four columns in depth: the area of the crescent was intended to have been ornamented with the statues of St. Peter and Paul, raised on gigantic blocks of granite ten or twelve feet high: one of them, however, was unfortunately sunk in crossing the Neva, and the other still rests on the rollers by which it was conveyed, in one of the by streets near the place of exercise.

In point of architecture, the composition of the building is not quite harmonious throughout; and the dome is so contracted in its dimensions, as to give, in some points of view, an air of insignificance to the whole. It deserves, however, notwithstanding these defects, considerable praise for the chastity of the decoration, as well as for the noble effect of the approach: in each line as the eye is directed, it is met by a forest of lofty columns, which form, at every step, combinations of the most classical variety.

On entering the interior the spectator is struck by a blaze of pomp and magnificence that would ill assort with any structure, other than the temple of religion. The columns of the aisles are of purple granite highly polished; their capitals of brass and gold; rich paintings line the walls, and a dim, mysterious gloom pervades the whole fabric.

Even more important to the skyline and planning scheme of the city was the Admiralty. Like the Kazan and Isaac churches, the Admiralty underwent considerable changes and reconstruction. It was during the reign of Anna Ivanovna that Ivan Korobov had rebuilt Peter's original shipyard fortress and gave it the gilded spire that looked across the river to the spire towering above the Peter and Paul Cathedral. It was essentially Korobov's Admiralty, which Porter described as 'one of the most extensive in St. Petersburgh. It was planned and built by Peter the Great. At present, the architecture is not very striking; but it is undergoing alterations, which, we hope, will render it worthy of the navy of which it is the head'. The vast reconstruction was to begin in 1806 according to the design of the Naval Ministry's chief architect Andreian Zakharov, who died in 1811, some years before his masterpiece was finally completed. Robert Johnston, a recent Oxford graduate, saw it in the summer of 1814:

The Admiralty stands in the centre of the town, on the south side of the Neva. It exhibits a light square building of immense extent; on every side forming a front of nearly six hundred feet in length, but of no height, and that considerably concealed by a heavy earthen mound, thrown up around it. In the centre of the south front, the principal entrance passes under a magnificent arched gateway, supporting a splendid square basement of Doric pillars, surmounted by a rich cupola, and slender spire, the top of which is crowned by a vessel under full sail, emblematic of the building. Along the outside of the earthen mound and ditch, delightful gravelled walks are laid out, shaded by double rows of clipped poplars, while the borders are beautifully relieved by low green painted railings, and sweet scented flowers. The extreme care with which these walks are kept, reflects the greatest credit on the police, and forms one of the most delightful lounges imaginable. Every morning, the inferior officers of the police are regularly seen cleaning and sweeping these walks, and trimming the flowers.

The boulevards around the southern and western sides appear on a drawing by James, with a view across the river towards the western end of Vasil'evskii Island, known as the Strelka, where one of the other great monuments of Alexander's reign stood. James ascribes the building to the Italian architect Quarenghi, but it was Quarenghi's Exchange (*Birzha*), which he had begun but never finished for Catherine the Great, that was demolished on the orders of the tsar and a new building commissioned from the French architect Thomas de Thomon. Thomon's great Stock Exchange, which was completed in 1810, is positioned on the true axis of the island and fronted by two red rostral columns near the junction of the Great and Little Nevas and took its inspiration from the mighty Greek temples of Paestum, with its continuous Doric colonnade raised on a mighty podium. Johnston, however, was far from impressed by it or its surrounding buildings:

> The Exchange and Custom-house are situated on the west end of the lower island called the quarter of Vassili Ostroff, at the separation of the branches of the river, and immediately fronts the citadel, which is situated on the opposite corner of the upper island, named the St Petersburg quarter. A new Exchange was erected a few years ago, but, from some singular motive, has never been opened; the merchants in consequence, continue to meet in the open air, in front of the old house. The new Exchange consists of an oblong square, surrounded with a broad piazza, supported on numerous pillars, with large figures emblematic of ships, but more like some nondescript monster. Nothing can be more ludicrous. Behind the Exchange is the Custom-house, warehouses, quay and docks; this range of buildings is probably more contemptible than those in any of the trading towns along the barren shores of Sweden.

Johnston was much more enthusiastic about Nevskii Prospekt and appreciated that 'from the Admiralty, the principal streets diverge, as from a general centre; so that from each, its gilded spire forms the terminating view. Among the streets leading from the Admiralty, that, called the Perspective, is the longest and most elegant in the city. A gravelled walk, shaded by trees, extends along its centre, occasionally interrupted by the massive granite bridges over the canals'. But one man's delight was another man's complaint. Carr's view was that

> The late Emperor [Paul] very materially affected the beauty of this street by destroying the foot-paths which were formerly on each side, and forming a very broad path in the centre of it, which he planted with Linden trees, and guarded by a low railing. The idea was evidently taken from the beautiful Linden walk at Berlin, which originated in the exquisite taste and genius of Frederic, so justly called the Great. The trees look very sickly, and for want of soil and moisture never can flourish, and cannot atone for the violation which is offered to taste. If this great nuisance was removed, the perspective would be one of the finest in Europe.

Incidentally, it was on Nevskii Prospekt that the 'English Shop', 'very dear & all the rage', continued to prosper, and, again in Carr's words, 'an Englishman of the name of Owens carries on a prodigious trade, chiefly in English manufactures; his house, which is a very magnificent one, has twenty-four rooms *en suite*, which are filled with the most beautiful merchandize; each room is a separate shop, and attended by persons who are solely attached to it: the promenade, through magazines of music, of books, of jewels, of fashions, &c. is very agreeable, and I believe perfectly novel. The respectable and enterprizing proprietor is said frequently to receive one thousand pounds sterling in one day: it is the constant and crowded resort of all the fashions of Petersburg'.

It is Carr once more who has left an invaluable description of another building that is connected with the name of Thomas de Thomon but was gutted by fire in 1811 and only rebuilt after several years. A little removed from the heart of the city on what became known towards the end of Alexander's reign as Theatre Square and on the site where there now stands the St Petersburg Conservatoire, there stood for more than a century the Grand or Stone Theatre. The first theatre, designed by Rinaldi, was opened in 1783, but it was decided to rebuild and enlarge it in a style more appropriate to the high classicism that was to mark the new reign. In a matter of months in the second half of 1802 the rebuild-

ing, to the design of Thomas de Thomon, was completed, and Carr
visited it on no less than three occasions during his stay:

> Soon after our arrival, we visited the Grand Imperial Theatre, or Opera
> House, called the Stone Theatre, which stands in a large open place,
> nearly in front of the Marine Garrison, formerly the New Goal, and
> the Nicholas Canal. At four angles in this spacious area, are four pavil-
> ions of iron, supported by pillars of the same metal, within which, in
> winter, large fir fires are constructed, the wind being kept off by vast
> circular moveable shutters of iron, for warming and screening the
> servants of those who visit the theatre in the winter. Previous to the
> erection of these sheds, many of those unfortunate persons were frozen
> to death. The government, attentive to the lives of the people, has
> interdicted performances at the opera, when the frost is unusually
> severe. The front is a noble portico, supported by doric pillars; the inte-
> rior is about the size of Covent-Garden, of an oval shape, and
> splendidly but rather heavily decorated. The lower tier of boxes project
> from the sides, at the back of which are pilasters, adorned with appro-
> priate decorations, richly gilded, above which are three rows of boxes,
> supported by corinthian pillars, each of which, as well as those below,
> contain nine persons. Nothing less than the whole box can be taken. It
> frequently happens that servants stand behind their masters or
> mistresses in the boxes, during the performance, and present a curious
> motley appearance. The Imperial box is in the centre of the first tier,
> projecting a little, is small, and very plainly decorated. The pit has
> seven or eight rows of seats with backs to them, in which a commodious
> portion of space for each spectator is marked off by little plates of plates
> of brass, numbered upon the top of the back seat; this part is called the
> *fauteuils*. Such is the order observed here, and in every theatre on the
> continent, that however popular the piece, a spectator may, during any
> part of the performance, reach his seat, in this part of the theatre,
> without any difficulty. Behind but not boarded off, is the pit and the
> parterre. The price of admission to the boxes and *fauteuils* are two silver
> rubles, little more than five shillings. There are no galleries. The massy
> girandoles, one of which is placed at every pilaster, are never illumi-
> nated but when the Imperial family are present, on which occasion
> only, a magnificent circle of large patent lamps is used; at other times its

place is supplied by one of smaller dimensions, when the obscurity which prevails induces the ladies to appear in an undress. Although this gloom before the curtain is said to be advantageous to the effect of scenery, yet the eye is saddened, as it runs its circuit in vain for forms adorned with graceful drapery, the glittering gem, the nodding plume, and looks of adorned beauty, that give fresh brilliance to the gay galaxy of light. The theatre is furnished with a great number of doors and passages, reservoirs of water, and an engine in case of fire, and with concealed flues and stoves, to give it summer warmth in winter. It is always strongly guarded by a detachment from the guards, as well as by the police officers, who preserve the most admirable order among the carriages and servants. It is not an ungratifying sight, after the opera, to pause at the doors and see with what uncommon skill and velocity the carriages, each drawn by four horses, drive up to the grand entrance under the portico, receive their company, and gallop off at full speed; pockets are very rarely picked, and accidents seldom happen.

Owing to the size and quantity of decorations, and the spacious arrangement of the boxes, I should not think the theatre could contain more than twelve hundred persons. Its receipts have never yet exceeded one thousand six hundred and eighty rubles, or two hundred and forty pounds. How different from a London theatre, which, on a crowded night, when a Siddons or a Litchfield delight their audience, is lined with faces, and the very walls appear to breathe!

The mishap to his theatre notwithstanding, Alexander could be well pleased with the face his capital presented to the world at what was to be the mid-point of his reign. An English naval surgeon provided a glowing tribute in 1814, although it is Peter I rather than Alexander I whom he extols:

If the mind finds, at the first approach to St. Petersburg, but little to admire, this feeling gradually gives way as we approach the city. Buildings of solid granite, as extensive as they are elegant, bridges, palaces, quays, churches with gilt domes, and turrets glittering in the sun, the banks of the river faced with the solid rock, and a succession for a mile or two, of splendid and costly mansions, which it requires some persuasion to believe are the residences of private individuals, all strike upon the eye with irresistible grandeur and a decided feeling in the mind that there is nothing equal to it in Europe. Every thing we see has an air of magnificence; perhaps the size of some, the materials of which they are constructed, and the idea of the labour necessary to give them their present form, may also impart sensations of the sublime. The Imperial Academy of Arts, the Marine Cadet Institution, and other noble edifices on the left, with the long line of the of the Great and English Quays, on the right, added to the gigantic facings of the Neva on both sides, are alone sufficient to confer celebrity on the city. But when we disembark near the bridge, rush into Isaac's Place, contemplate the admirable statue of Peter the Great, run our eyes over the Admiralty, up the grand Perspective street, along the Hermitage, Winter, and Marble Palaces, examine the hundreds of other mansions equal to palaces rising on every side, and enter the new Metropolitan Church, dedicated to the mother of the God of Kazan, all other faculties are absorbed in those of unfeigned admiration and astonishment. Other capitals may be larger and richer, but in beauty none for a moment can come in competition with this Queen of the North. Hers is the triumph of Architecture. In this respect she not only is, but ever must be the first in Europe, or indeed in the world, because the plan and much of the execution were the work of one extraordinary man, whom no future sovereign, however superior in ability, can equal in the means of accomplishing his designs. Regularity pervades the whole; the parts are so well fitted and adapted to each other that we can scarcely find any thing to condemn. It is a city of palaces rising in the midst of marshes.

This is essentially an update of the descriptions already quoted from Coxe and other late eighteenth-century travellers, but Alexander was far from finished. The last years of his reign saw the emergence of one of imperial St Petersburg's most influential architects, Carlo (Karl Ivanovich) Rossi. Although some of his major buildings were begun only in the reign of Nicholas I, three were started in 1818–19, of which two were completed and a third virtually so by 1825. The Elagin Palace on Elagin Island, which he completely rebuilt for the Dowager Empress Maria Fedorovna, was completed by 1822, while work continued in the centre of the city on the General Staff Building, the defining element in the planning of Palace Square, and the Michael Palace

(*Mikhailovskii dvorets*), situated between the Catherine Canal and the Fontanka and separated from the Michael Castle by its extensive gardens, also designed by Rossi in collaboration with Joseph Bush, the son of Catherine the Great's head gardener. Benjamin, Lord Bloomfield, the British ambassador to Sweden, paying a short visit to Russia in the summer of 1825, 'went to see the new Palais Michel, which is very fine inside and out, and suitable for a Prince of a great Empire, but the scaffolding had not been removed. It has been built by contract, and the architect said it would cost about 4,600,000 roubles, probably less than the alterations to Buckingham House'. On his return from Moscow two months later, he again 'went over the Grand Duke Michael's magnificent new palace. The scaffolding was all removed and much of the furniture in place. I have never seen so much comfort and magnificence combined so successfully. Sixteen fine rooms are allotted to the ladies-in-waiting. The stables very fine, and arranged upon a new principle, worthy of imitation. I complimented the architect greatly who was called upon to furnish the plan in four days. On the Emperor's next birthday, the 1st (13th) of September O.S., he is to present this cadeau to his brothers, who will only have to walk in and take possession! It is furnished with the most minute details by the Emperor, plate, china, etc., etc.'

The out-of-town residence of Alexander's younger brother Constantine is mentioned by George Matthew Jones a few years earlier, when he travelled down the Peterhof Road. Strel'na, the palace begun but left unfinished by Peter I, was given by Paul I to his son Constantine, for whom the palace and its gardens were restored by the architects Voronikhin and Ruska and where, as Jones notes, the Uhlan cavalry regiment was quartered during the war against Napoleon. Jones's admiring description of the Peterhof Road recalls Dashwood's a century earlier (see chapter 2), but the road now ended with a new structure from Alexander's reign: the Narva Gates, designed by Quarenghi and built in 1814 (but in wood) in time to welcome home the victorious guard regiments.

Hence [from Peterhof] to Strelna, the road continues for eight versts rich in variegated prospects. This imperial villa has the same origin, and nearly the same situation as Peterhof, but its fate has hitherto been very different; what it was under Peter, it remains to this hour, abating the dilapidations, which it has suffered from time. It has never been finished, which is extraordinary, as its situation is highly romantic, and it lies in the neighbourhood of a large well-built town, the first post station on the Riga road. It now belongs to the Grand Duke Constantine, and is the quarters for his own regiment of cavalry.

We soon after passed the monastery of St. Sergius; the road improved, and even at this gloomy season we came to a scene, continuing to the Riga gate, which, for the idea it presented of taste and art, stands unrivalled in any country we have visited. Conceive ten miles of an uninterrupted series of elegant country-seats and villas, surrounded by lawns, plantations, basins, statues, vases, cannon, &c.; in short, every thing calculated to produce the most striking effect. No expense has been spared by the respective owners, to convert this steril [*sic*] ground into, at least, by comparison, a perfect paradise. In summer, when all these delightful seats are animated by nature, they are the residence of the principal nobility, who hurry out of Petersburg the moment stern winter disappears. The rent of these houses is said to be the most exorbitant, and the foreign ministers are glad to get them at any rate. Sir Charles Bagot [the British ambassador before Disbrowe] had just moved into town before our arrival; indeed, when we passed, the houses were all closed for the winter. [...]

The winding of the road just before entering the city brought us suddenly up to a triumphal arch, and the effect was very fine. It was erected by the inhabitants of Petersburg, upon the return of the emperor, in 1814: the ornaments are allegorical. It was proposed to be built of stone, but for want of sufficient time, it was run up *pro tempore*, in brick, and stuccoed, which now begins to look shabby; and as their ardour is much cooled, I doubt its ever being finished according to the original plan.

Within the imposing imperial capital that St Petersburg had become, the British colony continued to occupy a conspicuous place. Ker Porter's description of their way of life at the beginning of Alexander's reign is reminiscent of the enthusiasm expressed by Lady Craven and others from the time of Catherine:

In the families of our English merchants resident at St. Petersburgh, you may still recall the simplicity of home, in the chastened elegance of their abodes. Their tables, as well as those of other foreign merchants, are always open to their friends; and the warmest hospitality ever ready to welcome all who bring introductions from their correspondents abroad. This truly estimable order of men are held in the highest esteem by the nobles of a metropolis which they so truly benefit and enrich. Many of them possess little paradises on the road leading to the imperial palace of Peterhoff, to which their families resort for the hot and short-lived months of summer. Since my arrival I have paid several visits to these charming retreats, where every thing around reminded me of dear England. The house embosomed in trees, and furnished in the English style; the gardens planted in the same taste; and the language and manners of the inmates; all would have persuaded me to forget I was in a strange land.

The community continued to grow during Alexander's reign, reaching perhaps 2,500, and a fourth (and final) commercial treaty was signed in 1813, in the wake of the great allied victories over Napoleon. Russian enthusiasm for things English – from the goods on display in the English shop on Nevskii Prospekt to the novels of Walter Scott and the poems of Byron – reached a new high, but the community had always been fearful that relations in the political sphere would have repercussions for its position in the Russian capital. The embargoes of 1800 under Paul and again in 1806 under Alexander and the repressive measures against British subjects were obvious signals of how quickly things could change for the worse. A more sober note was sounded by George Matthew Jones, who visited the capital between November 1822 and March 1823, highlighting the fact that the English Embankment, now officially so named, was inhabited by far fewer British:

The quay above the Palace is called the Russian, and that below, the English quay. The latter name is given to it, because the large houses on it were originally built, and inhabited by wealthy English merchants. I lament to say, that very few of them have been able to retain their houses, but have gradually ceded them to the Russian nobility, and, in some instances, to German merchants, while they have themselves been obliged to retire into secondary streets, particularly one called the Back Line. This falling off in our merchants, so annoying to British feelings, may be attributed to various causes; but, I believe, principally to the severe treatment they met with at the hands of Paul, in 1800, and to the subsequent war between Great Britain and Russia, which obliged them to leave the country. These changes so disgusted them, that when peace was restored the principals of the firms did not choose to return and again subject themselves to similar treatment, but sent junior partners, who were not entitled to, nor could they afford, such sumptuous residences, and, I fear, there is too much reason for supposing that the stability and credit of the English mercantile houses have sunk in proportion as the respectable appearance of their dwelling-houses has declined: indeed, it could hardly be expected to be otherwise; for, surely, the head of a house is always better calculated to support its dignity and appearance, than a junior partner or clerk.

However, there are still mercantile houses as respectable as any which are to be found in Europe, and they yet retain possession of dwellings on the quay, particularly the houses of Thornton and Melville, Thompson, Bonner, and Venning. The first is conducted by Mr. Henry Caley, one of the most intelligent merchants I have met with in any country, possessing not only mercantile but general information.

At Kronstadt, however, the presence of the British seemed as dominant as ever, registered in a diary from 1814:

The great basin or wet-dock for the reception of merchant-men, is unequalled by anything of the kind in Europe, except our own docks at Blackwall, which are, however, of recent date compared to that of Cronstadt. It affords infinite facility of commerce, by carrying vessels nearly into the heart of the town, and may contain, perhaps, three or four hundred sail. At this time it was so well filled that I could scarcely discover a vacancy. Never, even in the Thames, did I observe a more extensive or denser forest of masts. It was gratifying to find that they were nearly all belonging to our country, and of course so many practical testimonies to our wealth, reputation and enterprise. Besides the crews of these vessels, every second person we saw was English; the beach, quays, streets, and taverns (their keepers and servants also of the

ᴠᴇ: The Peter and Paul Fortress and
ᴄhedral. Signed Whymper. Frontispiece
Thomas Michell, *Russian Pictures
ɪwn with Pen and Pencil* (1889).

ʜᴛ: The Alexander Column on Palace
ᴜare. Drawn by H. de la Careerif for
ᴏmas Michell, *Russian Pictures Drawn
ʰ Pen and Pencil* (1889).

St Petersburg Scenes. Drawn by H . Hewley for Thomas Michell, *Russian Pictures Drawn with Pen and Pencil* (188

vskii Prospekt, *c.*1900. Photograph by Henry Norman in his *All The Russias* (1902).

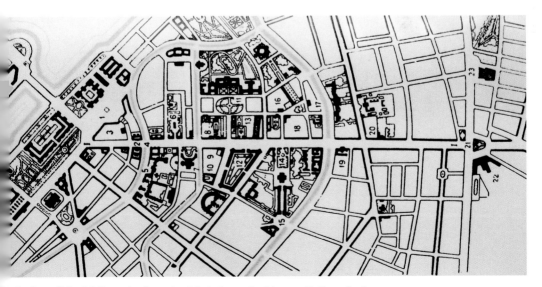

ch plan of Nevskii Prospekt, from the Admiralty to the Moscow Railway Station.

Members leaving the Duma (Taurida Palace). Watercolour by F. de Haenen. Published 1910.

cutting on the Neva. Watercolour by F. de Haenen. Published 1910.

The Bronze Horseman and St Isaac's Cathedral. Watercolour by F. de Haenen. Published 1910.

renadier by the Alexander Column on Palace Square. Watercolour by F. de Haenen. Published 1910.

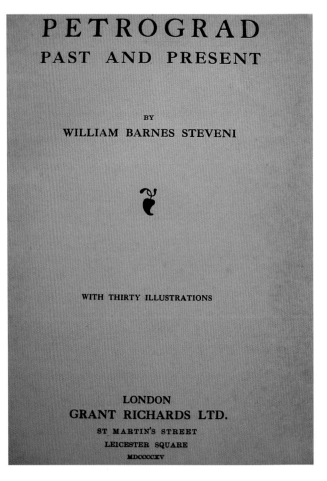

PETROGRAD
PAST AND PRESENT

BY
WILLIAM BARNES STEVENI

WITH THIRTY ILLUSTRATIONS

LONDON
GRANT RICHARDS LTD.
ST MARTIN'S STREET
LEICESTER SQUARE
MDCCCCXV

LEFT: Title page of William Barnes Steveni, *Petrograd Past and Present* (1915).

BELOW: The English Street, formerly Prospe in present-day Murino.

...aying golf at Murino, 1910s. Photograph from the Leeds Russian Archive.

...he site of the golf course in present-day Murino.

The English Church on the newly renamed English Embankment (contemporary view).

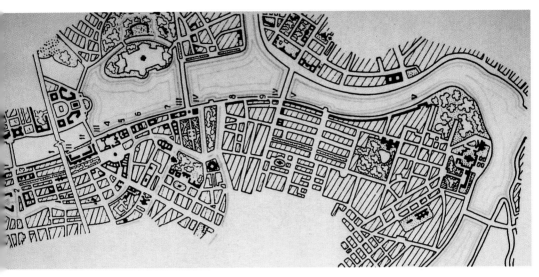

etch plan of the English Embankment, showing the approximate position of the English Church (near no. 3).

e British Embassy on Palace Embankment, originally the Saltykov Mansion (rented 1863–1917).

The drawing room and ballroom of the British Embassy.

LEFT: Sir George Buchanan, British ambassador in St Petersburg/Petrograd from 1910 to the October Revolution.

BELOW LEFT: Title page of Meriel Buchanan, *Petrograd the City of Trouble 1914–1918* (1918).

BELOW RIGHT: William Gerhardi (1895–1977), aged ten, ready for tennis in St Petersburg.

PETROGRAD
THE CITY OF TROUBLE
1914-1918

BY
MERIEL BUCHANAN
DAUGHTER OF THE
BRITISH AMBASSADOR

LONDON: 48 PALL MALL
W. COLLINS SONS & CO. LTD.
GLASGOW MELBOURNE AUCKLAND

LEFT: Lady Muriel Paget (1876–1938).

BELOW: The English house or dacha at Sosnovka. Photograph from the Leeds Russian Archive.

ENGLISH HOME, SOSNOVKA, LENINGRAD.

RIGHT: The former Swedish Embassy, no. 64 English Embankment. Contemporary view.

BELOW: 'The last Britishers in Leningrad': Mrs Fanny Morley (matron) and Miss Rose Healey (interpreter) leave Sosnovka, June 1938. Photograph from the Leeds Russian Archive.

Alexander Nevskii Monastery in the snow. Oil on canvas by John James, 2001.

Fishing in the city. Oil on canvas by John James, 2001.

same nation) were crowded with them, bustling to and fro with the characteristic hurry of commercial business, and occasionally, it must be confessed, dealing out to each other, or to strangers unluckily in their way, some of the choicest flowers of nautical eloquence. This is not an occasional, but on the contrary, a constant scene all the months in which, from the absence of the ice, the Gulph of Finland is open to traders; so that the place might be taken for an English colony. For so exclusively is the trade of this port in our hands, that of a thousand foreign vessels which enter, it is calculated 930 are British. What a pity that two nations so useful, and almost necessary, to each other, and whose real interests in all ordinary conditions of the world, present so little chance of interfering, should ever have been inconsiderate enough to go to war!

[. . .] The town occupies a considerable extent of ground, the streets irregular and often dirty, and the houses straggling. Many of the latter seem much neglected and going to decay, the access to some being quite ruinous or filthy; others again are not merely of an opposite description, but really elegant, among which may be ranked all those owned or occupied by our countrymen, who carry their characteristic comforts and neatness every where with them, though they seldom make proselytes to their practice. Besides two or three Russian churches, is an English one with a resident Clergyman, supported by contributions from the merchants [. . .]

Two very tolerable inns, kept by Englishmen, afford pretty good entertainment, when not crowded so much as they were at this moment. Scarcely a vacant corner – nay not even, as they say at the London theatres, 'standing room,' could be procured without some difficulty during the day, from the influx of masters of merchantmen, full of bustle and business, cargoes, freights, and insurances, profits and losses from their private adventures, quarrels with their seamen, and appointments to dinner with the merchants, interlarded with jokes and bantering anecdotes, arguments and scolding, loud laughter and occasional swearing, the whole washed down by copious libations of bottled *swipes* (porter) and grog. Such a Babel I never saw before. When the evening called these sons of Neptune on board their vessels, we found both room to breathe as well as very good beds, and when not chusing to dine alone, a very tolerable dinner at the *table d'hote* for the moderate sum of two and a half rubles, which at the then rate of exchange was about half a crown.

[. . .] The English form a numerous and important body, highly respected by the natives and visitors of all nations, for their attention and hospitality. Nearly the whole, are of course, mercantile men, and several are reputed very rich.

It was, incidentally, at this period that the Scot Charles Baird, who during Alexander's reign had become one of the capital's richest and most influential entrepreneurs, built Russia's first steamship, the *Elizaveta*, and inaugurated a service to the islands and Kronstadt, as Jones noted: 'we determined upon a visit to Cronstadt, while the gulf was yet open; and for that purpose embarked in a steam-boat belonging to Mr. Baird, an Englishman, who has a monopoly of them throughout the empire for seven years. The distance is twenty-two versts, and is usually performed in two or three hours'.

It is in Jones's book that we also find a description of the model Aleksandrovskii textile mill, visits to which in the early nineteenth century became as much a part of the tourist's itinerary as visits to the Smol'nyi Institute for Noble Young Ladies had been during Catherine's reign (the descriptions in both Coxe and Howard are particularly notable). The mill had been established at the end of the eighteenth century on a site along the Schlüsselburg Road on the left bank of the Neva beyond the Alexander Nevskii Monastery. It enjoyed the patronage of the Dowager Empress (Paul I's widow) and served as a source of employment for children of both sexes from the Petersburg Foundling Hospital. In 1817 a playing-card factory was added, where, as Jones notes, the young workers excelled in the colouring of cards. The British presence was much in evidence. The Engineer General Alexander Wilson had come as a young boy with his father and family to work for the architect Charles Cameron at Tsarskoe Selo, just as Charles Baird and his brother had arrived to work for Charles Gascoigne, the former director of the Carron ironworks in Falkirk and possibly the most important figure in introducing some of the successes of the British Industrial Revolution to Russia. It was Wilson who designed the building with its innovatory iron frame for the Aleksandrovskii works in 1812 and it was Baird who produced the ironwork.

On the 21st of October, O.S. [2 November 1822], we visited Alexandrofski, where there is an imperial cotton and linen manufactory, under the immediate patronage of the dowager empress. It stands on the left bank of the Neva, at twelve versts from the city. The establishment consists of six hundred and seventeen boys, and two hundred and fifteen girls, all selected from the foundling hospital, and who are employed in manufacturing linen and cotton, comprising every branch of the work, even to constructing the machinery.

We arrived just as they were going to dinner; this was cooked by steam, and the kitchen was beautifully clean. The dinner consisted of beef and soup, with a kind of rice, which grows in Siberia (but much more succulent than that of America), with plenty of bread and grass.

They marched in regular order, the boys separated by a screen from the girls; being arranged at table, the head attendant rang a bell, when grace was sung in chorus, after which they attacked the dinner with a good will. We were particularly struck with their healthy and clean appearance, although both sexes appeared small for their age. The girls were dressed very neatly, in white; their hair was arranged with elegance and uniformity, each having a large tortoise-shell comb on the top: none were strikingly handsome.

The boys and girls have every thing found for them, and receive two or four rubles a month, according to their diligence, which accumulates till their time of servitude expires, when they are manumitted. The dormitories were well ventilated and clean to a high degree; each had a separate bed, of which the blankets and bedding were as white as snow. They have a large play-room, which also serves as a theatre, and behind it is a drawing-school, ornamented with plans and models, executed by them, some in superior style. In short, it is an establishment which does honour to the empress; the children being, in the first place, in all probability, rescued from starvation or death, and then clothed, educated, taught a good trade, and made useful and respectable members of society. The establishment (as well as others which she protects) is under the general superintendence of General Wilson, a Scotchman, but it is directed immediately by a younger brother of his. A variety of articles are manufactured here, but the staple commodity is cotton and flax-twist; of the former a great quantity is sent into the interior, and a good deal of the latter to England: the whole is pressed by a hydraulic machine, as is practised by us. Three beautiful steam-engines are employed of seventy, sixty, and thirty horse power. The gasometer is on a large scale; the whole establishment is lighted by it, but as the gas is purified, nothing disagreeable arises from it: the coal is sent from England. The dowager empress has several monopolies, in order to support her philanthropic establishments (particularly the founding hospitals), throughout the empire; and amongst others, is an exclusive privilege of making playing cards, the whole of which are coloured here, and are said to produce more money than it is possible to conceive from such a source.

Mr. Wilson wore the order of Vladimir: he was very obliging: we left the manufactory highly delighted, and we are bound in justice to say, that in no country have we seen any thing to approach to it, in point of the comfort and cleanliness, which reign amongst the children. The far-famed establishment of Mr. Owen, at New Lanark, in these respects ranks far below it.

The British contribution towards the increasing 'industrialization' in the Russian capital and a more efficient running of its services had been noted by James, who visited various factories and mills a decade before Jones:

At the head of those we inspected, there was always most invariably seen a Scotchman or Englishman employes as superintendant. The integrity of these men, as agents, makes them invaluable in Russia; while the regularity and preciseness of arrangement which they introduce still more enhances the value of their moral qualities. Nor [. . .] have they been found less serviceable in matters of a higher description than the conduct of commercial business. Several Scotchmen are now high in the military service; and at the head of the medical profession, in its several branches of military, naval, and civil, are placed three gentlemen of the same country. I could indeed instance a department in which the expenses of the office were reduced by no less a sum than 22,000 R. within the first year of the administration of the present governor, nor did any diminution ensue of the advantages to be received from the establishment, but it was placed in a more efficient state, notwithstanding the economical plan which had been executed. [. . .]

Steam engines were in use at many of the manufactories, having been for the most part imported from England: though we saw an example (at the arsenal) of a machine which had been constructed on the spot under the direction of a Scotchman; and it seemed (which is an uncommon case with those made abroad) to answer extremely well. [. . .] The introduction of English machinery at the Mint is mentioned here, but merely as an instance of the esteem in which our countrymen are held for the perfection of their mechanism. The whole of the apparatus employed in coinage was constructed by Messrs. Bolton and Watts, and is precisely similar to that erected in our splendid edifice on Tower-hill, London.

In the capital, the British enjoyed their customary easy intercourse with the Russian nobility and the visiting British, particularly from the top echelons, were freely admitted to society salons and gatherings and presented at court. Descriptions of such events are usually trite, but the diaries and correspondence of Sarah, Lady Lytellton, who was in the Russian capital in the last months of 1813, offer refreshingly amusing pages on the social whirl which she entered. She describes to her mother her first visit to the Winter Palace and her presentation to the Dowager Empress and the Empress Elizaveta, wife of Alexander I:

I have already prosperously completed my payment of the toll which almost all foreigners pay on arriving here; it is a very trifling complaint, and I am now entirely recovered. I patched myself up one day to be presented, and came away quite blinded with splendour. The palace is magnificent, beyond even what its outside led me to expect. The vast size of the rooms, their immense number, the quantity of attendants, the fine solemn pomp of the High Mass of the Greek Church, performed by priests dressed in cloth of gold, with golden censors, book bindings, and taper stands, all in a perfumed mist of incense within the chapel, while very fine voices sang chaunts [sic], and though last, not least, the sight of the Empress herself, are really like a dream. It was not a regular Court day, so that there was nobody there but the usual attendants and officers of State, and four ladies and two gentlemen besides ourselves to be presented. We stood in a row in one of the rooms, and after the entry and procession of the whole Court, who ranged themselves opposite, in came the Empress-Mother, a woman of fifty five, with a fine large figure and a very cheerful blooming countenance, dressed in plain mourning, and covered – her head, neck, arms – with long rows of enormous pearls. She gave her hand to kiss to each of the two women presented, then embraced them, and said a *petit mot*. When she came to me, as I had seen two Countesses perform, I made no blunder luckily, nor even called Her Majesty Madame la Comtesse, though I was much inclined so to do. She vouchsafed to talk to me a very long time – I dare say ten minutes – asked me the usual questions, and then began talking about you, Papa, about your *carrière si brilliante et si belle*, and your being now so fond of the country; and no wonder in England, *où les châteaux sont tant d'agréments*. And, in short, I might, if I was not the most humble of all courtiers, boast of a very great favour; ahem! Well, then off she walked, and we proceeded to the antechamber of the chapel to wait till Mass was over for the second presentation to the young Empress.

All this time Mr. Lyte was performing elsewhere; he began with the *régnante*. The ceremony was the same with her; but she is so beautiful! Not her face, because she is very red – of late only; but her figure I think the very prettiest I ever saw, even in England. She came into the room with the lightest and most graceful step; she is tall, *élancée*, with the prettiest small head placed beautifully on her shoulders, and nothing can be more graceful than her manner. She is only rather too modest, shrinking from everything like ostentation; she won't suffer any woman to kiss her hand, but always embraces quite cordially. A few years ago her features show how extremely handsome she must have been. There was a Grande Duchesse and her gouvernante to be presented to besides, and the two Princes of the blood royal, *chez qui se faire écrire*, and as they all live at about three miles distant from each other, through halls, saloons, corridors, presence chambers innumerable did we march, till our chaperon, the Princess Prosorowsky, an old rouged lady, was obliged to smell at her bottle of eau-de-Cologne, and most loudly to lament the duties of her high office. The Empress has been pleased to say Monsieur Lyte is the most *aimable* Englishman she has seen this great while, and that his talking French so well put her much at her ease. I likes a bit of praise of 'im, though it is from an Empress and through a courtier that I get it.

She is soon visiting salons and soirées and notes that 'the general of what little society I have seen is, I think, formal and circular when it is numerous; men and women always in two distant and unjoinable squadrons at the end of the room. This is a new fashion, and fresh from Paris; and as the women so secluded are placed in an unmovable form, it is rather apt to wax dull. Small parties are, however, infinitely more agreeable than large ones are dull, and much more agreeable than the common run of English society, from the want of all affectation among women, and the general talkativeness and civility among men'. She has a talent for succinct characterizations that are never far from caricature:

Sunday night to Mme. Lounine's concert – very hot and brilliant. Mme. Narychkin *la belle* – face like the Apollo of Belvedere, exceedingly beautiful, modest manner; very plain, decent dress. Prince Kourakin, large head, fat figure like an elephant. Dressed in a blue uniform embroidered with gold, two stars of fine diamonds, an order hanging to his neck of large garnets and diamonds; epaulette of six rows of fine pearls hanging all over his shoulder, festooned up with a diamond brooch. Too dazzling to look at in bright light. . . . Princess Serge Galitzin arrived at twelve o'clock; very beautiful, quite eclipsed them all – most beautiful! Crown on her head; a little rouge on; fine gown and shawl. Men a parcel of figures! Senateur Abreskoff – some such name – with a wig like a very thick black broom, all *ébouriffée*. M. Demidoff, like a gnu, head in bosom. We came away before supper, past one.

Pen-portraits of the tsar himself were inevitably essayed by all who were presented to him or simply glimpse him at official functions and ceremonies. Carr was among the first to offer a detailed description to the British public:

The present Emperor Alexander is about twenty-nine years of age, his face is full, very fair, and his complexion pale; his eyes blue, and expressive of that beneficient mildness which is one of the prominent features of his character. His person is tall, lusty, and well proportioned; but, being a little deaf, to facilitate his hearing, he stoops: his deportment is condescending, yet dignified. In the discharge of his august duties he displays great activity and acuteness. But without shew and bustle: the leading features of his mind are sound discretion and humanity, qualities which cannot fail to render an empire flourishing and a people happy! He is so much an enemy to parade, that he is frequently seen wrapped up in his regimental cloak, riding about the capital alone, upon a little common droshka: in this manner he has been known to administer to the wants of the poor. It is his wish, if he should be recognized in this state of privacy, that no one will take off their hats; but the graciousness of his desire only puts the heart in the hand as it uncovers the head.

Carr mentions the emperor's predilection for the English and suggests that he 'has often been heard to say that "The man within whose reach heaven has placed the greatest materials for making life happy, was, in his opinion, an English country Gentleman"', an interesting variation on Peter the Great's famous wish to be an English admiral. Alexander, of course, was to visit England in 1814, when countless eulogies appeared in the press and his portrait appeared in numerous coloured plates.

It is, however, not with descriptions of the tsar, but with a demonstration, as Pushkin would have suggested, of the tsars' inability (the great Peter excepted) to tame the elements that besiege St Petersburg that this chapter ends. On 7/19 November 1824 there occurred the greatest flood in the history of the city. It is an event that is best remembered for providing the background to Pushkin's great poem *The Bronze Horseman,* but there were to appear in English at least four eyewitness accounts, all detailed, but all published long after the flood itself. By far the most graphic was included in Robert Lee's *The Last Days of Alexander, and the First Days of Nicholas* (London, 1854), but, as he makes clear, it was not by the good doctor himself, but by a British medical friend (possibly Alexander Crichton), working at the time in the Naval Hospital.

The autumnal equinoctial gales most generally prevail at St. Petersburg from the south-west, by which the waters of the Gulf of Finland and Neva are much increased. So it was in 1824; and for some weeks the wind continued from nearby the same quarter. The night of the 18th of November was very stormy; and at daylight of the 19th it blew a hurricane from WSW, by which time the stream of the river – the upper part at least – was reversed, and the waters, running higher than ever remembered, soon caused the lower parts of the city and neighbour-hood of the embouchure to be inundated. At nine o'clock in the morning I attempted to cross the Voskresenkiy Bridge of boats, on my way to the General Naval Hospital, on the Vyborg side, but was unable owing to the great elevation. I then paid some professional visits; and at eleven called on Prince Naryshkin, who had already given orders to remove the furniture from his lower apartments, the water then being above the level of the Fontanka Canal, opposite to his residence. From this time the rise was rapid; and at halfpast eleven, when I returned to my house, in the Great Millionaya, the water was gushing upwards through the gratings of the sewers, filling the streets and court-yards with which every house is provided. A Servant took me on his back from the drozhki, my horses being at that time above their knees, and conveyed me to the landing of the staircase. The wind now blew in awful gusts; and the noise of the tempest with the cries of the people in the streets was terrific. It was not long ere boats were seen in the streets, with vast quantities of fire-wood and other articles floating about. As there was an ascent to my coach-house and stables, the water there attained but to four feet in depth; in most, however, it was necessary to get both horses and cows up to the landing-places of the stairs in order to save them, though the loss of animals was great. Now and then a horse was seen swimming across from one pavement to another, the deepest part of the streets of St. Petersburg being in the centre. The number of rats drowned on this occasion was inconceivable; and of dogs and cats not a few. The crisis seemed to be from one to three in the afternoon, at which hour the wind having veered round a couple of points to the northward, the waters began to abate; and by four o'clock the tops of the iron-posts, three feet in height, by the sides of the pave-ment made their appearance. The reflux of the water was tremendous, causing much damage, and carrying off fire-wood, boards, lumber, and all sorts of rubbish, with various articles of furniture. From the commencement of the inundation the report of the signal cannon, fired first at the Galleyhaven, at the entrance of the river, then at the Admiralty dockyard, and lastly at the fortress, was continued at inter-vals as a warning to the inhabitants, and added not a little to the horror of the scene. At five o'clock persons were seen on the pavements carrying lanterns, and the rattling of equipages was heard an hour afterwards. The depth of water in the different parts of the city varied from four to nine and ten feet; but along the border of the Gulf of Finland, and especially in the low suburb of the Galleyhaven before alluded to, the depth was from fourteen to eighteen feet, and many of the small wooden houses built on piles were carried away, inmates and all. A few were floated up the Neva, rocking about with poor creatures clinging on the roof. Some of these perished; others were taken off, at a great risk, by boats from the Admiralty yard, which had been ordered out by the express command of His Imperial Majesty, who stood during the greater part of the day on the balcony of the Winter Palace, giving the necessary orders. The government ironworks, near the shore of the gulf, and two miles distant, were almost annihilated, and the loss of life was great. This establishment was afterwards removed to the left and elevated bank of the Neva, five versts above the city. Vessels of various kinds, boats timber, &c. floated over the parapets of the quays on the banks of the Neva and canals, into the streets and squares, and were for the most part afterwards broken up for fuel. As the lower part of most houses in St. Petersburg is occupied by shopkeepers and artizans of various descriptions, so these unfortunate people sustained much loss, and until their dwellings were considered to be sufficiently dried by means of stoves, found refuge and maintenance with their neighbours in the upper apartments. A German shoemaker with his family lived below me, and in this way became my guests for the space of eight days. The wind continued providentially to get round to the north during the night of the 19th, and a smart frost taking place on the following morning, rendered the roads and streets extremely slippery, but doing much good by the dryness it produced. On the 20th, the Emperor Alexander, ever benevolent and humane, visited those parts of the city and suburbs most afflicted by this catastrophe; and in person bestowed alms and consolation to the sufferers, for the most part of the lower classes, and in every way afforded such relief, both then and afterwards, as won for him the still greater love and admiration of his people and of the foreign residents of St. Petersburg. To assist the Emperor's benevolent views, a subscription was entered into, and the British residents came forward, as usual, with their wonted liberality.

As nothing official was published as to the actual loss of lives on this melancholy occasion, it is impossible to state otherwise than by report. The authorities were shy on this subject; but from what information I could obtain, twelve or fifteen hundred persons must have perished. Owing to the damp and unwholesome state of the lower parts of the houses and cellars, the mortality during the subsequent winter was nearly doubled, from typhus chiefly, as also from affections of the lungs; and many dated their rheumatic pains and various other maladies to the sufferings they then underwent.

CHAPTER 5

THE CITY UNDER
NICHOLAS I, 1825–55

A year after the mighty flood St Petersburg was witness to another great cataclysmic event, but this time it was of man's devising. On 19 November/1 December 1825 Alexander I died in distant Taganrog. When the news reached the Russian capital, it gave rise to a series of events that were registered with obvious bewilderment by Charlotte Disbrowe, wife of the British Minister Plenipotentiary. On 2/14 December she was writing that

> Never was a monarch so mourned; but it is not as their Emperor that they deplore him, it is as a common friend. Every individual weeps as for the loss of their dearest, best friend. He was loved for himself; was so affable, so benevolent, interesting himself about his lowliest subjects; entered into the concerns of all around him in the most affectionate manner; and in short completely identified himself with his people. Mr Law (the English chaplain) gave us a most impressive sermon on Sunday, and passed a beautiful eulogium on the late monarch. The church was hung in black, and it was altogether extremely affecting.

She notes that all were swearing allegiance to the new Emperor, Constantine, but twelve days later, she began another letter with the words: 'Long live the Emperor Nicholas! Ignoramuses that we were to suppose that Constantine meant to govern us. We were fifteen days in this pleasing error'. The date was 14/26 December, it was the day of what became known as the Decembrist Uprising, and Mrs Disbrowe proceeded to record what she heard and subsequently saw:

> I had got to the top of the stairs, when, lo and behold! appeared Sir Daniel Bayley [the British Consul-General] with a tremendously long face, to tell us not to stir, for one of the regiments had refused to take the oath to Nicholas, bayonetted two of their officers and a general; say

that Constantine is shut up in Petersburg, and that they will have no other Emperor but him. They are now this very minute drawn up in square, on the Place d'Isaac, have loaded with ball, and Heaven knows what will follow! The Chevalier Guards took the oath to Nicholas very quietly, and are assembling to quell this insubordination. The general is killed, but I believe the officers are only wounded . . . Half-past three. I have been walking on the Quay. The revolt is in the same state; frequent cheers are heard, but they will not receive the Emperor's aides-de-camp. It is said that General Miloradovich (Military Governor of the town) is wounded in the side. Troops are marching up from all sides to surround the rebels. They hardly deserve that name, poor misguided people.

Half-past nine. It was dreadful to hear the firing. Every round went to my heart. I do not know particulars for certain, except that at this moment all is quiet, and some say the mutineers have retreated across the river and dispersed. They were the Moskovskiy Regiment, joined by a battalion of the Fin Regiment. Do you remember our listening to their band at the camp? More spectators than soldiers have been killed, about a hundred they say. There are no hopes of General Miloradovich and a wounded officer who was carried to Count Laval's. Both the bridges close to our house were guarded, and the principal firing was down the back lane, and all communication between this cut off. Every approach to the Place d'Isaac was prevented.

Nicholas's reign thus begun in blood and was so to end in 1855 with the Crimean War at its height. During the nearly three decades of his rule Anglo-Russian relations were to fluctuate, founder and finish in free fall, but his capital was still visited by many British travellers who recorded some of the many changes and additions that occurred during this period, although inevitably their attention was focused on the great monuments of earlier reigns.

It was a period that saw the emergence of the English guidebook to St Petersburg. To be sure, there were many works, both English and translated, from earlier reigns that sought to offer comprehensive introductions to the city's topography and institutions, but the tourist's handbook came to the fore from the 1830s in keeping with a general trend to provide guides to all the European countries and capitals and profiting from new printing techniques that lowered the costs of production. Already in 1813 George Green, a merchant, produced an 'original journal' of the, or rather, *a* route from London to St Petersburg, with descriptions of posting stations, distances, costs, and other information, as well a listing of useful words and phrases in English and Russian, that had the virtue of being in small format for the traveller's pocket. It was, however, two mighty tomes published in 1828 that sought to fill a perceived gap in existing literature. The author, A.B. Granville, a doctor in the employ of a Russian aristocrat, asks in his introduction that his *St. Petersburgh* 'may be received for what he intends it – a minute, and, he hopes, a tolerably accurate account of the actual state of the Imperial Residence of Russia; embracing every subject which is likely to be of service to a traveller visiting that Capital, where he will find no Cicerone, or modern printed description of the city, to guide him' and he suggests in the text that 'the number of English who visit that city, either from curiosity or on account of business, is yearly increasing, owing to the greater facilities of communication now existing between the two countries'. He acknowledges the usefulness of Tooke's version (1801) of Storkh's work on St Petersburg, but he rightly emphasized how much the capital had altered during Alexander I's reign and for good measure he enumerates many of the changes – new palaces, new institutions, new bridges. He also usefully supplies a new map of the city, based on the Russian Ministry of the Interior's map of 1827. Granville obviously aspired to more than he achieved: as he readily acknowledged, he had resided in St Petersburg for only a few months at the end of 1827 and the errors he inevitably made were eagerly pounced upon by subsequent writers. Nevertheless, expanded and corrected, Granville's work enjoyed two more editions, in 1829 and in 1835, when the title was changed to *Guide to St. Petersburgh: A Journal of Travels . . .*

This modified title anticipated *A Guide to St. Petersburg & Moscow* which was published in 1836 by Francis Coghlan, already author of guidebooks to London and Paris and intent on contesting Granville's information at every opportunity. Coghlan seems to have spent as little time as Granville in the Russian capital, although nearly a decade later, but his book conforms more readily to the modern idea of the guidebook, opening with information on passports, customs and accommodation. A more satisfying variant, particularly as regards the early development of the city under Nicholas, also appeared in 1836. It was entitled *A Journey to St. Petersburg and Moscow through Courland and Livonia*, but it was in a series known as Heath's Picturesque Annuals. Its author, Leitch Ritchie, a seasoned traveller-writer, emphasized that his volume was 'entirely of information' and differed from earlier ones in the series by not being a 'drawing-room table book', but its appeal lay precisely in the intimate combination of text and illustration.The illustrator was a professional artist, A.G. Vickers, and his contribution will be assessed in a later chapter, but Ritchie's commentaries on Petersburg sights will be used here as appropriate.

It was in 1839, however, that there appeared the first edition of a guidebook that eclipsed all others, became the traveller's indispensable *vade mecum*, and was simply known as Murray's, after its publisher rather than its changing authors and editors. Originally entitled *A Hand-Book for Travellers in Denmark, Norway, Sweden, and Russia, being a guide to the Principal Routes in those countries, with a minute description of Copenhagen, Stockholm, St. Petersburg, and Moscow*, it devoted to St Petersburg a mere seventy pages (out of 125 on Russia in total), minute not in the sense intended. In 1848 it was vastly enlarged and renamed *Handbook for Northern Europe; including Denmark, Norway, Sweden, Finland, and Russia* with the Russian and Finnish sections available separately. In the period following the Crimean War, edited by Thomas Michell, it appeared, 'thoroughly revised' virtually every decade, under the title of *Handbook for Travellers in Russia, Poland, and Finland*. The first Murray's was published at a time when British suspicions of Russia had deepened and the rigours of the censorship were ever emphasized. Murray's first editor, known only under his initials T.D.W., wrote in the Preface:

In the direction given for travellers in Russia, I have studiously avoided touching upon any matter which might render the 'Hand-book for Northern Europe' an object of suspicion to the police, and thus make it, instead of a useful guide to a wanderer in a strange land, an additional source of trouble and difficulty to him. My object is here simply to impart information, and not to express or disseminate any peculiar opinions upon political questions.

Later travellers were to report that Murray's was nonetheless confiscated by Russian customs.

British hostility towards Russia or rather to its officialdom and autocratic regime was fuelled by the translation in 1843, and a re-issue the following year, of the Marquis de Custine's *La Russie en 1839*. Travellers in the 1840s were as likely to quote Custine as they were to refer to Murray and to be influenced by the perception of Russian society as façade and surface. Edward Thompson pointedly entitled his book *Life in Russia: or, the Discipline of Despotism* (1848) and suggested that 'display and external grandeur give the appearance of substantial wealth and happiness, but, alas, it is a hollow mockery'. To be sure, British comment on the insubstantiality of Petersburg architecture had become almost a cliché since Catherine's reign but it was now an element in a general mistrust of appearances. This is apparent in the following passage from Thompson, which is interesting nevertheless for the first detailed description in English of a phenomenon of Nicholas's Russia – the building of three- and four-storey buildings along Nevskii Prospekt beyond the Catherine Canal and elsewhere in the city, the tenement buildings that were to become part of the Dostoevskian landscape:

Most of the houses are built in quadrangles, having a large court-yard in the centre, which is used for stabling and for housing the enormous piles of wood laid in for winter fuel. They have common-stairs like those in Edinburgh, or the inns of court in London, and each floor often contains many separate tenements. They are generally of vast size, of three or four stories high, and accommodate an incredible number of families: one house, for instance, in the Nefskoi Prospeckt, where I had to deliver a letter, was occupied by 170 different sets of tenants, and, as there was no register of their names, I found it impossible to execute my commission. The ground-floor facing the street, even in the houses of the highest nobility, is used for shops: but the uniformity of the building is not disturbed by this arrangement; for the windows are not altered to form what are called shop-fronts in England. Indeed, any deviation from the usual form would be impossible, as there would be no means of putting in the double sashes or frames, which are indispensable preservatives against the severity of the cold in winter. The furniture, paper, and other hangings in the houses are flashy but not substantial, and many little articles which are seen in the meanest lodgings in England, such as window-blinds, bed-curtains, wash-hand stands, &c., are not to be found; but there are mirrors, sofas, lustres, French engravings, and other ornamental things, of ten times the value of those essentials that are wanting. This is typical of the state of things throughout the country; which seeks, by imposing on the eye by external effects, to blind the judgment to the moral and physical characteristics of things beneath the surface. The principle of government and the regulations of society know no other object: and to descend to realities, the glittering and noble-looking edifices, unsubstantial mockeries of Italian splendour rising from an arctic morass, are but so many incrustations of plaster, crumbling under the rigours of winter, and requiring to be renewed and restored again, to cheat the eye with a mask of magnificence.

Thompson, interestingly, was more disturbed by St Petersburg's spaces, commenting that

Vastness and space are the most prominent features in St. Petersburg: the scale on which the buildings are planned, the extreme width of the streets, and the prodigious extent occupied by the squares and public places, weary and bewilder the eye. Elegance and harmony are not obtained, because proportions are not kept; for, however colossal the buildings, the effect is marred, either by distance or by the uncircumscribed space around them.

It was a reaction shared by, for example, Richard Cobden, M.P., advocate of free trade and author of *Russia by a Manchester Manufacturer* (1836), who wrote to his wife in August 1847 that

The houses are lost and the palaces look insignificant in such vast open spaces. Peter's Statue, on a granite rock, which would look sublime at Charing Cross or Waterloo Place, is here a diminutive looking affair. The appearance of the city altogether is that of a parvenue who has just entered fashionable life and has copied all the newest modes, but there is too much gloss and glitter generally about such imitations.

Cobden did, however, concede that 'there is no city in Europe with so noble a stream flowing through it. Should another Liverpool one day grow up at Birkenhead, then the Mersey will alone outshine the Neva at St. Petersburg'. The Neva indeed received unexpected praise for the quality of its water, Ritchie asserting that

> To drink the water of the river is worth a journey to Russia of itself. It is the most delicious draught imaginable, and has besides a medicinal property favourable to most constitutions. Strangers, indeed, are cautioned against using it too freely; but in my own case, although I drank of it almost to excess, I found no bad effects whatsoever.

Within a few decades the pollution of the Neva rivalled that of the Thames. A young aristocrat visiting the city in 1845, Richard Bourke jokingly suggested that

> The constant repairs, plastering, roofing, building, and repaving that we saw going on in St. Petersburg are inconceivable; we scarcely found a street wherein several houses were not being either remodelled, rebuilt or newly plastered. From the different facades of elaborate scaffolding brick-bats and mortar perpetually descended and the stranger of a contemplative turn, 'whose eyes could scarcely serve at most,/ To guard their master 'gainst a post,' while studying the fall of a brick, would, ten chances to one, find himself either stumbling over a heap of stones, or the body of a prostate paviour.
>
> I suspect the long winter of the north is an excellent friend to the tribe of masons, plasterers, &c.; for a town whose buildings are composed exclusively of brick and plaster is not likely to escape unscathed the attacks of six months of frost. Marble statues lose their noses as well as the inhabitants, and the skin equally peels off the faces of churches and Christians.

The need for constant repairs was inevitably noted by most travellers, but there was also much new building in central St Petersburg during this period. Dominating all else was St Isaac's Cathedral, designed by Auguste de Montferrand, which remained a major attraction throughout Nicholas's reign, although it was begun in 1818 under his brother, Alexander I, and consecrated only in 1858 under his son, Alexander II. The Marchioness of Westminster, arriving in St Petersburg in the summer of 1827, first went to see

> the model for the scaffolding of the outside colonnade of the Eglise Isaac, and a beautiful model it is. The architect, Monsieur de Montferrand, then went with us to the place itself. The church was originally begun by Catharine II., in marble; finished by Paul in brick. It is now pulled down, all but a very small part, which, in church, must always be left, to begin an entirely new one. The columns for the colonnade, by which it is to be entirely surrounded, are magnificent; each of a single block of granite fifty-five feet in length, and sixteen feet in diameter. The machinery and method of placing each pillar on its base is very curious. The capitals and bases are of bronze, and it is to take, at least, ten years in building.

She was well advised to have added the 'at least'. Some eighteen years later, Richard Bourke found it still far from finished and far less impressive than other cathedrals he had seen on his travels, although he emphasized the important contribution that Baird's ironworks made to its construction:

> The interior is far from finished; but if the present design is carried out, it will be a mass of precious metals, and stones.
>
> We went to see, at the manufactory, the malachite columns for the front of the Eikonast, or screen; these are fifty feet in height, and will far exceed anything that has yet been done, in that beautiful fabric. All the iron and bronze work has come from the foundries of Mr. Baird, a Scotchman, residing in St. Petersburg, through whose kindness we were enabled to see every thing connected with this great work.
>
> Notwithstanding that the Russians are naturally so proud of this immense structure, I can hardly say that it quite answered our expectations. Whether it is that excessive simplicity defeats its purpose, or that the great size of the building is lost in the enormous place wherein it stands, I certainly did not look at it with the same feelings of awe, and exquisite admiration, with which I have regarded the grandeur of St. Peters, or the elaborate beauty of Milan, Westminster, York, or the scarcely begun Cologne.

There was, however, another project by Montferrand that was completed within a much shorter timespan. Leitch Ritchie was witness to the unveiling of the Alexander Column in the middle of Palace Square on 31 August/11 September 1834 and provides a graphic description of the events:

Opposite the Winter Palace, and midway between this edifice and the palace of the Etat Major, where the military business of the empire is transacted, stands the monument commonly called the Alexandrine Column, from its having been erected to the memory of the late emperor.

This object has a truly noble and majestic appearance from which ever point of view it is beheld. The shaft is formed of a single block of marble brought from the quarries of Finland, and, exclusively of pedestal and capital, is eighty-four feet high. The pedestal is of granite, with allegorical bas-reliefs in bronze; and on the summit stands an angel, holding a cross with the left hand, and pointing to heaven with the right. The inscription, on the side of the pedestal next the palace, is nearly as simple as that of the monument of Peter the Great. It contains merely these words: To Alexander I. grateful Russia.

On the eleventh of September, 1834, the consecration of this column took place [. . .] The day before, much anxiety and uncertainty had prevailed in St. Petersburg; for it seemed as if Heaven itself was about to impose. The beautiful, but terrible Neva, forced back by the waters of the Gulf of Finland, had risen upon her granite quays, and threatened once again to devour the city which so often before had been the victim of her wrath. The alarm-cannon were fired; and the population, already looking forward with intense longing for the scene of to-morrow, were thrown into dismay.

The Neva, however, was more placable than on former occasions; her swoln waters retired majestically; and that important morrow dawned upon the metropolis in peace.

If the reader will only remember the description which I have attempted of the grand square where the ceremony was to take place, he may form some idea of the scene it presented. Estrades were formed all round that immense area; and these, with the boulevards of the Admiralty, were crowded with spectators. The windows in like manner, were stuck full of human heads; and the flat roofs of the houses swarmed with their inhabitants. But in the middle space, from side to side, from end to end, nothing was to be seen but the glitter of arms and the waving of military plumes.

At ten o'clock, the troops assembled at their quarters; and, at eleven, on a signal from the guns of the light artillery, already planted at the corners of the boulevards, they all debouched at one moment by the several issues appointed, and drew up in the square.This imposing mass was formed of eighty-six battalions of infantry, and one hundred and six and a half squadrons of cavalry, with two hundred and forty-eight pieces of artillery. All these various bodies were drawn up, facing the Alexandrine column, the pedestal of which was concealed from their view by flags.

The Emperor, who had attended divine service at the monastery of Saint Alexander Nevskoi, soon appeared upon the scene, with the Heir of the crown, and the Grand Duke Michael, and surrounded by a brilliant staff. All eyes were then turned towards a large verandah, in the form of a tent, at the window of the palace above the great gate, directly opposite the column, and provided with a flight of stairs descending to the street. There already stood the high civil functionaries, the members of the diplomatic body, the marshals of the nobility, and the deputies of commerce; and, precisely at noon, the high clergy were seen filing into it in procession, from the grand chapel of the palace, with their crosses and banners displayed, and followed by the Empress and the whole court. The business of the day then commenced.

The moment the procession appeared, the Emperor gave the word of command; and the whole array of troops presented arms like one man. The priests then thundered forth the Te Deum; and emperor, empress, court, soldiers, spectators – every living soul in that mighty concourse of human beings – sunk upon their knees.

After the hymn, and a prayer for the imperial family, the archdeacon recited prayers for the soul of the Emperor Alexander; and, as he pronounced the last words, the flags which had hitherto concealed the pedestal of the column fell, and disclosed the monument. At this sight the troops again presented arms; a tremendous hurra rose from every lip; and a burst of military music shook the square, almost drowned by the thunder of the artillery, and the deep roar of the cannon of the fortress.

Prayers were then recited for the Russian army; and, when these were concluded, the clergy, followed by the Empress and her whole train, descended from the balcony. They walked in procession round the column, the metropolitan sprinkling it with holy water. The troops then defiled before it, and the ceremony was finished.

The Winter Palace, from the balcony of which the imperial family watched the ceremony, was of course unmissable for all tourists, not least by its position and its size, the exterior of which 'would of itself form a very tolerable forenoon's walk for a lady'. It continued to receive a generally bad press from the British, 'remarkable for its size, its dingy colour, and its bad taste' and, in the opinion of William Kinglake, author of *Eothen*, who visited the capital in 1845, it 'looked as if it had been dressed into line by a drill serjeant'. But only Elizabeth Rigby, later Lady Eastlake, drew attention to the great fire that had virtually gutted the palace on 17/29 December 1837, a year before she visited the capital:

A casual observer would hardly remark the traces of fire in the grand structure of the Winter Palace. The entire shell stands perfect, though, within, not a stone is left in its place. Two thousand workmen are now swarming about this vast hive, and the architect Kleinmichael, straining every nerve to redeem his pledge of presenting this palace, ready inside and out, as it stood before, for the celebration of the Easter fêtes. In one light this destructive fire has proved a blessing; for the custom of consigning to solitude those suites of rooms occupied by a deceased Sovereign had here closed so many of the finest apartments, that in a few more successions the reigning monarch would have been fairly turned out by the ghosts of his predecessors. The gilt cross, on the cupola of the private chapel of the palace, resisted the fury of the element, and glowed with increased brilliancy in the light of the furnace around it, was watched by many an anxious eye in the crowd of believers beneath, who ascribe its preservation to miraculous intervention. This idea has proved a powerful engine in the hands of the architect, for under the conviction that a blessing rests on the palace the workmen toil with double assiduity at its renovation.

The fire raged for some thirty hours and reduced the palace to a shell, but through the heroic efforts of soldiers and fire crews, almost all the precious furniture, ornaments and fittings were saved and piled on Palace Square around the Alexander Column. The restoration was begun under the supervision of General P.A. Kleinmikhel' and brought to a successful conclusion in 1840. Under Nicholas, many new buildings and projects were effected but no British visitor during his reign seems to have recorded impressions of the New Hermitage he commissioned in 1849–52 from Leo von Klenze, the architect of the Munich Art Gallery.

Among the items that were safely evacuated from the fire were the portraits in the famous Military Gallery that commemorated the generals in the victorious struggle against Napoleon in 1812 and the subsequent campaign in Europe. The original gallery was the work of Carlo Rossi and was only opened in 1826: it housed full-length portraits of Alexander I, his royal allies and other leaders including the Duke of Wellington, but along the walls in five ranks were 332 half-length portraits of Russian generals, heroes of 1812–14. The portraits were the work of the English artist George Dawe, whom Edward Morton, another British doctor in Russian service, met in his studio in the palace in 1827 and was very impressed by this 'gentleman of rather retired habits, of modest and unaffected demeanour, and of independent feelings, which his residence for a period of eight years at the court of a despotic sovereign could not alter or subdue'. Morton was setting out for Odessa and Dawe asked him to contact the widows and relatives of the few generals he had not yet painted for 'family portraits, or sketches, from which he might be enabled to complete the "Gallery of the Generals"'.

The Hermitage itself that housed the great art collections had not been damaged during the fire and, both before and after, it was a necessary visit for all, although many visitors then as now were overwhelmed by its riches and preferred to leave it to others to enumerate more than a few of the paintings they saw. Leitch Ritchie 'entered, with the intention of taking rough notes of the remarkable works of art, or rather of the impression they produced on me; but I speedily found that more days than I could afford hours would have been requisite for such a task'. Elizabeth Rigby, who was to marry an artist who became

President of the Royal Academy, also had a bout of cultural indigestion, but could not resist the almost requisite plaint for the loss of the Walpole/Houghton collection:

> After undergoing the positive labour of viewing a palace of this description – after running through forty magnificent and glittering apartments, beyond the first ten of which the powers of attention can no longer possibly be commanded, the miserable sight-seer returns with a head swimming with the colours and forms of every school, through which the delicious Alba Madonna, by Raphael – the pale fast-worn Christ, by Leonardo da Vinci – a whole succession of valuable lights, by Rembrandt – a never-to-be-forgotten Pordenone – and, for the sake of nationality, the Infant Hercules strangling the Serpent, by our Sir Joshua, though not among the most attractive of his productions, are dimly struggling. [. . .] No, the Hermitage must be left to those who have given, or can give, it all the requisite time. But no English heart will traverse this gallery without murmuring at the national indifference which could allow the Houghton Collection to be transported hither [. . .]

In 1832 the architect Carlo Rossi completed one of his last impressive projects which belonged wholly to the reign of Nicholas. His great theatre which became the home of the imperial drama and opera troupes was named the Aleksandrinskii, a title it retained until the Soviet Period, when it was became the Drama Theatre named after A.S. Pushkin. It faced Nevskii Prospekt across the square where later was to be erected the famous statue to Catherine by M.O. Mikeshin and it was flanked by the Anichkov Palace, also reconstructed by Rossi, and the Public Library. Behind it was Theatre Street, which in 1923 was renamed Rossi Street in honour of its architect, and leading to Chernyshev, later Lomonosov, Square. It was in the 1839 edition of Murray's *Handbook* that one of the earliest English descriptions of the theatre, or at least its interior, is to be found:

> The Alexander, unlike almost every other continental theatre I have seen, has chandeliers round the boxes – in my humble opinion, a great improvement upon the 'palpable obscure' of many theatres where the

entire blaze of light is concentrated on the stage. The entire pit is filled with arm-chairs, (Kraslya) numbered on the back, the numbers commencing from the orchestra, and on obtaining your ticket at the Kassa, on which your number is likewise specified, a servant in the imperial livery at once conducts you to your appointed seat, and in case it is already occupied, ejects the intruder in the most summary manner. [...]

There are no stalls in any of these theatres [he refers also to the Bol'shoi or Great Theatre and the Mikhailovskii], but quite the back part of the pit is fenced off, as a parquet, and contains seats at a lower price; about two thirds of the parterre are occupied by officers wearing uniforms of all fashions and colours, and almost universally muffled up in long bluish grey cloaks, without which no Russian officer seems to consider himself fully accoutred. On several occasions, when the house was so hot as to be quite oppressive, I have seen five or six of these sons of Mars, with their cloaks drawn tightly over them as if to exclude every breath of fresh air; and then no sooner has an act concluded, and the curtain fallen, than a universal rush takes place, as if the house were on fire. Six or seven times in the course of each evening's performance, you are obliged to make way for whole troops of these moving nuisances, trailing their swords after them, and thrusting their huge cocked hats in your face; though I am most willing to admit that they never fail to apologise if conscious of having given you any annoyance.

The Great or Stone Theatre had been built in Catherine's reign and continued to be the home of the imperial ballet and opera troupes and also of drama (up to 1832). Following the completion of the Aleksandrinskii, it too underwent major reconstruction between 1835 and 1838 under the chief architect of the imperial theatres Albert Kavos. In 1836, however, it staged the première of Mikhail Glinka's *Life for the Tsar* (*Zhizn'za tsaria*), otherwise known as *Ivan Susanin*, hailed as the first Russian national opera. A performance was witnessed three years later, in the winter of 1839, by Elizabeth Rigby:

Occasionally Taglioni's ballet gave place to a very different scene, both as respects actors and audience – namely, to the performance of a Russian opera, the first ever written, called *Jishn za Zara*, or 'Your life for your Zar': the music by Glinki, the words by Baron Rosen. This opera, equally from the popularity of the subject and the beauty and nationality of the music, has met with the utmost success. The plot of the piece, as far as we could fathom it, was the concealment and subsequent discovery of the true Zar, and his final coronation at Moscow, with a splendid representation of the Kremlin. This is woven up with a love-tale, and rendered interesting by the fidelity of a fine old Russian with a long beard and a bass voice, who eventually pays for his adherence with his life.

The music was strikingly national, and one trio in particular appeared to combine every peculiar beauty of Russian melody and pathos, and will doubtless acquire a European celebrity. It was very strange to see true Russians imitating true Russians – gallery, pit, and stage being equally filled with the same bearded and caftaned figures. The national feeling seemed in every heart and on every lip; any allusion to the Zar – and the subject was thickly strewn with them – was pronounced by the actors with the utmost animation, and responded to by electric shouts from the audience. Nor was there any casual inducement for this display of loyalty, for neither his Majesty nor any of the Imperial family were present.

It was a mere two months after the first performance of *Life for the Tsar* that Glinka's friend, the great poet Alexander Pushkin died in a duel. The capital's theatres were much frequented by Pushkin who was prepared to strut his stuff along with the best of the guards officers. It was in Murray's (1839) that there was an interesting long article on Russian literature which did not suffer from the generally patronising tone adopted by most English writers and there is a long and appreciative footnote on 'the Byron of the North', which mentions the circumstances of his death. However, an Englishman who actually met Pushkin was Thomas Raikes, although his description of the encounter on 23 December 1829 was not published until a decade later, in the same year as Murray's appeared:

I met last night at Baron Rehausen's the Byron of Russia; his name is Pouschkin, the celebrated, and, at the same time, the *only* poet in this country. His fame is established and unrivalled; no competitor attempts to win the laurel from his brow. His poems are read with delight by his countrymen, who alone can appreciate their merit; and his labours are not without reward, – he can always command ten roubles for every line from his publisher. In such a dearth of literature and literary taste, it will be no great injustice to suppose that his compositions may be overrated by his readers; and, as his genius is not likely to be excited by emulation, they will probably not be voluminous, particularly as, content with his present fame, he seldom has recourse to his muse except when his finances begin to fail. I could observe nothing remarkable in his person or manners; he was slovenly in his appearance, which is sometimes the failing of men of talent, and avowed openly his predilection for gambling: the only notable expression, indeed, which dropped from him during the evening was this, '*J'aimerois mieux mourir que ne pas jouer.*' Though a decided liberal, and *sourdement* implicated in the late conspiracy, he has always been treated with great attention and kindness by the Emperor; his muse, also, was enlisted in the revolutionary cause, and produced a poem which, under such circumstances, no other despotic sovereign could ever have forgotten or forgiven. It made a great sensation here: it bears the trait of genius; and as it has never been printed, I have obtained a copy of the French translation. [There follows the translation of 'Kinzhal' – 'Le Poignard'.] Under so arbitrary a government I know not what is the most extraordinary, – the audacity of the poet who composed, or the magnanimity of the sovereign who overlooked, such a violent and treasonable production.

Elizabeth Rigby makes no mention of Pushkin or of his death in her book first published in 1842, but she is very informative about another cultural luminary in the 1830s, the artist Karl Pavlovich Briullov, and in particular, about his best-known work, *The Last Day of Pompeii* (1830–3), which caused enormous interest when it was put on public display in the Academy of Arts in 1834:

[. . .] we proceeded to the Academy of Arts on the Wassili-Ostrof. This is one of those outwardly splendid piles, with ten times more space than in England would be allowed for the same object, ten times more out of repair, and ten times dirtier. [. . .] the halls and staircase are all on a grand scale, and appropriately adorned with casts from the Laocoon, the Gladiator, and other celebrated statues of antiquity [. . .] The walls are lined with eight cartoons of boar hunts and sylvan sports by Rubens and Snyders – the latter quite undeniable – of great merit, though we could procure no information of their history. Also a fine marble bust of this magnificent Emperor [Nicholas I], which, had it been dug up in classic ground, would have been declared a Grecian demi-god – it was impossible to pass without admiration. I wish his Douane [the Customs] were a little milder.

But the great attraction was Brüllov's picture of the fall of Pompeii – an enormous canvass – at least twenty feet wide by fifteen high, which now ranks as one of the lions of the capital. This picture is a gallery in itself, and one of absorbing interest. [Here follows a very detailed description of the painting.]

The critics have been busy upon the redundancy of interest and the multiplication of groups which the artist has crowded together; but as these strictly unite in telling the same story, and as the interest is chiefly concentrated in the principal group, this objection does not seem more legitimate here than in any of the crowded scenes of adoration, terror, or rejoicing, those of Mr. Martin omitted, which are familiar to the world. The more objectionable parts are the disjointed buildings on the right and left, with statues bending forward in the act of falling, which interrupt rather than heighten the intended effect. Living objects may be given in every transient movement; the momentary flash may be portrayed because never viewed in any other form; the rocking billows may be imitated because seldom seen at rest; but to fix a mass of stone in a position which it can neither sustain nor the eye follow for one instant, is as much in opposition to the laws of art as to those of gravity. Otherwise the drawing is magnificent – the colouring vividly true, and the effect of light and shade, and the meretricious glow afforded by the nature of the subject, sufficient to have seduced a less masterly artist from the severity of design which Brülloff has observed. At the same time it would have been physiologically more interesting had this first Russian painter of any eminence evinced a distinctive national character, however meagre or stiff, instead of continuing in the long-worn elements of the Occidental schools. But this may be simply accounted for by the supposition, generally adopted here, that Brülloff's nationality lies only in an assumed termination to his name, after the precedents of Madame Bellochi and M. Turnerelli, familiar to the

English world; though the object here sought being precisely inverse, it is more creditable to the sense of the nation.

This picture was painted for M. Demidoff, for the sum, it is said, of 80,000 roubles, or nearly 4,000, and by him presented to his Imperial Majesty, who placed it in this Academy.

Rigby also comments, critically, on another Briullov painting – an altarpiece placed in the newly built Lutheran Church on Nevskii Prospekt, which she also disliked and the architect of which was the painter's brother Aleksandr Pavlovich. The church was built in 1832–8 on the territory of the old church, dating from 1728–30:

Another [picture] just completed, a Crucifixion, by Brülloff, forms the altar-piece to the new Lutheran church. The body of the Saviour is splendidly drawn, but otherwise he has infused no freshness of idea into this oft-used subject – and a Predella picture below, the adminis-tration of the Sacrament, is infinitely higher in interest. Inferior, however, as this altar-piece is to the his Fall of Pompeii, it is neverthe-less ill bestowed; or rather it would be difficult to say what grade of merit would be compatible of abject architecture, only to be classed with the mountebank of our George the First's time. Alternately Grecian and Saxon, and painted within in a gewgaw taste, better befit-ting a theatre than a place of worship, this edifice unfortunately occupies a conspicuous position on the Nevskii Prospect.

Miss Rigby has also left a short account of a trip on the Petersburg–Tsarskoe Selo railway, the first stretch of line in Russia. It was begun in May 1836 and officially opened on 30 October/10 November 1837 but only in 1838 was steam traction used consistently, when the line had been extended to Pavlovsk, where the terminus was to become one of the centres of musical life in succeeding decades.

A day has been devoted to Zarskoe Selo – literally Imperial village, to which a railroad from Petersburg offers the easiest access. It was a sharp frost with a beautiful sun, the steam pouring off against a hard bright sky. The moment of starting being delayed, we quitted the carriage to hasten to the station-house. Here was congregated together that pictur-

esque crowd which the variety of Russian costumes always offer – officers in grey military cloaks – women with every bright colour on their
persons – priests in Rembrandt colour and costume – Mougiks with
aquiline noses and long beards, and even a Russian specimen of
Pickwick! We placed ourselves in the fourth carriage, commodiously
fitted up with soft easy seats, and pulling down the glass, braved the
frost for a short time to contemplate the peculiarity of the landscape.

Russia is the country for railroads – no hills, no vales – no beautiful
parks to intersect – no old family hearts to break. On either hand was a
plain of snow, so devoid of object as hardly to indicate the swiftness of
our movements. Above half-way appeared in the distance a castellated
mansion, where Catherine II was wont to relax from the Empress; and
upon the horizon was the slight but only elevation of Zarskoe Selo. The
distance, about twenty-five wersts, we accomplished in twenty
minutes.

Elizabeth Rigby was among the not inconsiderable number of
British visitors who were favourably impressed by Nicholas I, despite
the tensions between Britain and Russia that noticeably increased in the
late 1830s. The tsar was in fact an Anglophile, who had first visited
England when still Grand Duke in 1817, and Lady Londonderry, visiting Tsarskoe Selo in the autumn of 1836, recalled that 'He conversed a
great deal of England, his residence there, his recollections of the
country, and talked over the most remarkable beauties he had known
and admired, Lady Peel, Lady Mount Charles etc.' Her assessment of
his character led her to suggest that

The Emperor Nicholas is not like his brother Alexander. He has
neither the softness, the gentleness, nor the winning smile; he is taller
and larger, a perfect colossus combining grace and beauty. His face is
very handsome; if it has a fault I should say it was too long. His countenance is severe, his eye like an eagle's and his smile like the sun
breaking through a thundercloud; and on the whole, I think everyone
must admit he is a singular and magnificent looking being, and if seen
among hundreds and thousands would, from his personal appearance
alone, certainly be selected as the one best fitted for the situation he was
born to fill.

The following year, another English lady met him at a concert in Peterhof and fell under his spell:

> Even among the youthful branches of a family so famous for beauty, the Emperor shines preeminent, as well by the majesty of his deportment, as by the Jove-like beauty of his countenance. Towering above every one in the room, his well-proportioned figure glided through the crowd; and the extraordinary grace of his manner, is only equalled by the superiority of his manly form. A kind word, a cheerful remark, or a glad smile, greeted and delighted every person he addressed; while with rare talent, he seemed to unite in one, the host, the master, and the companion.
>
> Never in any rank of life, have I seen a man so admirably fitted for the position in which he is placed; and when we consider what that position is – the absolute monarch, the wielder of the destinies of a seventh part of the habitable globe – we must think him great indeed, on whom such a dignity can suitably rest. His eagle eye, on this night, wandered over the room. He directed everything even to the smallest minutiae; while never, for a moment, could I detect a movement or a gesture, unworthy the dignity of the Emperor. Truly Nicholas is the first gentleman of the age.

In 1844, the tsar was to pay an official state visit to England, thirty years after his brother Alexander I, and was well received. The Crimean War, however, was soon to turn charmer into ogre and the butt of numerous caricatures in *Punch*.

The English colony during Nicholas's reign lost some of the pre-eminence it had enjoyed over other foreign groups, but its numbers were still significant and it continued its traditional rituals. At its heart, as ever, was the English Church, which had been rebuilt in 1815 in accordance with a design by Quarenghi. In 1827 it was visited by Dr Granville, one of many British medics in Russian service:

> On the Sunday immediately after our arrival, I attended service in the English church, a very handsome and substantial edifice, situated about the centre of the English Quay, where it presents a noble front to the river, being decorated by a colonnade, placed on a massive and well-distributed basement story, in which are the apartments of the Rev. E.

Law, nephew of the late Lord Ellenborough, and Chaplain to the Factory. This church was first built in 1754, and reconstructed in its present form in 1815. The entrance, properly speaking, is from a street at the back of the Quay, through a handsome gateway. The interior is neat and simple, and has the great advantage of being well warmed and comfortably fitted up. There is a state pew for the British Ambassador on the right of the altar, and opposite to the pulpit: it is surmounted by the Royal Arms of England. The altar-piece is a Deposition from the Cross, a very creditable painting, on the sides of which are two handsome Corinthian pillars of marble. The part of the congregation, as in the Lutheran churches, sat apart from the rest, and occupied the left side of the church. Mr. Law is an impressive reader, and a clear expounder of the holy writings, and of the principles of morality as well as religion; and the congregation appeared evidently interested in the matter as well as the manner of his pulpit eloquence. In the Royal or Ambassador's pew sat Mr. Disbrowe, the Minister from the British Court, with whom I had an opportunity of conversing after the service, and from whom I received every possible civility during my stay at St. Petersburgh. The church has no gallery, and, although capacious, is insufficient to accommodate more than a part of the English residents. The resident English at St. Petersburgh are, I am told, about 2500 in number. It is the custom of this church, in the prayer for the King, to introduce the name of the Emperor: in the Litany, also, after the Royal Family has been prayed for, the clergyman says, with emphatic voice, 'that it may please thee to bless and preserve his Imperial Majesty, and all the Imperial family.' The same custom of praying for the health of his Majesty the King of England, I am informed, is also observed in the Russian Ambassador's Chapel in London. After the conclusion of the service I paid my respects, at their handsome apartments on the basement story, to the clergyman and his lady, to whom I had brought letters of introduction from his brother. The house of the Chaplain to the Factory, as well as the church, is exempt from the perquisitions, or domicilary visits of the police.

It was, incidentally, in 1827 that the much-admired Rev. Edward Law, whose sermon on the death of Alexander I had so impressed Mrs Disbrowe, published in London a collection of the sermons he had delivered to his ever-attentive English congregation.

Miss Rigby attended the church a decade later, while she was residing at Mrs Wilson's boarding-house on Galley Street, the back street running parallel to the English Embankment, which she found a 'well-conducted and most respectable establishment'. Coghlan declared that 'both the quantity and quality of her table, the regularity of her arrangements, and cleanliness of her house, were as good as the most fastidious can desire' and Ritchie considered it 'an establishment which every one must have pleasure in praising; the traveller finds there not only all the comforts of an English inn, but many of the advantages of a private circle. The terms for board and lodging on the most liberal scale are eight rubles a day'.

If the boarding-house pleased, the English Club at this period did not: Coghlan, for instance, 'could not discover any thing attached to it to justify the name – few, if any of its members are English. They do not serve up English dinners – the servants cannot speak English – it is not situated on the English Quay – I beg pardon, I had almost forgotten, there are generally one or two English newspapers lying on the table, and English gentlemen, to avail themselves of the accommodation, must be introduced daily! Verily, they ought to call this the *stiff* club'. In contrast, the Commercial Club was composed principally of English and German merchants, was situated on the English Quay and was 'hospitable and friendly'. These were the merchants Elizabeth Rigby so admired:

> In truth, nowhere can England be seen to better advantage than in the person of the British Factory [. . .] Every charitable custom is perpetuated – every hospitable anniversary celebrated – and every public rejoicing or mourning observed with jealous loyalty. The families, most of them highly aristocratic in descent, keep carefully aloof from all Russian society, and an intermarriage with a Russian is a circumstance of the rarest occurrence. At the same time this very adherence to national forms – prejudices if you will – has procured them universal respect. It is a mistake to suppose that foreigners like us the better for imitating them.

For Lady Londonderry there were, however, limits to intercourse with merchants and shopkeepers: 'We dined at Lord Durham's [the British ambassador] and met a large party of English bankers and merchants. I was much surprised to meet Mr. Nicholl, one of the proprietors of the English *magasin* and who literally stands behind the counter'. This was Constantine Nichols, joint owner of the fashionable English Shop at the corner of Nevskii Prospekt and Bol'shaia Morskaia, much frequented by Pushkin during his lifetime and to which he was in considerable debt when he died. Her ladyship failed to appreciate the easy social relationships that had existed within the British community at least since Catherinian times, exemplified here in the description of a boat-race between merchants and members of the British embassy in the summer of 1835:

> In the afternoon I went to a boat-race between English amateurs that had excited some interest among the English residents. The boats were badly matched; a six-oared boat thirty-two feet long, and weighing 230 pounds, being pitted against three pairs of sculls, with a boat twenty-eight feet long and weighing only 108 pounds. One belonged to the English legation, and the other to some English merchants. The race was from the English Quay to the bridge opposite the Suwarrow monument at the foot of the Summer Garden, and back, a little more than two miles each way. The rapidity of the current was between two and three miles an hour, though its full strength was avoided by both boats keeping to the eddies along shore. It was a beautiful place for a boat-race; the banks of the Neva were lined with spectators, and the six-oared boat beat easily, performing the distance in thirty-one minutes.

The outbreak of the Crimean War inevitably strained relations between the British community and the Russians. It is with the bleak picture of the situation painted by Rebecca McCoy, an English governess who had been in Russia since 1844 and left St Petersburg soon after the outbreak of hostilities, that we leave the reign of Nicholas I. Her book was published anonymously in 1854 and enjoyed no less than four editions and a long and favourable review by Charles Dickens in *Household Words*:

> The English in Russia have always been much more respected than liked; and latterly they have become most intensely hated, from the political position in which Great Britain stands towards that country.

Among us, if a Russian were in company, it is not probable that he would find any difference in the manner in which he was received because the two governments are at war; but the Russians are really not enlightened enough to separate the individual from the nation, and think it a proof of patriotism to show their resentment to any son or daughter of England whom they may chance to meet. As soon as the Declaration of War was known, there was a marked and very disagreeable change in the manners of even my oldest and attached friends: it seems that those few words were sufficient to sever the bonds of amity, and to place a barrier of ice between those who had previously been on the closest terms of intimacy; indeed, I verily believe that they would just as readily have touched a toad as have shaken hands with an English person. This intolerant feeling of course found vent in words, as well as in silent indications; and at last it reached so great a height, that it became almost impossible for any one to remain in the country who was obliged to come into daily contact with them. No opprobrious term was too coarse for us: 'those dogs,' 'those swine the English,' were expressions so general, that we were not surprised to hear them even from the lips of ladies of rank and education. Added to this was the impossibility of making any reply, unless in the most guarded terms; for the immense number of spies, and their excessive pleasure at catching a stray word or so, would have subjected either a lady or a gentleman to the most disagreeable visits of an emissary of the secret police, and a summons to Count Orloff's office.

CHAPTER 6

THE REIGNS OF ALEXANDER II
AND ALEXANDER III, 1855–94

Two years after Miss McCoy quitted the Russian capital, the war was at an end and a new tsar was on the throne. British visitors were soon arriving in numbers and were being assured that

> The number of English residents in St Petersburg is much larger than a stranger would have anticipated, and even during the recent war the majority of English residents preferred remaining in the capital to returning to their native country. It is highly to the credit of the Russian Government that throughout the whole of the war, the English in St Petersburg pursued their usual avocations without any interference more than usual from the authorities.

The author of these lines was James Mahony, who visited Russia in the summer of 1856 and produced the following year his modest *Book of the Baltic*. As the subtitle indicates, this traced the 'North of Europe Steam Company's Route to Denmark, Sweden and Russia, Norway, Prussia and the Hanseatic Ports' and was both a promotional document for the company and a celebration of the shrinking world brought about by travel on steamships. St Petersburg was now less than six days' sailing from Lowestoft and Mahony was providing information for the new flood of tourists. There is a distinctly modern feel to his guide with its emphasis on 'doing' the sights in order to get the most out of a short stay. Indeed, the mere thirty-five pages devoted to the Russian capital finish with 'hints' for the tourist who has only five days before the boat leaves for Denmark, beginning with advice on how to avoid clashes with officialdom, before naming the sights one should not miss, a necessary excursion to Peterhof, and a final day's shopping recommendations.

Another manifestation of the new world of tourism was the series of volumes entitled *Vacation Tourists and Notes of Travel* and edited by

Francis Galton, author of *The Art of Travel* (1855). In the second volume, published in 1862, the selection of essays of tours and travels in different areas of the world contained the Rev. Archibald Weir's 'St. Petersburgh and Moscow' with his impressions from a visit in 1861:

> To describe a city is the province of guide books; to relate his impressions and experiences may be allowed to the ordinary traveller. My first walk in St. Petersburg was at the time of twilight; and I think it was a most favourable time for the purpose. Twilight in the northern latitudes means much more than we understand by the word. It is all the summer night they have. Unlike what we call twilight, which is only day shading into night, the northern twilight has a permanence about it which gives to everything a very singular and beautiful appearance. It is not the interval between light and darkness, but between light and light. You do not feel that it is growing dark, but rather that it will grow no darker; and this gives you time to look around and observe at leisure. Twilight magnifies; it also deceives. In St. Petersburg there is full scope for its producing these effects. For St. Petersburg is a great, and yet not a great, city. In population and the number of dwellings it is comparatively small; in area it is superlatively large. In short it is a small city built on a grand scale. In a narrow, confined town the thickly blending shadows of the crowded buildings make all dark below when the sky is only half-dark above. But in St. Petersburg the spaces are much too broad for the shadows to deepen the actual gloom. Never shall I lose the impression of vastness and solitude which my first walk gave me. We seemed to be crossing a desert when approaching, from the river-side, the church of S. Izak. A strange sense of loneliness also presses upon one walking through the great streets and across the broad plains, with no sound to catch the ear but the occasional responsive clapping of the watchman's rattles, and one's own foot-fall.
>
> But here is another view. It is mid-day, and we take the opportunity of a cooling shower to make the toilsome ascent to the top of the dome of S. Izak's. We are guided by an old soldier, whose hand one is obliged to hold in order to be led through the perfectly dark passages. When we come to climbing the ladder which carries us up inside the dome, the heat is fearful. It feels as though the gold plates on the outside are all molten. But the summit is gained, and the reward is rich. The sun has

broken through the cloud, the sky is undimmed by smoke, the city lies out-spread around you. Look northwards and you see the beautiful, tranquil Neva, with its many mouths, flowing towards the gulf. Just below you the Great Neva, bordered by splendid quays and faced by palace-like buildings: further off the Little Neva, the Great Nevka, the Little Nevka, intersecting the land in their course, and forming the 'islands' so much resorted to in the evening by the citizens for the cool retreat of parks and woods, which they afford from the dust and heat of the city. The chief part of the town lies on the left bank of the river, but a considerable portion also stands upon the Vassilieostroff, or William Island, embraced by the Great and Little Nevas. Look around you, and you will see the many-coloured roofs of the houses; the spires and domes, gold and silver, of the churches and public edifices; making the whole seem like an illuminated page in an ancient missal. 'this alone is worth the voyage' – so I said, and so I now think.

The panoramic view of the city from the dome of St Isaac's or the spire of the Admiralty was much admired by visitors, but St Isaac's itself, although featuring in travellers' accounts in its various guises and stages of building since the reign of the great Catherine, was now at long last completed and ready for judgment. The cathedral was consecrated on 18/30 May 1858; a year later, C. Piazzi Smyth, the Astronomer Royal for Scotland, paid a visit and published in 1862 a detailed description of both the building and its new life:

Many were the bells of St. Petersburg, ringing all the livelong Sunday morning; rich-toned and solemn all of them, but most attention did we pay to those of St. Izak, so close to us and almost above our heads. [. . .]

Before these national chimes were quite exhausted, we had arrived in front of the church; but though there were still many persons entering its precincts; though carriages and droshkies in number were waiting outside; though the magnificent granite steps (towards the middle of the porticos supplemented with smaller steps, and covered over their glassy surface with thick matting,) were still lined with hermit-like beggars in long beards, flowing garments, and big boots, and holding out, for charitable additions, little trays of cloth with a cross worked thereon and several *kopeeks* already received; though the doorways were still beset with other and some ancient nun-like beggars, with similar cross-emblazoned trays, (clothed in black dresses, and with black velvet caps on their heads like Norman helmets in shape, were these nuns,) – yet the great tide of worshippers was evidently coming out, and we were too late for witnessing the forms of their religious service.

We looked, therefore, at what was about us, and there was much that was extremely touching, especially in the inquiries that were perceptibly made by many a fine lady as she passed some time-worn nun, or other poor female with her little begging-tray, and added thus, by kindly sympathy and timely consolation, seven times to what she gave. Something of this sort must have been the effect; for the countenances of the sickly old creatures beamed up with a joyful confidence, as if expressing that they now knew that the populous city was not to them, any longer, the heart-desert it once had been; and that such being the case, the merest pittance to keep them alive was enough to make them happy also. Many a long tale of illness, or thanks for relief received, seemed to be poured out, and to willing ears, in these majestic vistas formed by the several ranks of awful granite columns we were standing under; monoliths all of them, seven feet in diameter and fifty high.

When the outgoing stream had nearly subsided, we ventured to enter the church by a small side-door which was alone open; and as we advanced over the polished pavement, where, after the morning's flood of human beings, liveried servants were sweeping up long ridges of sand and dust, like abundant gatherings from a turnpike road, – we found ourselves in a dimly-lighted and vast space; vaster indeed, than we could well have expected, for the inside of the church is nearly free from every impediment, and measures almost the full size of what it is outside; being there rather more than three hundred feet in diameter, and in shape like a short-armed, and what is called in England, a Greek cross. Little daylight enters, except towards the summit of the great central dome, eighty-seven feet in diameter; and in that, the illumination comes in chiefly behind a large emblem of a winged dove, which appears just about to descend on the congregation from a height of three hundred and seventeen feet above the ground.

By the chastened light thus thrown down from on high, we saw the pillars and internal walls on every side adorned with large fresco paintings of the better French Academy school, interspersed with gilding and variegated marbles, which increase in splendour as the eye travels towards the eastern side, where at last it is bewildered in the unsurpassed richness of nothing but malachite and lapis-lazuli, gold and sacred historical portraits. Here too, as it appeared to us at the time, a portion of the service of the church was still proceeding; so we slowly approached. It was but a small extraneous part, for there were only two priests engaged at it, and they were standing outside the railed-off altar and *ikonostas* enclosure on the general floor-level of the whole church; and that is perfectly free from pew, chair, or bench of any description. A little crowd was collected about the priests, chiefly of men and of the lower orders.

One priest was reading, with his back to the people and with astonishingly quick utterance, out of a huge old volume on a portable reading desk; and the other was offering a golden crucifix to be kissed, as each worshipper left the church. Near them, on a sort of easel, was a picture of the Virgin and Child; showing, as usual, only brown faces and hands, and being elsewhere covered up with plated garments adorned with jewels; but before it was a candle-stand, with a silver circular plate about it, set with numerous sockets for small candles, of which many were already burning there. The people were bowing and crossing themselves to the rapid reading that was varied by a musical intonation occasionally of one or two words, then kissing the crucifix, kissing the frame or plated garments of the Virgin's picture, and going in peace.

Gorgeous as money can make a building, and complete at all points, as far as the unlimited payments and personal inspection of an Emperor can command, is this St. Izak's church. Precious materials are everywhere employed; everything is solid, massive, and rigorously finished; the several bronze doors are wonders of art for their alto-rilievos, both inside and out. Excepting only the peculiar religious pictures, which are ancient, Byzantine, and on portable stands, all the others, that is all those attached to the body of the church, frescos or oil, were every one of them painted expressly for their architectural positions; and there is not a single weal one, or a single small one. The malachite columns, green to an intensity and richly marbled, in front of the *ikonostas* or more sacred altar portion of the church, exhibit shafts nearly fifty feet high, with bases and Corinthian capitals of massy giltwork; while at the very entrance into the holiest of holies, the doorposts of the golden gates, – now closed and further shut in behind by a curtain of crimson silk, more richly blushing by reason of a light that is streaming through it from behind, – are formed of pillars of the rich blue which lapis-lazuli alone can show, and must be something above twenty feet in height. Everything looks new, very new, too new; and so it may, seeing that the interior was only opened to the public last year (1858): but though so new, nothing has been slurred, nothing forgotten, over the whole extent.

Then making our exit through the ranks of monolith pillars, with dark bronze bases and capitals of the same, and down those illustrious steps of far-reaching, glossy red granite, we wander around. Round and about the whole vast structure extend the same glossy steps, of material as hard as adamant, and never worked on so large a scale since the Pharaohs held their state upon earth; and to every side is a similar portico, and with similar monoliths. Every pediment is filled with congeries of graduated figures in bronze; and each corner, each apex, each niche, has always its group or single figure, colossal in size. Above all this main portion of the building rise, at the four principal corners, open-work cupolas, capped with polished gold, and containing all the rich-sounding bells; and in the centre rises the cylindrical base of the great dome, ringed by more monolith columns of polished red granite, each of them surmounted with winged angels in bronze; and then above all these is the great dome, a ribbed mountain of gold, bearing a little golden chapel on its summit, with the final cross standing on a crescent culminating the whole.

To appreciate these higher splendours, it was necessary to depart to a distance from the base of the building, and this is possible to an extraordinary extent, so vast is the open space that spreads all around, and forms a plain, a wilderness paved with little granite boulders; and where one meets, here and there, with a droshky track connecting the streets on one side with those on the other, like the footsteps of a caravan in the desert. A view more or less from the south, was that we most preferred, on the account of the remarkable effects of sunlight on the golden domes; for the very part of a western cathedral building, which with all other nations is dark, dingy, and blank, was here pre-eminently the richest. 'Glitters like the sun over a mountain,' is an expression we have seen applied to St. Izak; but it is strangely inapplicable, you will find, with the reality before you. Each lesser cupola, with its perfectly smooth golden cap, reflects its imitation of the solar orb, and the large dome has something similar from its general surface; but what constitutes the crowning glory of the whole, is the veritable 'crown of glory' formed by the several optical images which are reflected from the gold-covered ribs of the dome. Each of these ribs reflects its little sun, and the suns of several ribs arrange themselves always to the eye of a spectator below, as an elliptical crown of just so many jewelled points of light laid obliquely, and as it were a testimony, on the general golden dome. The crown is thus simple, spiritual, but veritably glorious – truly a crown of glory; and as we looked at it, now under one degree of perspective and consequent ellipticity, and now under another, we could speak of it under no other name, and never could see it without being set thinking of the scriptural crown of thorns to which man's redemption is owing.

The detail of this description notwithstanding, we should not leave the cathedral without also recording the reactions of two visiting Oxford academics a few years later for whom the service rather than the building was the principal attraction and its interpretation became the subject of earnest debate. The Rev. C.L. Dodgson, undoubtedly better known as Lewis Carroll, and the Rev. Henry Liddon, soon to become Canon of St Paul's, were fellow Students at Christ Church but were far from united in their reaction to what they saw, Liddon noting that 'after church a long argument with Dodgson'. Liddon wrote in a letter to a clerical friend on 29 July 1867:

I wish you could have been with me yesterday morning at the Great Celebration on St. Isaac's Cathedral. Of course, the ritual was elaborately complex – bewildering – indeed, to an English mind. But there was an aroma of the fourth century about the whole which was quite marvellous. The vast Church was crowded with people of all classes, from the lowest to, I imagine, the very highest. The Archbishop was present – assisting on a throne in the middle of the church looking toward the holy gates. The choristers wore bright gold-coloured dresses, shaped liked dalmatics; the celebrant and deacons were, of course, very gorgeous.

There was a short sermon in modern Russian, which, I believe, is very different from the old Church Slavonic; but, of course, I know nothing of either. A number of very young children communicated; and troops of infants in arms were brought by their mothers and soldier-fathers to kiss the Icons which were on the Iconostasis, and indeed all about the Cathedral. The devotion of many of the people was exuberant, passionate. They threw themselves flat upon the pavement where there was room; they kept their heads *close* to the stones for minutes together; they crossed themselves with a kind of business-like energy, which would be equal to some mechanical labour, such as working at a pump.

I got between three cabmen, as I imagine them to have been, who were doing this; and the practical result was – in a crowd – very appreciable. But one would not have had them stop for anything. The entire absence of seats in the churches, the extraordinary glitter of the screens and Icons, and the invisibility of the ministering clergy during large parts of their ministrations, make the appearance of the Eastern Services very unlike anything in the West.

I cannot understand anybody coming here and saying that the Eastern Church is a petrifaction. Right or wrong, it is a vast, energetic, and most powerful body, with an evident hold upon the heart of the largest of European empires; indeed, a force within the limits of Russia to which I believe there is no moral parallel in the West.

This may *seem* a rash conclusion after so short a visit; I shall retract if necessary. But the churches yesterday surprised and impressed me greatly, and would account for a rash generalisation of this sort, if it be rash.

Dodgson on the other hand recorded his impressions in his diary (in which, incidentally, there was very little of Lewis Carroll other than an amusing passage on the 'alarming' nature of some long Russian words):

July 28. (SUN) We went in the morning to the great Isaac-Church, but the service, being in Slavonic, was beyond all hope of comprehension. There were no musical instruments whatever to help in the chants, but they managed to produce a wonderful effect with voices alone. The church is a huge square building, running out into 4 equal pieces for the chancel, nave, & transepts, the middle being roofed by a great dome (which is gilt all over outside), & there are so few windows that it would be nearly dark inside, if it were not for the many Eikons that are hung round it with candles, & these are supplied by those who pray before them, each of whom brings one with him, & lights, & sticks it in. The only share the congregation had in the service was to bow and cross themselves, & sometimes to kneel down & touch the ground with their foreheads. One would hope that this was accompanied by some private prayer, but it could not have been so in all cases: I saw quite young children doing it, with no expression on their faces which even hinted that they attached any meaning to it, & one little boy (whom I noticed in the afternoon in the Kazan Cathedral), whose mother made him kneel down & put his forehead to the ground, could not have been more than 3 years old. They were doing all the bowing & crossing before the Eikons as well, & not only that, but when I was waiting outside for Liddon (I went out when the sermon began) I noticed great numbers do it while passing the church-door, even when they were on the opposite side of an enormously broad street. A narrow piece of pavement ran from the entrance right across, so that every one driving or walking by could tell the exact moment when they were opposite.

The crossing, by the way, is hardly to be so called, as it consists of touching, with the right forefinger, the forehead, breast, right shoulder, & left shoulder: this is generally done 3 times, followed by a low bow each time, & then a 4th time without a bow.

The dresses of the officiating ministers were most splendid, & the processions & incense reminded me of the Roman Catholic Church at Brussels, but the more one sees of these gorgeous services, with their many appeals to the senses, the more, I think one learns to love the plain, simple (but to my mind far more real) service of the English church.

It seems appropriate to introduce here a passage from the writings of an even more senior and eminent Oxford Anglican cleric, the Dean of Westminster, Arthur Penryn Stanley, who was witness to an Orthodox marriage ceremony in St Petersburg and then officiated at the ensuing ceremony according to the rite of the Church of England on 11/23

January 1874. The marriage between the Grand Duchess Maria Aleksandrovna, daughter of Alexander II, and Alfred, the Duke of Edinburgh, son of Queen Victoria, took place in the chapel of the Winter Palace. It was a union that caught the imagination of both the Russian and English publics and Stanley's account provides a unique perspective on the events:

> The morning of a mighty day – dark, dull, thaw. Yesterday was spent almost entirely in preparations – the arrangements of the Hall, the rehearsal of the Russian singers, the negotiations between the Grand Maréchal de la Cour and the Metropolitans for their coming to our service; and – not last, not least – the endeavour to find a bouquet of white roses in which to entwine a sprig of myrtle which had come in a box from Osborne, to be presented to the Grand Duchess. [...]
>
> Tea as usual with Countess Bloudhoff; then dinner; then to the play – one I had long wished to see, 'The Life of the Czar,' [sic] a most instructive national story from the times of the first Romanoff, all in Russ, but admirably explained to us by one of the angels of the Court, one of those wonderfully intelligent ladies. It represented three things all in one – the hatred to the Poles, the devotion to the Emperor, and a Russian marriage. Then to an evening party at Count Adelsberg's, the most influential of the Russian grandees – music, ending with a supper, which lasted till 2 a.m. The Prince of Wales was there, the Duke of Coburg (whom I had not seen since Egypt), and a vast succession of Russian magnates.
>
> And now we are all arrayed – I in my red robes for the Russian service, to be exchanged for white for the English, Augusta [Stanley's wife] in lilac and resplendent with diamonds, Lady Emma in pink. At 12 we start – I with my two chaplains, the two English clergymen.
>
> The marriage is over! At twelve we started – i.e. I and my two assistants were conducted to our places in the Imperial Chapel, close to the chancel rails, where all the clergy, not of the Greek Church, were placed. It commanded the whole view of the ceremony, which I need not describe. It was a very pretty sight. All the old metropolitans were there, even the blind Innocent of Moscow, and stood round in their splendid vestments, whilst the venerable chaplain, Bajanoff, formed the centre of the bridal group.

It was much more like a family gathering than anything in Western Churches. The bride and bridegroom were closed round by the four groomsmen (for there are no bridesmaids), as if protecting them, and the crowns are held over their heads so long as to give the impression of a more than fugitive interest. The walking round and round the altar, with these four youths pacing with them, had quite the effect of what originally it must have been, a wedding dance. The sunshine, which after a dull, gloomy morning had gradually crept into the dome, at this moment lighted up the group below, and gave a bright, auspicious air to the whole scene. The singing was magnificent. The Lord's Prayer again struck me as the most beautiful vocal music I had ever heard.

At a given moment, just before the conclusion of the service, one of the Court officers came to summon me away. With difficulty we found our way through the crowd to the antechamber, where I changed my red robe for my white one, and immediately took my place on the high platform which had been made in front of the altar that stood against the screen. All the curtains were drawn down, and all the candles lighted, so that the whole place was transformed.

The Hall was full from end to end – far more than the English Church would have accommodated – and as I looked down the vast array of officers, &c., it was a splendid sight. The Russian choir was on my right, the English residents on my left; the two English clergy on each side, and the five Russian clergy, who came in with changed garments as soon as their service was over.

Then came up the Hall the bride and bridegroom, and stood before me, the Emperor and Empress on their right. The music of the choir broke out with Psalm XXII as they advanced.

It was a thrilling moment when, for the first and last time in my life, I addressed each by their Christian name – 'Alfred' and 'Marie' – and looked each full in the face, as they looked up into mine. The first part of the service I read from the Coronation Prayer-book. The second, from one lent by Lady Mary Hamilton, out of which were married George IV, the Princess Charlotte, William IV, the Duke of Kent, and the Prince of Wales. At the very end came the Prayer, which you will doubtless see in the newspapers; then the final benediction and the chanting of Psalm CXII. 1, 2, 3.

When his was over I bowed to the Emperor and Empress, and they returned it; and ten I turned round to the metropolitans and kissed their hands. Immediately afterwards I was summoned away to sign the leaf of the Register, which had been brought from the Chapel Royal. All the Princes were there, signing as witnesses. The Grand Duke Constantine was exceedingly kind, and begged to see me on the first opportunity. 'There is so much,' he said, 'that we have in common.'

At 4.30 p.m. followed the banquet of 800 guests. I sat by the Danish Minister; opposite me were the Emperor and the whole line of Princes and Princesses. The four heirs of England, Denmark, and Germany, all so different, each from each, but, of all, certainly none to compare with the last. He is like a sunbeam wherever he goes. These were all waited on by the high dignitaries of the Court, who stood behind and talked to them. Then at 9.30 a ball, or rather an immense evening party, multitudes and multitudes spreading through hall and galleries, in one of which the Princes danced, or rather walked, the Polonaise – once, the Emperor with Augusta. Even if it were only for the new acquaintances we have made, what a wonderful episode this will be!

The last years of Nicholas's reign had brought a spate of buildings and monuments that contributed significantly to the appearance of the city but were to be mentioned, if at all, only in English accounts following the end of the war. New churches, public buildings, palaces, embankments, bridges all added to the city's image. There was now, for instance, the first permanent bridge across the Great Neva, between Blagoveshchenskaia Square (in Soviet times, Labour Square) in the middle of the English Embankment and the 7th Line on Vasil'evskii Island. In 1850 the Blagoveshchenskii Bridge, designed by A.P. Briullov but built by the engineer S.V. Kerbedz, was completed, but was soon to be re-named the Nikolaevskii in honour of the late emperor, and so it remained until 1918, when it became the Lt Shmidt Bridge. It was Professor Smyth who provided the first detailed description for British readers:

Soon we came upon the Nikolayevski Bridge, and though from the western side there was a rich and busy scene of shipping, steamers, and commerce, yet we rather dwelt on the view to the east, whence comes that never-ceasing flow of pellucid water that forms the majestic stream of the Neva; and towards which quarter are directed long abutments from the several piers, like so many gigantic knives of granite, edge upwards, for breaking in pieces the floating fields of ice that at certain seasons come whirling out of Ladoga lake, and sweep out the whole breadth of the river before them.

In length about twelve hundred feet, with seven arches of elegantly flattened ellipsoidal form, and a ship drawbridge portion at the northern end, where the roadway, single and imperially broad before, sparates into two diverging branches, – this bridge is a beautiful construction to look upon from far and near; so lightly and airily does it span the waters, and yet show such a grip of the earth below, with wide-reaching solid masses of ponerous stone. And it is the only stone, the only permanent bridge, over any part of the Neva – a glorious triumph, therefore, for the late Emperor to have achieved.

[. . .] Three sets of piles, each, if we heard aright, seventy-five feet long, had to be driven in, one on top of the other, and in such numbers as to touch side by side, all across and along that part of the river, before the engineers had a sufficiently secure under-stratum to begin their work upon; and then they commenced laying down their Cyclopean blocks of Finland granite. A valuable material, this granite, without which, indeed, modern St. Petersburg would not be possible; for travel forth far and wide as you may in Russia proper, and dig down deep through her generally soft alluvial soil, and you seldom find anything better than thin, flaky limestone. This sheety stuff has been tried for the side-pavement of the noble bridge; unfortunately, for it is already exfoliating and breaking up under the mere feet of passengers; but all the ferocious attacks of the impetuous ice-rams in winter have not yet dulled the edge of the granite knives, or perceptibly scratched the polished surface of the stately granite archways. [. . .]

He mentions the two Egyptian sphinxes erected nearby on the granite embankment in front of the Academy of Arts, and then the Chapel of St Nicholas (not of Alexander Nevskii) which was built on the Nikolaevskii Bridge itself. This was designed by A.I. Shtakenshneider and finished in 1854, although it was demolished when the bridge was rebuilt in 1936–8:

An excellent example of this grey Russian granite is fortunately offered to view on the Nikolayevski bridge itself: for just at the junction of the drawbridge roadways, there is erected in this material, a dedicatory chapel to St. Alexander Nevski. An excellent example, too, it is, though lilliputian in size, of ecclesiastical architecture thoroughly adhered to in principle, at the same time that it is boldly executed in the improved manufactures of the present day. The east and west sides of the chapel are accordingly filled with magnificent arch-shaped sheets of the finest plate-glass, while a mural painting of the military saint fills the external wall on the north. Then the pillared corners and door-posts of the chapel, in polished grey granite, rise from the base of the same, and support an entablature of similar material; above which is a steep conical roof with golden tiles, surmounted by a glittering little gilded dome, and a richly ornamented cross.

The whole building, which is not more than four times the linear dimensions of a sentry-box, is thus finished and perfect to the last degree, and shows brilliantly as well as elegantly in the sun. But among the mass of the people it excites some far deeper feeling; for, as we stood there for a few minutes in a neighbouring niche, observing, hardly a second elapsed without some person being in the act of bowing and tossing, with bare head, as he passed the hallowed precincts.

Smyth is also an excellent source for a somewhat unusual description of Nevskii Prospekt, particularly its upper reaches beyond the Fontanka River, past the Nicholas (Moscow) railway station and on towards the Alexander Nevskii Monastery:

[. . .] that long, long street, which slowly and steadily increases in breadth and magnificence, as you trudge past verst after verst of its broad blocked houses in your way from the Admiralty Square outwards. Thus do its proportions continually enlarge until, after having passed innumerable cross-streets, churches, theatres, library, the third canal, and that by a bridge decorated with four spirited groups of wild horses and their tamers, in bronze by a native artist in the person of a veteran subaltern, you arrive at the Prospekt's fashionable conclusion, in the Annichkoff Palace; residence of the Emperor Nicholas before his accession, and retreat to which he afterwards carried his Empress, in 1837, on the night of the destruction of the Winter Palace by fire; and since then the abode of Russian diplomacy. From this point forewards, and to the large and airy Liteinaya Street, the same aristocratic character extends; freed from the bustle, business, and shoppy character of the more central regions, and not yet arrived at the unarchitectural negligence of the suburbs, or the outskirt poverty of every great city. In fact, in this region, and eastward of it, are most of the mansions of St. Petersburg-residing nobles; here, probably, quite safe from those floods of the Neva's mouth, which have from time to time done so much mischief to the lower part of the city, and which foreigners do so delight to detail the proofs of, that they must some impending day sweep away the whole of this metropolis, and leave not a wreck behind to show where once St. Petersburg stood.

By the time, however, that we had arrived at the third verst and a fourth canal lo! a citizen air again begins to creep over the houses, and presently, a large open place presents itself, with the Moskva railway terminus on one side, and shops, with railway hotels above, on the other. Beyond this point, the Nevski Prospekt continues, but at an angle with its former self, and in rapidly increasing deterioration. The bakers, with gracefully painted representations of abundance and with gilded signs, much in the shape of a solid true-lover's knot which passes here as the typical form for a loaf of bread, still occasionally deck the scene; but *modes et robes* are gone; no more does the legend 'Fotografiia' catch the eye; and there are instead, whole rows of old iron shops, and then whole rows of harness shops, dealing largely in the brass roses and other ornaments of country horses; then comes a large damp market-place, for diseased and broken-down carts, one would think; then a continuation of the broad street, but marked now only by garden walls, and an occasional monumental stone-cutter's cottage; and finally the whole concludes in the semi-circular entrance-gate of Alexander Nevski [...]

An amusing companion piece to the above is the description of the shops on Nevskii Prospekt and adjoining streets, penned by Fred Whishaw, a member of a long-established British family in the Russian capital, and author of innumerable boys' adventure yarns about Russian life and history:

At least two circumstances will probably strike the tourist promenading the streets of St. Petersburg for the first time as being peculiar and remarkable: one is, the amazing number of drinking shops which are able, presumably, to support themselves upon the darling vice of the country; they abound throughout the town; here and there the stranger may count two or three within a few yards. These drinking-shops are of all grades, and to accommodate all classes; they range from the dark and grimy and evil-smelling Kabak of the slums, to the stately Pogreb of the Nefsky Prospect. St. Petersburg is evidently not a stronghold of teetotalism.

The second striking circumstance referred to is the curious custom, designed, apparently, for the convenience of an uneducated population, of hanging outside the shops enormous pictures representing the wares which are procurable within. Thus the baker displays large posters upon which the cunning artist has depicted clusters of tempting rolls; a dish of cakes piled up in great profusion, and coloured with the most lavish disregard for expense; and a loaf or two of black bread modestly concealing its humble personality in the background. The butcher, again, hangs out the counterfeit presentment of an animal, intended by the artist to impersonate a bull in a pasture field; the terrible animal is apparently filled with sinister intentions, directed against nothing in particular, and is portrayed with head down and tail up, evidently in the very act of charging, but wearing for all its truculent mien, the mildest aspect and quite a benevolent expression, which says as plain as words: 'Don't be afraid, my dears, I wouldn't hurt a fly: it's only my way'. The trader who deals in all sorts of linen clothing reveals the facsimile of these without regard to the modesty of the public; while every little jeweller displays the portraits of golden and jewelled wares such as, did he really possess their actual counterpart, would enable him to ransom every crowned head in Europe if he were desirous of doing this kindness to royalty in distress. The drinking-shop generally presents an extremely realistic poster, showing, besides mugs of impossibly frothy beer and porter creaming up in a manner to tempt the austerest of abstainers, the portrait of an uproariously happy moujik engaged, presumably, in singing, as moujiks love to do, over his vodka, with enough liquour arranged around him, in bottles and decanters of all sizes and shapes, to keep him singing for a fortnight. In a word, each shop, excepting those whose customers are derived from the aristocracy alone, adopts this simple method of making known to the public the nature of articles which may be had for a reasonable equivalent within. The tourist should bear in mind that on entering a Russian shop, however humble, dirty, or stuffy that shop may be, he is expected to remove his hat; and that great offence will be given if he neglects to perform this customary act of courtesy.

In his description of Nevskii Prospekt Smyth made mention of the equestrian statues at the Anichkov Bridge over the Fontanka that were but one of the sculptural ensembles produced by Baron Petr Klodt in the 1840s and 1850s. Mahony called it 'a pretty stone bridge, guarded by a series of equestrian statues in bronze, the work of a Russian artist of considerable talent'; the Rev Archibald Weir was intent on seeing Klodt's statue of the beloved Russian fabulist Ivan Krylov 'which was put up in the Summer Gardens in 1855. As a work of art it is highly creditable. The poet is represented sitting, reading a book. The pedestal is adorned with very clever groupings of animals in high relief, the personae of his admirable fables'; while William Laurie, touring the city with his father in 1861, wrote of Klodt's equestrian statue of Nicholas I that was erected in front of Shtakenshneider's new Mariiskii Palace on Isaac Square:

> [. . .] we soon behold the new monument of the late Emperor Nicholas. Having been so recently erected, this splendid equestrian statue is not mentioned in any of the popular works on Russia. Nicholas, in full Guard uniform, mounted on a spirited charger, in a less daring attitude than Peter's, the hind legs reposing on a richly adorned pedestal, with at each corner a classical figure, and on the sides the imperial eagle, with various devices; then below, as it were, another larger pedestal, on which the former rests, this also richly carved; and an elaborate railing with elegant lamps on its crest, round the whole; such is the Russian tribute to the Czar Nicholas, who, whatever his failings may have been, endeavoured well for his empire!

It was in 1870 that a young English art critic, J. Beavington Atkinson, visited St Petersburg and wrote a rather less enthusiastic appraisal of Klodt's achievements, at least of his monuments to Nicholas and Krylov, within the context of his review of monumental statuary in the city:

> St. Petersburg is considerably indebted to the art of sculpture: public monuments adorn her squares and gardens. Indeed the art of sculpture has, like the sister arts of architecture and painting, been forced into preternatural proportions. In the large area within sight of the church of St. Isaac and of the Admiralty, stands conspicuously one of the few successful equestrian statues in modern or ancient times, the colossal bronze to Peter the Great. [...]
>
> The monument to the late Emperor Nicholas is a sad falling off from the manly and heroic style of the memorial to Peter the Great, the reason being that while the design of the latter is due to a Frenchman, the equestrian statue of Nicholas, with surrounding bas-reliefs and emblematic figures, is the work of the Russian sculptor Baron P. Clodt. This productive, hard-working, but not original artist naturally proved himself wholly unequal to an undertaking so arduous. The style embodies weakness with affectation; the work, in short, is a failure, as all such art compilations in St. Petersburg or elsewhere are bound to be. Other public statues help to people the solitudes of the city: the Suwaroff monument, destitute, almost as a matter of course, of art merit, stands on the open space at the flank of the British Embassy. The monument to the Scotchman Sir James Wylie is in the court of the Imperial Academy of Medicine: the memorials to Field-Marshals Tolly and Koutousoff surmount pedestals opposite the Kazan Cathedral. Of these collective works, certainly not less than respectable, perhaps the worst that can be affirmed is that they but exchange servility to the Byzantine school for equal servility to classic and Italian styles. The misfortune of these Russian sculptures is that they seldom succeed in establishing an independent individuality or a distinctive nationality. The best means of escape from this dead-alive condition seems to be in the direction of naturalistic and pictorial treatment. As favourable exceptions to the dull conventionality of Russian sculpture may be quoted four groups of horses reined in by attendants: these compositions, which tell with admirable effect on one of the many bridges in St. Petersburg, are wholly exceptional in this local plastic art

for free movement, bold action, and faithful transcript of nature. The sculptor, Baron Clodt, has deservedly won for himself renown. Also exceptional for manly, robust, and individual treatment is the bronze statue to the well-known popular fabulist Krilof, surrounded by bas-reliefs illustrative of his works. Here again Baron Clodt proves command of character, action, incident. The reliefs surrounding the figure illustrate Krilof's animal fables and other tales, which have recently been translated into English by Mr. Ralston. These reliefs are evidently most popular with the common people; indeed uneducated Russians I have found in no material degree to differ from the uneducated classes in England or other countries: all alike know a spade or a besom when they see one, and little more. Sculpture has always been to the illiterate of all nations a dead letter so far as it is an art.

Atkinson was the first British visitor to leave a really substantial description of the paintings of the Hermitage, which, he believed, 'alone repays a journey to St. Petersburg; for a whole fortnight I visited almost every day the picture and sculpture galleries of this vast and rich museum, and in the end I left with the feeling that I had done but inadequate justice to these valuable and exhaustless collections'. He was no less attentive to the essentially new building that housed them: the New Hermitage, opening on to Palace Square, was begun a year after the great fire (described by Elizabeth Rigby in the previous chapter) and was opened to the public in 1852:

Before I enter into detail as to the contents of the Hermitage it may be as well to describe the building, which by its art style and its palatial magnificence has brought great éclat to St. Petersburg. When I say that Ritter von Klenze, of Munich renown, was the architect, the reader may be able to picture to himself the structural and decorative aspect. Klenze has written his name in sufficiently large and legible characters on the face of modern Europe [. . .] No architect in one century has revived so many dead traditions, or given such grandiloquent expression to worn-out commonplaces. Klenze had already won his laurels in the service of King Ludwig of Bavaria, when he was summoned, in the year 1839, by the Emperor Nicholas, to St. Petersburg. His duties became onerous; he had to carry out the interior arrangements of the

Cathedral of St. Isaac, and he was entrusted with the design and construction of the Hermitage, a work of ten years, begun in 1840, completed in 1850, and formally opened in 1851. Previous structures had to be swept away which dated back to the time of Catharine II, who here made for herself a refuge from burdens of government called the Hermitage. The palatial Museum, which takes the place of the previous structure, shows itself in every sense span new; from toe to top, from basement to roof, it is bedizened with ornament and polichrome, after the manner has become notorious in Munich. The style is bastard Grecian, degenerating in the portico and the interior into the grotesque and florid renaissance. The portico is sustained by ten caryatides, tortured in form, and of more than usual dimension. These monolith colossi were cut in granite by the Russian sculptor Terebenieff, from a small model by the Munich sculptor Halbig. Niches in the walls are occupied by statues of historic artists; the sculptures at the sides are by Schwanthaler. The collective effect, though far from mean, wants character and originality. The stranger may safely reserve his emotions for the interior. The entrance-hall presents a truly noble appearance: the roof is supported by sixteen monoliths of the finest granite from Finland, and the whole interior boasts of an aggregate of no fewer than 140 granite monoliths. A stately flight of marble steps, second only to the monumental Treppenhaus in the New Museum, Berlin, conducts from the basement to the picture galleries. The visitor when he reaches the summit finds himself on a plateau adorned with modern French and Italian sculpture, and supports for candelabra of violet jasper from Siberia. The traveller feels he is no longer in a museum but in an imperial palace; the Pitti Palace in Florence is in comparison small and simple. Yet the architectural ideas are not so striking for novelty, as the decorative materials are astounding for boundless expenditure. It is easy to see whence the conceptions have been borrowed; – Klenze in fact not unnaturally thought he might steal from himself without charge of larceny, accordingly the sculpture galleries on the basement are indebted to the Glyptothek in Munich, while the picture galleries are a free and florid adaptation from the Old Pinakothek. The three large central galleries severally assigned to the Spanish School, to the Italian School, and to Rubens and Vandyck, are crowned by coved ceilings, enriched with gold and polichrome, and lighted from the top.

Blinds are need in the Russian summer as in the dog-days in Burlington House. The side rooms which branch off as in the Old Pinakothek from the lofty central halls, are of the nature of cabinets suited to small pictures; here the windows are on the side, screens intrude in the centre, the light, as in Munich, is capricious and poor.

The decorations of the galleries, cabinets, and corridors, may astound strangers not accustomed to the elaborate ornamentation of galleries and palaces in Munich. Mural colouring is known to have been reduced by Germans to a system or science, and Klenze being a painter as well as an architect, has heightened by his brush the work of his chisel. But he had less occasion for the use of paint, by reason of the rich-ness and the variety of the solid materials at his command. Whoever has visited the Mineralogical Museum in St. Petersburg, the richest in the world, with perhaps the single exception of the collection in the British Museum, must have been astounded with the amazing mineral wealth of the Russian empire. From Finland in the north, to the Ural Mountains southward, and to Siberia stretching towards the east, supplies reach St. Petersburg from quarries and mines which yield gran-ites, marbles, malachite, lapis lazuli, crystals, precious stones, gold, and other metals. With these materials in lavish profusion it is not surprising that Klenze was able to throw into the decoration of the Hermitage an opulence in excess of even the ornate Bavarian interiors. Moreover in staircases and other large surfaces and spaces, he has seen no objection to the use of scagliola, and thus an unbroken aspect of marble halls is main-tained throughout. Klenze, in the design and decoration of the Old Pinakothek, and of the Glyptothek, had learnt the utilitarian distinction between a picture and a sculpture, and accordingly, when he came to St. Petersburg, he wisely kept his basement, which was to be reserved for ancient marbles, solid and comparatively sombre, while the topmost story, devoted to the pictorial arts, naturally assumed a more festive and aerial aspect. Yet the architect has shown his knowledge and discretion in keeping down any undue splendour in his materials and appliances, thus, although each part is forced up to the highest pitch, the whole is balanced and brought into tone, so as to enhance rather than to militate from the effect of the pictures hung on the walls. The background of silk hangings, against which the gold frames rest, inclines to a uniform scarlet red. But any monotony involved in this invariable colour of the wall linings, is relieved by the variety thrown into doors, ceilings, and floors. The floors, the only wood in the building, are of marquetry, of which we have a comparatively humble example in our Royal Academy. In some of the rooms the patterns both in arrangement of form and colour, are highly effective. [...]

It remains to notice that the galleries are furnished with a taste and magnificence in keeping with the structure. The chairs and couches are covered like the walls with rich silks. The vases and tables of porphyry and malachite, the candelabra of violet jasper and of rhodonite, the tazzas of lapis lazuli, syenite and aventurine, have the value of scientific specimens as well as of art products. These mineralogical monuments are in fact the only strictly national works in the Hermitage, except Russian pictures. But I need not here dwell on a thought which I fear will have to be oft repeated in this volume, that the arts are in Russia exotics imported from afar. The Hermitage happens to be in St. Petersburg only because there was money to rear it. As I have already signified the structure has been transported from Munich, the contents are foreign, and the style is but the usual eclecticism from Italy.

Atkinson would have obviously preferred to have seen the Hermitage's great collection of paintings in Europe whence they had come and he travelled to Russia to see what he considered to be truly Russian, truly national. Inevitably, it was the onion dome that attracted him, even to the point that he exaggerated what is for many its alien presence in St Petersburg:

I can scarcely refrain from again referring to the fine fantasy played by many-coloured domes against the blue sky. The forms are beautiful, the colours decorative. The city in its sky outline presents a succession of strange pictures, at one point the eye might seem to range across a garden of gourds, at other positions peer above house-tops groups which might be mistaken for turbaned Turks; and when the sun shines vividly, and throws glittering light on the 'patens of bright gold', over these many-domed churches, a stranger might almost fancy that above the city floated fire balloons or bright-coloured lanterns. The large cupola of St. Isaac, covered with copper overlaid with gold, has been said to burn on a bright day like the sun when rising on a mountain top.

In his impressions of the city as a whole, Atkinson conceded there was 'no capital more imposing when taken from the strong points of view' and that 'almost without parallel is the array of palaces and public buildings which meets the traveller's eye in a walk or sail from the English quay to the Gardens of the Summer Palace' and the views from the three bridges across the Neva 'are eminently palatial and imperial'. Nevertheless, 'few cities are so pretentious in outside appearances as St. Petersburg, and yet the show she makes is that of the whited sepulchre: false construction and rottenness of material, façades of empty parade, and plaster which feigns to be stone, constitute an accumulative dishonesty which has few parallels in the history of architecture'. Few would-be authoritative judgments are more damning, although the British military attaché at the time felt able to pronounce that 'no description of the town of St. Petersburg appears necessary, as it has no features peculiar to itself, but is a sort of mixture of all the other principal capitals of Europe'. The Hon. Frederick Wellesley was nevertheless able in at least one area to draw a positive out of an initial negative:

> St. Petersburg is, I suppose, the worst paved capital in Europe. The roads are made of large cobble-stones, and much domed in the centre. When you add to this the holes caused by traffic and frost, it can be imagined that jolting over such thoroughfares in a crazy vehicle like the droshki, which answers to our cab, is not a pleasant experience. Such means of locomotion, however, are fortunately restricted to the summer months, for when the snows fall these horrible roads are, sometimes in twelve hours, converted into the most perfect and smoothest streets in the world. The change is really quite extraordinary, for not only have all the roughness and jolting disappeared, but the noise of carriages and carts bumping along has given place to the quiet and noiseless progress of the sledge. In other words, the streets of St. Petersburg, from having been the worst in the world, have suddenly been transformed into the best and easiest roads imaginable [...]

The reign of the tsar-liberator Alexander II came to a sudden and bloody end on 1/13 March 1881, when he was assassinated near the Catherine Canal. George Augustus Sala, who had first visited St Petersburg in 1856 to write a series of gossipy and whimsical articles for

Dickens's *Household Words* that were subsequently recycled for his book *A Journey Due North* (1859), returned as the correspondent of *The Daily Telegraph* to report the tsar's funeral:

He [Lord Dufferin, the British ambassador] helped me to a material extent in March, 1881, by obtaining for me an invitation to the house of a wealthy English merchant whose windows commanded a near and clear view of the Winter Palace, whence the corpse of the Tsar was to be borne across the bridge which spans the Neva, to be interred in the chapel, or rather the cathedral, of the fortress of St. Peter and St. Paul. I could have procured one from the Russian Minister of the Interior, or from one of the Imperial Chamberlains, a card of admission to the church; but I should have had to wait two or three hours in the crowded edifice, and should only have witnessed the funeral ceremony itself, whereas from the merchant's residence I could see the whole stately procession winding its way from the palace to the fortress. [...]

The thoroughfares through which we drove were densely crowded; while the route of the funeral *cortège* was lined on each side by troops, including several batteries of artillery. A special police permit had to be obtained before a window in a house in the line of procession could be opened, since there was no knowing from what casement a murderous shot might be fired. The pageant was magnificent in the extreme; but the most touching part of the spectacle was the illustrious group who followed on foot on the snow-covered roadway the funeral car of Alexander II – the young Emperor Alexander III, a numerous body of the princes of the imperial family, and our own Prince of Wales supporting the chief mourner. It was awful to think when the procession had entered the fortress, and the minute-guns were sullenly firing at the close of the ceremony, that the dull roar of the cannon must have been audible to the accomplices of the assassin of the Tsar, who were immured in the stone casements of the citadel.

As I have said, the funeral itself I did not see, but on the Sunday following the deposition of the body I witnessed the lying-in-state of the dead Tsar in the Cathedral of St Peter and St Paul. The coffin was placed on a dais, forming an inclined plane, in the middle of the church, which was hung with rich sable draperies, while on either side the bier were lighted wax candles in towering candlesticks of silver-gilt.

The lid of the coffin had been removed, and as the spectators passed in single file they were expected to incline themselves and kiss the right hand of the corpse, which hand was covered with a piece of silk-yellow gauze. The remains of him who a few days before had been Autocrat of All the Russias were clad in full military uniform, and with a constellation of stars and medals on the breast. The body had been embalmed, and the injuries in the face skilfully plugged and painted over; below the waist, I was told, the limbs of the victim of the devilish bomb outrage were only so much padding, cloth, and leather.

The dispatches of the British ambassador and the letters of his wife record the turmoil of these years, when attacks by the 'Nihilists' became more and more frequent. Lord Dufferin, whose embassy in St Petersburg lasted from the spring of 1879 to April 1881, had spoken with the tsar just hours before his murder. Dufferin was anxious that the Prince and Princess of Wales (the future King Edward VII and Queen Alexandra) should be present at the funeral and meet the new tsar, whom the prince invested with the Order of the Garter at 'really a very striking ceremony. Though the company was small it was composed of very distinguished personages, and the quaint and novel features of the ceremony were an agreeable change from the gloomy pre-occupations and funeral services of the last fortnight'. A week before he left Russia for a new posting in Constantinople, Dufferin wrote to a friend:

For the past fortnight I have been terribly busy. In the first place Greek affairs took up a good deal of my time, and then I had to look after the Prince and Princess of Wales. Their visit has gone off very well, and it has been a great comfort to these poor people. The Princess returns tomorrow. I was all in favour of the Prince coming, and of bringing his wife too. I knew that the risk, though not absolutely nil (for no one can calculate upon what these fanatics will do), was almost inappreciable, and considering what near relations our Royalties now are to those in Russia, and the fact that all the other Princes of Europe were flocking to St. Petersburg, it would have looked very ill if a brother-in-law and sister had been deterred from coming by the fear of any personal risk. Consequently I telegraphed to the Queen in that sense, in spite of the responsibility. Her Majesty telegraphed back that she would hold me personally liable for any harm that might happen to either of them, which under the circumstances is not a very pleasant message.

Tomorrow we are to be received by the emperor. The town is full of stories of bombs, and mines, and explosions, and conspiracies to blow up everybody. The other day it was reported that a dog was heard howling on some small tenement near the great powder magazine. On breaking open the door they found the house destitute of any human inhabitant. They cut the string by which the dog was tied, and the animal at once ran off. But on further examination it was observed that the other end of the string led down through the floor. This excited suspicion, and on following the clue it was found to be attached to a detonating apparatus, the calculation being that the straining of the dog at his collar would pull the trigger. It appears, however, that instead of contending with fate, the dog contented himself with howling, and so half St. Petersburg has been spared.

Before he left, Dufferin also 'looked in at the trial of the Nihilists. One of them was very distinguished looking, with a countenance of a high type. The others were merely moujiks, one woman a disreputable looking Jewess, and Peroffsky, the lady, a bosomless, sexless creature of the true Nihilistic type with a huge forehead, small intelligent eyes, and a hideous face'. Also present at the trial were members of the European press corps, including, among the British representatives, John Baddeley, reporting for the *Standard* and producing for it his own impressions of the accused, which included an almost equally negative description of Sof'ia Perovskaia: 'Contrary to report she is not pretty, but quite the type of the female nihilist, with high, massive forehead, straight hair, nose turned up, a firm mouth, and a pointed chin'.

It was only in 1921, near the end of his life, that John Baddeley published his *Russia in the 'Eighties'*. It is an interesting fact that there were few British first-hand accounts of St Petersburg published during the twelve-year rule of the new tsar, although American publications abound. What British writers who had known the previous regime seemed unanimous about was that it was 'a very different Russia' – Sala's verdict on his return to Russia for the coronation of Alexander III, echoed by Baddeley, and by E.A. Brayley Hodgetts. Hodgetts, who had been the resident correspondent of the new *Daily Graphic* from

1889, contrasted the 'brilliant' capital he had known under Alexander II with what he now encountered:

> It was as though a pall had been cast over the town. One felt at once that Russia had been plunged back into the Middle Ages. To me, who had been away so long, and had not therefore witnessed the gradual transformation, step by step, the change was all the more striking. What was noticeable was the extent to which German methods and manufactures had ousted those of France and England, which had previously prevailed. This was all the more noteworthy seeing that Alexander III and his Danish consort both cordially detested everything German. Alexander III wanted to make Russia Russian, and tried hard to act up his watchword of Russia for the Russians, but failed in this, as he did in most things.

It was inevitable in the context of Russianization that when a monument to the murdered Alexander II was planned it was to be in the ancient Russian style and not in the international neo-classicism that was St Petersburg's trademark. However, only the foundations of the church were laid by the death of Alexander III and its first description in English belongs to the following reign and chapter.

'Sport and Politics' (such was the sub-title of Baddeley's book) rather than architecture and the usual tourist sights were the dominant topics. Not only the domestic situation within Russia but Russia's role in the 'Great Game' and its alleged pretensions to Constantinople and the riches of India, concerns stretching back, of course, to the end of the eighteenth century but receiving intensified resonance as Russia and Britain moved to the brink of war, preoccupied British writers and readers, particularly through the growing influence of newspapers and journals. Sport, however, was an equal passion and the British were as happy recording their slaughter of bears, elk and wolves in Russia as of other unfortunate creatures in India and Africa. Baddeley, writing about his hunting of bears near the Finnish border, proudly writes that 'my friend and I in the course of twelve days' actual hunting killed twenty-three, of which eleven were cubs from one to two and even three years old, the rest grown bears of from four to sixteen *poods* (144 to 576 lbs.) weight' and his book abounds in similar listings. He also shot vast amounts of game birds and fished for mighty trout in the lakes and rivers around St Petersburg. If politics divided the British community from the Russians, sporting activities tended to unite them.

Sport had always occupied an important place among the leisure pursuits of the British community. Ambassadors fished and played real tennis and attempted to organize rowing races on the Neva already in the eighteenth century; the British organized horse races and awarded cups; they formed a Piscatorial Club in the 1820s and a hunt near the capital. In the reigns of the Alexander II and Alexander III clubs prolif-erated, inspired by British example and as often as not British-run. It was in connection with the establishment in 1846 of the exclusive Imperial Yacht Club (and the spread of race-meetings) that a Petersburg paper suggested that 'English sport has begun to spread' (using, incidentally, the neologism 'sport'), but it was in the 1860s that the British themselves founded at least two new-style sports club that were to prosper for over fifty years: the Neva Tennis and Cricket Club and the Arrow Rowing Club. The first report of a cricket match dates from 1875 when an English Petersburg XI played against a team from the Royal Yacht *Osborne* on the Cadet Corps square on Vasil'evskii Island, where football and hockey were also played. Krestovskii Island, separated from the Vyborg District of the city by the Malaia Nevka River, became the centre of much sporting activity, organized and less formal. It was on this island (where today the Kirov Sports Stadium is to be found) that the St Petersburg Circle of Lovers of Sport (founded in 1888) acquired a large area and encouraged tennis, cricket, soccer, athletics, and shooting. A secluded corner of the island was also every winter 'made over to the British colony as a site for their ice-hills'. The British were to be found at play played not only within the city but also in villages which became virtual summer colonies.

Baddeley remembered with warmth life in the British colony in the 1880s:

[. . .] the British colony had passed through many vicissitudes to reach at the time of my arrival in Russia [1879] a stage that as far as regarded social amenity left really nothing to be desired. There were very few old people, the great majority of the leaders of the community being, by chance, young married couples, nearly all in receipt of good incomes and possessed of spacious apartments in St. Petersburg and pleasant country quarters at Ligovo, Mourino, or elsewhere – with tennis lawns – where they spent the summer months and where they delighted to entertain their friends. There were pretty girls about, too, and altogether a more pleasant society, for a young man, it would have been difficult to find anywhere.

Moreover, there were clubs of all sorts connected with the colony – famous clubs, some of them – for shooting, fishing, cricket and lawn-tennis, ice-hilling, skating; and I myself with three others founded, a little later, the Yukki ski-ing club, the first of its kind. The Gorielovo Hunt, in which Russian aristocrats such as Vorontsoff-Dashkoff rode side by side with the British colonists, had just come to an end, the last master being Evelyn Hubbard [...]

Count Vorontsov-Dashkov, scion of a distinguished aristocratic family that had had close links with the British since Catherinian times, owned the village of Murino, some twenty kilometres to the north-east of St Petersburg on the River Okhta (which falls into the Neva opposite the Smol'nyi Cathedral). James Whishaw, a cousin of the novelist Fred, was one of those British families privileged to rent a summer house there and his memoirs conjure up something of the magic of those long past summers as well as highlighting the close-knit family ties that frequently united British families in the Russian capital:

My own family, as well as several of our relatives, lived in a village called Mourino, 18 versts from St. Petersburg. I can well imagine how and why this spot became the country place chosen by the early English in Russia, for 100 years ago [c.1830?] the country between St. Peterburg and Mourino was practically a succession of woods with open spaces here and there interspersed. I can imagine my antecedents going in this direction and suddenly coming upon a small village at the foot of which ran a river, the banks of which were honeycombed with springs of the most glorious water. My wife's cousin, Alfred Cattley, had a small book written by a great-uncle of his, one Stephen Cattley, which he had illustrated with pen sketches, one of which is supposed to represent himself riding on horseback to Mourino. How long we had been established there I cannot say, but my grandmother Anastasia

Henley (born Whishaw, a sister of my grandfather Bernard Whishaw) told me of her memories of Mourino when she was a child of six years old. My grandmother was then in her ninety-fourth year, and as I was then at Sutton Valence and was about fifteen years old, it brings back our connexion with Mourino to a period which, to my younger readers, must sound prehistoric. At the time my grandmother mentioned, her father – my great-grandfather William – was living at what was called the Count's House.

The estate of Mourino, and a vast amount of the property surrounding this and neighbouring villages, belonged to the Vorontsov-Dashkoff family. We paid practically no rent for the houses on the estate, but we were bound to keep them in good condition. The Count's House was in ruins when I first saw Mourino, but parts of the old house and the large stone steps leading to the balcony remained, and I have no doubt are standing to this day. [...]

In the Mourino gardens were living in 1877 the Robert Andersons, next to whose house stood the Old house in which my Father, Miss Potter and my sister were living, while Uncle Jim slept in the lodge belonging to this house. Next came another very old house in which the Fred Raitts were living. Then, a short distance from them was a more modern house, built by Fred Cattley, my wife's uncle, in which house the Arthur Raitts lived. Alongside this stood Uncle Bernard's house. These different houses were separated either by a row of trees or by hedges. As you can imagine, life there really [...] was that of a large family. There were no doubt small tiffs at times, but these served perhaps to keep away monotony. Outside the garden and along the main road, bordering on the old Count's garden, stood the house in which my uncle Alfred Whishaw lived with his large family, and on the opposite side of the road stood a small *datcha* in which Charles Sanderson and his wife lived, and after they left St. Petersburg it was inhabited by my cousin Fred Whishaw and his wife.

I cannot imagine any place in England or in any continental country where more delightful picnics could be taken than those we had from Mourino, for the country all round, though mostly flat, was exceedingly picturesque – parts indeed (but those parts were somewhat far distant) being really beautiful. The little River Ochta, which had its source in the region of the Toxova Lakes (about 15 miles north of

Mourino) meandered in a tortuous course through many parts of the country which we visited, finally becoming the boundary of the Mourino gardens and ultimately making its way until it joined the Neva, by which time it had become quite a large river.

One of Murino's great attractions, mentioned elsewhere by Whishaw and by Baddeley, was 'the first and only golf-links in Russia'. There is no information about precisely when this nine-hole course was laid out, but Whishaw recalls how a member of the imperial family, Grand Duke Kirill, came to Murino 'probably as a guest of a member of the Embassy, to get his first instructions in golf' and, looking ahead, it proved irresistible to the British ambassador on the eve of the October Revolution.

Ligovo on the Peterhof Road had no similar memorialists, although Baddeley provides the following pen-picture:

At Ligovo, some dozen miles from the centre of St. Petersburg, on the road to Peterhof and Oranienbaum, was another small colony of the well-to-do English, a rival to Mourino. The great Empress Catherine, it seems, disliking the dull monotony of the coast-road, caused the land through which it runs to be cut up into transverse strips, and distributed amongst her courtiers with command to build houses, and lay out parks and gardens, on them. Several of these houses were still standing in my time, and in one of them, known as Litania, lived E.H. Ebsworth, as genial a man as ever lived – outside his office – local chief of the great industrial firm [Sir William Miller & Co.] from which Millers, Cazalets and others drew millions in the second half of the nineteenth century. Here, in summer, he and his clever wife, dispensed lavish hospitality to their many friends, and to strangers who were lucky enough to bring introductions to them, while nearby dwelt others of the British community hardly less hospitable. There were tennis-lawns in plenty, gardens, pine-woods, ornamental water, and, across the highroad, meadow, marsh and sea – or rather the rush-bordered fresh-water gulf at either end of which lay St. Petersburg and Kronstadt.

The tense political situation notwithstanding, the British seemed content with their favoured place within Petersburg society. The English church, which had fallen into disrepair during the last decades of the reign of Nicholas I, was substantially rebuilt in the 1870s under the architect F.K. Boltenhagen, who removed the third floor of the building and enlarged the windows on the second floor. In 1877 an organ, built by the firm of Brindley and Foster of Sheffield, was installed. Thomas Michell, the British Vice-Consul in St Petersburg and author of the 1865 edition of Murray's, was unimpressed, however, with the new interior:

> In 1873 the interior was renovated, and unfortunately rendered very bare and cheerless-looking, notwithstanding the addition of stained windows, at a cost of 10,000, defrayed from the funds accumulated by the so-called 'British Factory', in the form of a compulsory tax on British shipping, which at last became obnoxious to the tax-payers, and injurious to our trade. The capacious and valuable premises enjoy the boon of ex-territoriality, on the ground that the chapel, like our other Anglican establishments in Russia, is a chapel of the Queen's Ambassador. A boys' school, and an extensive circulating library for the benefit of the two thousand British subjects who reside at St. Petersburg and its vicinity, are also on the premises, and render complete the arrangements made by our countrymen for the spiritual and moral welfare of the British colony.

The library, which had existed since the beginning of the reign of Catherine the Great, was, indeed flourishing, and in 1882 a catalogue of some 400 pages and listing 10,000 titles was published.

What was new, however, on the English Embankment was the establishment run by Mrs Benson (and then, seemingly, by her daughters) that was particularly commended and frequented by the visiting British. Mahony's guidebook of 1857 notes that 'persons intending to stay more than a week can be accommodated with bed, breakfast, and dinner (exclusive of wine or malt liquor,) at two roubles a day', but the most amusing and extensive evocation of the Benson boarding-house occurred in the anonymous *Half Hours in the Far North* of 1877:

> But before we part for the present, please, reader, take in fancy a chair with me on the balcony, entered from the dining-room, on the second story of Miss Benson's excellent boarding-house.

The guests who are seated beside me and in the room are all English, with one exception, who shall be mentioned. Almost all of them are commercial men. Two or three of them with unrevealed names are probably not so. They maintain the usual silence and reserve of Englishmen on their travels; talk among themselves, and gaze around them with eyes educated to express a vacant stare. Yet these are very likely fine fellows, if you only knew them. They have travelled before now, have just come from a fishing tour in Norway, have 'done' Sweden, Finland, and intend visiting the great fair of Novgorod. They study to appear unconscious of the presence of any other human being in the room, and it is to be presumed that 'you must love them, ore you know that they are worthy of your love.' Pray don't trouble them, and they won't trouble you. Yet, ten to one the ice will be broken between you, if you are not intrusive, and you will find Jones and Robinson right good fellows.

Sitting in the corner of the balcony, slowly whiffing his cigar, is a British naval officer who has been for many months in St. Petersburg. He was one of the commissioners for arranging the boundary between Turkey and Persia. He, too, is silent and reserved, though an Irishman; but only draw him out, and you will soon discover what a mine of inexhaustible information there is in him, and what sly, *pawky* humour. [...]

Below is the street, with a drosky-stand, bounded fifty feet across by the granite quay, and beyond, the Neva flowing past, broad, deep, and swift. There are no vessels so high up, except a steamer or two on the opposite wharf.

'What a stupid, dull place,' exclaims the naval officer; 'how I hate it!'

'And I.'

'Ditto, ditto,' exclaim others.

'Please give me a light for my cigar,' asks a commercial man of his neighbour, 'I am dying of *ennui.*'

'What a glorious evening! What a sunset! Only look!' cries an enthusiastic new-comer.

It is indeed a glorious evening. Just watch across the Neva the remains of the sunset over Vassali Ostroff! What a marvellous combination of colour in the sky! How deeply calm and lovely are the heavens, from the horizon to the zenith! What exquisite colouring of blues, purples, reds, yellows, greens, and tints of yellow-green, with broad streaks of light, widespread oceans, golden islands, amethyst promontories, unfathomable abysses of glory – all are there, and they will remain there till early dawn, at two o'clock, in unchanged, undecaying beauty, while we bid them good-night, and go sleep!

Disgruntled or content, the British, visitors and residents, had relatively few years to enjoy the view and the peace.

CHAPTER 7

STRADDLING THE CENTURIES: THE REIGN OF NICHOLAS II, 1894–1917

Oscar Browning, a Fellow of King's College, Cambridge, who in 1898 had published a life of *Peter the Great* which included a brief chapter on the Russian capital, visited St Petersburg for the first time a decade later to deliver a series of lectures on English literature. He was so taken with the city that he composed a sonnet in its honour:

> Fair child, engendered by a despot's thought,
> Queen of the North, enthroned on confluent streams,
> Goal of his strivings, pagod of his dreams,
> From churlish nature by persistence wrought.
> Prove worthy of thy mission, slowly taught
> By triumph and disaster, wear thy crown;
> Clutch not at hasty issues, be thine own,
> Too oft by misdirected good distraught.
>
> Then the bright spirit of the Slavic mind,
> Condemned too long to an unworthy part,
> Led by thy gentle governance, shall find
> New worlds in letters, music, life, and art.
> Awake, proud city of the golded domes!
> Thy winter past, the joy of harvest comes.

It was with this poem, perhaps the only one ever written in English about the city, that George Dobson concluded his book on St Petersburg, published in 1910. Dobson, who had been the special Russian correspondent of *The Times* from 1876 to 1901, had a deep knowledge and love of the capital. The closing chapters of his book, enhanced by thirty-two coloured and black and white illustrations from original watercolours by F. de Haenen, provides an interesting insight into the speed of change in the capital during the reign of Nicholas II but in particular in the years following 'Bloody Sunday', the massacre of 9/22 January 1905.

He highlights, for example, the introduction in 1907 of electric trams (imported, incidentally, from Britain):

> The most remarkable of the new features of outdoor life in St. Petersburg are those resulting from the successful operation of the new electric trams, which, since they began to replace the old horse traction at the end of 1907, have accelerated locomotion to a degree little short of producing a revolution amongst easy-going pedestrians and careless droshky drivers. They seem to have stimulated the life of the city in general. They are also enabling the population to spread out wider afield, away from the congested and expensive centre, for the sake of cheaper house accommodation. The city, which, without its suburbs, covers an area of about forty square miles of land and water, is now being supplied in all directions with neatly appointed electric trams. Only a few of the old horse tramcars are still running, while on the lines extending to the remoter outskirts of the city steam-traction has long been in use. The public are taking fullest advantage of the new method, for it offers the only expeditious means of locomotion combined with cheapness, with the exception of about a dozen motor-buses, there being no overhead metropolitan railway, and, considering the nature of the ground, it is not likely there will ever be any twopenny tubes. During the busy hours of the day the new cars are everywhere over-crowded with strap-hangers, and it is not unusual to see as many as fifty or sixty tramcars at one time along the Nevsky Prospect, a thorough-fare as wide as Portland Place, running right through the heart of the capital for over two miles.

Nevskii Prospekt had been illuminated by electric lighting back in 1884, shortly after the construction of St Petersburg's first electro-generating station, but during Nicholas's reign it was being introduced ever more widely:

> For one thing, there has been a great extension of electric lighting and the use of other bright illuminants, although in the suburbs and on the edges of the city kerosene is still used in many of the streets. All the

principal thoroughfares are now brilliantly lighted at night, and, weather permitting, present a very gay and lively appearance. In winter the effect is heightened by the reflection from the snow and the frequent flashing of blue sparks from the overhead conductors as the contact rods of the tramcars slide along them.

The city had become an animated European capital:

Any observer who remembers what the Neva capital was like only a few years since cannot fail to be struck with the evident increase of population and activity. Less than ten years ago it could still be said with a certain amount of truth that St. Petersburg consisted of only two main avenues, towards which everybody seemed to gravitate – the Nevsky Prospekt and Great Morskaia Street – the Oxford and Regent Streets of the Russian capital. To-day many other important thorough-fares, such as the Sadovaya and Gorokhovaya Streets and the Litainy, Soovorofsky and Voznesensky Prospects, are equally busy and crowded arteries of traffic. The crowds also have considerably mended their pace, which was formerly a crawling one in comparison with the bustling throngs in other European capitals.

Despite the Russians' inveterate love of small shops, there was the promise of large trading establishments such as found in London and Paris:

A variation has also begun to show itself in the peculiar tendency of St. Petersburg to multiply indefinitely the enormous number of its small and badly aired shops, many of them having their floors much below the level of the pavement. Nothing gives such a good idea of the addict-ness of the Russians to small trading, and of their lack of the enterprise necessary to build up large retail businesses, as the great extent of the petty shopkeeping still carried on in St. Petersburg. Had it not been for Imperial prohibitions against trading in some of the more aristocratic parts of the city in the early days of its existence, there would probably not be a single house or street to-day without some kind of small shop. As it is, there are few houses and streets without them. One or two big firms, like Elisayeff Brothers and Tcherepenikoff, have long been famous as very large dealers in all kinds of fruit and native and foreign dainties, but the creation of a Russian Maple, Shoolbred, Waring, or Peter Robinson, seems at present to be rather a remote possibility. Still, as already mentioned, there are signs of a change in this respect. It would seem that capital is beginning to find its way into retail trading, as a number of large stylish establishments, and one or two huge stores, especially one belonging to the Army and Navy Cooperative Society, have lately sprung into existence.

This was the period of '*Modern*', Russia's 'Art nouveau' or 'Secessionism', when on Nevskii Prospekt there was built, for instance, P.Iu. Siuzor's Singer Building (1902–4), which in 1919 became the House of Books, and the store built for the Eliseevs by G.V Baranovskii in 1903–7 (No. 56 Nevskii, later housing a State Food Store and the Academic Comedy Theatre):

Another notable development, adding to the architectural embellishment of the two principal streets and to the advantage of the community in other respects, has taken place of late in the insurance and banking businesses of St. Petersburg, the increasing prosperity of which may be inferred from the construction of many handsome and palatial buildings for office accommodation, in spite of revolutionary troubles and 'expropriations'.

Dobson also notes 'an extraordinary development of much-patronized cinematograph shows and cafés, the latter being a business in which St. Petersburg was, until quite recently, very deficient'. The first cinematographic projection in St Petersburg had taken place at the very end of 1895, four months after the invention of the cinema. By 1913 there were 134 cinema halls in the city.

The 'modern' developments Dobson described in the city in the first years of the century are to be seen in the context of vast demographic changes. The population of the capital stood at nearly one and half million in 1901 and by the beginning of the First World War it was approaching two and half million. Even since the Emancipation of the serfs in 1861 there had been an increasing drift of poor peasants to the cities and as the tempo of industrialization rose, the drift became a flood of potential workers for the factories and mills and menial employ. Harold Williams, a brilliant New Zealand linguist, who had arrived in Russia as correspondent for the *Manchester Guardian* in December 1904 and was soon widely acclaimed for his authoritative commentaries on Russian affairs, published in 1915 his book *Russia of the Russians*, the last chapter of which was devoted to 'In the Chief City', where he painted a vivid picture of the impact of the peasant immigration and their accommodation to the new patterns of life:

> The thousands who have hitherto seemed as mere human material for writing 'St Petersburg' in big, bold letters are ceasing to be a mere indiscriminate mass. Most of the working people of the city are of peasant origin. Year by year they come to St Petersburg from Riazan, Orel, Kaluga, Yaroslavl, Kostroma, Tver, Novgorod, Viatka, Perm, Vologda, Archangel, come with their bundles in the third-class carriages of the slow trains, or else trudging on foot, in top boots or in bast shoes. Many find work as factory-workers, as cabmen, as Swiss or concierges, as dvorniks or house-yard servants, as messengers, floor-polishers, stone-masons, carriers or draymen, while many of the women become domestic servants. They live poorly at the best in dark, tiny flats in the back-yards of big houses, or in tumble-down wooden houses on the outskirts of the city; at the worst in 'corners', paying for the corner of a room from a rouble and a half to two roubles (three to four shillings a month), and living on herring, black bread, and tea, with various additions proportioned to their earnings. To a large extent they maintain their peasant outlook, associate with their zemliaki, their compatriots, people from their own village or government, throng to the churches early on Sunday morning, watch the weather and the passing of the seasons, thinking 'now is the time for haymaking, now for harvest,' and maintaining the peasant accent, the peasant decorum. Naturally they drink more in the city, and on Sundays and holidays staggering figures are to be met at every turn. The city does its fusing, levelling work upon them; they gather together in traktirs or teahouses, and over glasses of weak tea slowly exchange and interpret the impressions that now come crowding in the shock of great events, now flow in a steady stream in the regular course of daily labour. They grow accustomed to the cheap amusements of the city. Hundreds are attracted to the

Narodny Dom, the People's Palace, with its plays and operas at extraordinarily low prices of admission. In the summer evenings, or on Sundays and holidays, there are guliania, 'walkings' in the public gardens, which are lamentably few and far between, and in the Petrovsky Park on the Petersburg Side. Here they walk in pairs, eating sunflower seeds, listening to the music of a military band, or else standing watching some melodrama on an open stage. And now there are scores of cheap cinematographs in all parts of the city, with scenes of blood-curdling tragedy, and pictures of all the wonders of the wide world. Cheap newspapers have appeared and cheap books, and there are night-schools and popular lectures, and the children go to school and grow up to be true city folk, and all kinds of new ideas spread swiftly amidst this busy, moving, alert, and endlessly communicative mass. Now they are carried away by the preachings of Father John of Kronstadt. Then comes the political upheaval with all its perplexing problems and wild hopes and bitter disappointments. Lay brothers come preaching temperance, and move hundreds to shake off their slackness and live a cleanly life. A wave of pessimism passes through the mass, and the police records daily tell of suicides of working people – a workman jumps into a canal, a woman drinks acetic acid. It is a swift transformation of the neighbourliness of village life into a big city neighbourliness, confused, uncertain of itself, with many relapses into vice and much groping after goodness, with an inevitable urban vulgarisation and debasement of feeling, but at the same time with a sharpening of the intelligence to eager inquiry that is sometimes raised in a volume of collective emotion to the point of passionate moral questioning.

While there were many developments in the city to enthuse about, observers such as Dobson and Williams were very alive to the vast problems that remained, not least in the area of public health and sanitation:

No other capital city in the world has ever been criticized as much as St. Petersburg. Russians themselves have always complained of its defects, and not without good reason. Foreigners also have given it a bad reputation, and its ruin has often been predicted. Its depreciation by English and other foreign writers, however, was more in fashion when Russophobia was rampant. Russian constitutional reform and popular liberty, although as yet existing more in principle than in practice, have taken the political sting out of foreign criticism. The evil spoken and written of St. Petersburg today is chiefly in reference to its inherent failings, which it must be admitted are very great. In spite of all its external splendour, it has come to be known as the unhealthiest and most expensive capital in Europe. It stands first among the large cities of Europe, and even of Russia, both as regards the rate of mortality in general and the high death-rate from infectious diseases. Typhoid and cholera are the periodical scourges of its population. Since the thirties of the last century there have been seven outbreaks of cholera, and the epidemic has prevailed altogether no less than twenty-five years.

The foundations of public health have been too long neglected in favour of the outside glitter of modern civilization. Although the subject of sanitation has been under discussion for the last quarter of a century at least, there is still no proper drainage and no pure water-supply. St. Petersburg is now the fifth in point of size among the great capitals of Europe, with nearly 2,000,000 inhabitants, and yet this mass of humanity, in addition to the rigours of the climate and the insalubrity of the situation, is obliged to put up with primitive arrangements for the disposal of sewage which in these days constitute nothing less than a national scandal. These arrangements may be briefly referred to as a system of filthy cesspools in the back yards of all houses, with rough wooden carts to carry away the contents at night and pollute the atmosphere by the operation. At the same time, as though this were not enough, the citizens are supplied with water which nobody valuing his or her life dares to drink unboiled, and which is drawn from a river contaminated by human dirt and teeming with bacteria and the vibrion of cholera. This is the Russian scientific opinion of the beautiful, fast-running, and limpid stream of the Neva during the cholera epidemic of 1909.

The situation Dobson was describing was far from the lyrical descriptions of the Neva water found in so many British accounts from the eighteenth century up to the first decades after the Crimean War. The Neva had inevitably fallen victim to the vast population increase, to the proliferation of factories and mills along its banks and its tributaries, to the woefully inadequate infrastructure. It was only fifty years earlier that a bill had been passed in Britain to build a proper sewer system, devised by the Victorian engineer Sir Joseph Bazalgette, which put paid to cholera and typhoid. At last there were signs in St Petersburg that the new government under Prime Minister Stolypin was intent on tackling problems that other major European capitals had long since faced. This was a view shared by Williams:

All imaginable defects of city government are, in fact, well represented in St Petersburg. After 1906 the population of the city grew restive under the misgovernment of the Council, the last cholera epidemic intensified the general discontent, and during recent elections the party of reforms has succeeded, in spite of the inequalities of the franchise, in securing a majority which includes a number of professional men and deputies and former deputies of the Imperial Duma. This new majority has pledged itself to effect a thorough renovation of the city. The changes in the City Council, the growing divergency between the burgesses and the governing classes, the increasing manifestations of individual taste in the architecture of private houses, the feverish building activity that has marked recent years, the general rise in the standard of comfort, indicate a growing determination to escape from the old abstractions and generalisations that have hitherto formed the staple of life in St Petersburg, and to live a full, many-coloured, many-sided life.

Williams was, however, a great admirer of the classical image of St Petersburg:

Catherine and Alexander I in determining the architecture of the capital followed Greek and Roman models. And the sternness, the severity of outline thus attained is entirely in accord with the predominantly abstract character of the city. It expressed the true St Petersburg. Buildings, especially churches, erected during the nineteenth century in a pseudo-Russian style are out of harmony with the St Petersburg character. St Petersburg is far less than itself when, instead of being broadly, powerfully, and imperially Russian, it sinks into a narrow and exclusive nationalism, forgets its native dignity and the manifold responsibilities of Empire, and, aspiring to be another Moscow, chills warm Russian nationalism into something lifeless and oppressive.

St Petersburg has its own very strongly marked style which aberrations mostly dating from the latter half of the nineteenth century spoil at many points but cannot obscure. This style finds its fullest expression on the Neva quays and in their neighbourhood. The long, dark-red façade of the Winter Palace with its outlook on the Neva, the iron gates and the fine iron railings around the Winter Palace garden – the beauty of St Petersburg is very suggestive of the beauty of fine iron-work – the Admiralty with its arched entrances and its spire whose graceful upward movement is a relief from the prevailing massivity of the capital, the long sweep of palaces and embassies along the Neva above the Winter Palace, the equestrian statue of Peter the Great in the Senate Square – these constitute the nucleus of the city. On the side of the Winter Palace, a fine open space which, with an admirable sense of fitness, is kept perfectly clear, except for one slender and lofty column in the centre commemorative of the victory over Napoleon in 1812, a column which expresses in its fine self-restraint the very best in the St Petersburg spirit. The column is the one architectural feature in St Petersburg suggestive of clear aspiration. Opposite the Winter Palace in the Palace Square are the Foreign Office and the War Office, the two ministries naturally most closely associated with the Monarch in the maintenance of a sovereignty essentially military in character. The Ministry of Finances is close at hand. An archway which pierces the line of government offices leads out from this centre of power into the business part of the city. It in the neighbourhood of the Winter Palace, the Hermitage, the Foreign Office, and that Bridge of Singers that leads over the Moika Canal to the buildings of the Court Choir that the impression of St Petersburg is strongest and most intimate. It is an impression of power firmly and consciously grasped. And this impression is strongest when the Palace, the Column, and the Ministries stand alone in the emptiness of the Square. The presence of human masses does not add to it.

Unlike the art critic Beavington Atkinson who loved nothing so much as the onion dome and the 'national' (however bogus), Williams was firmly opposed to aberrations on the city's skyline. He does not name the Church of the Resurrection (*Voskreseniia Khristova khram*), popularly known as the Saviour on the Blood (*Spas na krovi*), but undoubtedly had it clearly in his sights. Although it imitated the familiar outlines of the famous St Basil's on Moscow's Red Square, its rich external and internal mosaics and décor were the responsibility of a cohort of Russia's foremost artists, including Vasnetsov, Nesterov and Vrubel'. Begun back in 1883 as a monument to the assassinated Alexander II, it was only completed in 1907, when it was seen by A. MacCallum Scott during a short visit to the Russian capital:

> On the spot where Alexander fell, on the bank of the Ekaterininski Canal, over the paving stones stained with his blood, a magnificent memorial church has been erected, in the most characteristic Russian style, with a fantastic array of brilliantly coloured domes and cupolas. The Church of the Resurrection, dedicated to the memory of the Royal Martyr, is one of the most splendid sights in St. Petersburg. The work of decorating it never seems to be ended. In the Royal lapidary works at Ekaterinburg, in the Urals, workmen are still employed cutting and polishing granite, marble, and precious stones for this shrine. Many of them have been employed for years upon a single stone.

A year later, Etta Close, a Fellow of the Royal Geographical Society *en route* to Siberia, attended a service there:

> Tired of being pushed about amongst the crowds in the older churches, we one day found our way into the modern one built over the spot in one of the main streets where Czar Alexander was killed by a bomb as he was passing along in his sledge.
>
> The low September sun was pouring in through the windows when we entered; it lit up the priceless marbles with which the church is lined, especially one that is plum colour, with what appear to be small pieces of blue butterfly wings floating in it. Round the sides of the church are sacred pictures, many of them hung with strings of real pearls and other jewels, and in the midst of all this splendour, enclosed by a low bronze railing, is the six feet of the common cobblestones of the street where the Czar was murdered.

While we were gazing at this sermon without words a procession of priests and singers filed in, elderly men whose long black beards fell to their waists over their white woollen habits; they ranged themselves round the bronze railings and, without any accompaniment, one of the choir opened with a low deep note, which was taken up by another, and then another, until the sound, like that of a great organ, filled the whole of the vast church and lost itself in the cupolas far above our heads. Nothing could have been more impressive. When the deep bass voices died away, a priest intoned a prayer, and again the choir took up their Gregorian chant, and the volume of sound again filled every corner of the church.

In contrast, it was to a more distant and venerable church standing since Petrine times that Somerset Maugham, sent to Petrograd on a 'secret mission' in the revolutionary days of 1917, was drawn. His diary entry reads:

The Lavra of Alexander Nevsky. As you reach the end of the Nevsky Prospekt it grows shabbier and more dingy. The houses have the bedraggled look of those on the outskirts of a town, they suggest a sordid mystery, until the street ends abruptly in an oddly unfinished way and you come to the gateway of the monastery. You enter. There is a cemetery on each side of you and then you cross a narrow canal and come to the most unexpected scene in the world. It is a great quadrangle. Grass grows fresh and green as though you were in the country. On one side is a chapel and the cathedral and them, all around, the low white buildings of the monastery. There is something exquisitely strange in their architecture; the decoration is very simple and yet gives a sensation of being ornate; they remind you of a Dutch lady of the seventeenth century, soberly but affluently dressed in black. There is something prim about them, but not at all demure. In the birch trees rooks were cawing, and my recollection was carried back to the precincts of Canterbury; for there the rooks cawed too; it is a sound that never fails to excite my melancholy. I think of my boyhood, unhappy through the shyness which made me feel lonely among a crowd of boys, and yet rich with vague dreams of the future. The same grey clouds hung overhead. I felt homesick. I stood on the steps of the Greek church, looking at the long line of the monastery buildings, the leafless birches, but I saw the long nave of Canterbury cathedral with its flying buttresses and the central tower more imposing and lovely to my moved eyes than any tower in Europe.

The real attraction at the Lavra was, however, the grave of Fedor Dostoevskii:

It is surrounded by a neat iron railing and the plot of ground is neatly laid with sand. In one corner stands a huge round case with a glass front, containing an enormous wreath of artificial flowers, prim white roses and lilies of the valley larger than life; it is tied with a great bow and there is a long silk streamer on which is an inscription in gold letters. I wish the grave were as neglected, covered with fallen leaves, as are those that surround it. Its tidiness is distressingly vulgar. The bust is placed against a granite stele, a shapeless thing carved with meaningless emblems, and it gives you an uncomfortable feeling that it is on the point of toppling over.

It is a face devastated by passion. The dome of the head is stupendous and evokes irresistibly the thought of a world great enough to contain the terrible throng of his creatures. The ears are large, protruding, with the heavy lobes of the sensualist; the mouth is sensual too, with a cruel pout, but a pout like that of a sorrowful child; the cheeks are hollow, the temples deeply sunken; beard and moustache are long, bedraggled and unkempt; the long hair is lank; there is a great mole on the forehead and another on the cheek. There is agony in that face, something terrible that makes you want to turn away and that yet holds you fascinated. His aspect is more terrifying than all his works. He has the look of a man who has been in hell and seen there, not a hopeless suffering, but meanness and frippery.

This was the period when Britain was in the throes of Russomania and overwhelmed by Henry James's 'baggy monsters', the novels of Tolstoi and Dostoevskii, reaching the British public in ever increasing numbers of translations since the end of the nineteenth century, frequently in the versions of Constance Garnett. One English novelist able to imbibe Dostoevskii's St Petersburg at first hand was Hugh

Walpole, who arrived in September 1914 as correspondent for the *Daily Mail*, became an officer in the Russian Red Cross at the Carpathian Front, and finished up as Head of British propaganda in Petrograd, before leaving finally on 8 November 1917. The distillation of his Petersburg experience was the novel *The Secret City* (1919), his version of the 'Petersburg myth', in which the literary influences of Pushkin's *Bronze Horseman*, Dostoevskii, and Andrei Belyi's novel *Petersburg* are all too obvious. While Walpole's St Petersburg is not consistently Dostoevskii's, it embodies what may be said to be his understanding of Dostoevskii's 'fantastic realism' and of St Petersburg as 'the most fantastic city'. In the following passage he describes the area around the Hay Market (*Sennaia ploshchad'*):

> We had passed quickly on leaving the Market into some of the meanest streets of Petrograd. This was the Petrograd of Dostoeffsky, the Petrograd of 'Poor Folk' and 'Crime and Punishment' and 'The Despised and Rejected.' . . . Monstruous groups of flats towered above us, and in the gathering dusk the figures that slipped in and out of doors were furtive shadows and ghosts. No one seemed to speak; you could see no faces under the spare pale-flamed lamps, only hear whispers and smell rotten stinks and feel the snow, foul and soiled under one's feet.

There are many set pieces in the novel devoted both to familiar and much less-known areas of the city, none more vivid than a passage in which the narrator, during an illness, gives a bird's eye view of the city and, in particular, of Nevskii Prospekt:

> I was conscious also of Petrograd, of the town itself, in every one of its amazingly various manifestations. I saw it all laid out as though I were a great height above it – the fashionable streets, the Nevski and the Morskaia with the carriages and the motor-cars and trams, the kiosks and the bazaars, the women with their baskets of apples, the boys with the newspapers, the smart cinematographs, the shop in the Morskaia with the coloured stones in the window, the oculist and the pastry-cooks and the hairdressers and the large 'English shop' at the corner of the Nevski, and Pivato's the restaurant, and close beside it the art shop with popular past cards and books on Serov and Vrubel, and the Astoria

Hotel with its shining windows staring on to S. Isaac's Square. And I saw the Nevski, that straight and proud street, filled with every kind of vehicle and black masses of people, rolling like thick clouds up and down, here and there, the hum of their talk rising like mist from the snow. And there was the Kazan Cathedral, haughty and proud, and the book shop with the French books and complete sets of Tchekov and Merejkowsky in the window, and the bridges and the palaces and the square before the Alexander Theatre, and Elisseieff's the provision shop, and all the banks, and the shops with gloves and shirts, all looking ill-fitting as though they were never meant to be worn, and then the little dirty shops poked in between the grand ones, the shop with rubber goods and the shop with an Aquarium, gold-fish and snails and a tortoise, and the shop with oranges and bananas. Then, too, there were the Arcade with the theatre where they acted *Romance* and *Potash and Perlmutter* (almost as they do in London), and on the other side of the street, at the corner of the Sadovia, the bazaar with all its shops and its trembling mist of people. I watched the Nevski, and saw how it slipped into the Neva with the Red Square on one side of it, and S. Isaac's Square on the other, and the great station at the far end of it, and about these two lines, the Neva and the Nevski, the whole town sprawled and crept, ebbed and flowed. Away from the splendour it stretched, dirty and decrepit and untended, here piles of evil flats, there old wooden buildings with cobbled courts, and the canals twisting and creeping up and down through it all. It was all bathed, as I looked down upon it, in coloured mist. The air was purple and gold and light blue, fading into the snow and ice and transforming it. Everywhere there were the masts of ships and the smell of the sea and rough deserted places – and shadows moved behind the shadows, and yet more shadows behind *them*, so that it was all uncertain and unstable, and only the river knew what it was about.

The Neva and the canals are everywhere in Walpole's novel, concealing monsters in their depths, threatening to inundate the city, but always scenes of beauty:

Outside the cold air was intense. I walked to the end of the Quay and leaned on the stone parapet. The Neva seemed vast like a huge, white, impending shadow; it swept in a colossal wave of frozen ice out to the far horizon, where tiny, twinkling lights met it and closed it in. The bridges that crossed it held forth their lights, and there were the gleams, like travelling stars, of the passing trams, but all these were utterly insignificant against the vast body of the contemptuous ice. On the farther shore the buildings rose in a thin, tapering line, looking as though they had been made of black tissue-paper, against the solid weight of the cold, stony sky. The Peter and Paul Fortress, the towers of the Mohammedan Mosque were thin, immaterial, ghostly, and the whole line of the town was simply a black pencilled shadow against the ice, smoke that might be scattered with one heave of the force of the river. The Neva was silent, but beneath that silence beat what force and power, what contempt and scorn, what silent purposes?

(The mosque, incidentally, which Walpole mentions as prominent against the skyline, was built in 1910–14 on Kronverkskii Prospekt (present-day Gor'kii Prospekt) on the Petersburg Side or District. It was one of many new religious buildings appearing in the city: the Great Synagogue was opened in 1893 and a Buddhist temple in 1909–15.)

The Neva was always central to the impact the city produced on visitors and residents alike. Williams better than most evokes its significance and the attraction:

Without the Neva the city would be stiff and sombre, petrified in the consciousness of power. The Neva gives life and light and motion. Just above the city it takes a sudden bend and then its main stream flows out broad and majestic to the sea, sending off branches to the north-west and so forming islands on which part of the city and the suburbs are built. On the Neva the palaces, the St Isaac's Cathedral, the Bourse, and the Academies all gain the necessary perspective and relief. The river brings down a tremendous volume of water from that inland sea, Lake Ladoga, to the Baltic, and brings it down in a swift current. This swiftly-flowing mass of water and that fine expanse of sky which the river keeps clear right in the centre of the city have a liberating effect. They make distance sensible, real, and visible. The current is motion amidst immobility, a perpetual and living reminder of connections and relationships, of possible comings and goings, of the spontaneity in things that is so easily forgotten in the streets beyond the quays. Glorious sunsets are to be seen across the Neva, and the river broadening out below the quays leads into Western skies and the eager progress of the Western world. The river is incessant motion and stately impetus. And never is the feeling of liberation so strong as when the ice comes down in the spring. Gaps in the ice widen, the ice surfaces break and crumble, lose their brilliant white, become heaped-up clumps of dirt grey, and when at last their hold is loosed and the stream at last gains power, the tumbled mass yields to the mighty constraint and changes its immobility for movement, at first slow and uncertain, and then as it breaks up into floes and the floes collide and break and melt and the ice under the banks is loosened, the dark waters of the river appear at last after the long oblivion of the winter, and crags and patches and whirling blocks are borne down in the triumphant sweep of the current to be lost in the sea. And in the early days of spring the Neva, just freed from the ice, is majestic and powerful as at no other time of the year.

The Neva is all motion. But for all its vitality and volume it is almost motion in the abstract. There is little traffic on it in the region of the city. The port is at the mouth of the river and probably many residents have never seen it. Smaller coastal vessels, the steamers that ply to Reval, Riga, and Libau, to Helsingfors and Stockholm, berth under the Nicholas Bridge, the last of the bridges down stream. But higher up there are only the darting ferry-boats and the few steamers that maintain the Ladoga and Onega service and barges from the interior, though the barges mostly prefer the branches of the river and the canals, and rarely appear in large numbers in the main stream. The busy movement of human traffic is lacking, and the impression of pure motion given by the river is not diffused amongst the endless minutiae of human activities. It remains an impression of great possibilities, of latent power, of large scope for development. It reinforces by its vivid suggestiveness that sense of abstractness which dominates in the city.

In his poem on the city Oscar Browning predicted St Petersburg's 'new worlds in letters, music, life, and art', but he was writing at the very time of Russia's 'Silver Age', a blossoming of the arts – of painting and architecture, music and ballet, theatre, poetry and publishing. It was a time also of the flourishing of salon and café culture, as Dobson had noted. Nonetheless, there are few British contemporary accounts of the cultural life of the period, but there are pages worth quoting for their record of meetings with outstanding artists or of theatres or salons visited. Rothay Reynolds, yet another British correspondent in the Russian capital at the beginning of the century, was the author of two weighty volumes in 1913 and 1916. In the first, *My Russian Year*, he writes amusingly of the famous Mariinskii Theatre:

The fashionable world of St. Petersburg is comparatively small. The stranger who wants to see it should go to the ballet at the Marinsky Theatre on a Sunday night. Every opera-house is impregnated with the spirit of the city in which it is found. Foreigners leave Covent Garden on a big night, staggered by the richness, the luxury, and the elegance of the scene. In Berlin the people at the opera are so badly dressed that one is half surprised that they do not rise and depart in a body to show their disapproval of Salome or the Rosen Kavalier. Women dressed like the people in Ibsen's plays wander into the sumptuous foyer of the opera-house in Stockholm and look unhappy in a room that is shrieking for diamonds and the frivolities of the mode. There is repose in the Fenice Theatre, where the delicate loveliness of the Venetian ladies is framed in the faded gold of the boxes, like the portraits of bygone beauties. And the Marinsky Theatre has a character of its own. The scene in the house is less splendid than at Covent Garden, but more animated. The jewels are less magnificent, but the uniforms of officers, Court pages, and boys from the privileged schools make a blaze of colour in stalls and boxes. The entr'actes are long, and many people spend the time walking up and down the corridor behind the stalls and chatting to their friends. The foyer upstairs is left to those who know no better than to walk round it in a great circle. People from any part of the house can go there, and it is amusing to stand and watch them, but it would ruin a fashionable reputation to be seen promenading with them. The middle-class Russian has sketchy ideas of the proper way to dress, and I have seen some unbelievable disguises in the foyer of the opera. The most extravagant was a black frock-coat, a white evening waistcoat, a scarlet necktie in a sailor's knot, and light trousers. A cherry-coloured bow with an up-and-down collar, in conjunction with a dinner-jacket and brown boots, was another pleasing get up. It is a great responsibility for an Englishman in St. Petersburg to dress himself. Young Russians are apt to regard him as a living substitute for the fashion plates their tailors receive from London.

It is in his second volume, entitled *My Slav Friends*, that he gives an altogether more interesting account of his meeting with the famous actress Vera Komissarzhevskaia, who had graced the stage of the Aleksandrinskii Theatre (see chapter 5) for a few years at the turn of the century in such roles as Nina in Chekhov's *Seagull*, before deciding to establish her own theatre. In 1904 the New Dramatic Theatre (widely known as Komissarzhevskaia's Theatre) opened on Italian Street and staged premières of plays by Maksim Gor'kii, before moving two years later to new premises on Officer Street (now Decembrists' Street). Reynolds had seen her act for the first time in her famous role of Beatrice in Maeterlink's *Sister Beatrice* at the Aleksandrinskii, but it was at her new theatre that he first met her:

I was shown into her sanctum. It looked like a man's study. There was a desk with a roll-top and many books. A little woman with a colourless face and colourless hair came in. It was the great actress. She wore a plain stuff dress, the sort of dress a woman who is too much engrossed in helping the poor to trouble about clothes may have worn. She was not beautiful, but the sweetness of her expression, her air of gentleness, gave her a charm which one felt and found difficult to analyze. She sat down in a great basket-chair and learnt back, looking too fragile and too weary to get out of it again. I thought of all this when I saw her as Magda and she flashed on to the stage, brilliant, animated, vivacious. [...]

It [the Dramatic Theatre] was not in the least like any other theatre in Europe: a long hall, with unornamented white walls, a few boxes on a level with the stage, a gallery, supported on white pillars, running round three sides. A first night was extraordinarily interesting. French actresses from the Michail Theatre in the front row, a little bewildered, gave a touch of elegance to the house; but Vera Feordorovna did not trouble to invite the fashionable world, she asked men and women whom she believed to be striving for progress in letters, in politics, in the sister arts, as she was in the art of the theatre. It was the makers of a new world who met together, the men and women who are moulding the mind of the nation, standing aloof from the official and diplomatic society, the fashionable world of Petrograd. In the gallery were the children of the New Russia, students, student girls, and never has an actress found the gods more propitious to her than did Vera Feordorovna.

It was at exactly the same period that there flourished one of the most famous of St Petersburg's literary salons, hosted by the Symbolist poet Viacheslav Ivanov and his wife and frequented by leading writers and artists. Their apartment, known as the 'Tower' (*Bashnia*) was at No. 25 Taurida Street (*Tavricheskaia ulitsa*) and adjoining, as the name suggests, Potemkin's Taurida Palace and Gardens, which after the Revolution of 1905 became home to the State Duma. The Ivanovs not only entertained their friends but rented out rooms to long-stay guests who included Mikhail Kuzmin – and Bernard, later Sir Bernard, Pares. Pares, who later did so much to establish Russian studies in the universities of Britain, had been visiting Russia since 1898 and was a member of the press corps observing the workings of the Duma. It was in 1907 that he stayed with the Ivanovs for the opening of the Second Duma:

The Duma thus elected met on 5th March 1907. I arrived almost at the start, and only missed five sittings in all, of which three were held with closed doors. I wanted to be close to the Duma, and engaged a room in the flat of the distinguished poet, Vyacheslav Ivanov; he was married to a delightful authoress who wrote under her maiden name of Lydia Zinoyev-Annibal. The Ivanovs' flat was known as the Tower, and served as a meeting place for a number of the most distinguished writers of the time. Here I met Alexander Blok, a young Apollo and the greatest poet of his generation; the dreamy-looking Andrey Bely; the bearded religious thinker, Nicholas Berdiayev; and the eccentric novelist, Kuzmin, who lived in the flat. Kuzmin was a wonderful musician, and about three o'clock in the morning he would play the Appassionata of Beethoven on a fine piano, only just the other side of a door in my room, against which lay my bed; but it would have been quite impossible to have been anything but grateful to him. The family and their friends used to sit up all night, reading out to each other from their latest works, as yet unpublished, and criticising them in common. They begged me not to sing when I was in my bath in the morning, because that was the time when they were just going to bed. It was an exceptional and in some ways an eccentric environment, but it served admirably to balance the hysteria which filled the life of the poor Second Duma.

Ivanov's wife died a few months after Pares's visit, but the 'Ivanov Wednesdays' continued until Ivanov's departure from the capital in 1912. It was in that year that the legendary literary cabaret, 'The Stray Dog' (*Brodiachaia sobaka*) began its activities.

'The Stray Dog', founded as a club, meeting-place and stage for all interested in experimental art and attracting some of the outstanding poets, painters and musicians of the period, was located in the cellars of the second courtyard of house No. 5 on Michael Square (*Mikhailovskaia ploshchad'*, now *ploshchad' Iskusstv*). It was visited by H.J. Bruce, Head of Chancery at the British Embassy since 1913 and amateur painter, whose wife, the great ballerina Tamara Karsavina, introduced him to Alexander Benois and who was 'usually herself busy in declaiming somebody else's poetry from the little stage'. The twenty-one-year old C.E. Bechhofer, who was later to produce important translations from contemporary Russian literature, was also taken to the cabaret by Russian friends in 1915:

From the studio we went on to the 'Stray Dog,' which we reached at four in the morning. Its little cellars were draped and covered with paintings and patterns: Pierrot, Columbine and Harlequin; the poet's miserable life and fate; Don Quixote and his jade; the bourgeois with his gramophone and novel; and other phantasies. A bright fire burned in the grate; someone was playing the piano – ragtime; a poetess was reciting sentimental verses to an audience of officers and actresses. A youth with a powdered face and a stiff swallow-tailed collar asked his friends not to press him to read his poems now; 'in twenty minutes' – very good, said they; 'in a quarter of an hour' – our poet felt their lack of interest and attempted to revive them – 'well, as they so much desired it, in ten minutes – well, if they must' – and they began half-heartedly to applaud – 'very well, now.' He climbed upon the stage, called for silence, and began to squeak with his treble voice, 'Yes, dear, I will give myself to you to-night. 'Tis the hour, and I am prepared. I am more interesting than ever to-night' – he finished at last, was applauded and laughed at, regarded himself in the glass, patted his hair and smoothed his eyebrows and sat down. Everything was very thin – no wine, only tea and lemonade and omelettes and apples. And all the while a persistent voice in my ear, 'Why are you so silent? Oh, you say nothing. You are always thinking, always dreaming. And I am like a princess imprisoned in a castle; without ecstasy I cannot exist. Oh, you still say nothing. You are a dull Englishman.'

Then there entered a young volunteer – a poet fresh from the War. He recited a poem he had made on the field. It was quite good. 'I feel I cannot die,' was the burden, 'I feel the heart of my country beating through my pulse. I am its incarnation, and I cannot die.'

The young poet was Nikolai Gumilev, the first husband of Anna Akhmatova and leader of the so-called Acmeist Poets.

Perhaps not unexpectedly, there is a rich literature of meetings with some of outstanding political figures of the period during these years of political upheaval and revolution. Figures at the Court from the tsar downwards, members of the Duma and the Government, the choice is endless. There are many attempts to characterize Nicholas II and his consort, and while many are hostile, particularly those dating from the last years of his reign, there is in English accounts sympathy for a man who impressed not as a an absolute ruler but as a kind and caring pater-familias. Bernard Pares, along with Harold Williams and Maurice Baring, the best informed of British commentators with an easy command of Russian and years spent in Russia, met the tsar on several occasions and recorded his impressions on the occasion of the visit to St Petersburg in 1912 of a Parliamentary delegation, of which he was the secretary.

The Emperor's English was perfect and absolutely natural; indeed, it was the language in which he spoke and wrote to his wife, and to speak it must have given him a feeling of home. Practically all who have seen him closely agree that he had a remarkable personal charm, proceeding from an almost feminine delicacy which made him in advance anticipate the moods and feelings of anyone with whom he was conversing. It was not at all the official manner of sovereigns. On the contrary, it was extremely simple, and the feeling which it produced in me was curiously enough, one of pity. One saw his intelligence, one felt his weakness, and there was a certain quick movement of the head which suggested that he had a constant sense of insecurity. At the end of his long talk with us, he said very simply: 'Would you like to see my family?' The children were brought in, grouped together as if to be photographed, and a very charming family they were. This, we were told, was the greatest compliment he could possibly have paid us, and if one realises that the imperial family lived almost completely isolated, even from many of their own relations, and that every meal was a family meal, one could appreciate this compliment. Several of us were struck by the lack of distinction at Tsarskoe Selo – in the pictures, and in the faces of the courtiers. Except for the signs of wealth, it looked humdrum and ordinary; it was not a Court that drew distinction from the culture of the nation which it was there to represent.

As for the other 'celebrities', let two cameos suffice, one of which simply has to be of Rasputin. The young Bechhofer, who described himself as 'the only Englishman whom Rasputin ever kissed', records a meeting he contrived with the 'mad monk' at his flat at No. 64 Gorokhovaia Street (the middle of the three radials starting from the Admiralty):

The longer I remained in Russia the more I felt inclined to see this strange man for myself. I made careful inquiries, and at last found a way of reaching Rasputin, unapproachable though he was supposed to be. One morning I procured a copy of his book, *My Thoughts*, a diary of his journey to the Holy Land, which had just been published in a hole-and-corner way. When I had looked through it, I went to the flat of one of Rasputin's intimate acquaintances and rang up the telephone number he gave me. A gruff voice answered, and, by good luck, it was Rasputin himself. I hastily explained that I had been reading his book, and, as a foreigner, had been particularly impressed by his pleas for the unity of Christendom; could I come to hear more of this from him? He told me to come at once, and, after a certain time, I called at No. 64 in the

Gorokhavaya, where I knew Rasputin lived. When I rang the bell of the flat, the door was opened on a chain, and a slut of about fourteen asked me what I wanted. I recognised her from descriptions as Rasputin's daughter and housekeeper; after a parley she shut the door on me and went to make inquiries. While she was gone, a man approached me from the stairs, obviously a plain-clothes detective. He told me that it was useless to wait; Rasputin never received visitors. Then he rang the bell in a peculiar way, and was at once admitted by the girl. I waited a little while, and went away. I again telephoned to Rasputin, who promised to admit me. Surely enough, when I called again half an hour later, I was admitted at once and led into a kind of waiting-room. As I sat there, various important-looking men came out from a conference with Rasputin, and one or two ladies in fashionable clothes were admitted to the flat. After about a quarter of an hour, Rasputin came to me. He wore a not very clean blue blouse, breeches, and top boots, like a peasant, and walked with a clumsy roll. He drew up a chair in front of me and leaned forward on it, so that our eyes were less than a foot apart. I asked one or two questions, and he delivered emphatic answers not much to the point. He spoke the rather archaic Russian of the Church and the monasteries, and illustrated his meaning by waves and passes of his hands. These, combined with the closeness of his very bright and expressive eyes, made me feel a little uncomfortable. He had also the knack of answering my question before I had quite finished asking it, which is a very effective trick, and one not practised by Rasputin alone. Occasionally, he was inaccurate in guessing the unspoken rest of my questions; but, on the whole, he showed considerable shrewdness.

To be faced by two piercing eyes not a foot away from your own is excessively disconcerting; when, in addition, the person to whom the eyes belong is sitting in his own stuffy and (to you) unfamiliar room, and is making mesmeric passes with his hands, there is every excuse for confusion. I cannot deny that I felt horribly uncomfortable; finally, I pulled myself together with the thought that at least Rasputin could not be clairvoyant, since he did not realise my real purpose in coming to him. This notion saved me from losing my nerve, and I held out to the end of the conversation. I asked him to give me formal permission to translate his book. He did so and signed it; it is a curious and almost undecipherable scrawl.

As I said, we kissed when we parted, and he invited me to call again without the slightest desire that I should do so. I might have doubted the evidence of my eyes and ears, and have been so much impressed by his certainly hypnotic (if not clairvoyant) powers as to believe in his prophetic nature – had he not written that hopeless book. 'And I saw with my own eyes,' he wrote, 'that the Turks wear the same clothes as Christians and Jews. For the fulfilment of the word of Our Lord is at hand, that there shall be one orthodox Church without distinction of dress.' I agree that Rasputin did not write all the book, nor half of it, but he certainly claimed the authorship with considerable pride when I was speaking to him. He assured me that it was a good book, but I had already assured myself that it was a very foolish one – and that, there-fore, Rasputin was in sufficiently important respects a foolish man. I found him shrewd and probably hypnotic, but neither clairvoyant nor wise. And this, I think, is probably the true estimate of Rasputin.

As a coda to Bechofer's interview with Rasputin is Walpole's attempt to weave news of Rasputin's murder in December 1916 into the brooding atmosphere of his novel:

It was the evening of Rasputin's murder. The town of course talked of nothing else – it had been talking, without cessation, since two o'clock that afternoon. The dirty, sinister figure of the monk, with his magnetic eyes, his greasy beard, his robe, his girdle, and all his other properties, brooded gigantic over all of us. He was brought into immediate personal relationship with the humblest, most insignificant creature in the city, and with him incredible shadows and shapes, from Dostoeffsky, from Gogol, from Lermontov, from Nekrasov – from whom you please – all the shadows of whom one is eternally aware in Russia – faced us and reminded us that they were not shadows but realities.

In sober contrast, Pares's memoirs record unsensationally his numerous encounters with, and assessments of, all the leading politi-cians of the 1910s. He met Aleksandr Kerenski, the barrister who rose to be Prime Minister of the Provisional Government, on many occasions and wrote with admiration of his oratory and with reservation about his true significance:

I never set the same exaggerated value on Kerensky as was commonly set at this the highest point of his power [May–July 1917]. Why should one? Up to March of this very year he could have no experience whatsoever of administration. He was a fearless young lawyer and a really fine speaker. He could always touch the hearts of those whom he addressed by his simple and eloquent simplicity, and he always knew how far he could carry his audience with him. 'Is this a revolution,' he once asked, 'or is it a rising of slaves?' and it took some courage to say that. In appearance he was extremely simple and looked very young. His principal mentor, it was said, was that wonderfully plucky old lady, Catherine Breshko-Breshkovsky, called the grandmother of the Russian Revolution, who had been one of the Narodniks of the seventies, and was never daunted or depressed by a lifetime of political persecution and imprisonment. He was reputed to base his speeches on those of Danton, but how different was this slight, emotional boy from the towering front and figure of the Montagnard! Kerensky did a first-class service at a most difficult moment – at the outset of the revolution – when he decided, in spite of the prohibition of the Soviet, to take office with the Provisional Government, thus acting as the only possible link between the two bodies, for he was a Member of the Duma, and a Vice-President of the Soviet. He went straight off to the Soviet after disobeying its orders, and by a fearless avowal he won its approval. There were moments in his premiership when he showed equally high courage and intelligence. But the speech was almost his only weapon, and no one on earth could have mastered the chaos all around him by that alone. After all, he had pleaded all his life for liberty, and he was not going to be the first to cut it short.

The outbreak of war and the turmoil that followed marked the end of the tourist's St Petersburg. It was ironic that it was precisely in 1914 that there appeared *Russia with Teheran, Port Arthur, and Peking*, the first and only edition of the English version of Karl Baedeker's noted 'Handbook for Travellers' that would re-appear in 1971 as a historical curiosity, as a reminder of a world that was to disappear with frightening speed. 'Baedeker' briefly mentions buildings and monuments, old and new, in its succinct itineraries (there are only seventy-five pages devoted to the city as such and another twenty-five to its environs), but only one might detain us for a more detailed look at its changing fortunes and its very English associations.

Just beyond the Anichkov Bridge and Klodt's 'four colossal bronze groups of horse-tamers', much noted since their installation in 1841, there is on the right at the corner of Nevskii Prospekt and the Fontanka embankment 'an elaborate baroque structure', which, 'Baedeker' further informs us, was formerly the Palace of the Princes Belosel'skii-Belozerskii and in 1914 was the home of the Grand Duchess Elizaveta Fedorovna (which in fact it no longer was). There had been a mansion on the site since the very end of the eighteenth century but it was only after its reconstruction in the spirit of Rastrellian baroque by the court architect Andrei Shtakenshneider in 1846–8 that it became a notable Petersburg palace. In 1884 it was given by Tsar Alexander III to his brother Sergei and the palace thereafter became known as the Sergeevskii. The British connection began with Sergei's marriage to Queen Victoria's granddaughter Ella (Elizaveta Fedorovna), the elder sister of Alix, who as Aleksandra Fedorovna became the last tsaritsa. After the assassination of her husband in 1905, Elizaveta Fedorovna gave the palace to his nephew, the Grand Duke Dmitrii Pavlovich, who was to participate in the murder of Rasputin. During the last years of the First World War the palace, which was also known as the Dmitrievskii, became the home of the short-lived Anglo-Russian Hospital, established as the response of a British public and government, moved by accounts of the enormous Russian losses during the war. The hospital was officially opened on 31 January 1916 by the Dowager Empress and a Union Jack fluttered proudly from the flagpole on the roof of the palace. Stephen Paget, a doctor arriving from London to serve at the hospital at the end of 1916, describes the transformation of the palace into hospital:

> We are in the palace which once belonged to the Grand Duke Serge. One face of it looks across the canal Fontanka to the palace of the Dowager Empress. Where the road goes over the canal, there is a bridge adorned with bronze statues, men wrestling with horses. Doubtless this bridge looks well in summer: but to my thinking it must be at its best now, when snow and frost play tricks with the darkness of the bronze, and seem to heighten the conflict between the horses and the men.

The palace has two courtyards, outer and inner. The ground-floor of the palace is kept for the owner's use. The first floor is the Hospital. Above us are they whom we call 'the palace people': old servants of the household, pensioners and others, we know not how many: we meet them now and again on the back staircases, we hear voices, footsteps, drifts of balalaika-playing or of singing; we have learned to recognize one or two of our many overhead neighbours: but we do not know much about them, and it would be pleasant, some day, to be allowed to explore this settlement under which we live.

Those of us who came first, and made the Hospital as we have it now, worked through a long series of difficulties. We who come later admire what they achieved – the good arrangements, adjustments, and re-modellings; the mapping-out of new rooms with partition-walls, the covering of decorations and pictures with surface-walls, and all the difficulties overcome, and the fabric of a Hospital set within the fabric of a palace.

Out of the traffic and the crowd and the cold of Petrograd, you come, through a triple defence of glass doors, to the hall and the grand staircase. There may be staircases even more grand: but none, I think, of more beautiful design and proportion. It takes your breath away, not as do stairs at home, but with delight. The roof of the hall, and the dome over the staircase, are supported by towering white caryatid figures. They look at us, these imperturbable guardians of the palace, as if we were not worth looking at. Those that are nearest to the entrance look not at us but toward the doors, as if they were expecting a crowd of guests: the others guard the staircase. They have seen the pride of life at its height, and the grand staircase thronged with grand people: it is not surprising that they do think much of us. And they have seen tragedy: and if I had their eyes, I should see not only life but death going up and down past them and me. But they see now what they never thought to see; for it is convoys of wounded who now are guests of the palace. The wounded are brought in motor ambulances from this or that station in Petrograd, and the stretchers are laid down on the landings of the stair-case; and the dazed, cold, worn-out men lie there for a minute or two, wondering where at last they have come.

Our wards – three large and three less large – are the ballrooms and reception-rooms of the palace, all white and gold, lit with great chandeliers, and hundreds of lights on the walls. We are never tired of the magnificence of our wards. The ballrooms, which are the three large wards, open into each other by wide arches upheld by caryatides like those that guard the staircase. At the end of the largest of the wards there is an alcove, designed for an orchestra, but used now for the setting of an icon, and for a service every Saturday evening. The three reception-rooms likewise open into each other by double folding-doors, making a set of smaller wards, which are of the pleasantest size and very quiet. The six wards together take 190 patients. On the walls are carved and painted tablets, bearing the arms and the names of those [British] towns which have given one or more beds.

Prior to the opening of the Anglo-Russian Hospital, the British community in St Petersburg had responded to news of the outbreak of war by embarking on a series of voluntary aid initiatives. The wife of the British ambassador, the formidable Lady Georgina Buchanan, immediately organized a so-called Feeding Point for many of the refugees flooding into Petrograd and this was followed by a Maternity Home. In September 1914 Lady Georgina was largely responsible for the opening of the British Colony Hospital for Wounded Russian Soldiers (sometimes also known as the King George V Hospital). The hospital was located in a wing of the large Pokrovskii Hospital on the Bol'shoi Prospekt on Vasil'evskii Island. The patients marvelled at the chintz curtains, bright bedspreads, and crisp white linen and a degree of English comfort not to be found in other hospitals. The hospital continued its work until June 1917, when worsening conditions in the city led to its closure. At the beginning of January 1918 the Anglo-Russian Hospital in the Dmitrievskii Palace followed suit. The October Revolution also led to the break-up of the British Colony.

The British Colony during the reign of Nicholas II was no longer as monolithic as it had once appeared, although from the very beginning there had been social divisions, arising from class and wealth; there was more intermarriage, both with members of other foreign communities and with Russians; the edges at the perimeter were blurred, but even here a certain stubborn adherence to British traditional ways and customs was observed, even where command of the English tongue had ceded primacy to that of German and/or Russian. Illuminating insights into the community at the beginning of the twentieth century, differing perspectives and sometimes conflicting evidence are to be found in a number of accounts written by 'insiders', who were at different points in the social hierarchy.

There is no consensus about the size of the community at the turn of the century. Estimates range from four thousand ('The English folk in the capital, prior to the outbreak of war, numbered about four thousand, most of them living on the Vasilii Ostroff or in the mill districts, some in stately houses in the suburbs'), to two thousand ('The British colony in St. Petersburg in its time has numbered many thousands, but since the Crimean War its strength has gradually waned, while the German colony has proportionately increased in wealth and numbers. There are now probably about 2,000 British subjects in St. Petersburg, engaged principally in business'), and to as low as 'probably not more than four to five hundred strong'. This lowest estimate was provided by Herbert Swann, father of Donald of Flanders and Swann fame, who suggested nevertheless that a distinct line could be drawn between

> those who had integrated into Russian or Baltic German society, and those who held themselves aloof, mixing almost entirely with others of their own nationality. The head of the latter group can be said to be the British Ambassador, Sir George Buchanan, but personally I did not know any of them. When there were parties at the British Embassy, we were never invited – which perhaps was just as well, for until I was sixteen I could not speak English properly, and they knew little or no Russian or German.

Although he suggested that it was the majority in the community that became integrated into what he called 'local society', he nonetheless amusingly highlighted the identity crisis such attempts sometimes occasioned:

> My father was a typical example of those who became a part of German Baltic society. He married into a Danish–German family, and sent his children to a German school. At the same time, we spoke Russian among ourselves and tried to assimilate Russian customs and

habits. Yet Father also tried to maintain his links with his native country. He would say grace in English before dinner, though he would then immediately lapse into German or Russian. We would sometimes have English food – a Christmas pudding sent from the old country, or a Stilton cheese bought at the English shop (though Mother would then carefully remove the 'mouldy' green bits, for 'Surely that must be poisonous,' she would say).

A similar picture is painted in the memoirs of Elizabeth Hill, who became the first Professor of Slavonic Studies at Cambridge University in 1948. She was born in 1900 into a family which on her father's side had been in St Petersburg since the eighteenth century but whose mother was Russo-German and, she recalls,

spoke Russian with us, but kept insisting with a Russian accent, which we only realised was a Russian accent when we visited England in 1912, 'Children, speak English', her constant refrain. [. . .] The British side of us hybrids, strongly encouraged by my mother, was reflected in some foods: the daily porridge, often burnt because kasha, the staple diet of buckwheat, millet or barley, was cooked differently with every grain separate. No bacon for the children, but we watched our father eat bacon and eggs, and cold bacon which looked like an uninviting white lump of fat with a thin streak of meat. It seemed a revolting sort of food. Christmas with turkey and plum pudding; and Boxing Day, meaning-less in Russia, was meaningful to us who annually watched our father delight in a 'devilled' turkey leg smothered in mustard.

The Swanns and the Hills clung on to their British nationality, trying to keep English as a language and a culture alive also by sending the children off to England for schooling or stays with relatives. James Whishaw, the descendant of yet another old Petersburg family, used to spend every fourth year in England with his family, for 'we naturally did not wish our children to become what we termed "St. Petersburg" English, and I am glad to say that none of my daughters spoke with the curious accent acquired by even purely English people who rarely left the country. The accent was a peculiar one, being of a sing-song nature: I have only heard it amongst Anglo-Russians.'

English, albeit sometimes of the variety Whishaw describes, was of course the language of the British 'high society', presided over at the beginning of the century by Sir Arthur Nicolson and then by Sir George Buchanan, succeeding him as ambassador in 1910, although increasingly Yorkshire and Lancashire accents were much in evidence. James Whishaw, deciding to remove his family to England for good, clearly revealed his social prejudices in suggesting that the circle in which his daughters moved 'was diminishing very rapidly, and there were few girl friends or young men left whom we felt they should meet. The English colony itself was increasing, but this was in the direction of the factory quarters, for there were large families of Lancashire, Yorkshire and Scotch mill-managers and foremen'. Since the eighteenth century the British had owned factories and mills on Vasil'evskii Island and further afield, but it was in the post-Crimean War and Emancipation period, when St Petersburg spearheaded Russia's rapid industrialization and absorption of new technological advances, that British capital, expertise and entrepreneurial skills were at a premium and British mills and factories loomed large in the environs of the sprawling city. Some twelve kilometres towards Ladoga huge industrial complexes were developed on both sides of the Neva, but particularly on the left bank along the Schlüsselburg Road. W. Barnes Steveni, writing in 1915, commented that

> Here the Thorntons, Hubbards, the Becks and the Nevsky Stearine Company have several large mills and factories, their managers and foremen being generally Englishmen. The Russians have of late years become so skilled in the manufacture of cloth and cotton goods, and in the knowledge of machinery, that fewer Englishmen are required in these duties than was the case some years back. [...] There remain still, however, some English managers who earn princely salaries – men from Yorkshire or Lancashire, some mill-owners, who have made large fortunes. The wealthiest are the Hubbards, whose big mills are at Schlüsselberg.

The most famous of the mills was, however, on the right bank: the Thornton Woollen Mill, founded in the 1880s, stood in a vast compound, surrounded by a high fence, topped with barbed wire, where there were, according to the memoirs of the manager's daughter, also 'workers' flats, bosses' flats, and four beautiful houses – for the Thorntons, the manager (that was us [Willie Brooke]), the paymaster-treasurer-accountant (Edwin Coates) and the lawyer (that was Edwin Coates' brother)'. The British in the various compounds led a privileged life and were almost a self-contained community within the larger community in the Russian capital: 'we entertained ourselves with plays and concerts and tennis. There was a tennis court outside the compound where we had tournaments with all the English people in St. Petersburg. We all met at the English Church every Sunday in St. Petersburg; our lot used to cross the river in two ferry boatloads and go *en masse*.' A tourist to St Petersburg in 1905, Annette Meakin provides some further interesting details:

> On our way back to St. Petersburg we gave our attention to the factories, and noted, amongst other important ones, the government porcelain factory, a paper factory, a huge iron foundry, Messrs Thornton's immense cloth factory across the river, where some three thousand men are said to be employed, Messrs. Cooper and Maxwell's linen factory, and the government playing-card factory. In the steam tram which brought us back to the Nicholas station were two little English girls from the English colony, chatting away together, and making us feel as if we were on the outskirts of Manchester or Leeds rather than of St. Petersburg. Amongst the factories is a tiny English church, with its parsonage opposite, in which the factory chaplain resides, and near-by lives a retired English oculist, who practises only among the poor. There is also a school for English children, to which Russians are not admitted.

The church, as Steveni notes, was built, 'chiefly for the convenience of the mill population up the river', at Aleksandrovka on the Schlüsselburg Road, but there were also two Nonconformist chapels in the city itself, and, of course, the church on the English Embankment remained the focus for the British community, presided over by the ambassador from his ambassadorial pew. Elizabeth Hill, however, provides a far less reverential description, a child's-eye view, of Sunday matins, conducted in the years up to the October Revolution by the Rev. Bousfield Lombard:

The British Sunday meant arriving for Matins. Impossible to sit in our winter coats; these were left with the verger, Mr Woodward, always very obsequious in helping the important or self-important ladies to remove them. In we filed, in time or late, to the front of the church, which was a cold rectangular building, lofty and light. The Ambassador's pew was to the right, in front of it the choir where my brother Alfred would be singing if on holiday from his English school. The Bishop's throne was unoccupied, except for the occasional confirmation visit of the Bishop of Gibraltar, who evidently was the travelling bishop responsible also for Anglicans in Russia. The repetitive business of ritual kneeling, silent or mumbled responses, standing up to sing, or for the Creed, where at a certain point some flopped down on their knees and immediately popped up again, while others merely bobbed a curtsey, or bowed their heads solemnly, and then we sat down again. This ritual was so repetitive. The worst of all was sitting for a long time listening to the sermon, a voice coming from the pulpit, without ever being able to follow the thread because it was above our heads. I would sit facing the altar and my eye would travel automatically up above it to read the incomplete text 'The same-yes-ter-day,-to-day-and-for-ever'. This would fill me, week after week, with the deadly thought of how many years of Sundays were yester-days, the awful boredom of today, and the depressing misery of knowing the same would be repeated for ever and ever, amen.

The ambassador was also the honorary president of the New English Club on Bol'shaia Morskaia, formed to be the exclusive preserve of the British and some Americans and to promote the interests of British business. Such solid English institutions as the English shop and the English bookseller Watkin & Son on Nevskii Prospekt continued to flourish. There was also 'an English preparatory school to which their children could be sent until they were old enough to go to a public school in England'.

Where the British really made their mark, however, was in the creation and encouragement of sport and its attendant clubs and associations. 'They have also cricket and football clubs, tennis grounds, rowing clubs, etc.', wrote Steveni. 'Winter sports appeal strongly to the English. They hold skating competitions and amuse themselves by ice-yachting, ski-ing, tobogganing or hunting bears and wolves in the forests of Novgorod and Finland; also by shooting foxes on skis[!]' And, of course, the privileged few continued to play their golf at Murino, where a frequent visitor was the ambassador himself, Sir George Buchanan; indeed, on Sunday 9 September 1917 he was playing a round, while being sought in vain by a Russian Foreign Office, anxious to inform him of Kornilov's march on the capital.

It occasions little surprise that Steveni felt able to paint such an idyllic picture of life in the community, believing that its members

> show more hospitality and sociability in their daily intercourse than do their compatriots at home. Freed from the deadening effects of the strenuous existence, the struggle for life, which too often spoils Londoners for any enthusiasms when work is done, they uphold, as do other Englishmen in our colonies, some of the best traditions of the race. [...] Once these delights have been tasted, with the sense of enjoyment which is such a feature of Russian life, not many Englishmen care to return for good to their native land. Many I have known who went back, but Russia called them and they left the old home once more.

He little knew when he wrote these lines (published early in 1915) how soon the idyll would be shattered, first by war and then by revolution.

There are many pages devoted to events in the capital as law and order broke down in the last years of the First World War, written by journalists, members of the British embassy and residents. Stinton Jones, a businessman who had been in the Russian capital since November 1905, was witness to the sacking of the Astoria Hotel near St Isaac's Cathedral on 28 February/13 March 1917. The Astoria was an excellent example of Petersburg 'modern' and, designed by F.I. Lidval', had only been completed in 1912, but it had become essentially an officers' club during the war years:

> One very notable incident of this day was the sacking of the Astoria Hotel. This was the largest and most modern hotel in the city, which some months previously had been commandeered by the Military Authorities as a place of residence for officers on leave with their families, also for officers of the Allied Armies. On the previous

evening a deputation had approached the hotel and stated that, provided no resistance was offered from those in the hotel, the Revolutionists on their part would refrain from violence towards the building or its inmates.

On the Tuesday morning an enormous crowd made its way to the hotel, and a deputation was sent in to ask for the surrender of the Russian officers in the building. The deputation promised that every possible facility would be offered to the foreign officers to leave the building with their effects, and that motor-cars would be placed at their disposal. While the deputation was in the hotel a Russian general performed the mad act of firing into the crowd from one of the windows. At the same moment a machine-gunner stationed on the roof poured a stream of lead into the dense mass below, killing and wounding a large number of people.

This infuriated the mob, who returned the fire of the machine-gun with tremendous interest. They simply poured volley after volley into the building, and then rushed the place. This hotel had enormous plate-glass windows reaching to the level of the roadway. These windows were very soon broken and the crowd poured into the building, where a most terrible struggle took place, numbers being killed on either side as the Russian officers offered stout resistance. The worst of the fighting took place in the vestibule, and in a short time the big revolving doors were turning round in a pool of blood.

Quite a number of English officers were resident in the building at the time, but naturally did not attempt to join in the fighting. Their chief concern was for the women and children in the building. These they collected together and formed a guard in front of them. They then informed the mob who were in the hotel that they themselves would not in any way interfere with their programme provided that the women and children were not molested, but in such an event they would defend them to the last man. This called forth great cheers from the crowd, who promised that they would not interfere with the English or other foreign officers or any of the women and children. This promise they religiously kept, but insisted that all the Russian officers must give themselves up without further delay. This they were persuaded to do, with the result that they were all immediately placed under arrest and taken from the building.

In the square outside a number of these officers were shot, while others were taken to places of detention under a strong escort of soldiers. Several generals were taken out and shot, including him who had first fired on the crowd, and his body was thrown into the adjoining canal. The mob then looted the building, with the exception of the rooms occupied by the foreign officers. They also broke into the wine cellars, freely consuming all intoxicants. Thus very shortly quite a number of the mob and soldiers were reduced to a state of intoxication. Some of the soldiers, after they had drunk as much as they possibly could, poured the wine into their top-boots and then wandered away to consume more elsewhere.

Eight months on, the February Revolution was overtaken by the events of October. H.J. Bruce of the Embassy was staying at a flat on the Millionnaia, the street that runs from Palace Square, across the Winter Canal, towards Suvorov Square. It was the evening of Wednesday 26 October/8 November:

The last thing we heard last night (the wildest contradictory rumours were the order of those days) was that everything was going in favour of the Government and that the Revolutionary Committee had been arrested. This morning early nobody knew what had happened, though it seemed pretty clear that the Government was down and out. This became increasingly clear as the day went on, until in the evening we heard that the whole town was in the hands of the Bolsheviks who had taken the State Bank, Telephone, etc. At 7 o'clock I left the Embassy to go to the ballet where I arrived peacefully by tram. The others arrived later, having all been arrested *en route* and taken to the barracks of the Pavlovsk regiment, where they were apparently treated quite civilly and given a bit of paper to allow them to proceed. The ballet was *Casse Noisette*. T. [Karsavina] danced magnificently and had a tremendous reception. But the poor Marinsky was the ghost of itself, the stage half empty. After the ballet, T., Madame B., C. and myself went by tram up to Suvoroff Square and proceeded to walk down the Millionnaya, barred by pickets, to C.'s flat (where I had spent my early days in 1913). The first person we met was a completely unperturbed Havery [the Chancery servant] engaged in explaining to a soldier in his peerless Cockney Russian that he couldn't help his (the soldier's) troubles; he had some letters to post, battle or no battle. Everything had been quiet in the rest of town, so we were surprised to find the Lord's own holy racket going on round the Winter Palace, where the Government were putting up a last stand – field-guns, machine-guns, rifle fire, a destroyer from the river *et tout le tremblement*. Never heard such a row. Altogether the walk a very jumpy business. After supper escorted Madame B. home to a machine-gun obbligato and so to a very noisy bed.

His diary entry for the next day read simply: 'Arrived safely at the Embassy to learn that Lenin was Prime Minister, Trotzky Foreign Minister.'

The months from February to October 1917 sounded the death-knell of the British community. Meriel Buchanan, the ambassador's daughter, who had continued working as an auxiliary nurse, described how by the autumn

people began to talk of a possible bombardment of Petrograd from the sea; others made elaborate calculations as to how long it would take the Germans to reach the capital if they continued advancing and the Russians continued retreating as they were doing at that moment. Everybody who could go was leaving. Nearly all the women and children of the British Colony were being sent away, though several wives refused to leave their husbands and preferred to stay on, braving the discomforts and hardships of daily life in Petrograd. It was a tragic breaking-up of little homes, a constant bidding farewell to those who were going, leaving behind all the associations of their childhood, all the treasured possessions of many years of work and pleasure. Every Sunday the church on the English Quay got emptier, every Monday the work party at the Embassy got smaller.

One of the young daughters of a Thorntons' foreman, Dorothy Shaw (aged thirteen in October 1917) recalled that the ambassador 'had instructed the English colony to leave with dignity, as if they would soon return, which meant not scuttling with everything. We left in September (October), I was wearing all my clothes, I couldn't bend my arms at all, and I had gold sovereigns stitched into my coat lining. Mother carried her precious silver-wedding teapot'.

Meriel Buchanan also recalled the last days of the occupancy of the British embassy. The embassy occupied No. 4 Palace Embankment by the Troitskii Bridge and near the Field of Mars, a mansion which since 1863 had been rented by the British government from the Saltykov family. It was there that the ambassador and Lady Georgina hosted a final Christmas party on the eve of his recall to England at the beginning of January 1918:

The increasing stress and strain of the situation was beginning to have a serious effect on my father's health, and early in December [1917] he became so ill that the doctor declared that he would not be answerable for the consequences if he did not take a complete rest and leave Petrograd altogether. In answer to a telegram, asking for permission to come home on leave, the British Foreign Office sent back a ready agreement, at the same time urging my father not to delay but to leave for England at the first opportunity, and accordingly it was settled that we were to start as soon as the Constituent Assembly had met.

On Christmas night we invited the members of the Chancery and of the various Naval and Military Missions, as well as some of our Russian friends who had not yet left, for a party that was to prove itself, I think, the last party ever given in the British Embassy. Luckily it was an evening when the electricity was not cut off, so the great glass chandeliers blazed with light, the big rooms were crowded and filled with laughter, and though every officer present had a loaded revolver in his pocket, though there were rifles and cartridge cases hidden in the Chancery, for the moment we tried to forget the ever-present lurking danger, the sadness of approaching good-byes, the desolation and want hidden behind the heavy red brocade curtains which were drawn across the windows.

We began the evening with a variety entertainment got up by Colonel Thornton and ended with a supper, which if it did not live up to the former meals at the Embassy, was a proof of the ingenuity and astuteness of our *chef*, who had somehow been able to overcome the difficulties of obtaining provisions and had managed to send up an extraordinary variety of dishes. We danced old Russian folk-dances, we sang English songs, we drank each other's health and wished each other a Merry Christmas and a happy meeting in England during the coming year. We tried to believe in the infallibility of that meeting, we tried to keep away the thought of danger or sorrow, but the shadow of death was very near some of the men who were there that night and it was impossible not to feel a chill of foreboding, a presage of tragedy, underlying the wishes for 'Good Luck' on heard on every side. Cromie, Valentine, Dennis Garstin, these were never to reach England alive. The Russian officer who sat next to me at supper was imprisoned by the Bolsheviks scarcely a month later and was tortured to death. The husband of the friend with whom I stayed in the country was murdered by the peasants on his estate. Princess Soltikoff with her white hair and beautiful tragic eyes, was to die of want and starvation within the year. Even the Embassy was not to escape the relentless fury of the Red Terror; sweating, expectorating soldiers were to invade the big rooms, silence and decay were to follow, mildew rotting the heavy brocade curtains, dust griming the windows, burst pipes spoiling the silk-covered walls.

A few days after Christmas my father had a bad relapse and the doctor urged the need for his immediate departure and we therefore decided not to wait for the opening of the Constituent Assembly, and after some difficulties with Trotsky our departure was finally fixed for January 8th [1918].

The attempt to establish some *modus vivendi* with the new regime saw the British government send Bruce Lockhart to Moscow as its unofficial diplomatic agent, but during the summer allied troops landed in North Russia and soon afterwards in Vladivostok. The ill-fated Intervention had begun. Suspicions of Lockhart's activities led to the sacking of the Petrograd embassy on 18/31 August (the day after the assassination of the Cheka boss Uritskii), when the British naval attaché, Captain F.N.A. Cromie, was shot dead by Red Guards, and to the arrest of Lockhart three days later.

CHAPTER 8

THE CITY FROM REVOLUTION
TO CLOSURE, 1917–38

St Petersburg had become Petrograd on 18/31 August 1914, a patriotic change to emphasize the Russian rather than the German resonance, while preserving the name of the city's founder. The change from Petrograd to Leningrad on 24 January 1924, three days after the death of Lenin, banished Peter and substituted the name of the Bolshevik leader, who had *de facto* deprived the city of its status as capital with his removal to Moscow in March 1918. In pre-Soviet days, British visitors to St Petersburg were wont to compare what they saw and experienced with things back home; after 1918 (although it was only in the 1920s that they came again and in very small numbers), the comparison was of the city of the Soviets with the great capital they had earlier seen or read about.

While there was a spate of books appearing in the 1920s about the 'old Russia' and about the Revolution, one of the first accounts of a visit to the 'new Russia' was that of H.G. Wells, who had been there for the first time in January 1914 and returned for two weeks in September 1920. He wobbles between the names of Petersburg and Petrograd as he looks with some equanimity at the scenes on the streets:

The dominant fact for the Western reader, the threatening and disconcerting fact, is that a social and economic system very like our own and intimately connected with our own has crashed.

Nowhere in all Russia is the fact of that crash so completely evident as it is in Petersburg. Petersburg was the artificial creation of Peter the Great; his bronze statue in the little garden near the Admiralty still prances amidst the ebbing life of the city. Its palaces are still and empty, or strangely refurnished with the typewriters and tables and plank partitions of a new Administration which is engaged chiefly in a strenuous struggle against famine and the foreign invader. Its streets were streets of busy shops. In 1914 I loafed agreeably in the Petersburg streets

– buying little articles and watching the abundant traffic. All these shops have ceased. There are perhaps half a dozen shops still open in Petersburg. There is a Government crockery shop where I bought a plate or two as a souvenir, for seven or eight roubles each, and there are a few flower shops. It is a wonderful fact, I think, that in this city, in which most of the shrinking population is already nearly starving, and hardly anyone possesses a second suit of clothes or more than a single change of worn and patched linen, flowers can be and are still bought and sold. For five thousand roubles, which is about six and eight pence at the current rate of exchange, one can get a pleasing bunch of big chrysanthemums.

I do not know if the words 'all the shops have ceased' convey any picture to the Western reader of what a street looks like in Russia. It is not like Bond Street or Piccadilly on a Sunday, with the blinds neatly drawn down in a decorous sleep, and ready to wake up and begin again on Monday. The shops have an utterly wretched and abandoned look; paint is peeling off, windows are cracked, some are broken and boarded up, some still display a few fly-blown relics of stock in the window, some have their windows covered with notices; the windows are growing dim, the fixtures have gathered two years' dust. They are dead shops. They will never open again.

All the great bazaar-like markets are closed, too, in Petersburg now, in the desperate struggle to keep a public control of necessities and prevent the profiteer driving up the last vestiges of food to incredible prices. And this cessation of shops makes walking about the streets seem a silly sort of thing to do. Nobody 'walks about' any more. One realises that a modern city is really nothing but long alleys of shops and restaurants and the like. Shut them up, and the meaning of a street has disappeared. People hurry past – a thin traffic compared with my memories of 1914. The electric street cars are still running and busy – until six o'clock. They are the only means of locomotion for ordinary people remaining in town – the last legacy of capitalist enterprise. They became free while we were in Petersburg. Previously there had been a charge of two or three roubles – the hundredth part of the price of an egg. Freeing them made little difference in their extreme congestion during the home-going hours. Every one scrambles on the tramcar. If there is no room inside you cluster outside. In the busy hours festoons of people hang outside by any handhold; people are frequently pushed off, and accidents are frequent. We saw a crowd collected round a child cut in half by a tramcar, and two people in the little circle in which we moved in Petersburg had broken their legs in tramway accidents.

The roads along which these tramcars run are in a frightful condition. They have not been repaired for three or four years; they are full of holes like shell-holes, often two or three feet deep. Frost has eaten out great cavities, drains have collapsed, and people have torn up the wood pavements for firs. Only once did we see any attempt to repair the streets in Petrograd. In a side street some mysterious agency had collected a load of wood blocks and two barrels of tar. Most of our longer journeys about the town were done in official motor-cars – left over from the former times. A drive is an affair of tremendous swerves and concussions. These surviving motor-cars are running now on kerosene. They disengage clouds of pale blue smoke, and start up with a noise like a machine-gun battle. Every wooden house was demolished for firing last winter, and such masonry as there was in those houses remains in ruinous gaps, between the houses of stone.

Two years after Wells's visit, Thomas Preston, who had been British vice-consul in Ekaterinburg at the time of the assassination of the imperial family, returned to Petrograd (which he had visited several times before the First World War) in the post of British Official Agent and remained until 1927. In his memoirs, published in 1950, he recalls his shock at seeing the state of streets and buildings nearly a decade after his last visit:

On the following morning [11 November 1922] we were up at 10 a.m. to see the sights. We found, however, to our surprise that the great Nevsky thoroughfare was deserted, save for a tram and stray *izvoschik*. We were then told that the shops did not open until eleven, and life did not start in the streets until 4 p.m. My impression of Petrograd, as I saw it, was that of a very shabby and dead city by comparison with the former smart and lively St. Petersburg, plus a good many ruins caused by the destruction of houses during the street fighting in the early days of the Revolution. Most of the street paving (blocks) was in a terrible state of disrepair. All the signboards on the great shops of the former St. Petersburg had been changed, being replaced by abbreviated words to represent the Soviet trusts in their new nomenclature. In every way the old had been eradicated; something new and strange that confused, and to a foreigner, at least, although perfectly fluent in Russian, much of it was unintelligible. It took at least weeks or months to get accustomed to all the alterations. But I think the most gruesome sight of all was when, on passing the Admiralty at the end of the Nevsky, we came upon the famous Angliskaya Naberejknaya [*sic*], or English quay, the beautiful embankment along the great Neva River where almost every house was formerly a palace, and the town house of some noble Russian family. The whole of this quay was now like a graveyard, and many of the beautiful houses which were entirely unsuitable to the purse of Russia of the day were destroyed, at least in part. During the days of the 'Terror' many of the workmen attempted to live in these houses, but got out upon finding it impossible to heat the enormous rooms. Before doing so, however, they frequently left some souvenir of their temporary domicile by destroying a work of art or even setting fire to a parquet floor.

The road itself, along which one would have seen in the old days carriages and pairs of sleighs drawn by blood trotters, covered with beautiful snow-nets, was now completely deserted.

Even with no danger of arrest and with food and lodging guaranteed, Petrograd was a city to depress. The state of the English quay may be said to apply to many of the great streets where there were formerly very large houses, i.e. the Sergieffskaya, which was also like a graveyard,·except for a few houses where the members of the old families still lived in the quarters formerly occupied by their servants. Of the great public building of former St. Petersburg, the Winter Palace had been turned into a museum, called the 'Museum of the Revolution', and Smolny, Catherine the Second's institute for young ladies, had been seized as headquarters for the Soviet; here Zinoviev reigned supreme as Governor of the district of Petrograd. The former Foreign Office building was used as a police station, whilst many of the enormous old government buildings, formerly housing various ministries, were entirely empty. Seeing them deserted, forcibly reminded one of the impracticabilty of Moscow, with its terrible overcrowding, as the seat of government. All the Embassies, with the exception of the German, where the newly-appointed Consul-General was residing, were empty and going to rack and ruin. They were under the administration of a Soviet institution known as 'Burobin', which was short in Soviet Russian for *bureau dlya obsloujivanya inostrantsev* or 'bureau for the service of foreigners'. This worthy society, incidentally, eventually became known as 'bureau for robbing foreigners' which, to judge from my own experience, seems to have been its chief occupation.

Lancelot Lawson, who had lived many years in Russia before the October Revolution and who was married to a Russian, made a long visit to the city soon after its re-naming in 1924 and wrote a series of articles for *The Daily Chronicle* and used much of the material for a book published in 1927.

The contrast between Moscow and Petrograd, now named Leningrad, was always marked – Moscow with its air of 'the big village', so typical of Russian disorderliness; Leningrad, an Imperial capital, with broad streets and Western aspect. But to-day the contrast between the two cities is still more striking; for it is the contrast between life and death itself. Leningrad is a dying city. Never did I feel so depressed as during my stay there.

I knew Leningrad well in its prosperous days. Life was never too happy in Russia. But it was always possible to extract some delight from the mere contemplation of Leningrad's stylish beauty. No city in the world contains more eighteenth or early nineteenth century architecture, nor can show more romantic gardens of the same epoch wherein are graceful pavilions set on columns. How well its slender golden spires and Byzantine domes fit into this lyric setting. And then there is the Neva – a river of magnificent decorative qualities, and the broadest and handsomest on which a capital ever stood! And the canals!

To-day Leningrad reminds one of a beautiful woman suffering from neglect. It is still beautiful, very beautiful; but so inexpressibly sad. As one approaches the city in the train one sees lines of deserted factories with smokeless chimneys.

The Neva, which at this time of the year was always so animated, is now almost deserted; a few broken and waterlogged barges are moored at its wharves; the palaces on its quays are empty and in decay; a sunken steamer lies in the fairway; at night no rows of twinkling lights; the darkness over the scene is almost unrelieved, and as one walks along the embankments one sees only silhouettes.

Elsewhere are many deserted dwellings, and hundreds of buildings are in ruins; in some parts of the city one might imagine that an earthquake had taken place; skeletons of houses and heaps of debris everywhere. The centre of the city suffered little, and already has returned to something like a normal aspect; that is to say, most of the shops are open, and their windows are filled with the customary array of articles displayed in a European city.

But even here rows of shops may still be seen closed and shuttered-in; in the Morskaya, for example, which was noted for its jewellers' shops, and which was Leningrad's smartest shopping street. Many banks and houses are also empty and deserted.

At the Nevsky end of the Morskaya the same policeman stands on point duty who was there in the Emperor's day – the policeman with the side whiskers who was one of Petrograd's characters. How strange that he should have survived when so many of his kind have vanished!

Grass may be seen growing, not only in the streets of the outlying districts, but also in some of those in the centre. The square of the Kazan Cathedral, adjacent to the Nevsky, looks quite green; it might well be the square of some ancient cathedral square. At one time botanists discovered in the heart of the city plant life such as is only found growing in wild countries.

The traffic has diminished and the streets are silent. In the old days one had to walk warily when crossing the Nevsky and other main streets; the traffic was not thick, it is true, but it was swift-moving, and the danger of being run over by some smart equipage drawn by high-stepping horses was considerable.

To-day one may stroll at leisure across the Nevsky, and the 'traffic', like the crowd in the streets, looks worn out. The roads in Moscow are bad, but in Leningrad they are far worse – full of great cavities. In the black days of the Revolution the wooden blocks were pulled up and plundered for firewood.

In many open spaces outside museums and other public buildings immense piles of logs are stored in readiness for winter. One would not be surprised at such a homely sight in a small village, perhaps – but how strange in Leningrad!

In the daytime the streets in the centre are animated enough; the Nevsky, for example, is almost as crowded as it used to be. But it is a different crowd; no military uniforms, and few elegantly dressed women The proletariat, as Dostoevsky prophesied, is on the streets: arm in arm, they parade up and down – sometimes six or seven in a row. They jostle one another, talk and laugh loudly, and sing revolutionary songs.

The women have abandoned the peasant shawl and taken to cheap hats. High heels are in fashion, and painted faces more common than in former days. In summer time the crowd is everywhere; all open spaces are filled; people sit on the steps of the cathedrals, and perch themselves on the ledges of shop windows in the principal streets; and when they go they leave behind on the pavements a litter of husks from the sunflower seeds which they have just munched.

All these three observers were struck by the emptiness of a city that had seen a dramatic decrease in its population since 1915, when it had reached a peak of some 2,300,000. By 1920 the figure had fallen to 722,000, but had climbed back to 1,616,000 by 1926.

A visitor of a somewhat different type was Allan Monkhouse, an engineer whose main base was Moscow over a long period of years stretching from 1911 until 1933, when he was one of the engineers deported after the notorious Metro-Vickers trial in Moscow. He had visited Petrograd on business several times between 1914 and 1918 and remembered it as 'a city of extraordinary beauty and interest'. It was in December 1925 that he saw it for the first time under Soviet rule and he was to live there for some three and a half years, coming 'to know the city well and form[ing] many associations'. Monkhouse notes not only the general dilapidation in the city but also the depredations caused by its traditional foe, the Neva in flood. On 23 September 1924 there occurred the second highest flood in the city's history (following that of 1824, described in a previous chapter), covering half of its total territory, sweeping away some twenty bridges and affecting over 5000 buildings.

At the end of 1925, Leningrad presented the appearance of being a derelict. The extremes of the Russian climate cause rapid deterioration to paint and plaster unless careful maintenance work is done almost yearly, and thus the ten years of neglect from 1916 onwards had resulted in the majority of the buildings falling into a state of dilapidation and disrepair which was pitiable to behold. The situation had not been improved by the disastrous flood of September 1924, when a strong westerly wind had brought the waters of the Gulf of Finland into the city, flooding the main streets to a depth of several feet. This flood had destroyed the gas-works, and consequently, at night-time, the streets, which had previously been gas-lit, were in total darkness. The flood had also washed away the wood-paving of the majority of the main thoroughfares. In many districts the destruction wrought during the fighting of the revolution and the civil war was still apparent.

The world famous Nevski-Prospect – that great street which, in Tsarist days, had been so full of colour and the busy life of a great capital – was now almost deserted. Its surface was still only partially restored after the flood. An occasional motor-car passed along, but over-crowded tramcars formed the greater part of its wheeled traffic. The bright uniforms of the officers of the Imperial armies and the Parisian dresses of the women of St. Petersburg's aristocracy had given place to the simple khaki of the Red Army and the drab clothing of a distinctly proletarian population. The name of the street itself had been changed. It was now 'The Prospect of the 25th October.'

Re-naming of streets and buildings (to say nothing of cities!) had always been part and parcel of revolutionary change and the Soviets proved particularly adept and prompt at the practice. Lancelot Lawson commented in 1924:

In Leningrad, as in all Russian towns, the streets have been renamed; the Nevsky has become the October Twenty-fifth Prospekt! (the date of the Bolshevik Revolution); other streets are named after famous revolutionaries; one street, for example, in memory of the man who assassinated Alexander II, a second after Rosa Luxembourg; and a third after Robespierre.

Then there is a 'Street of Young Proletarians,' a 'Place of Communards,' a 'Square of Red Commanders,' a 'Street of Brotherly Love,' and a 'Bridge of Freedom.' If one went only by the names of many of the streets one might well imagine one was strolling in the highways of Paradise itself.

Some streets are named after well-known writers and composers, Turgeniev, Tchekov, and Tchaikovsky amongst others; and there is a Rontgen Street in memory of the X-ray inventor.

In addition to re-naming, the transformation and adaptation of many of the distinguished buildings of an earlier era to the needs of the first generation of Soviet citizens proceeded apace. Monkhouse describes how many of the great houses and flats had been converted into communal dwellings (*kommunalki*) to meet the housing crisis in the capital and his own successful acquisition of a flat belonging to the old aristocratic family of the Obolenskiis.

In January 1926 it had become apparent that my stay in Leningrad would last for a year or more, hence I commenced to seek for suitable housing accommodation. In the course of my enquiries I found that the great majority of the spacious flats and residences of the old aristocracy and the wealthy residents of St. Petersburg had already been converted into communal dwellings for Leningrad's workers. In pre-revolutionary days the majority of the workers had lived on the outskirts of the city in wooden two-storey dwellings. During the winters of 1919, 1920 and 1921, when famine and disorder reigned, many hundreds of these wooden dwellings in the outlying districts had been pulled down and used for fuel, and their occupants had moved into the city and had been housed in the accommodation left vacant by the dispossessed and scattered aristocracy. The sanitary condition of the city at this time was alarming.

The flat which I ultimately rented, and made into a headquarters for the British engineering staff employed at Volchovstroi [the hydro-electric station], had previously belonged to the Obolenski family, who, in pre-revolutionary Russia, had occupied a unique position among the titled families surrounding the Tsar's Court. During the time which had elapsed since its original occupiers had fled from St. Petersburg the flat had been used to house troops; and latterly had been a communal dwelling for work-people. The condition into which it had been allowed to lapse was appalling. The figures on the artistically painted ceiling of the drawing-room had obviously been used for target practice. Expensive mirrors had been wantonly broken, and apparently no effort whatsoever had been made to maintain any part of the premises in a clean and sanitary condition.

Requisition for an altogether different purpose had taken place with the old British embassy building by the Trinity Bridge (*Troitskii*, later, *Ravenstva*, and after Kirov's murder in 1934, *Kirovskii*). H.G. Wells recounts how Maksim Gor'kii had established there the headquarters of the so-called Expertise Commission which was responsible for saving and cataloguing all the furniture, paintings and other *objets d'art* that had adorned the former mansions and palaces.

It is not simply scientific and literary work and workers that Maxim Gorky is trying to salvage in Russia. There is a third and still more curious salvage organisation associated with him. This is the Expertise Commission, which has its headquarters in the former British Embassy. When a social order based on private property crashes, when private property is with some abruptness and no qualification abolished, this does not abolish and destroy the things which have hitherto constituted private property. Houses and their gear remain standing, still being occupied and used by the people who had them before – except when those people have fled. When the Bolshevik authorities requisition a house or take over a deserted palace, they find themselves faced by this problem of the gear [. . .]

For greater security there has been a gathering together and a cataloguing of everything that could claim to be a work of art by this Expertise Commission. The palace that once sheltered the British Embassy is now like some congested second-hand art shop in the Brompton Road. We went through room after room piled with the beautiful lumber of the former Russian social system. There are big rooms crammed with statuary; never have I seen so many white marble Venuses and sylphs together, not even in the Naples Museum.

There are stacks of pictures of every sort, passages choked with inlaid cabinets piled up to the ceiling; a room full of cases of old lace, piles of magnificent furniture. This accumulation has been counted and catalogued. And there it is. I could not find out that any one had an idea of what was ultimately to be done with all this lovely and elegant litter. The stuff does not seem to belong in any way to the new world, if it is indeed a new world that the Russian Communists are organising. They never anticipated that they would have to deal with such things. Just as they never really thought of what they would do with the shops and markets when they had abolished shopping and marketing. Just as they had never thought out the problem of converting a city of private palaces into a Communist gathering-place.

'Confiscated Treasures' is the title of a chapter in Sir Martin Conway's *Art Treasures in Soviet Russia* (1925), which describes a journey he made to Moscow and Petrograd in the summer of the previous year. Conway, a M.P. and a former Slade Professor of Art at Cambridge, travelled only 'to see the works of art in Russia and to record the manner and prospects of their preservation' and he 'employed the whole of every day – and the days in Russia are very long – from early morning till late in the evening in passing from one collection to another, and either beholding or even having in my hands a countless succession of precious objects'. His descriptions of the Hermitage and of other imperial palaces are the most detailed since Atkinson a half century earlier and he enjoyed unprecedented access and was allowed to roam at will through the galleries of the Hermitage 'smoking my pipe and sitting at will now before a gem-like Raphael, now inspecting the magic mystery of the great Rembrandts'. *Pace* reports in Western newspapers, 'the escape of such a multitude of valuable objects from theft and destruction' seemed 'almost miraculous'. Like Wells before him, Conway was simply agog at the quantities of preserved and confiscated works of art – in the Hermitage inventory before the Revolution there were 11,000 pictures, to which 4,000 had been subsequently added. He was at the same time acutely conscious of the inferiority of much that had been confiscated from private collections and was now heaped at the top of the Winter Palace in former living quarters:

Nothing can be imagined more dreary than this sad assemblage of pictures, most of which were of no value from the point of view of a public collection, though good enough for private houses. The still-lifes would have sufficed to decorate a dozen dining-rooms, but I doubt whether three of them would have been worth hanging in any public gallery. The reader will easily imagine the bewildering effect produced upon one's eye and mind by passing in review so great a multitude of pictures. One wandered through the derelict rooms with a dim consciousness of the lives that were led in them, of the people who occupied them, of the aims and heartbreaks and the triumphs they had experienced; a sense that all this was gone, utterly dead and vanished into the past, and that nothing of it remained beyond the parquetry floors, the tattered wall-papers, the decorated ceilings. The whole place seemed peopled by ghosts. A deadly silence reigned. No one came there; no one had any business there except the curators who were studying pictures. It was a sort of Hades into which one might imagine the dead pictures passed in some after-life of unbroken sleep.

In another chapter, entitled 'Confiscated Houses', Conway writes that

In Petersburg [he always used the old name] many of the big houses were burnt down during the tumultuous days of the Revolution and they remain gaunt shells open to the sky or heaps of overthrown ruins. A larger number have become uninhabitable through neglect or mishandling. It will be remembered that Petersburg passed through a terrible winter of starvation and cold. Fuel was not to be had for love or money and the people were perishing. Why none went a mile or two out into the islands and cut down the trees I was unable to discover. Apparently the disorganization was such that even so simple a procedure could not be organized. The proletariat was accordingly permitted to enter empty houses and tear up floors and any wood they could lay hands on. Many large houses were thus ruined. Other removables – taps, door-handles, pipes, everything – were also carried off and these buildings are now uninhabitable.

He did, however, manage to visit three of the largest aristocratic palaces within the city that were still 'maintained with scrupulous care' – the Iusupov, the Shuvalov and the Stroganov, the first of which, however, was soon to be re-assigned, as a later extract will reveal.

Palaces apart, there was an embarrassment of cathedrals and churches within the city, some of the most famous of which were soon put to new uses. Reader Bullard, who became British Consul-General in Leningrad in July 1931, looked from his office windows on the former Nevskii Prospekt at the Kazan Cathedral and noted

> The cathedral opposite – the Kazan – is open: it rings a bell (rarely) and services are held, and I even saw the priests on the steps in full robes holding a funeral service. But the great cathedral of St Isaac is an anti-religious museum; some churches are closed and the tower of the Dutch Reformed church is being pulled down and the building turned into some sort of club. The general weapon now against religion is taxation. The authorities levy taxes they know cannot be paid and then seize the church in satisfaction of the debt. But communists still make merry on their name days – possibly because this provides an excuse for drinking.

But just over a year later, the Kazan followed St Isaac's:

> The Kazan Cathedral – a cathedral no longer – is being got ready for 7 November. The text in gilt letters is being scraped off the architrave. Yesterday I could just read 'Blessed . . . in the name of the Lord'; today the inscription has quite disappeared.

Further along Nevskii, across the Anichkov Bridge, the former Belosel'skii-Belozerskii Palace (also known as the Sergeevskii and the Dmitrievskii, after its subsequent royal owners), which had housed the Anglo-Russian Hospital during the First World War, had once again undergone a radical change of use. Lady Muriel Paget, who had been one of the driving forces behind the establishment of the hospital, had first come to Petrograd in April 1916, dividing her activities over the next eighteen months between the hospital and its mobile field hospital at the Russian front before she returned to England after the October Revolution. In 1926, she returned after an absence of nine years and published her impressions in a series of articles published the following year in the *Daily Telegraph*.

> Everything was quiet now, as I again walked across the Fontanka bridge to visit the house which had once been a palace and our hospital. I found a soldier on duty in the hall, looking as if he might have been one of our patients. He explained that the premises were converted into clubs and recreation-rooms, which would not be open to the public for another hour, but when I explained my reason for wishing to see the place he was very interested, and immediately gave me permission to do so. I dashed up the great staircase and through the room that had been our dining-room, into the big wards, which were now comfortably furnished as club rooms. But a picture of Lenin hung in the alcove which had formerly been a chapel. I went out again, realising that things had indeed changed.

Grand Duke Dmitrii Pavlovich, the owner of the palace up to the October Revolution, was involved in the murder of Rasputin and it was memories of that event that excited the artist Robert Byron as he made his way at the beginning of 1932 to the palace where it had taken place. The Iusupov Palace stood on the Moika Embankment towards the south-west, beyond St Isaac's (Senate) Square. The site had been acquired in 1830 by the fabulously rich Count Nikolai Iusupov, the hero of Pushkin's poem 'To a Grandee', and the mansion was greatly enlarged and its delicious little rococo theatre added later in the century. The palace housed the famous Iusupov collections of paintings, porcelain and furniture. For a few years after October it was a museum, but by the time Byron saw it, it had become a club for workers in education and propaganda.

> The streets and squares of Leningrad have not only good architecture, but poignant associations. In them were achieved the twin Revolutions of March and October. The ideas which produced that upheaval germinated in the previous century. But the history of its actual events dates from the night of December 16 by the Old Style, 1916, when the deputy Purishkevitch, drunk with his own heroism, proclaimed to a bewildered policeman that Rasputin was dead and Russia saved.

Fifteen years and a fortnight later I was walking by the side of the narrow, frozen River Moika, through the Mayfair of old St. Petersburg. 'Our house on the Moika', writes Prince Yusupov in his account of the affair, 'was chosen as the place where our project was to be carried out.' And unchanged the house on the Moika still stands, a long perspective of yellow stucco with the ornament picked out in white. Above the entrance a coat-of-arms on the attic storey recalls the magnificence of the family of Yusupov-Sumarokov-Elston. But below this, two plac- ards, bearing white letters on a red ground, inform the passer-by that here may now be found the Club for Scientific Workers and the Club for the Trade Union of Educationalists. The afternoon was sad and dark. Nevertheless, I experienced, as always in Russia, that incommu- nicable exhilaration associated with a first sight of scenes often and untruthfully imagined.

It happened that my guide was a a member of one of the clubs now contained in the palace, and he thought that, though foreigners were not usually admitted, an exception would be made in my case. A fat comrade, golden-haired and rubicund, greeted us with effusion, then galloped up the main staircase to switch on the several hundred lights of the central chandelier. Dazzled by the blaze, we proceeded to the state rooms on the first floor, through double doors of mahogany set with ormolu rosettes, through room after room, each richer than the last, furnished in the manner of palaces with silk hangings and gilt cupids, with tables of agate and porphyry, aubusson settees and chairs of Spanish leather, and mantelpieces of porcelain and malachite. Through the small and the big ballrooms we went, through the picture gallery, and down into the miniature theatre, a rococo auditorium about fifty feet long, lined with three tiers of boxes. Prince Yusupov himself could not have exhibited more pride in his surroundings than did our guide, who begged us to note how the precious chairs were kept in dust-sheets. On reaching the theatre he jumped on the stage and let down a drop-curtain depicting the Yusupov country house as though it were his own.

Only two or three of the state rooms were occupied. In one of them we found an artist who had just returned from a scientific expedition to Kamchatka and was hanging a series of landscapes illustrating the behaviour of volcanoes in those parts. Since he looked under-fed, I asked if he hoped to sell many. 'Certainly not', he replied. 'The workers must not be deprived of culture.' Half of the pictures would go to the institute that had financed the expedition; the other half would remain his. Then his dream was to hold an exhibition abroad.

On returning to the ground floor, a series of passages led us to the winter garden, where the Scientific Workers and the Trade Union of Educationalists were eating soup. Beyond this was a billiard-room copied from the Alhambra, and beyond that the apartments of old Prince Yusupov, where they had recently discovered a safe under the floor. I asked about the great hoard of treasure that had been found walled up in the palace three or four years ago, and our guide replied that the whole place was honeycombed with secret passages. In fact, only the other day as workman had lurched into the building drunk and said he could show them some new ones, which he himself had built. But next day, when he returned sober, he had been unable to find them after all.

The way now led through a series of locked doors and empty rooms, till suddenly we found ourselves in a small octagon about ten feet across and eight feet high. Each of the eight sides consisted of as wooden door painted white and inset with a broad panel of plate glass, behind which was a curtain of frilled blue silk. One door led into a still smaller bathroom, beyond which was a no less diminutive bedroom. The walls of both these sinister little apartments were thickly padded. A second door revealed a plain square room with two windows looking out on the Moika. This was now used as a military class-room; there were posters on the walls of tactical exercises, first-aid, and how to affix your gas-mask; a rifle on a stand was pointing into the street. A third door opened on to a cavern of darkness. But the other doors gave access to blank walls only, so that, once in the octagon, it was a matter of some minutes to find which door provided a way out of it. In addition, I had noticed that one of the previous doors leading to the octagon hand had to be carefully propped open, as it was self-locking.

These were Prince Yusupov's private apartments, and here came, on the night of December 16, 1916, the Grand Duke Dmitri Pavlovich, Purishkevitch, and Dr. Lazovert.

Of course, many establishments in Leningrad continued to function more or less as before, if under different ownership and with a very different clientèle, as Thomas Preston discovered on revisiting in November 1922 the famous Hotel Europe (*Evropeiskaia*) on Brodskii Street (in pre-Soviet times, *Mikhailovskaia*) which leads to Nevskii Prospekt. The hotel, which has recently been restored to its former glory, was created in the 1870s and at the beginning of the twentieth century received 'style modern' interiors, including stained-glass windows to designs of Benois:

We found that in spite of the fact that it was very dirty and was full to the brim with communists of all nationalities, who glared at us every time we encountered them, it still bore some of the signs of its former splendour. We had, however, nothing to complain about. The word from the powers-that-be has been passed round. The management was polite, and we were offered five of the best rooms in the hotel – the so-called *bel-étage* or first floor – for the sum of eighteen million roubles per diem.

A word about the rooms: I should say they had been beautiful; under the old régime they would have cost at least from seven to eight pound per day. As we got them they were the remnants of beautiful rooms, richly upholstered and carpeted, but the curtains gone, stolen during the Revolution. A picture which adorned one of the walls had a couple of bullet-holes in it. There were traces of many orgies on the richly upholstered furniture. On the whole one would have preferred something more modest, but less remindful of the days in which we lived.

We were next to encounter our first Soviet waiter, a tall fair-haired man properly attired in a dress suit. I should perhaps point out that the entire staff of this hotel (there were 400 rooms and several hundred servants) were in the pay of the Cheka, it being their duty to furnish reports on the visitors in the hotel, if possible obtaining copies of any documents they could find lying about in their rooms; in fact one's locked portmanteaux were not safe. It was, however, incriminating documents, i.e. in the eyes of the Soviet Government, and not valuables, that they were looking for. Many of the walls of the hotel were said to contain dictaphones which recorded conversations resulting afterwards in arrests [...]

On returning to our hotel, after our first long walk round Petrograd, we encountered, in the vestibule of the hotel, the most exotic collection of human beings it has been my lot to meet. There were some 200 of them, and in reply to our enquiries as to who they were we were informed that they were members of the *chornaja birja* or 'black-exchange', which was a kind of money-exchange – under the auspices of the Cheka.

In the evening, which happened to be a Saturday, we dined later in the public dining-room. There were the same Tartar waiters in their white suits as we had been accustomed to see them in the old days. One of them recognized me but was afraid to show any outward signs of having done so. Except for a few Soviet officials with their ladies (many of them obviously had seen better days) the dining-room was fairly deserted. An excellent string orchestra performed throughout the meal on a small stage at the end of the room. The music was of the highest order: trios, violin and piano solos, with an occasional piece of more frivolous strain. There was a strange incongruity about this good music in this proletarian paradise, but it is probably accounted for by the number of Jews (always admirers of good music) to be found amongst the Soviet officials; furthermore, there were a great many first-class musicians in Russia who were out of work, and only too glad to perform at restaurants.

Later that evening, Preston and his colleagues witnessed an excellent cabaret, but it was the audience that provoked his strong class prejudices:

They were the most extraordinary mixed crowd we had ever set eyes on. There were workmen in Russian shirts and *valenki*, or warm felt top-boots – *valenki* have a way of making the feet perspire profusely, an unpleasant addition to the atmosphere which was already heavily charged in a hall where all the windows were sealed for the winter; Soviet officials in their leather jackets and equally obnoxious Russian top-boots – cleaned with a strong-smelling kind of boot polish. A few Russians appeared in smoking jackets, obviously of pre-war cut. A sprinkling of foreigners, mostly Germans and Swedes, looked particularly immaculate in their well-cut suits and 'smokings'. The ladies ranged from the coarsest members of the worker class, attired in their factory best, to Russian Princesses in décolleté and jewellery.

The cabaret, Preston further suggests, was, on the one hand, designed to impress foreigners but, on the other, was catering for the tastes of the new Soviet 'bourgeoisie' during the period known as NEP (New Economic Policy). Monkhouse, who was there at the same time, noted, however, some of the benefits that accrued to the infrastructure and fabric of historic buildings:

It must be remembered that during these years the results of the New Economic Policy were more apparent than at any other time. Shutters were pulled down and private shops were opened. House Committees commenced to make repairs to the houses under their charge, and the city authorities themselves gave the Winter Palace, the old General Staff, the Admiralty and other great public buildings, a much-needed coat of paint. New sewerage and street-lighting systems were proceeded with as quickly as possible in order to replace the damage done during the floods of 1924. Several large restaurants reopened, and, generally speaking, there existed a feeling that conditions were steadily improving.

E. Ashmead-Bartlett, who had visited Russia (but not Petrograd) in 1919, paid his first visit to Leningrad in 1929 as correspondent of *The Daily Telegraph*. Noting that 'the city gives you the impression of having recently been excavated after being buried for centuries by an earthquake or volcanic eruption', he added nevertheless that 'all who knew Leningrad four years ago tell me it is vastly more alive to-day, although the facades of the houses are crumbling day by day. The authorities are trying to clear the main buildings, and force the industrial workers into the suburbs, where some new model dwellings have been erected.'

Many British visitors rued the passing of the old, but were nonetheless attentive to the new ways. They could hardly ignore the parades that were instituted for May Day and to commemorate the October Revolution. Lawton was witness to the May Day parade of 1924:

The May Day procession, which took place some days after Easter, was a monster affair; it occupied nearly the whole of Nevsky, which is not far short of three miles long, before it passed into the big square outside the Winter Palace.

The atmosphere of a festival was completely lacking. Masses of black-garbed people wearing red favours moved slowly in detachments behind red banners on which were inscribed such mottoes as these: 'Every cook must know how to govern the State'; 'The Red Army, Fleet and Air Force are for the Service of the World,' and numerous denunciations of Rumania's retention of Bessarabia. Grotesquely painted representations of the faces of Christ were held above the heads of the crowd; also grotesque masks of the Emperor and Empress were exposed to view on the ends of high poles.

At intervals, groups of young factory women, wearing leather coats, short skirts, and with red handkerchiefs on their heads, marched past at a swinging pace, singing revolutionary songs in chorus. They were small of stature, and most of them had ill-shaped figures and embittered faces. Life had left its mark upon them.

On motor lorries 'living pictures' were staged: a fantastic capitalist beating the head of a worker with a colossal hammer; bourgeoisie in top hats and evening dress, looking half-drunk and behaving in clownish fashion; a 'bourjoui' hanging from a gibbet; a black coffin containing the corpse of the Second International; an Englishman in white helmet and white clothes, a Frenchman in military uniform, and an American wearing a morning coat, check trousers and white spats, sitting at a table beneath a palm tree, drinking champagne; and revolutionaries waving red flags between the bars of a prison surmounted by skulls.

The procession was composed, not only of workers, but also of university students and middle-class employees in government departments, and artists in the state opera houses, theatres and choirs. Large numbers were there simply because they had no other choice; attendance was compulsory.

Bullard had to endure the October (November) Parade in 1932:

It was a cold, raw day yesterday, but there was one consolation: the official parade was scheduled to last only two hours instead of the usual four. I noticed that the horses were all half-starved. Three tanks broke down in the square and had to be towed off under the eyes of the army commander and the foreign visitors. It was perhaps sabotage which caused a failure of current in an essential letter of an illuminated slogan, whereby 'Forward to new victories!' read 'Forward to new dinners!' I wish the Soviet Government had a shorter official song and that they would not play it so often. It is no joke to keep your hat off while the 'International' is being played in the open with a cold wind blowing. I noticed that most of the hundreds of Soviet citizens in the next block of seats had their cloth caps firmly on their heads, so I put my hat on again and never moved it after that, however much they played the 'International'. I am not called upon to be more Bolshevik than the Bolsheviks.

He was somewhat more impressed by his visit to a Pioneer camp outside Leningrad in July 1931:

The camp we saw is for children who are not well – undernourished in many cases, I suspect. The children come for a month and then another lot take their place – 160 at a time, all the year round. This fine weather they are only in their rooms for an afternoon rest and at night. The rest of the time they are in the open air. They gave us lunch – cabbage soup, coarse meat with carrot and potato chopped up – not very appetising but not bad, and a water ice which was perhaps put out for our visit.

The children looked well and the dormitories were light, airy and clean. All the children are Pioneers. They are taught that the Party is above all everything and (according to Radek) they despise a teacher (and presumably a parent) if he is not a member of the Party. There are four such organisations. The tiny children – corresponding to our Wolf Cubs and Brownies – are called Octobrists, after the month on which the Bolshevik Revolution occurred. Then come the Pioneers, boys and girls of ten to fifteen. Then the League of Communist Youth, which takes the young men and women past the age of twenty-one. Last of all there is the Communist Party. I have not yet heard whether there are any camps for those who are simply children and not Pioneers. I found it rather shocking to find a political camp supported by the Red Cross, but in Soviet Russia everything is subordinated to the Communist Part.

259

The camp occupies several *dachas*, i.e. Russian country villas, and the land between and around them. The food is simple and the children wear clothing belonging to the camp. One of the staff apologised for its condition. It was sketchy and ragged in many cases, but adequate for a summer life out of doors. In the reading-room was a pile of Soviet newspapers (chaffy diet even for grown-ups), and over the door was an inscription: 'We Pioneers protest against the murder of the eight young negroes'. When Lady Astor saw this a few days later she was furious, and asked the people in charge what they would think if we put up inscriptions in Boy Scout camps: 'We protest against the shooting of their political opponents by the Bolsheviks'. [. . .]

I got the impression that the doctors and the housekeeper (a most efficient man) got much satisfaction from seeing the children happy and improving in health without troubling much about politics, but the 'cultural' work of the camp is in the hands of a very young Jew who is very much the Party man. He had all the catch words of the Party propaganda. Pinned on the wall, to serve as subjects of discussion, were Stalin's latest speech and extracts from the Soviet press about the crisis in Europe. It is evident that the children are stuffed with propaganda the whole time.

It was places outside Leningrad that were formerly on every tourist's itinerary rather than pioneer camps that Ashmead-Bartlett was anxious to see. He managed to get to Tsarskoe Selo, which in 1918 had been become Detskoe Selo and in 1936, to mark the centenary of the death of Pushkin, it was to receive the poet's name. The most detailed and interesting pages are devoted not to the Catherine Palace but to the Alexander Palace (*Aleksandrovskii*), built by Quarenghi in 1792–1800, where Nicholas II and his family were held under house arrest from 9/22 March to the beginning of August 1917. For the English visitor it was a sort of tragic pilgrimage:

Once again in the hall, the attendant hands you a visitors' book and says: 'Please sign your name and write a few words of comment on your visit.' As you cannot write what you really feel you merely sign. You have paid your last mark of respect to a dynasty that is no more. You have signed a dead Emperor's visiting-book. You hasten to leave this, the most melancholy spot on earth, and pass out into the fresher air of the park.

How strange is the Bolshevist psychology. They take great pride in showing the home of the last Tsar. Yet I know nothing more calculated to give a pleasing picture of domestic bliss ruthlessly shattered than the Alexander Palace. The petty tyrant has already vanished into the dim pages of history, and only the memory of a devoted father surrounded by his happy family remains at Tsarskoe-Selo.

It was to another of the great imperial palaces that Peter Stucley, a young novelist and travel writer, made his way with some difficulty in 1936.

Everyone said it was impossible for me to go to Pavlovsk. No tourist ever went there; I should never find my way [. . .]

None [in Pavlovsk] seemed to know the whereabouts of the palace but, following a vaguely pointing hand I found myself, after a few minutes' walk, in a park with a little valley crossed by a stream.

Presently, the yellow façade of the palace showed itself close on my left hand, standing on a high rise of land. Rank grass grew thickly on the slope leading up from the stream to the house. Grass grew right up to the walls of the palace and the palace itself appeared as though on a high island of green. Through the windows I could see thick silk curtains and the glint of a chandelier. But none moved, either before the house or inside it. The sun shone very bright and warm on the grass, and very bright on the circle of white pillars bearing up the dome of the house.

I walked up the rise and round to the front of the house, where I experienced a shock of pleasure at first seeing the main façade.

Stucley managed to get into the palace and was simply charmed by its interiors. He then wanted to see the gardens and parkland:

Attempting to penetrate into the garden of the palace, I was confronted by an old man of ruffianly appearance, who, with a pipe in his mouth and a rifle in his hand, rose from his bed in the grass and forbade me to proceed a step further. Explaining, with the rifle pointing at my stomach, that I was a foreigner and harmless, I begged permission to pass, which was at length granted me, after the ancient sentry, still directing his weapon at me, had shouted to a comrade in the palace for counsel and explained to me that he was on the watch for thieves breaking in through the lower windows, or damaging the statuary.

The garden was charming enough, but had a sadly unkempt appearance. Plaster crumbled from Cameron's elegant little pavilion, and paint had fallen in chunks from Gonzago's *trompe l'oeil* on the walls of the colonnade. In the little closed garden where Paul had talked with his ministers the flower-beds were empty and dishevelled and weeds grew thickly at the base of the statues. But there was an enchantment even in the decay.

From the main entrance of the house an avenue of linden trees led to the park, and at the end of the avenue I found a bench and rested there for a little. Close by me an old woman was laboriously planting pansies in a flower-bed shaped like a five-pointed star. It was very soothing to be alone, and without the attendant chatter of the guide. One was able to enjoy the country as country, pure and simple, and not a few more square yards of the Soviet Union.

And how exhilarating it was to let the eye travel over so civilised a landscape! The park was arranged with dells and valleys and set with little temples and pavilions. On either side of a green valley grew firs and birch trees, not in thick barbaric woods, but pleasant, domesticated groves. The grass was thick with buttercups.

For a long time I wandered in the park, coming sometimes to little lakes on which there were boating-parties, mostly of men and boys, and sometimes to a clearing in the trees adorned with the statues of antiquity. Of all the places I saw in Russia, I shall remember the park and the palace of Pavlovsk with the greatest affection.

He made his way back to the railway station, the famous Voksal (modelled on the English Vauxhall), which once 'was the resort of rank and fashion; now, with its rows of empty seats, its faded wooden rostrum, its occasional lamp-post, it is reminiscent of a seaside bandstand out of season. The solitary patron, I sat at one of the rusty tin tables and drank some beer as I waited for my train back to Leningrad'.

It was Pavlovsk that Dame Una Pope-Hennessy most wanted to see out of all of St Petersburg's great palaces and estates. It was, indeed, mind's-eye images of St Petersburg rather than of Leningrad inspired by her assiduous reading of a tattered Murray that persuaded her to spend the months of August and September 1937 in the northern city. Much that she wished to see was for various reasons off-limits or restricted access. 'The palace of Oranienbaum, it transpired, was permanently out of bounds for foreigners.'

Then we were informed that the Michael Palace [in fact, the Michael Castle] was never shown, though in Mr. Murray's day one merely had to present a card to be taken all over it. The Smolny Institute, too, was barred to tourists, whereas formerly, when it was serving as a kind of Hampton Court for gentlewomen, it had been accessible to all comers and even in post-Revolution days it had been customary to show the plainly furnished room in which Lenin, the saint of modern Russia, worked and slept. We learnt that since the murder of Kirov [at the end of 1934] it had been closed to all comers. As for Smolny Cathedral, both the main church and its apanages were declared to be in a dangerous condition and portions might become dislodged at any moment. Ropsha and such once private properties as the Serge, Yussupov, Sheremetiev, and Stroganov Palaces were not to be visited, and it was doubtful if we should be allowed inside the Taurida Palace where the first Duma had met. For one reason and another we found that many former sights were closed for ever to the tourist.

She did, however, manage to see a great deal, not only Pavlovsk and Tsarskoe Selo, but also Peterhof and Gatchina, and much within the city itself. At Gatchina, which was not as much visited and described by British over the decades as other palaces, she provides, in addition to her typically well-informed and informative commentary, a very Soviet-museum cameo such as to bring a smile to subsequent generations of similar sufferers:

After paying our entrance money we were given pieces of felt to tie on our feet and then set out on our round. [. . .] In each room was a custodian, a woman looking drab, tired, and under-nourished. There was no smile on any of their faces, but they were very watchful, and though it was a warm day one of them objected to my carrying the coat belonging to my skirt and ordered me to put it on at once, which I hastened to do, as rules of this kind are I am told very strictly enforced in this country. [. . .] My felt foot-coverings were not very satisfactory and kept coming off, even though I had been given a child's size. To try to adjust them I sat down on a red velvet settee which looked to me as if intended for use, but Sophia Ivanovna pulled me up just as the crowd was beginning to groan out a sort of Oo-oo sound, as if I was doing something nefarious or destroying the property of the proletariat.

Dame Una's descriptions of the palaces are especially interesting and important as being virtually the last to be produced by a British visitor to Leningrad before the city was closed to foreigners and, crucially, before, a few years later, Tsarskoe Selo, Pavlovsk and Peterhof were reduced to burnt-out shells during the Second World War. Her book, entitled *The Closed City*, appeared at the end of 1938 and was dedicated to the memory of Lady Muriel Paget, who had died earlier in the year and to whose activity in Leningrad over the previous decade a long chapter is devoted. It is to the fate of the remnants of the British community in Soviet Leningrad, intimately connected with the endeavours of Lady Paget, that we should now turn.

A graphic account of the situation in Petrograd in the first few years following the October revolution is provided by Meriel Buchanan, retelling the story of Violet Froom, who had been the matron of the British Colony Hospital until its closure. After some months in the south of Russia Mrs Froom returned to the city only in September 1918 and made her way to the English Church to find that the chaplain, the Rev. Bousfield Lombard (mentioned in the memoirs of Elizabeth Hill in the preceding chapter), had been imprisoned. She decided to set up a makeshift sick ward and soup kitchen in one of the rooms of the chaplain's quarters to try and alleviate the sufferings of just a few of the remaining British, estimated to be well over a thousand, and for two years she and a few helpers struggled against all the odds, succouring the ill and the hungry and successfully hiding from the searches of the Red Guards others' jewellery and even a Stradivarius behind the organ pipes in the church. As a consequence of improved Anglo-Soviet relations after Lloyd George's 'Guildhall' speech of 8 November 1919, British nationals were given permission to leave Russia and Mrs Froom supervised two large groups that left in the spring of 1920 and in December a final exodus, which included herself and the Stradivarius (which she was later to hand to the widow of its British owner who had died in a Soviet prison). Some two hundred British subjects were left in Petrograd. The darkest page in the history of the British community was still to be written.

The seesawing in Anglo-Soviet relations over the next two decades until the Second World War exceeds anything previously experienced in the contacts between our two countries, not least because of the rapid changes in the 'colour' of British governments. The down that soon presented itself in the form of Lord Curzon's 'Note' or 'Ultimatum' in May 1923 was followed in February of the next year by the *de jure* recognition of the Soviet government and subsequent trade agreements and treaties, only soon to be disrupted by the so-called 'Zinov'ev letter'; then, in 1927 came the Arcos raid and the rupture of diplomatic relations. Thomas Preston, the British Official Agent, was accused of being a spy and was obliged to quit the city:

I left Leningrad in somewhat tragic or shall I say melodramatic circumstances. [. . .] At Leningrad, at the time, a rumour – a fantastic one – to which a great many Russians gave credence was that the British Fleet was going to bombard Kronstadt. In both Leningrad and Moscow the Soviet authorities staged giant anti-British demonstrations. In Leningrad I sat for four hours on my balcony at the Mission in Alexieffskaya Street watching the endless procession in which I saw many of my Russian friends who had been obliged to participate on pain of the usual penalties – loss of ration cards, or worse. To make the demonstrations more realistic the local authorities insisted on giving my house police protection – mounted and foot police; although I never felt the need of them, for I always found there was no real anti-British feeling among the rank and file Russian population. [. . .] I was honoured with the usual designation of the arch-British spy. Here again, if I had any feelings at all in the matter, they were of contempt for such nonsense. I must say in all justice to the authorities that beyond publication of my photo and the letter in the paper, I was subjected to no inconvenience and was given every facility to leave Leningrad with all my furniture and effects.

Three years earlier, in March 1924, Preston had written to Lady Paget in London, drawing her attention to 'quite a number of British subjects here who are in the most deplorable plight' and proposing that a home should be opened 'for ten or more confirmed invalids' and daily dinners supplied for a further twenty. In 1926 she visited Leningrad, as we have seen, and wrote movingly in the *Daily Telegraph* of the fifty or so 'families of British nationality who are living in terrible conditions'. A British Subjects in Russia Relief Fund was set up at this time, but it was only in 1930, subsequent to a further visit by Lady Muriel after a four-year gap, when the Fund was transformed into an Association, that the real work of effective on-the-spot aid began. Lady Muriel embarked on seven years of frequent visits (sometimes three times in a year) to see her British charges, who were now widely referred to as the D.B.S. (Distressed British Subjects), but the day-to-day responsibility for their care was shouldered by her permanent representative, Miss Dorothea Daunt, a Quaker who had taken part in the Famine Relief Mission to South Russia in 1922–5 and who proved an exceptional and resourceful woman during the three years (1931–4) she spent in Leningrad.

In late 1929, diplomatic relations were resumed when the USSR was represented for the first time by an ambassador to the Court of St James's. In July 1931 Bullard, the new British Consul-General, arrived in Leningrad and was soon allocated spacious accommodation on the former Nevskii Prospekt:

I have an immense flat to live in. The position is excellent (26 Nevsky Prospekt): we look out in front on a garden between the curved wings of the Kazan Cathedral; at the side we appear to look out mainly on a lady who on sunny days sits on her window-sill baring her back to the waist. The huge premises easily accommodate myself and two vice-consuls (one married). My flat is exactly opposite the Greek portico in the middle of the cathedral. In the foreground is a statue of Barclay de Tolly balanced on the left by the statue of Kutuzov. They it was who, with the help of the Russian climate and of whoever it was gave the order for the burning of Moscow, brought about the defeat of Napoleon in 1812.

For over a week I have been busy unpacking, rearranging rooms, sorting out and reading up the files. A large corridorful of cases is packed with all kinds of junk. There was a mass of dusty stationery left behind when the Embassy left after the Revolution, cases and cases of archives going back to the earliest years of the 19th century, boxes of books belonging to a defunct English club, bound volumes of *Punch*, a billiard-table in bits with twenty cues, rusty fenders, a broken weighing-machine, curtain-poles without brackets and brackets without poles, tin trunks full of waste-paper and old photographs, and so on.

Sadly, at least for the historian, the archive and much else were to disappear, probably during the siege years, when anything that might provide heat was duly burnt. It was, however, in Flat 16, House No. 26 on the former Nevskii Prospekt, adjacent to the Singer Building, that Lady Paget was given office space, but it proved inadequate for the welfare activities of her Association.

In May 1934 she leased from the Swedish Consulate a large flat at No. 36 Red Street (*Krasnaia ulitsa*) that became the new heart of the British community, a social, welfare and medical centre, and a lunching club, as well as providing a much-needed room for Miss Daunt. It may be re-called that under its earlier name of Galley (*Galernaia*), Red Street had been at the centre of the British Community in far happier times and the main building, which had housed the Swedish Embassy, was No. 64 on the English Embankment (in Soviet times, the Embankment of the Red Fleet), a few doors away from the English Church. Street It was in the flat on Red Street that Una Pope-Hennessy stayed in 1937.

The flat in which we are staying is the relief Centre for British Subjects in the Soviet Union, in other words the headquarters of the Paget Mission. Once part of the Swedish Legation, the living-room contains some of the former furnishings and presents with its deep arm-chairs, sofas, and grand piano a comfortable appearance. It is on the second floor of an apartment house in the Krassnaya Ulitza of which the first floor is occupied by the British Consulate. The street is one of shabby façades from which plaster peels and stucco crumbles. The rest of the houses in the street are fully inhabited even by Soviet standards, and as the weather is warm the babel from open windows makes sleep difficult. Hooters and sirens sound at midnight and at unexpected intervals. [...]

Despite the easy comfort of the sitting-room, the flat turned out to be a hive of industry in which a zealous staff seems to be on duty for unspecified hours. There is a book-keeper, a secretary, a hospital nurse, all of them British subjects, and all hard at work keeping the accounts, writing up card indices, replying to correspondence, and dealing with supplies such as tea, coffee, rice, and other groceries, clothing, money, drugs, and medicaments. It is their duty to see that the hundred-odd impecunious British nationals, who are, for various reasons, still residing in the Soviet Union, do not suffer hardship and privations. A doctor and his wife, both British subjects, attend at the flat twice a week to diagnose cases and they also visit patients in their homes. The services of a dentist, too, are available when required. One hears a great deal of discussion about teeth here, as stoppings are scarce and sets of teeth said to be unprocurable.

The first thing one notices about the flat is the maddening telephone which is used with exemplary forbearance but with ever-rising voice by the secretaries; the second thing is that open house is kept at luncheon and tea for the persons we hear spoken of as the D.B.S.s, which is short for Distressed British Subjects. Five sat down with us to luncheon on the first day. They seem to drop in when they like, for they know they are always welcome. At every meal during our stay at least three of them were present, sometimes there were ten or twelve. The dining-room table is long, the simple rations equal to extending occasions, Lady Muriel's smile a benediction.

In observing the activities of those who run this centre one learns that the work is never-ending, for the simple reason that every negotiation in the Soviet Union is dragged out to the limit and that neither time nor days of the week are taken seriously. To-morrow is always better than to-day. This means the simplest matters of routine, such as the inscribing of a cook who has moved from one district of Leningrad to another, may take several visits to the police to put in order. No one seems to get impatient here, a kind of fatalism that takes the edge off irritating situations has been acquired by all.

It had also long been recognized that there was little chance of repatriating most of the remaining British subjects and that it was desirable to build a home for some of them. Torgsin, the official soviet Agency for Trade with Foreigners, eventually agreed to build what became known as the 'datcha', a ten-roomed wooden house with a glazed verandah on a two-acre site at Sosnovka on the Vyborg Side of the city (and not all that far from the former 'British' summer village of Murino). Completion was promised for early 1932, but the optimism was misplaced and it was only in June 1934 that the Association in London could be informed that 'the Datcha is now habitable & Miss Ferrell [one of the resident British] has arrived there to convalesce'. The appointment as matron in early 1934 of Mrs Fanny Morley, a trained nurse, was crucial to the success of Sosnovka. She was to be Sosnovka's Mrs Froom. Habitually dressed in her uniform of grey faced with blue, designed and also worn by Lady Muriel herself during her visits, Mrs Morley brought order and discipline and great humanity to the running of the dacha. 'She never makes any fuss; every instruction carried out to the letter; great loyalty and devotion to duty, and nothing ever too much trouble.' The number of permanent residents grew from the original four to over ten, as well as Mrs Morley's daughter with her two children. Most of them had little or no English, but everyone had to try to speak English at meals. In October 1936, one of the London newspapers, *The Daily Sketch*, published a full page of photographs of life at Sosnovka, showing residents on the sunlit verandah and at table, and several of Lady Muriel herself, including one where she sits by a veritable cornucopia of fruit and vegetables gathered from the garden.

Although life in Leningrad was desperately hard and there were numerous frustrations, difficulties, and palpably increasing tension, life at Sosnovka could not but seem an oasis of peace, a little English island where order and reason, decency and rituals were carefully preserved. Even modest idylls, however, come to an end and already in late 1937 Lady Muriel was facing the possibility of withdrawing from Leningrad and setting up a small colony in the Russian-speaking part of Estonia. She paid what was to be her last visit to Russia in October 1937; on 16 June 1938 she died in England, having suffered from cancer for over eight years. In the intervening months the Soviet authorities had decided for reasons of national defence and security to close Leningrad to all foreigners. The British Consulate was closed on 15 March 1938 and moved to Moscow; the Swedish Consulate, which occupied the first floor of No 36 Krasnaia, followed suit on 15 May. The Association was allowed to continue to occupy the flat until the end of June and it was left to Mrs Morley to supervise the shutting down of both the flat and the dacha at Sosnovka as well as the evacuation of members of her ailing flock to Estonia. There is preserved a wonderful photograph of Mrs Morley standing with her interpreter Rose Healey in front of the house and holding a Union Jack; the photograph bears the handwritten caption 'The last Britishers in Leningrad June 1938, leaving Sosnovka'. The history of the British colony was at an end.

CHAPTER 9

FROM LENINGRAD UNDER SIEGE TO ST PETERSBURG REBORN, 1938 TO THE PRESENT

Leningrad, closed to foreigners since the summer of 1938, was within three years completely cut off not only from Europe but also from the rest of Russia. Since June 1941 thousands of citizens had been mobilized to build fortifications around the city as the German armies spread through the Baltic Soviet republics. The shelling of Leningrad began on 4 September but it is 8 September, when the last land connection was severed, that marks the beginning of the siege that was to last 900 days until 18 January 1944. The first winter was the most horrific: the ice road across Lake Ladoga, the Road of Life, was not established until the end of November and thousands died, overwhelmingly more from starvation than from bombing. It was a winter that has been poignantly and imaginatively caught in recent times in the novel by Helen Dunmore, *The Siege* (2001), but there were no first-hand British accounts. There were, undoubtedly, some British who died during the siege or even survived it, not only a few members of the former community who for reasons of health could not leave the city in 1938 but possibly also individuals who had come to Russia for political reasons: Lidiia Ginsburg in her memoirs writes, for instance, of a certain Winscott, an English communist who arrived in the city in the 1930s, married a Russian, and died during the blockade.

It was to the besieged city that the Reuters war correspondent Alexander Werth came in September 1943. Werth, a Petersburg-born British citizen, who had left Russia in 1916, describes how

The Leningrad Writers' Union organised one evening a reception at which I was guest of honour. It was a great event for me, and I was assured that it was also a great event for them. I believe it. Not because they considered me a famous journalist or eminent author – I don't

271

think any of them had ever heard of me before – but because I was the first British correspondent, in fact the very first person from England since the war, to have turned up in Leningrad. The fact that I was also originally a 'native' of Leningrad seemed to make me doubly welcome.

In an interesting and in some respects prophetic passage he addresses the vexed question of the Soviet 're-naming' of cities and streets and emphasizes that 'Leningrad' is a name that had its own particular resonance and distinction:

The next day was that in which I fully realised that the shell was still the same, but that this was a very different city from what I had known it to be. St. Petersburg, Petrograd had gone for ever. This was Leningrad. It had inherited many things from the other two, but it had its own substance, its own personality. Leningrad was not just a new name for St. Petersburg; it was a name that meant a hundred things that the other did not. Similarly, there were a hundred things that belonged to St. Petersburg which could not be found in Leningrad. Perhaps this distinction was not so sharp three years ago, but to-day Leningrad had acquired the same distinctive personality as Stalingrad. One no more felt like calling Leningrad 'St. Petersburg' or 'Petrograd' than one felt like calling Stalingrad 'Tsaritsyn.' Perhaps, in the course of years, when thoughts of the siege and the blockade fade in people's memories, they may again colloquially refer to the city by its own name; but it is significant that throughout my stay not one person should have called the city Petrograd or St. Petersburg, though everybody without exception continued to call the principal streets and most of the others by their old names. It was always the Liteiny and the Nevsky, and the Morskaya – never the Volodarsky Avenue, or the October Twenty-fifth Avenue, or Herzen Street. People had not accepted these artificial innovations; they had, however, accepted the city's new name – a name full of new associations. St. Petersburg now belonged to literature, and to history, but no longer to real life. And nothing convinced me more of this than the curious personal experience of revisiting the house where I had spent the first sixteen years of my life, and which I had not seen for more than a quarter of a century.

Incidentally, by a decree issued on 13 January 1944, many of the old street names were restored, among them Nevskii, Liteinyi, Sadovaia, although that of Mokhovaia, on which Werth was born, had never been changed.

Werth was in the city during what had become by then a routine shelling of Nevskii Prospekt near Sadovaia and the Public Library, first opened in 1814 and continuing to serve its readers throughout the siege. He describes the almost miraculous survival of one of the best-loved squares in the city, which he calls by its old name, Aleksandrinskaia (*Aleksandrinka*), but which since 1923 had been renamed Ostrovskii Square, in the centre of which still stood the statue to Catherine II, designed by M.O. Mikeshin and unveiled in 1873.

What was interesting that day was our visit to the great Leningrad Public Library. This great library, at the corner of the Nevsky and the Sadovaya – one of the 'danger corners' during the shelling – claims to be, with its nine million volumes, the largest library in the world, or at any rate in Europe, with the exception of the British Museum. [. . .]

It was a beautiful sunny day when we drove up to the public library, but as the Sadovaya street corner is a dangerous one, and shelling has been going on since morning, it was decided that we park the car in the Alexandrinka Square on the other side of the library. Here we were, standing outside the car, and looking at the beautiful building of the Alexandrinka, with its freshly painted yellow stucco, and with the whole exquisite ensemble of Rossi's stucco buildings beyond, and to the left of us the little square in front of the Alexandrinka Theatre, with the bottle-shaped monument of Catherine, with Rumiantsev and Potemkin and other great men nestling below the sovereign's equally bottle-shaped skirt. It seemed almost miraculous how this beautiful corner of old St. Petersburg had escaped without a scratch. Although the streets were now very deserted – for the shelling was becoming heavier and heavier – this Alexandrinka Square looked more beautiful than it had ever looked. And just then one shell, and then another, crashed into something quite near, perhaps five hundred yards away, on the other side of the Nevsky, somewhere behind the enormous granite pavilion with its plate-glass windows, which was once the most Gargantuan delicatessen shop in Europe – Eliseyev. Two clouds of what looked like brick dust shot up into the air. The tramcars in the Nevsky stopped and the few passengers came running and dived into houses. A few other people could also be seen running for cover. We waited beside the car for a few minutes, not feeling too comfortable, but perhaps reassured by the extraordinary 'luckiness' of the Alexandrinka Square. An ambulance dashed past, turning into the Nevsky. I uncomfortably recalled Major Lozak's experience of the man who had staggered two steps down the Nevsky already without his head. The firing continued, but the shells were no longer exploding in this part, so we walked into the Nevsky – I had the feeling of slinking rather than walking – and round to the other 'unlucky' side of the State Library at the corner of the Sadovaya where, according to Leningrad hearsay, the Germans had a special knack of landing their shells in the middle of the crowd at the tramstop. Actually it did happen once or twice – hence the legend.

But now there was no crowd at any tramstop, the Nevsky was still deserted except for an occasional army car, half a dozen people on the allegedly more sheltered side of the street, and a girl policeman who continued to stand on point duty. Then one of the tramcars with two passengers inside began to move. Clearly Leningrad had learned not to be too lighthearted about shelling.

The trams mentioned by Werth had been re-activated in the spring of 1942; although they were few in number, they were the only form of public transport in the city.

Some six months later, in February 1944, Werth was again in Leningrad, just a few weeks after Soviet forces had broken the blockade. His book, *Leningrad,* was published in London at the end of the year and gave British readers their first eye-witness account of the devastation that had occurred in and around the city, including the destruction of the great palaces at Peterhof, Tsarskoe Selo and Pavlovsk.

Though I didn't see very much of Leningrad on this second visit, I spent two days in the wasteland around it – in those places which in September I'd only been able to see from that observation tower near the Narva Gate. Snow had fallen since the great battles of January, and had modestly covered up the earth. Even with the snow covering it the terrain was irregular – ploughed up by that fantastic Russian barrage.

And here and there a leg or a head was still protruding from under the snow. All around Ligovo and Pulkovo, where the main battle had been fought, there was nothing but a strange white lunar landscape with a few fantastically shaped fragments of brick walls standing (I identified one of them as Ligovo station). But already the trains were running among the ruins, running westwards towards Estonia. Here and there also a tree stood raising its bare shattered arms helplessly in the winter sky. Such was the immediate neighbourhood of Leningrad. Verdun – worse than Verdun after the last war. At Strelna, among what had once been cosy-looking country houses (many of these were still standing, for there hadn't been much shelling here) stood monstruous German siege guns inside concrete blockhouses eight inches thick. The Germans had certainly put in a lot of time and trouble to shell Leningrad. Beyond that was Peterhof with the pathetic remains of the great Rastrelli Palace, and a canal denuded of all its statues and fountains to show where the centre of Peterhof had been. The town of Peterhof had disappeared with the exception of a shattered church and a few other buildings. Tragic in a different way were the numerous villages, with their high-gabled huts, in the snowy plain between Peterhof and Tsarskoye Selo and Gatchina. They looked normal and intact. Yet there wasn't a soul to be seen anywhere. Everyone had been driven away into the rear by the Germans. Gatchina was the first place where 'native' population could be found – a couple of thousand people who had lived through two and a half years of the usual Nazi terror – with the concentration camp, still with barbed wire round it, occupying one of the main buildings of the town. [...]

The quiet charm of Pavlovsk and the splendour of Tsarskoye Selo, with its beautiful baroque Palace built for Catherine [Elizabeth] by Rastrelli and the classical colonnade built by Cameron, the Scottish architect, and all the rest of that wonderful ensemble of eighteenth-century art – all was now in ruins. True, part of the Catherine Palace had escaped complete destruction. That was only because some German sappers had been caught and had been ordered to remove immediately eleven delayed-action mines they had placed under the Palace. However, everything inside had been looted. Pavlovsk Palace had been set on fire the day the Germans left. Most of the trees in those poetic parks of Tsarskoye and Pavlovsk which had been sung by

Catherine's Poet Laureate, the great Derzhavin, by the young Pushkin and much later by Innokenti Annensky, the great symbolist poet, who was headmaster of Tsarskoye Selo high school and who in 1909 collapsed and died while wandering through the park – most of the trees had been cut down by the Germans. Most of this damage will never be repaired. The destruction of these palaces and parks has aroused among the Russians as great a fury as the worst German atrocities against human beings.

Even as the war drew to a close and in the months following the Allies' victory, Leningrad again received visitors, few in number and carefully monitored, coming as members of official delegations (parliamentarian, trades union, etc.) or, occasionally, as individuals at the invitation of VOKS, the Soviet bureau for cultural contacts. John Parker, Labour MP for Dagenham and Parliamentary Secretary, Dominions Office, was a member of the All-Party Parliamentary Delegation that visited the Soviet Union between 11 January and 25 February 1945 and spent a brief four days in Leningrad (21–4 January). He found the city centre 'not much damaged as Germans hoped to capture it to begin with and were unable to damage it when in retreat' and noted in his diary that

the re-colouring has already started on some of the palaces and apartment houses. The town should look very gay in summer when fully painted. The City Architect showed us the City plan and we then went to see new blocks of flats to south of city. These were more damaged by gunfire. New flats are also to be colour-washed but of rather uninteresting 'classical style' – French Empire – which is now the official style. Few good modern style buildings either here or in Moscow. The immediate post-revolution stuff was usually eccentric without being good. Some cottages to be built on outskirts and population limited to three and a half millions.

The delegation visited the Permanent Exhibition of the Defence of Leningrad, soon to be re-named the Museum of the Defence of Leningrad (*Muzei oborony Leningrada*), which had been founded as early as the beginning of 1942 and occupied a building in the so-called

Salt Settlement (*Solianoi gorodok*) on the left bank of the Fontanka near the Summer Garden. It says little for Parker that he 'spent a very boring time' there, although Walter Elliot, M.P. for Lanark and leader of the delegation, 'spent hours admiring guns whilst we wanted to get on. The relief across Lake Ladoga provided the most interesting set of plans and photos'. Parker was more moved by the trip the following day to Peterhof:

In the morning we motored south through the Russian and German lines. Here destruction was complete. Trees were practically all shot away in the woods and a suburb of 20,000 people was level with the ground. It was curious to see ruined tramcars almost all the way to Peterhof left along the track which runs beside the road, in groups (they run in threes or fours) just where they were when the Germans broke through suddenly and cut off their electricity. They seem to have survived the gunfire much more than buildings although some had been burnt out. Young trees were planted last autumn all along the main roads out (and many in Leningrad streets). We were told they took a long time to grow and so were the first things to be thought about. None appeared to have been destroyed by small boys. After passing the German lines we stopped some miles on and walked to see one of the gun emplacements from which Leningrad had been shelled. [. . .]

We reached Peterhof and are taken around the palace by the mayor and councillors. It was built by Peter the Great and was a magnificent eighteenth century show-place with well-laid-out gardens where Leningrad people came by boat in summer on a Sunday for the day out. The Germans set it on fire when they took the town and blew it up when they left. Nearly all the houses in the town had been fired. Some of the inhabitants had been deported to Germany for labour; some had returned who had fled before the Germans or had been released when the Russians reconquered Estonia. These had either made some part of their homes habitable or else had built dugouts below ground to live in for the winter. We were told that the whole palace was to be rebuilt as it was. It seems difficult to believe this possible particularly as far as the eighteenth-century interior is concerned. They have already begun to restore the park for use in summer.

No excursions outside the city were made by the novelist J.B. Priestley during his short stay in Leningrad as part of a visit to the Soviet Union at the invitation of VOKS in the autumn of 1945. Unquestioning, he was wined and dined to excess:

At the hotel there we had delicious food, the best I have ever had for years, but it arrived in so many courses and in such quantities that finally we had to explain to the young man in charge of our arrangements there that we could not cope with such gigantic meals. What, we asked, had given him such a notion of our appetites. Then he explained that, as a diligent student of English Literature, he had been looking into the works of Dickens and Thackeray, as guide to English taste in eating. So we had to explain that we were not the trenchermen our great-grandfathers were.

He paid a visit to the University of Leningrad, housed in Domenico Trezzini's famous Twelve Colleges on Vasil'evskii Island, and pronounced:

Personally I prefer Young Russia [as opposed to pre-Revolutionary Russia], especially as we saw it in the University of Leningrad, an old building that has the longest corridor I ever remember seeing. Along that astonishing corridor we were mobbed enthusiastically by students, who apparently made up their minds to compensate themselves for a shortage of English books by having a roaring good afternoon with English authors. This shortage of English books, especially textbooks and editions of our classics for students, was referred to wistfully in a dozen different places.

His general view of the city was that 'in spite of the long siege, the war damage is not very noticeable, although when you visit a number of the larger buildings you soon discover that most of them still contain wrecked rooms, chiefly the result of shellfire. And we did go in and out of a great many buildings – factories, schools, clubs, hospitals, theatres – because the Leningrad folk, perhaps our most enthusiastic hosts, were determined that we should see as much as possible.'

He did not highlight, however, the enormous amount of clearing and cleaning, reparation and restoration that had been carried out virtually from the moment the siege had ended. Isaiah Berlin, who was in Leningrad shortly after Priestley, on the other hand, noted that

> The centre of Leningrad shows virtually no destruction, and the restoration and renovation of public buildings, to which much attention has been devoted, seems now to be complete; they glittered with pride and splendour in the clear wintry air. The public statues and monuments are once again exposed to view, the Hermitage is open (all save the Spanish, French and English rooms), and is said to be preparing its German acquisitions – apparently for the most part drawings from Dresden and Berlin – for exhibition fairly soon.

Both Parker and Priestley published their accounts in 1946, but Berlin's comments with their reference to the art treasures removed from German museums were contained in an official memorandum that saw the light of day only in 2000. Born, like Alexander Werth, in Russia, which he left for England at the age of eleven in 1920, Berlin worked during the war for the Foreign Office. After visiting Moscow, he moved on to Leningrad, accompanied by Randolph Churchill, and they stayed for a week at the end of November 1945. His attempts to get to Pavlovsk and Oranienbaum were blocked, as Una Pope-Hennessy's had been nearly a decade earlier, but his visit left a profound impression on him, not least for his meetings with Anna Akhmatova about which he published elsewhere (and which, incidentally, were the subject of a recent Radio 4 play). It was 'three long evenings which I was permitted to spend among writers, occasionally tête-à-tête' which gave him an insight into the hardships and horrors of the siege, the rivalry between Leningrad and Moscow that was to worsen in the near future, the state of Soviet literature and its censorship, Leningrad's 'westernism' and the interest in English (and European) literature. Many of his memorable encounters were engineered through his acquaintance with the manager of the city's leading second-hand bookshop, the Writers' Shop (*Lavka pisatelei*) that occupied No. 22 Nevskii Prospekt, where in the 1830s–1840s A.F. Smirdin had a famous bookshop, frequented by the poets Zhukovskii and Pushkin and other leading literary figures of the day:

Gennady Moiseevich Rachlin is a small, thin, gay, baldish, red-haired Jew, noisy, shrewd, immensely and demonstratively affable, and probably the best-informed, best-read and most enterprising book-seller in the Soviet Union. Although, like other managers of State bookshops, he makes no official commission on his sales, and says that he subsists entirely on his official salary, his interest in and passion to promote the sale of books is at least as intense as that of any bookseller in the Western world. As the manager of the two most important bookshops in Leningrad, he is the official dictator of book prices in the city, and is evidently able to get books from other shops at very short notice, and thus to supply the needs of his clients more efficiently than any other known agent. Having certain vaguely romantic literary ambitions, founded on the memory of the famous booksellers of the nineteenth century who acted at once as the publishers, distributors and patrons of literature – his own bookshop is on the site of Smirdin's famous establishment – he has converted one of the rooms in his bookshop into a kind of club for writers and other favoured visitors, and in this room, which Miss Tripp [the British Council representative in Russia] and I were kindly invited to frequent, I was enabled not only to purchase books with a degree of comfort unknown in Moscow, but to make the acquaintance of several well-known literary persons, such as Zoshchenko, Akhmatova, Orlov, Dudin. Whenever I called, there were some three or four people in the room – artists, academic persons, writers – ostensibly looking round the bookshelves, but, as they very rarely carried anything away, perhaps more anxious to meet their friends in a warm room during the winter weather than to make any purchases. Conversation ran easily and freely in this little salon on literary, academic and even political subjects, and it was as the result of an acquaintance formed there that I visited an eminent literary person-age at home, and there met other members of the Leningrad intelligentsia. Rachlin himself took a lively part in these conversa-tions, though it was quite evident that his clients did not look upon him as an intellectual equal, but rather as an exceedingly capable literary factotum (which he is) with whom it was a good thing to keep in, since he acted as a kind of general Leningrad Figaro, procured theatre tickets, arranged lectures, gave monthly literary suppers, carried intelligence, disseminated gossip, and in general performed innumerable small services which made life more interesting, agreeable and indeed tolerable.

The visits of such as Parker, Priestley and Berlin came at a time when Leningrad half-opened its doors to foreigners, but they were soon closed shut not only as a result the 'Iron Curtain' that Winston Churchill discerned as stretching from 'Stettin in the Baltic to Trieste in the Adriatic' and the onset of the Cold War that destroyed the fragile bonds of war-time allies, but also of the savage repressions against Leningrad writers and, later, party officials that had their precedent in Stalin's mass repressions following the murder of Sergei Kirov in 1934. It was precisely Akhmatova and Mikhail Zoshchenko, whom Berlin had met at the end of 1945, who were attacked and abused less than a year later by A.A. Zhdanov, the former First Secretary of the Leningrad Communist Party and later, as Secretary of the Central Committee in Moscow, responsible for ideology. The notorious 'Leningrad Affair' (*leningradskoe delo*) followed in 1949–52, when, at the instigation of Stalin and Beria, cases were fabricated against almost all the leading political figures from the time of the Second World War, leading to imprisonment and execution. Lev Rakov, for instance, who was responsible for the Defence of Leningrad Exhibition visited by Parker and later became Director of the Museum and then of the Public Library, was removed from his office in 1950 but survived and was rehabilitated after the death of Stalin. It was Stalin's death in 1953 and Khrushchev's subsequent denunciation of him that led to a renewal of contacts with the West. Delegations once more visited Leningrad; Intourist 'welcomed' tourists; cultural agreements were signed.

Allan Chappelow led a group organized by the National Union of Students in the summer of 1954, the first tourists to visit the Soviet Union since 1939 and the first in Leningrad since early 1938. Seemingly expecting the worst, he found much to admire:

Reconstruction of the city, including the entire replacement of its water, gas, and electricity systems, and rebuilding and restoring of tens of thousands of houses and buildings, was begun in 1944, immediately after the siege was lifted. The miracle is that to-day, only one decade later, hardly a trace of this terrible damage and hardship is visible. Milling crowds throng the Nevsky Prospect and other thoroughfares with serene and happy expressions, as though nothing had been.

The food shops (*gastronoms*) we entered were very well stocked. Poultry, meat, and fish of various kinds; a large assortment of sliced sausages and cold meats (salami, ham, galantine, and so on); vegetables in abundance; different kinds of cheese; caviar, wines, butter, eggs, chocolates and sweets. Little, if anything, seemed scarce or not readily available. In one shop [formerly, Eliseev's on Nevskii Prospekt] I noticed drinks like Coca-Colas and some tins of *English* corned beef (the trade mark was Fray Bentos–Oxo). The five women cashiers were housed in five separate glass-fronted cubicles adjoining each other in the form of a pentagon, and raised about seven feet above the floor like a kind of multiple pulpit, with steps leading up – presumably to save floor space.

He was similarly impressed by the restoration of the exterior of the palace at Peterhof, which Parker had seen in ruins a decade earlier, although he was doubtful about the possibility, even the desirability, of restoring the interior. However, within another decade, much of the work had been done and some 5,000 fittings and objects that had been saved before the arrival of the Germans were returned to their pre-war positions.

The Palace has now been completely restored – externally – and looks majestically down over the fountains and gardens in its gleaming coat of cream-yellow paint, against which the white columns and window edges, and grey-tiled roof, contrast in a most elegant pattern. But nothing is left of the former splendour of Peterhof's interior decoration, furniture, and objets d'art. After attack by three thousand machine-gunners the Palace, originally constructed in 1706, was fired and completely gutted and the fountains wrecked by the vandal Nazis, who, all too frequently when they gained territory during the War, seem to have taken a special delight in desecrating its churches and historic buildings, and burning or otherwise ruining works of art. The intention is to restore the interior also. But this is an infinitely more difficult and inevitably less satisfactory matter than restoring the outside, since the imitations can never equal the original paintings, or Peter's various personal belongings – whose intrinsic interest would for most people derive from the very fact of their being original and genuine articles.

Richard Edmonds was a member of a different category of delegation, British town planners who were invited to Russia in May–June 1958 as guests of Gosstroi, the Soviet government building agency. So it was with a professional eye that he looked on the new buildings swiftly erected to meet the post-war shortage of housing in the context of a rapid growth in population – Leningrad's population, which had shrunk by an estimated 600,000 by the end of the war, was approaching three million by the end of the 1950s, and by the end of the 1970s was over four million. After visiting a vast pre-fabrication building plant, Edmonds and his colleagues moved on to see one of the major new areas of urban development. Ivanovskaia Street is in the Nevskii Region in the south-east of the city and crosses the Neva near the present-day metro station of Lomonosovskaia.

From the factory it was only a mile or two to one of Leningrad's largest new housing estates, Ivanovsky Street, where it was possible to see the pre-fabricated materials being put into use. The first impression on this estate is of rather poor workmanship, the blocks of flats being hastily thrown together. The flats, too, are on the whole dull and stereotyped, and they clearly have not come under the new influences now abroad in Russia. On examining finished work, however, the impression is rather better, a certain amount of moderate craftsmanship being neatly concealed. The one, two, and three-bedroomed flats (priced at 33, 70 and 105 roubles per month) are really very pleasant. Within the estate is a creche for the children and also a kindergarten. The essential criticism that can be levied at the Ivanovsky Street scheme is that it needs more of a neighbourhood spirit, a humanised modernism. There is reassurance in the fact that this new approach while not apparent in work done in Leningrad is clearly revealed in what is going on to the drawing board in the department of the City Architect. Russians, when they seize on new ideas are quick to implement them.

Of particular interest in Edmonds's book are his impressions of the Leningrad Metro, which he was seeing prior to his subsequent visit to the more famous and extensive metro in Moscow. The first eight stations on the Avtovo-Vyborg Line had been opened three years earlier, on 15 November 1955. The line then stretched from 'Avtovo', at the Square of Strikes (*Ploshchad' stachek*) in the south-west of the city, to the 'Square of the Uprising' (*Ploshchad' vosstaniia*) by the Moscow Station on Nevskii Prospekt, a distance of some eleven kilometres. The metro now boasts four lines and over fifty stations and is still being extended. A museum devoted to the history of the metro was established at 'Avtovo' in 1967. Edmonds describes two of the first stations, the 'Technological Institute' and 'Pushkin', where the bust of the poet is the work of A.K. Anikushin.

The morning ended with a journey to Metroland. 'What Moscow can do we can do better' say the people of Leningrad about most things, whether it be in the realms of sport, the arts, or production, and Leningrad's Metro is held to be no exception. Moscow's subway, which I have as yet to see in detail, is vast and elaborate. Leningrad's is also on a generous scale; but there is as yet no major network, the total distance of completed track cutting right through the centre of the city for 11 1/2 kilometres.

The circular domed booking hall of the Technological Institute Station must be fifty or sixty feet in diameter. The station itself is even more surprising, with a great central corridor running between the platforms and greatly embellished. The platforms and station corridors are bare of all advertisements and, as in the streets, as in the sports stadia, as everywhere there is no litter. People just don't drop paper and cartons about; they put it in the numerous but not obtrusive bins which are freely provided.

We got out at the first station up the line, the Pushkin Station, having noted that the trains travel smoothly and comparatively fast. They are not as comfortable as those on the London Underground, but are neatly upholstered in good leather cloth.

The Pushkin Station with its chandeliers and colonnades, is certainly opulent. At one end of the long central gallery between the platforms is a sculpture of Pushkin himself set in an elaborate marble bower with a scenic backdrop. Pushkin, the revolutionary poet, stands very high in Russia to-day, and after Lenin, a long way after Lenin, and after Stalin must be one of her most commemorated citizens.

They say that the Moscow and Leningrad metros are built in the lavish way that they are as a symbol to the people of the sort of targets the Revolution can achieve in every field. They are a harbinger of future excellence in every department of Russian life. This is no doubt quite true, but looked at more simply, here is a good service built to last and to meet future needs, and there is no reason at all why the underground stations should not be suitably embellished. Sometimes, perhaps, we are all too busy probing for motives, and over-anxious to make comparisons.

Bernard Newman prided himself on being a rather different type of visitor; indeed, he presented the sort of challenge that the Soviets were keen to discourage. In 1937 he had managed a bicycle tour through Europe to Kiev and Odessa and, twenty years on, he resolved to visit the Soviet Union once more, despite having been refused a visa during Stalin's lifetime, and to be as independent as possible, despite what he considered were prohibitive costs for the individual traveller. Seasoned traveller and author of a string of travel books, Newman, nevertheless, managed to 'see a good deal more than They [Soviet officialdom] want[ed] him to see', joining a small tour group in Leningrad itself but 'escaping' at every opportunity. It is encounters with people rather than descriptions of places that distinguish his book which distils an admiration for Leningraders and their proud cultural heritage – a superiority that was remarked upon by almost every visitor at this period. Nevertheless, he felt strongly that

Ghosts walk the night streets of Leningrad: Anna Karenina, vainly searching for happiness: Dr Pavlov, who experimented with more dogs that the whole city now possesses – the Communists 'adopted' him, and strove to fit his theories to human beings, but he refused to associate with the régime: Gogol, surely the saddest humorist the world ever knew: Pushkin, who died in St. Petersburg from wounds received in a duel: Dostoievski, who was educated at the Engineers' College and wrote 'Crime and Punishment' in the city. But he is regarded by the régime as a 'pernicious' writer, and is much more highly esteemed abroad than at home.

The 'literariness' of classical St Petersburg coloured visitors' perception of the Soviet city. Colin Wilson, author of *The Outsider* (1956) and categorized as one of the 'Angry Young Men' of English literature of the late 1950s, was inevitably alive to any Dostoevskian, and not only Dostoevskian, associations:

> Soviet propaganda accustoms us to thinking of men and women in overalls, with molten iron glowing in the background, and the shadow of Big Brother is over everything. But Leningrad is still, in every essential, the St. Petersburg of Dostoievsky. It is still the hopelessly inefficient and incompetent country that you find portrayed in 'Oblomov'. And there are still the same appalling little rooms with nineteenth-century wallpaper and unbelievably smelly lavatories.

As soon as he set foot on Russian soil, having arrived by boat from Helsinki, Wilson and his group of writers, who included John Braine, already well-known in Soviet Russia for his novel *Room at the Top* (1957) and even more, for its film version, 'found our way out of the docks and into the city of Gogol, Rasputin and the last of the Tsars':

> I had been told to expect a city of imposing prospects and some of the most magnificent architecture in the world. No doubt we went the wrong way. The dock area was exactly like the streets described by Dostoevsky in 'Crime and Punishment': wooden pavements, enormous but filthy tenement buildings, cobbled streets, giant drainpipes a foot in diameter that stop dead at the pavement and have no channel to carry their rain to the gutter; kvass tanks at the corner of many of the streets, all attended by very old women who sell the brown, fruity tasting drink (like plum jam in water) at a few copecks a glass; and the typical Leningrad smell of gasworks, the smell you never escape completely – it may be due to the bad petrol.

In his two articles for the *Sunday Times* in 1960 Wilson strove to convey his very mixed reactions to the people and their city, 'built by gods and now inhabited – by a race of troglodytes'. He seemed very disappointed in the Leningraders he observed, not least because of their clothes:

I found it very difficult to find a word for my feeling about Russian people. They seemed on the whole friendly enough, but somehow entirely preoccupied with their own business – there is none of the live-liness one finds in the French or the Italians.

This impression may be due partly to the appalling quality of the clothes in Russia. It is easy to spot a foreigner in Leningrad; he is better dressed than any Russian.

But apart from this, the 'average Russian' (if I may be allowed that dubious expression) seems still very close to the peasant. Their lumpi-ness, their lack of smartness seems bound up with a complete lack of sophistication. Women walk around with their babies wrapped in a giant cocoon of blankets, looking like a bundle of washing. Soldiers and sailors looked fantastically ill-dressed, as if uniforms too large for them had been stuffed with straw to fill in the spare space. And I, who am used to being regarded by my friends as incorrigibly scruffy, found myself in the position of being stared at because my clothes fitted.

What is more:

Oddly enough, I saw no pretty girls in Leningrad. At first I thought this impression must stem from the poor clothes, but a closer study of the girls who passed us in the streets made it apparent that this was not so. The reason baffles me; it may be simply that so many Russians are peasant types; perhaps all the 'beautiful, aristocratic' Russian women were driven abroad by the Revolution.

Shabby clothes equally impeded his appreciation of the Russians' love of literature and poetry in particular. Riding on a tram, 'I noticed that the woman in front of me was reading a volume of poetry; she looked an ordinary Russian housewife, the usual bundle of rags'. However, after successful forays into record stores and bookshops, he concluded on a more positive note:

The books and records were a part of the generally favourable impression made by Russian culture. It is obvious that by making no effort to cater to the cheaper public tastes (trash magazines, scandal newspapers, sensational films), the Russians have succeeded in raising the standard of general culture enormously. We passed open-air book-stalls where books were being bought as avidly and continuously as newspapers in the Charing Cross Road.

But this favourable impression was dissipated as soon as I settled down to study the Russian literary magazines printed in English. The Communist propaganda was unutterably trashy and stupid: the stories all full of oil derricks and collective farms and healthy, public-spirited young Communists. My main consolation was that Russia itself is nothing like this. We met no ardent Communists, and the few cultured Russians we talked to seemed unprejudiced and broad-minded.

Wilson wrote little about the city, except to record his admiration for Nevskii Prospekt, 'the gigantic avenue that is the Oxford Street of Leningrad and perhaps the most famous thoroughfare in Russia. I had not dreamed that it would be so magnificent. The huge curved façade of the Kazan cathedral is the most impressive piece of architecture I have seen'. Writing in December of the same year in *The Observer*, Sir William Hayter, author of the famous 'Hayter Report' that recommended the expansion of Russian studies in Britain's universities, was not at all impressed by this 'disappointing street. Of immense length and width, totally straight, it is flanked by buildings that are for the most part insignificant. It is on the quays and squares to the north of it that the best architecture is to be found'. He did concede, however, that 'few towns have better bones than Leningrad. Its shape and plan are superb'.

It was to write articles for *The Sunday Times*, which seemed to lead the way among numerous British newspapers eager to feature stories on conditions in Soviet Russia, that Ronald Hingley visited Moscow and Leningrad in the summer of 1960. Hingley, an Oxford don, best known for his studies and translations of Chekhov, offered in his subsequent book *Under Soviet Skins* (1961) perhaps the most informed and no-nonsense appraisal of contemporary Russia, but included little specifically about Leningrad. It did, however, include a vignette about its Palace of Matrimony (*Dvorets brakosochetaniia*), which was housed in the imposing mansion built in the 1890s by A.F. Krasovskii in the Florentine style for the wealthy P.P. Derviz on an embankment that has loomed large in these pages:

> In matters matrimonial Moscow has been put in the shade by Leningrad, which has instituted on the Embankment of the Red Fleet, formerly the English Embankment, a Palace of Matrimony in a pre-revolutionary building. This was started because of resistance among young Soviet couples to marry in the more sordid *zagsy* [registry offices].
>
> In the Leningrad Palace a distinguished-looking male Councillor performed the ceremony, making a longer address to bride and groom. I noted some of his phrases, which were spoken with great dignity.
>
> 'You are embarking on a union which will last all your life ... Yury Mikhaylovich, you are a very nice young man ... Do you promise to cherish and look after your lovely young bride? Will you promise to avoid quarrelling, that unhappy residue of the past in family life? Will you hand down the traditions of a firm family life to your children, grandchildren and even great grandchildren?' He also asked each couple sternly: 'Have you thoroughly pondered this serious step?' These Leningrad ceremonies were the only ones I saw at which such spoken affirmations were required, and also the only ones at which Mendelssohn's Wedding March was played on the gramophone as each couple arrived in the wedding hall.
>
> Here they have a doorkeeper who asks for your invitation card, but past whom the word 'tourist' guided me. The palace is overwhelmingly luxurious with glittering chandeliers, sparkling mirrors, marble columns, separate waiting rooms for bride and groom – and even high fidelity musical reproduction.

Alan Sillitoe, the poet and novelist, whose *Saturday Night and Sunday Morning* (1958) brought him fame and, a few years later, an invitation to visit the Soviet Union, which by his own admission he had long been eager to see, spent a week in Leningrad in the spring of 1963. He was impressed by the new Leningrad suburbs. 'New building didn't begin till six years ago. Before that industry was being rebuilt from the war. Now the construction fever is on, cranes are everywhere, tall thin machine-birds building living space.' He was no less taken with the 'luxurious' Astoria Hotel: 'I have a sitting-room, bathroom, and bed-alcove. I've never travelled in such style. Telephone, desk, wardrobe, sofa – the best Portobello Road antiques. There is a statue: *Phryné devant ses juges, par Campagne*, a naked figure done in bronze, modest in face, voluptuous in body'. Sillitoe acutely felt the history of the city around him, the city of revolution and of the siege, but in contrast to many visitors, he did not seek the exotic or the strange, but 'was heartened when the same connections [in his observing of faces] leapt the condensers of national and racial barriers'. His most detailed description is of his visit to the Smol'nyi (the former Institute for Noble Young Ladies, designed by Quarenghi) for traces of Lenin, but it is his cameo, capturing the end of winter, that provides a more fitting farewell to the city:

> Spring is flowing along the Neva, taking the last black snow off the streets. Cleaners heap up their carts with blocks of dirty ice and, when loaded high, slide the whole lot onto the still solid ice-surface of the canals. The tipped ice lays there like a load of coal. Some, though, is melting, changing from coal to mounds of dark wax, as if fires have been lit below it. Suddenly the ice breaks like thin glass, and the pile slides under. The city is thawing, and next week a general spring clean is in order, all citizens working to beautify their city for when leaves come out on the trees.

The late 1950s and early 1960s saw a veritable spate of accounts and impressions of Leningrad, but the Cuban Missile Crisis of 1962 (which I remember vividly, 'marooned' as I was at Moscow University) moved the world into a more confrontational phase of the Cold War, which was followed by the uneasy years of the so-called détente in the 1970s, before the situation worsened again in the early 1980s. During these decades, British visitors still came to Leningrad via the normal channels of group travel, delegations and student exchanges. Intourist was encouraging tourism while dictating what was to be seen, what could be photographed, what questions could be answered. The situation was not promising for the would-be independent traveller. As Colin Thubron recorded in one of the more engaging accounts of the 1980s:

'"Are you a group?" she asked. It was a quintessential Russian question. I glanced down at myself. No, I was not a group. Solitariness here is rare, odd. It was not catered for. I found myself apologizing for it.' But Thubron travelled alone, in his old battered car, and despite all the points of his itinerary carefully pre-arranged through Intourist, he still managed, in the spirit of Bernard Newman, to see far more than he was supposed to.

Thubron was much taken with Leningrad. The chapter he devotes to it opens in a way reminiscent of the classical British accounts of the late-eighteenth and nineteenth centuries:

Leningrad is like no other city in Russia or on earth. It seems to reject the half-Asiatic hinterland on whose rim it hangs, and to have exchanged this troubled parentage for the grace of eighteenth century Europe. On the northernmost limits of the ancient Byzantine world, it lies like a pale and beautiful question-mark. In 1917 the Bolsheviks repudiated it as capital, and it is touched now by the sad, patrician glow of an Istanbul or an Alexandria. However important its present, its past seems to saturate it. Bathed in the lost harmony of Europe, it symbolizes the paradoxical leaning of Russia towards the West, spurred by an atavistic dread of China and a centuries-old longing for civilized recognition.

Whereas the streets of most old Russian cities radiate out from a crumbling or vanished kremlin, those of Leningrad echo the centripetal grace of its canals. As I drove in deeper, its office and apartment blocks gave way to a glimmer of nineteenth century mansions, seedy and blemished now, along the outer waterways. Then, in an ever-tightening rhythm of alternate water and stone, the city's heart came beating round in its saddened splendour. All the way to where the Neva river wound beneath a rank of water-reflecting palaces, and the Gulf of Finland opened to the west, canals and avenues succeeded one another in long, shining arcs of ever-increasing beauty.

Leningrad ineluctably has been called the Venice of the North. In fact it resembles Venice little more than Paris or London does. No Mediterranean warmth overhangs the measured glory of its canals, but a clean, unenchanted Nordic light. Palace follows palace, terrace follows terrace, with the impersonal radiance of a Bach cantata. All is cool, balanced, spacious. Under a coldly luminous sky, the thousands of quiet dwellings line the waters without appearing to partake of them. Even in summer the fogs and ice of the Neva seem to pervade the streets. These mansions reject any charm of southern ornament or light, and hold their place by elegance of proportion alone. Here and there the curve of a pedimented window or a lightly-moulded frieze breaks the stone serenity, but all the rest is a soft interplay of chromatic squares and rectangles. Their colours are wintry pale – gentle and reticent in the summer sunlight, as I first saw them: pastel yellows, ochres and oranges. The quays and pavements beneath are shod in pink-grey granite, and the bridges reach over the canals in single spans of handsomely-wrought iron, forged with winged heads and long redundant coats-of-arms.

It is a city, however, into which the present intrudes:

Trams and concertina-like Hungarian buses wobbled along the streets; but often the ways were half deserted. In every other lane my car would hit a heaving slipstream of cobbles. Open manholes gaped without warning in the middle of the thoroughfares, and twice I nearly dropped the car into one. Every street was a long, seductive ambush. Tram-lines erupted like swords from their cobbled beds; and once I almost crashed into one of the official black limousines, bullying its way down a road's centre.

Thubron brings life and verve to descriptions of even the most familiar tourist sights. Having quoted 'blinding statistics' about the size of the Hermitage, he was still unprepared for the impact the palace made:

Yet inside, its sheer immensity comes as a shock. Long before I had traversed the vaulted and galleried halls of the ground floor, where the kitchens and services once spread, I was drowned in an ocean of variegated marble, my eyes aching and dazed with colour, drenched by ceilings which burst into a delicate glory of plasterwork or arched overhead in rococo vines and a blaze of armatures. Dragons and lions and a hundred mythological beasts stiffened among the foliage; cherubim kicked and squirmed; and the twin-headed Romanov eagle, talons sceptred and orbed, raked the void with his double gaze.

After five hours I was washed up in stupefaction at the foot of the ceremonial stair. Circled by alabaster nymphs, its marble steps lifted in mountainous serenity towards painted ceilings where the ancient gods tumbled over Olympus. By now I was wandering in stunned anaesthesia. Around and above me, in room after room, there unfolded a panoply whose every square inch glittered with an insect's toil of gilded appliqué, the whirl and shreik of stucco griffins and thunder of gold-entangled lions. Raphael, Rembrandt, Leonardo, Rubens – their masterworks swam by me in a pageant of indigestible glory. I simply stared at the ceilings, the columns, the floors under my senselessly trudging feet. I wandered by fantastic torchères and caryatids sleepy with gold, and slithered over shining lakes of precious inlaid wood. All around me crowds of Russian tourists were tramping through the glamour of their repudiated past. Their mild, rustic faces, and the portraits of imperial courtiers, contemplated one another with mutual astonishment. On and on went the rooms, flowering into marble and porphyry stage-sets, reproducing themselves in ormolued mirrors, opening onto parquet pools of ebony, mahogany and amaranth, sinking under the drip and gush and crystal. In the Malachite Room, where vistas of the grey Neva and a troubled sky hung like pictures in the windows, the mantelpieces and columns were vivid with two tons of their green treasure, dug from the Urals. The great ballroom, scene of the innocent transvestite banquets of the empress Elizabeth, shone miraculous with 116 fluted pillars and pilasters and its mammoth chandeliers, blazoned with the arms of all the Russian provinces, filled the room with a ravishing incandescence, like frosted, aerial Christmas trees.

Thubron's contacts opened up to him homes in city and suburbs whose occupants were far less concerned about the attentions of the K.G.B. than he was. In the suburbs, he furtively visited the flat of a dissident, where a group of young people smoked and sang and passed around typewritten copies of Solzhenitsyn and other forbidden authors, *samizdat*; later, he attempted to negotiate a cluster of apartment blocks in a 'planetary landscape' to the north of the city and reflected that 'for the past quarter century, the government has launched a titanic rehousing campaign. Every year between two and three million new apartments have been built. They are aesthetically null, and poorly constructed; almost before they are up, the bricks drop off, the concrete cracks, the paint flakes away. But they have transformed their people's lives'. He also describes a flat

in a nineteenth century apartment house in the city's centre, four storeys up magisterial stone steps with elaborate iron banisters, dark and filthy now, the windows cracking. Their three-room flat looked down into an echoing courtyard piled with crates. The living-room was monopolized by two huge beds raised on blocks of wood. The curtains were gossamer thin. Heavy furniture stood about, its drawers crammed with worn blankets, pillows, books. A budgerigar perched dumb in a cage. There were no carpets, no ornaments, no pretence at decoration at all. The Russian aesthetic sense seemed to have died with Lucia's [his friend's] ancestors.

It was, however, in a similar flat that Duncan Fallowell, novelist and travel writer, was to rent a room and live for the summer of 1993:

The flat is of the Dada school of art, having a quality of makeshift in many of its accoutrements. Water pipes are visible, and rusty or badly painted. Rigmaroles of electric wiring and socketry are pinned to walls like ivy. The bathroom is basic, home to a degenerate gas heater which after various jabs and strokings can be persuaded to spout a curmud-geonly amount of warm water. The loo likewise is basic, home to a cat tray. Furniture, some pieces quite noble, is either damaged or brand new, mostly the former. An array of glum ornaments stands about. Few of the movables have any connectedness: random totems triumphantly connived for in the social struggle. The wall plaster is in bad condition, papered over but the paper peeling here and there, patched with diverse rectangles, the whole disintegrating faster than it can be disguised. These motley walls enclose a general high-ceilinged dimness, and dimness was at first my most vivid impression, of the city as we drove into it, of the flat as we entered it, as though everything were dissolving into everything else in a haze of dust and faded colours. It is a dimness which immediately absorbs the attention, for once the eyes have adjusted, they discern an extreme and lively mellowness, a visual world animated by having no hard edges.

Thubron had been in Leningrad during the period known as 'stagnation' (*zastoi*), when the greyer than usual men in the Kremlin suffocated the country and the unrest was palpable; Fallowell arrived a decade later, when the Soviet Union was no more and the atmosphere was so very different, if the living conditions had hardly changed. 'Before, one could *visit* Russia (although I only ever had 1 day in Moscow). Now, for the first time in nearly 100 years, it is possible to *be* here.' In March 1985 Gorbachev had been elected First Secretary of the Communist Party and embarked on a programme of economic and policy reform. *Glasnost'* (openness) and *perestroika* (restructuring) were the order of the day and led to unexpected and unforeseen consequences. Within five years Gorbachev and President George H.W. Bush had declared the Cold War was at an end, but, two years later, so was the Soviet Union. In June 1991 Boris Eltsyn was elected President and in December the USSR was transformed into the CIS, the Commonwealth of Independent States. What is more, Leningrad became St Petersburg again, when on 6 December 1991 just 54% of those voting agreed to the change. *Catastroika* (catastructure) was the word coined to denote the disastrous economic situation that prevailed, but it was the new sense of liberation that Desmond Hogan, visiting the city on two occasions in 1989, mirrored in a description of the city's famous 'white nights':

In the week of white nights, everything seems to converge on the evening, when the band started up with 'I celebrate my love for you' at the Metropole where Rasputin and Nicholas II dined, hands in the air, against the lamé backdrop.

But of all places at evening, it is the Leningrad Jazz Club in Zagorodny Street, near Restaurant Troika, which seems to capture the spirit of Leningrad, red shaded lamps on the tables, pictures of black American jazz artists around the walls – Dave Brubeck, King Oliver and his Creole Band, Billie Holliday, Ella Fitzgerald, Count Basie – Greek sailors drinking white wine in the generous light of the foyers, Elvira Trakhova singing 'Sweet Georgia Brown', people dancing the samba on small platform; some women in low-cut, black Fifties dresses, some in early Sixties pedal-pusher trousers, some men in suits, others in shorts.

He also suggested that 'the soda and ice-cream parlours in Nevsky Avenue were the places to retreat for colour' and described how

> Often these parlours have no name, but they are nick-named. The one further down Nevsky Avenue, beside Zelabova [Zheliabov] Street, is called the Frog Café, perhaps because of the green festoons, green table coverings and green marble on the walls. Likewise with cafés. One, officially unnamed, is called the Saigon because the eating conditions are cramped; another the Gastric because the food is reputed to be indigestible. A café that is named outside The Black Coffee is more generally known as The Bell because there are bells in the patterns on the walls. Café names are a kind of samizdat in Leningrad.

It is, however, to Fallowell, whose evocation of life in the new St Petersburg is a stunning *tour de force*, that we go for a valedictory look at the scene on the great Nevskii Prospekt, where his attention is focussed not on the buildings but on the passers-by, in the spirit of Nikolai Gogol:

> Nevsky Prospekt incidentally is the only thoroughfare in St Petersburg which is busy – and it is *always* busy. The pavements are lined with market stalls, and alongside them chorus lines of individuals stand motionlessly, each holding up a single object for sale – a book, a bottle, a jumper, anything. The heterogeneous crowd surges past them – office workers, shoppers, families, students, tourists, old men with a row of military medals pinned to frayed jacket, gypsy beggars barefoot and filthy. The young people are strikingly sexy, with a dash of bravura or fierceness in them and something spaced-out too. Slavs often have remarkable eyes and mouths. The weakest feature is the putty nose but this often confers charm to a face which would otherwise be too superb. The racial mix is very apparent and their bodies are well-made, thanks to work, exercise, national service: straight backs, firm limbs, a natural physical confidence in the walk. Girls show their legs in very short skirts, and boys their muscles in tight coloured singlets. It is quite believable that these people have been Europe's most resolute 20th-century empire builders. But the hard life tells. Evidence of physical damage is widespread among all categories, often carried off with flair:

scars, bandages, arms in slings or plasters, bashed noses, black eyes, purple bruises. Yes, damage can be colourful – uncovered lesions are marked with medicated paint in red, orange or green.

And uniforms can be colourful. These are no longer the uniforms of cavalry officers of the Imperial Guard who wore white kaftans with gold belts and high white lambskin caps; but they are nonetheless very colourful by non-royal standards. Black, grey, white, blue, green, khaki, decorated with gold and red; caps forward over eyes or level or on backs of heads, belts round trousers or round the waist of jackets Cossack-style, trousers over boots or tucked into boots; uniforms singly or collectively wherever you look. This prevalence is not threatening because the men inside them do not strut. They are part of the normal human round. Picturesque, often at ease, chatting, smoking, sometimes relaxed to the point of loucheness.

Alan Sillitoe had stridden around Leningrad in 1963 with the 1914 Baedeker in his hand. Just as, twenty-five years earlier, Una Pope-Hennessy had clutched her Murray. During the 1960s and 1970s these guidebooks were not replaced by any adequate up-to-date English original and the visitor, preparing for a trip to the Soviet Union and visiting prior to departure Collet's Russian Bookshop in London, would find only poorly printed and worse illustrated semi-official and always approved guides translated from Russian that did their best to hide much that was really interesting in Leningrad's past – and present. The accompanying city maps always and only impressed with their simplicity and clarity, achieved by omitting most of the smaller streets and many historically significant buildings, particularly churches. The 1980s and certainly the 1990s changed all this. As Leningrad moved to become St Petersburg, so the guidebooks became more informative, ever more beautifully designed and illustrated. We have long had a Blue Guide to Moscow and Leningrad/St Petersburg and it has been joined by Fodor's, Lonely Planet, Rough, Everyman, and Nelles guides; Rose Baring, Chris Booth, Christopher Knowles, Catherine Phillips, Christopher and Melanie Rice, and Nick Selby have all edited or written guides in the 1990s, either on the twin cities and on St Petersburg alone. St Petersburg has even joined the short-break circuit and Reg Butler published his *City Breaks in Moscow and Leningrad* even before the name change in 1991. The maps are now helpful and detailed and we even have a *Traveller's Yellow Pages and Handbook for St Petersburg*, after all those years endured during the Soviet period with no telephone directories of any sort. Thirsty for so long for information, we are now also 'deluged', in the best Petersburg tradition, with Russian works on every facet of Petersburg life, old and new: we have detailed toponymies, registering the see-sawing in the names of streets, stations, squares and schools in imperial, Soviet, and post-Soviet times; we have fascinating booklets and brochures on the histories of house after house down the most famous streets; the city administration produces a regular quarterly *St. Petersburg: The Official Guide*, in Russian, English, German, Finnish and French, advertising events, restaurants, hotels. There are regular newspapers, both Russian and foreign, and journals, such as *Where St. Petersburg*, distributed *gratis* in the city's hotels, to inform the visiting businessman or tourist. In short, St Petersburg has enjoyed for a decade or more most of the things we take as expected of a great European city.

Twelve years after the city was re-named, it celebrated in 2003 the tercentenary of its founding, a mega-event, over a decade in the planning, that kept the eyes of the world on St Petersburg. A year earlier, in 2002, Robert Wistrich visited St Petersburg with a predominantly British 'senior citizen' tourist group, and in a 'Letter from St Petersburg' for the *Times Literary Supplement*, he described it as 'no longer the decaying backwater bequeathed by decades of bungled Communist planning, pollution and neglect. The signs of vitality are palpable – new industries, new roads and building renovations – as well as injections of fresh cash and new ideas'. He compared what he now found with the city he had seen on his first visit in 1992, shortly after the failed coup of 19 August 1991 and the emergence of Boris Eltsyn:

> [. . .] there were huge potholes in the streets, and the state of the buses was pathetic. The tap and bathwater in my hotel had a sickly yellowish-brown colour, and the local beer looked more like a bad urine sample. There was a thick grime over many of the public buildings, and infested waterways were a health hazard. Today, Petersburg streets look relatively well-paved, the Nevsky Prospekt seems reasonably well-stocked with goods, Russian youth are dressed more like their

Western counterparts and there is a certain liveliness in their gait. Many of the town houses have been redecorated and refurbished. The homeless, the destitute, the drunks, the prostitutes and the drug addicts are much less in evidence than they were a decade ago.

The 1990s had been a difficult time for St Petersburg, so much to do and so little money to do it. The 'window on Europe' was now, however, opened widely enough to allow through essential international funding to sponsor building and restoration projects and to provide expertise in fields in which Russia was deficient. The city's historical centre has become a UNESCO World Heritage Site. The Hermitage, the financial plight of which was first highlighted in a long article for *The Independent on Sunday* in April 1993 by Geraldine Norman, reached out for and attracted support from a network of 'Friends' in the U.S.A. and Europe. Among its initiatives was the establishing of the Hermitage Rooms at Somerset House in London, where the exhibitions served (alas, no longer) as a permanent reminder of the museum's vast treasures and its constant needs. The Prince of Wales's International Business Leaders' Forum has been very actively engaged in the city, for over a decade, promoting business skills and cultural enterprises. One of its earliest individual projects was the monumental facsimile edition in eight volumes (1995–7) of Pushkin's working notebooks, designed to benefit Pushkin House, the Russian Academy's Institute of Russian Literature (the former Customs House) on the Makarov Embankment of Vasil'evskii Island, where the originals are preserved.

HRH the Prince of Wales had himself visited St Petersburg to see the notebooks in May 1994. It was in October of the same year that Her Majesty the Queen paid a state visit to Russia, sailing up the Neva in the Royal Yacht Britannia, which moored by the newly renamed English Embankment. HRH Prince Michael of Kent, whose striking resemblance to the last Romanov tsar has endeared him to many Petersburgers, has visited the city on several occasions, attending the re-internment of the remains of the murdered Romanov family in 1998 and, five years later, leading a charity fund-raising rally of vintage Bentleys from Ekaterinburg to St Petersburg to mark the tercentenary. A return visit by HRH the Prince of Wales in July 2003 to attend a gala dinner in the Hermitage was the culmination of a decade of royal visits and recognition not only of the tercentenary but also of 450 years of Anglo-Russian relations.

There may no longer be an identifiable British community in the city, but many British, businessmen and students in the main, are temporary or, in some cases, permanent residents. Indeed, there are probably more British than at any time since the October Revolution, but they are now part of a much wider and amorphous international community. The English Church, for so long the epicentre of community life, was returned to British ownership, but the lack of church-goers has led to the building's present use as an uninspiring Russian souvenir centre.

British awareness of St Petersburg nevertheless is perhaps at an all-time high and British newspapers and journals have given, and continue to give, many column inches to events, both image-enhancing and potentially disastrous. Over the past few years there have been articles on the imaginative plans for the extension of the Mariinskii (Kirov) Theatre; on the successful completion of the restoration of the Amber Room in the Catherininan Palace at Pushkin in time for the tercentenary; likewise, on the Constantine Palace at Strel'na on the Peterhof Road which in 2001 President Putin had ordered to be restored as a presidential residence and which was to house some fifty heads of state during the tercentenary celebrations; and, indeed, on the playing of the band of the Royal Marines as they marched down Nevskii Prospekt on May 31 2003 (by a curious coincidence, almost fifty years since the Marines played in the Kirov Stadium on a goodwill visit in October 1955); and, more recently, on the fire that devastated the dome of the great Trinity Cathedral. This last catastrophe took place just weeks after the holding at Strel'na of the G8 summit in July 2006 had re-focused world attention on the city.

It was on the eve of the summit that Bel Mooney visited St Petersburg for the first time and was 'enthralled', 'gliding under the elaborate bridges that give the city its Venetian quality'. Hers was the enthusiasm of a neophyte: 'with almost nothing of the puritan about me, delighting in decoration, in the unnecessary opulence of a park railing, in rampant creativity, eccentricity and (always) an indulgent third glass of icy vodka, I was bound to fall for this strangest of cities'. At the bottom of the page in *The Times* where her article appeared,

Intourist was advertising the attractions of a discounted tour to St Petersburg and Moscow, as it had done for virtually fifty years (compare the advert on the same page as Sir William Hayter's article in 1960), but it has long since had more glamorous competitors among the great tourist firms and cruise lines of the world. It is virtually impossible to turn the travel pages and sections in any British newspaper without being offered the delights of a visit to St Petersburg. The stately city on the banks of the Neva, much more than an often brash and vulgar Moscow, is a magnet for countless visitors arriving by air, land and sea. The Baltic cruise with St Petersburg as one of its highlights is perhaps the most appealing way of approaching the city and one which British tourists have used since the early eighteenth century, when Sir Francis Dashwood proclaimed St Petersburg 'worth any curious man's while, going to See'.

CHAPTER 10

IMAGES OF ST PETERSBURG

It was the likenesses, often distant, of Peter the Great rather than of his city that adorned the biographies which began to appear after his death; at best and in a minority of examples, there was some gesture towards inhabited space in the background. No British artist or visitor with pretensions to draw what he saw seems to have left any sketches of St Petersburg (or indeed, of anywhere else in Russia) before the reign of Catherine. If we discount the image of the fortress of Kronslot on the map that accompanied the description of the city in Weber's *The Present State of Russia* (1722), the engraving of La Motraye's drawing of the Alexander Nevskii Monastery (1732) was the first representation of a building in St Petersburg to be published in England. It was similarly from a foreign source, the 1753 jubilee album, that the 'View of the Exchange and Warehouses at Petersburg in Russia' was re-engraved for sale as a separate print in London in 1754, aimed primarily, it would seem, at merchants sentimental about their days in the Russia capital. This engraving and others from the album, including the wooden Summer Palace Rastrelli had built for the Empress Elizabeth, were thereafter much used in popular publications such as Middleton's *New and Complete System of Geography* (1777–8) to illustrate the 'present state' of the Russian capital long after some of the buildings in question had disappeared or been radically altered. Two further engravings of notable buildings might be mentioned, although undoubtedly both came originally from foreign sources: the large quarto engraving of Rastrelli's Smol'nyi Cathedral that was the frontispiece to the Rev. John Glen King's book on the Orthodox church (1772); and the more humble image of the English Church on the Neva embankment, of which King was once the chaplain, appearing in *Gentleman's Magazine* in 1796. All these images were of pre-Catherinian buildings; the first monument of her reign to be drawn and engraved was, appropriately, Falconet's Bronze Horseman.

The first representation of the statue was published in England a few years before the monument itself was officially unveiled in 1782. The sculptor's son, Pierre, who had studied at the Royal Academy in London under Sir Joshua Reynolds before joining his father in Russia, produced a fine drawing which was engraved by the Royal Society's engraver James Basire for the Rev. William Tooke's *Pieces Written by Mons. Falconet, and Mons. Diderot* (1777) and repeated in 1783 in *Gentleman's Magazine*. Thereafter the statue became a favourite subject for the sketch-pads of British visitors, serving as the frontispiece to Andrew Swinton's *Travels* of 1792, for instance, when he took it upon himself 'to correct some errors' in Pierre Falconet's drawing, and also brought a very British response to too much fame, an anonymous and amusing caricature.

Catherine's reign had, however, brought to St Petersburg its first professional British painters. It was in the late 1770s that Richard Brompton, George Carter and Edward Francis Cunningham (often known as Francesco Calze) sought commissions at the Russian court and it was portraits of the empress that they painted. Brompton, appointed painter to the imperial court, was also allowed to 'to paint *en ville*', but aristocrats rather than the city itself provided the subjects for his brush. It was the next wave, a few years into the 1780s, that was to produce the first British 'topographical' artists, the little-known Joseph Hearn and the more talented and much better known John Augustus Atkinson.

It was only when the set of six acquatint engravings that Thomas Malton executed from Hearn's watercolour originals was published in London in 1789–90 that some of St Petersburg's most famous sights could be 'viewed' by the British public: the Academy of Sciences, the Academy of Arts, the *Gostinyi dvor*, the Fontanka, the Marble Palace on Millionnaia and the Arsenal on Liteinaia. Hearn's accurate drawings, enlivened by foreground scenes, capture the city at an important time during its 'improvements' under Catherine and only partially recorded in contemporary British written accounts. Thus, for example, 'A View on the Fontancka Canal St Petersburg' shows the Simeonovskii Bridge, built in 1784–7, and the iron railings, designed by Quarenghi, along the granite-clad embankment of the river; Quarenghi's classical Academy of Sciences with its eight-columned portico, completed in 1785, dominates the view across the Neva towards Vasil'evskii Island; while further west along the same embankment, the Academy of Arts, often called the most French of St Petersburg's great buildings and designed by Vallin de la Mothe but rarely described in written accounts, is the centre piece of another view. The only evidence we have of Hearn's continuing interest in Petersburg scenes is a watercolour of the ice hills on the Neva from the early 1790s, but no other engravings from his work seem to have been made.

A close friend of Hearn (he was a witness at his wedding in 1793) was the court engraver James Walker, who in 1784 had arrived in St Petersburg with his wife and nine-year-old stepson John Augustus Atkinson. One of Walker's principal tasks was to make engravings from paintings in Catherine's collections in the Hermitage and in 1792 he returned briefly to England to supervise the publication of the first two folders of *A Collection of Prints, from the Most Celebrated Pictures in the Gallery of Her Imperial Majesty Catherine the Second, Empress and Autocratix of all the Russias*. The eleven high-quality mezzotint engravings included works by Rembrandt, Murillo, Guido Reni, Greuze, as well as Sir Joshua Reynolds's 'Infant Hercules', acquired by the empress only four years previously. The publication gave a few privileged British collectors the opportunity to see some of the treasures of the Hermitage, such as described by countless British visitors to St Petersburg. It was also in its way a companion piece to the two-volume *Set of Prints Engraved after the most capital Paintings in the Collection of Her Imperial Majesty the Empress of Russia Lately in the possession of the Earl of Orford at Houghton in Norfolk* (1788), a reminder of the permanent loss to the nation of the 'Houghton Collection', thereafter also only to be seen by visitors to the Hermitage. Walker's contribution to the British awareness of St Petersburg lay, however, not in his engravings but in the extensive captions he was to provide for a publication by his stepson and in the series of lively anecdotes, entitled *Paramythia, or Mental Pastimes*, that he was to publish anonymously and many years later, in 1821.

Atkinson showed precocious talent as an artist and, still in his mid-teens, he produced a painting of the Easter festival in St Petersburg, which, apparently, attracted the attention of Catherine, and followed this with one of the ice hills which was very near in date and detail to Hearn's. It was, however, only in the early years of Alexander's reign and subsequent to their return to England in 1802 that he published in quick succession his *Panorama of St Petersburg* and *A Picturesque*

Representation of the Manners, Customs, and Amusement of the Russians.
There is some dispute whether the *Panorama* appeared for the first time
in 1802–3 or only in 1805–7, the latter date considered by some to be
that of a reprint; the plates are undated, which is not the case with the
hundred plates of *A Picturesque Representation*, issued in three volumes
in 1803–4. During the months before he left St Petersburg Atkinson
looked down on the city from the Observatory of the Academy of
Sciences and produced the drawings from which he etched the four
acquatints that were issued as a large oblong album, some 44 × 80 cm.
He thus provided a panoramic view of the city as it appeared on the eve
of its centenary and prior to the great structures of Alexander's reign. It
is an outstanding British contribution to a tradition of panoramas of the
Neva and its embankments started in Peter's time by the Russian artist
Aleksei Zubov, continued in the Makhaev album of 1753, and main-
tained in the paintings and watercolours of the Swedish artist Benjamin
Pattersen, whom Atkinson and Walker undoubtedly knew. The first
two plates depict the left bank from the Marble Palace to the Winter
Palace and from the Admiralty to the end of the English Line respec-
tively, and the remaining two, the right bank, from the Academy of
Arts to the Twelve Colleges and from the New Exchange to the Peter
and Paul Fortress, and under each plate Atkinson identified the main
buildings. The few buildings that coincide with those depicted by
Hearn, such as the two Academies and the Marble Palace, are seen from
quite different perspectives. Although the third plate, showing the
English Line, would have commanded particular interest, it is the
fourth which offers an unusual view of the Strelka or eastern end of
Vasil'evskii Island. This was very much the 'business end' of the city; to
the left, across a wide unbuilt space, are the old exchange and warehouses, and in the centre is the so-called 'New Exchange', Quarenghi's
building, approved twenty years earlier but still unfinished and soon to
be dismantled for a newer and differently sited temple to Mammon
designed by Thomas de Thomon.

Buildings were not the primary concern of *A Picturesque
Representation of the Manners, Customs, and Amusements of the Russians*,
as the title makes clear, but buildings in the capital had their role to play
as background and setting in many of the hundred plates. Atkinson
roamed wide in his choice of subject, depicting life in town and village,

sports and pastimes, forms of transport by land, sea, and river, winter and summer (no less than twenty-six plates), rites and rituals, including birth, marriage, and death, and, of course, inside a bathhouse, and a whole portrait gallery of 'types', from metropolitans to nuns, soldiers and sailors, merchants and mead-sellers, watchmen and yardmen, but, interestingly, no representatives of the gentry and aristocracy, except in the depiction of the wedding ceremony. Many of the scenes and people could be found in village or town, but a sense of place is basic to depictions of the Haymarket, the Frozen Market on the Neva, the horse races on the frozen river, the fish barges on the Neva and the Moika which 'serve the fishmongers at once for dwelling houses, shops, and fishponds', and of city types such as the watchman (*budochnik*) and the yardman (*dvornik*). 'The Consecration of the Waters', the ceremony on 6 January observed in many places in Russia and described in so many visitors' accounts, is depicted at its most famous spot before the Winter Palace, while 'A Public Festival on Palace Square' shows the curious public festivities or *cocagne* that accompanied 'the nuptials of a person of the Imperial family' and is described at length by Walker.

A Picturesque Representation was a unique publication, a blending of the work of a talented artist and of an engraver-turned-writer able to offer 'an accurate description of each plate' in an informative and lively way. Walker was later to write that reviewers 'had complimented Mr A. on the truth, freedom, and spirit of the etched prints' and the finished product gains immeasurably from Atkinson's supervising all the process from drawing to engraving and colouring. His nervous, impressionistic style gives a freshness and spontaneity conspicuously lacking both in the efforts of his immediate predecessors and contemporaries and in most of those who followed him.

Walker in his preface to *A Picturesque Representation* was anxious to contrast Atkinson's method with those books where 'costumes [are] treated in a geographic, rather than a picturesque manner', stressing that 'as character, action, and expression, and not the minute particulars of dress, have always appeared to us to form the distinguished features of nations, it is to that great object we have devoted our principal attention and effort'. He highlights 'the impossibility of seizing the character of the people, without an intimate acquaintance with, or a long residence among them; and its being so much easier to give a figure its appropriate dress, than its true character and expression'. Walker had costume-books in general in his sights rather than specifically on Russia, but the publication of *A Picturesque Representation* coincided in time with the appearance of a number of books purporting to show the costumes of the Russian empire and largely plagiarized from existing German works. The volumes issued by such publishers as Miller, Harding and Akkerman over the next few years have no relevance to our concern with the depiction of St Petersburg and its people but they do point to the growing interest in Russia that survived the blip of Tilsit to reach euphoric heights with our newly-recovered ally's struggle against the French on Russian soil in 1812, the subsequent defeat of Napoleon, and the tsar's triumphant visit to England in 1814.

The burning of Moscow evoked much interest in the old capital, reflected both in prose and pictorial descriptions, such as Akkerman's *Historical Sketch of Moscow* (1813), but St Petersburg was not forgotten. Atkinson and Walker's work was re-issued in 1812 and was soon followed by *Sketches of Russia* (1814) and *A Picture of St. Petersburgh* (1815). The text of *Sketches of Russia* and the fifteen original drawings, engraved by J. Bluch, were the work of the Russian diplomat and amateur artist Pavel Svin'in, and included six engravings of buildings in St Petersburg: alongside the familiar Bronze Horseman, the Ice Hills, and Kazan Cathedral, are the Field of Mars, the Summer Garden, and Thomon's new Exchange. More comprehensive coverage, as its title would suggest, is provided by *A Picture of St. Petersburgh*, in which 'the historical and descriptive account' of the city was by one W. Balston, but the twenty coloured acquatints were from drawings by the otherwise little-known French artist Mornay. The stylization and affectation of the eight engravings devoted to various sledges and carriages and their occupants only put in high relief the quality of Atkinson's etchings on the same subjects, but the twelve views of the city, 'taken on the spot', give the most up-to-date picture of Alexander's city available to the British public. They are arranged, calendar-fashion, according to the months of the year: thus, 'the Imperial Bank and the Shops' are shown for January, 'the Place of Peter the Great and the Senate House' for May, and so on. In addition to expected views across the river, there are others of the principal squares and streets. Several present what is to a certain extent an update of Hearn's views of, for example, the Arsenal on Liteinaia, Millionnaia Street, the *Gostinyi dvor* on Nevskii Prospekt, although among the new there is the quaintly and inaccurately titled 'View of the Canal of the Moika, the Bridge & the Police Establishment at St Petersburgh', which shows one of the earliest direct British contributions to the city – the iron bridge across the Neva, known as the Police Bridge, and later, as the Green Bridge and in Soviet times, as the People's (*Narodnyi*) Bridge, and designed by the architect and town-planner William Hastie, who had originally come to Russia to work for Charles Cameron at Tsarskoe Selo.

The names of Cameron and Hastie suggest another area in which the British made a pictorial contribution, although it remained out of sight of the British public and need not delay us. The British were prominent as architects and as landscape gardeners in the reigns of Catherine and Alexander and in both roles proved accomplished draughtsmen, leaving delicate coloured architectural drawings in the case of Cameron and Hastie and competent watercolours in the cases of the former master mason Adam Menelaws, another of Cameron's Scottish 'workmen' who achieved independent success and renown in Russia as both architect and garden designer and famous perhaps above all for building the 'Cottage' (1826–9) at Peterhof for Nicholas I, and of James Meader, who was responsible for the English garden at Peterhof. Meader left a series of unique watercolours of his creation at an early stage in its development, showing the cascade and an ornate bridge from petrified wood he constructed, as well as the Birch Cottage Quarenghi designed for Catherine.

The art of drawing was widely cultivated among the travelling gentlemen of the Grand Tour as an important aspect of their education. It gave them the opportunity to enliven their diaries and letters with drawing and occasionally watercolours of types and views and 'curiosities'. Among the first Russian examples was the diary of John Henniker during his northern tour in 1775–6, enlivened with coloured sketches of village scenes and modes of transport. Thomas Philip Robinson, Lord Grantham, arriving in Russia for the coronation of Alexander I, sketched similar subjects for his letters home, one of which, written on 11 December 1801, mentions that 'I have been this morning to see some drawings by a young Polish Artist named Soloffsky, lately come here; I admired them so much, for their spirit & boldness, very much in

Morland's style, that I have desired him to come & give me a few lessons'. The evidence would seem he was much in need of them, but he had found a skilled teacher in Aleksandr Orlovskii, soon to gain fame for his drawings of Count Platov and his Cossacks much engraved in London *c*.1814. A much higher degree of competence was exhibited, however, by several 'publishing' travellers during the same period, whose extensive narratives were quoted in earlier chapters.

The books of John Carr, John James, Robert Johnston and, of course, the professional painter Robert Ker Porter brought to the British public numerous coloured engravings based on drawings and watercolours they had made during their travels, complementing the detailed descriptions in the text. The sum total of plates specifically devoted to St Petersburg was not vast, but the subjects were only in part predictable. All the travellers had obviously made many more draw-ings, other than those selected for their books, and Porter referred to the many sketches 'taken in Russia' that he later lost at sea and elsewhere suggested that when words failed him, he resorted to conveying 'the visible form of the scene I have attempted to describe'. He was, however, twice blessed: he had the ability to evoke place both with pen and paint. The usually censorious *Edinburgh Review* went so far as to say that 'We really think a person who has never been at St Petersburgh, will rise, from Mr Porter's description, with a much more lively idea of the exterior of that magnificent capital than if he perused all the other accounts of it put together'.

Carr seems to have been the first to draw the famous 'little house' of Peter the Great', enclosed in its purpose-built protecting structure, on the Petersburg Side, as well as the interior and winter garden of the Taurida Palace. His third contribution was panoramic, a single large plate (18 × 5 inches) taken unusually from the steeple of the Peter and Paul Fortress and depicting square-on the otherwise familiar vista of the Hermitage and the Winter Palace, but without the talent and live-liness of an Atkinson. Out of the many coloured full-page illustrations in Porter only three are of St Petersburg, although one or two of the 'types' were urban. They are all wide panoramic views, but from the level of the river for the 'View from the English Quay' and 'Isaac's Place' or from the canal for the 'Stone Theatre', depicted for the first time by a British artist. Porter, achieving instant fame at the age of nineteen for his vast historical panorama, 'The Storming of Seringapatam', and invited to Russia by the tsar to paint a series of historical paintings of Peter the Great for the reconstructed Admiralty, saw the vistas of St Petersburg as so many theatrical back-drops; suggestive outlines, muted colours and vastnesses of virtually empty spaces – river, sky and square.

Johnston and James were drawn to post-1812 Russia and the melan-choly ruins of a burnt Moscow, but they also left conventional coloured plates of the capital, three in Johnston – the ubiquitous flying moun-tain, the Hermitage and the Kazan Cathedral – and two in James – the Kazan Cathedral again and the equally frequent Bronze Horseman, but under James's brush, acquiring a hint of menace and mystery and viewed from the front and from below, against a sky in which clouds obscure the late afternoon sun. It was to the Kazan Cathedral, both outside and in, that James was to return a decade later. His original volume, *Journal of a Tour in Germany, Sweden, Russia, Poland, during the Years 1813 and 1814*, proved very popular and went through three issues in as many years, but he expressed some dissatisfaction with the engravings that were made from his drawings by J. Clark. Perhaps the most talented of the amateur painters and watercolourists visiting Russia, he went to Italy soon after his return to study painting in Rome and Naples and he was also particularly interested in engraving tech-niques. A few years later, he decided to produce lithographs from his own drawings, some of which had been previously engraved in his *Journal*, others unpublished from his archive, 'so that they might not be subjected to such changes and variations of detail as too often occur when the original drawing and the print that is taken from it are furnished by different hands'. He produced some prints in chiaroscuro, after the example of artists in Munich and Vienna, 'many of whose productions are tinted with brown after the same fashion', but the four views of St Petersburg were all coloured. All the coloured lithographs were 'prepared after a manner that is, as far as I know, quite novel: though for such innovation, I ought perhaps rather to apologize to the public, than presume upon their approbation. They have been litho-graphed upon gray paper, and then tinted by the hand and touched with permanent white, and in some instances finished with the pen'. The lithographs were accompanied by texts, taken from the third edition of his own work or from the accounts of later travellers, and represented 'Mikhail Palace', which was in fact the Michael Castle, 'Newski Perpective', by the colonnade of the Kazan Cathedral and looking towards the Admiralty, 'Interior of the Kasan Church', and 'Boulevards', which was in fact a view between the Admiralty and the Winter Palace, looking towards the Strelka across the tree-lined boulevards installed by Alexander, but the Exchange it depicted was not 'built after a design of the late signor Guarenghi', but after Thomon's, and complete with rostral columns.

James's lithographs, published in 1826–7 as *Views in Germany, Sweden, Poland and Russia*, marked the climax of British architectural representations of Alexander's capital city. Among non-published watercolourists of the same period, one might point to William Markham (1796–1852), who visited Russia in 1823. A Russian watercolour by him was sold at Sotheby's on 5 November 1970 and a collection of his Russian watercolours was advertised for sale by Romulus of King's Road, London, in the 17–24 December 1970 issue of *Country Life* (including a photograph of a view of Vasil'evskii Island). A further curiosity is a watercolour of the Summer Garden, painted in 1821 by the sixteen-year-old John Cook, grandson of the author of the 1770 *Voyages and Travels*.

The first quarter of the nineteenth century had in general witnessed in Britain a great flourishing of sumptuously produced and illustrated books and editions in quarto and in folio, in which coloured engravings abounded and margins were wide and generous. We now enter a period when book production and printing was revolutionized and line-drawings in the text became popular and the feel and look of books changed. There were still to be well illustrated books, but mainly in black and white, unconsciously in tune with the perception of Russia during the reign of Nicholas I. If there were exceptions – and one might look, for instance, to Pinkerton's *Russia* (1833) with its eight coloured lithographs of types and pastimes from Russian originals – they were not relevant to St Petersburg. Siberia and, after the Crimean War, once more the Russian South were the exotic locales which brought more lavish productions from publishers (e.g. Thomas Witlam Atkinson's *Oriental and Western Siberia* (1858) and Carlo Bossoli's *Scenery of the Crimea* (1856)). The more routine travel accounts which included the capital, provided at best an uncoloured acquatint (William Rae Wilson's *Travels in Russia* (1828) with its view of the Admiralty), or a drawing of a *droshky* (John Barrow's *Excursions in the North of Europe* (1834), or disappointed expectations (George Francklin Atkinson's *Pictures from the North in Pen and Pencil; Sketched during a Summer Ramble* (1848), 'gathered from private letters, penned at the spot for friends at home, and drawn hastily, to render more graphic the account of those scenes they attempt to describe').

There were, however, two works, dating from the early years of Nicholas I's reign, that merit attention for their illustrations as much as for the text. The first was Dr A. Bozzo Granville's *St Petersburgh* (1828), where the author's gaze was directed 'to the more obvious features of "THINGS AS THEY ARE" during a brief residence in the autumn of 1827. To accompany his detailed descriptions, Granville supplied fifteen full-page drawings and plans as well as four in-text sketches of Russian 'types'. The drawings were very simple, designed to show the basic architectural features of the façades and few were enlivened by any allusion to their setting or by genre scenes. The black and white illustrations were taken from undisclosed sources with no indication of artist or, with three exceptions, of engraver. They nevertheless present a gallery of some of the impressive buildings that adorned the Russian capital by the end of the previous reign. Predictably, there were drawings of the Kazan Cathedral, the Winter Palace and the Hermitage Theatre on the mainland, and of the Academy of Arts, the Academy of Sciences and the Exchange on Vasil'evskii Island, but there were also drawings of Rossi's Elagin Palace on Elagin Island and of the Michael Castle, built for Paul I on the Fontanka. There was also an anticipation of the future: a completed St Isaac's Cathedral, obviously copied from Monferrand's model.

Much more distinguished for its illustrations was Leitch Ritchie's *A Journey to St. Petersburg and Moscow through Courland and Livonia* (1836) 'with twenty-five splendid engravings, by the first artists after drawings, by A.G. Vickers, Esq.'. It was a volume in Heath's Picturesque Annual series and followed earlier travel volumes by Ritchie, but it was the contribution of Alfred Gomersal Vickers which gave the work its lasting value and which, given his premature death within a year at the age of twenty-seven, became his memorial.

Ritchie and Vickers travelled together to Russia in 1833 and the resulting book is very much presented as a combined effort to the degree that Ritchie subordinates, as it were, his text to the accompanying engraving – or at least does so on twenty-five occasions. Ritchie is, however, at times very critical, determined to give 'a plain account of what I saw with his own eyes and heard with his own ears', whereas Vickers creates perhaps the most comprehensive British tribute to the beauties of the Russian capital (and, indeed, of the old capital, to which eleven of the engravings are devoted).

All the expected 'sights' are portrayed, the Admiralty, the Kazan Cathedral, the Fortress, Nevskii Prospekt, etc, but also more unusual ones (within the British tradition, at least), such as the cathedrals of the Trinity and St Nicholas, both on the Fontanka, as well as new additions, notably the Alexander Column. The architectural monuments, however, do not dominate, as a rule, they occupy the middle ground, while the foreground, river, canal, embankment, street, or square, is animated by scenes of workmen, tradesmen, boatmen, passers-by, road and river transport, even animals and birds (Ritchie calls attention to the pigeons strutting across Nevskii Prospekt near the *Gostinyi dvor*). There is much interplay between sky and water – this is a picturesque album after all. To the degree that the vast squares and streets are never left unpopulated, the immense sky is never without formations of cloud, filtering sun- or moonlight. Ritchie had suggested that 'it would be difficult, even for the talented artist whose productions grace these sketches, to convey an adequate idea of the scale on which this city is laid out; and yet, without doing so we do nothing'. Unlike some of his predecessors, Vickers does not provide panoramas and his is not a city that threatens, man is not overawed by buildings or the elements – even when the river is shown windswept and with high waves, as in the engraving entitled 'The Bourse and part of the Fortress' or, more so, in 'The Smolnoi Convent' (and memories of the great inundation of 1824 still very much alive), the people carry out their normal tasks. This is a lived-in, functioning city, where people also exist in harmony with the man-created monuments around them.

Each of the engravings was protected by tissue-paper; lifting it was to enter into a world of enchantment, a touch of the theatre, which is also part and parcel of St Petersburg's image. Vickers was well served by a bevy of engravers, no less than eight worked on the Petersburg plates alone, among whom the most notable were Thomas Higham and James Willmore. The engravings became even better known when they used soon after the end of the Crimean War in E.H. Nolan's *Illustrated History of the War against Russia* (1856). Vickers' original watercolours, including many scenes that were not engraved for Heath's annual and a few of which were exhibited during his lifetime, were sold soon after his death at Christie's in February 1837. Examples of his work are to be found in a number of private collections and public galleries (Brighton, York, Victoria and Albert). Most recently, three of his watercolours were sold by Agnew's in Bond Street, including the one of the parade at the unveiling of the Alexander Column, referred to 'by mistake' by Ritchie. Another of these watercolours is of the St Nicholas Cathedral which served as the frontispiece vignette to the album and reveals the sort of changes seemingly introduced by the engraver. In this specific case, the watercolour shows two workmen engaged in building over the canal in front of the cathedral's freestanding bell-tower the special pavilion, or Jordan, for the ceremony of the Blessing of the Waters; the vignette depicts the ceremony actually in progress, and watched by a small group of onlookers on the embankment.

The situation after the reign of Nicholas I and the Crimean War with regard to illustrative material on St Petersburg was gradually to change in one particular and radical way. The Crimean War, often called the first modern war for the application of new technology, was also the first war to be documented on the ground by newspaper reporters and photographers. The reports of William Russell of *The Times* were instrumental in convincing the publishing house of Thomas Agnew and Sons to send to the Crimea the photographer Roger Fenton, whose subsequent exhibition of 300 photographs aroused great public interest in London and the provinces in 1855–6. It was, however, to be several decades before photographs vied with, and eventually more or less replaced, drawings and engravings in books about Russia and its capital.

Nevertheless, a British photographer was soon to make a contribution of real importance, although not in the world of books.

William Carrick, a son of a Scottish timber merchant at Kronstadt, was a graduate of the Academy of Arts in St Petersburg and continued his studies in Rome throughout the years of the Crimean War. He was, however, drawn to the new-fangled photography and a visit to Scotland in 1857 gave him the chance to learn more about it and to make the acquaintance of a young photographer, John MacGregor. Carrick and MacGregor were to open a studio at No. 19 Malaia Morskaia, near the Nevskii Prospekt in 1859, and over the next thirteen years (until MacGregor's premature death in 1872) forged a strong partnership that was to bring recognition at the highest level. It was another Scot, C. Piazzi Smyth, the Astronomer Royal for Scotland, visiting Russia in that very year of 1859 'chiefly on scientific business', who subsequently wrote that 'Someone had told us on board ship that photography was miserable and hardly known in St Petersburg; that was, nevertheless, a decided mistake, for there is scarcely a more frequent sign to be met along all the principal streets, than PHOTOGRAPHER; and all the specimens exhibited outside the studios, chiefly large-sized portraits, were among the finest things we have ever seen in that line'. Competition was thus fairly severe in an as yet very restricted market and it was Carrick's willingness to look elsewhere for 'sitters', or a desire to fill an excess of spare time, that allowed him to create the particular niche that was to bring him lasting fame. When there were no middle- or upper-class commissions, he went out onto Nevskii and brought back to his studio the hawkers, pedlars, itinerant craftsmen, ordinary soldiers, and pilgrims in which the city abounded. He was to create a wonderful gallery of 'Russian types' or 'Hawkers' that he produced on 'cartes-de-visite'. It was a collection of some forty of them, 'representing peasants dressed according to their different trades and calling', that he presented to the heir to the throne, who rewarded him with a diamond ring. Carrick's 'types', to which later were to be added 'St Petersburg Scenes' (as well as scenes taken during his expeditions into the provinces in the 1870s), form a satisfying parallel to John Augustus Atkinson's coloured etchings from the beginning of the century; there is often a remarkable correspondence, a reminder of 'unchanging Russia', but also new types, new activities, in a changing Russia. Despite the fact that the original types were studio-staged, there is a freedom and naturalness that is reminiscent of Atkinson. The 'truth' and quality of Carrick's photographs impressed W.R.S. Ralston, a librarian at the British Museum and one of the pioneers of Russian studies in Britain. It was not by chance that Ralston, who is famous for his translations of the Russian fabulist Ivan Krylov, should follow his lively articles on the writer in *Good Words* in 1868 with an article on Carrick two years later. Ralston effectively introduced Carrick (whom he had met on a visit to St Petersburg) to the British public, suggesting that his photographs were 'as far as foreign visitors are concerned [. . .] of the highest value, teaching them so much while they are in the country, and enabling them after their return home, to recall to mind so vividly the forms and faces of the people among whom they have been sojourning'. Nevertheless, Carrick's work slid into obscurity following his death in 1878. It is only of quite recent times that the vogue for books of photographs of old Russia (such as Kyril Fitzlyon and Tatiana Browning's *Before the Revolution* and Marvin Lyons's *Russia in Original Photographs 1860–1920*) has brought wide use of photographs by Carrick and other masters like Bulla to evoke late-nineteenth and early twentieth-century St Petersburg, and the ceaseless activity of a descendant, Felicity Ashbee, has illuminated his life and career.

Piazzi Smyth, the astronomer, whose remarks on the proliferation of photographers in St Petersburg were quoted above, was, not unexpectedly, very interested himself in the new art. He mentions that the photographic equipment he had brought from Scotland was eventually delivered to the Pulkovo Observatory near Tsarskoe Selo and that thereafter 'day after day, as long as any chemical light endured, we hammered away with a couple of stereoscopic cameras, wet collodion and dry, at both the front and back of this splendid building and its various surroundings of interest'. The age of the book illustrated with photographs had not yet come, however, so he also amused himself with a sketch-pad during his visit. Publishing his *Three Cities in Russia* in 1862, he drew attention instead to 'the six wood-engravings [. . .] from sketches entirely original, taken by myself in Russia; and looked after unceasingly since, to ensure the engraver giving a faithful reproduction of whatever I had been able in the drawings to transfer from the natural scene to paper'. The two engravings on St Petersburg add little but a dash of humour to familiar scenes of transport in the city. In fact, the last decades of the nineteenth century brought little that was novel and new to illustrate its life and architecture. The city seemed to be held tightly in the straitjacket of its past. Drawings and photographs were predictable and the expectations aroused by promising titles were usually disappointed. Thomas Michell's *Russian Pictures: Drawn with*

Pen and Pencil (1889) was constrained by the format of the 'Pen and Pencil' series: the necessity to cover the whole of the Russian Empire meant restricting St Petersburg to drawings of the Alexander Column, St Isaac's, the Peter and Paul Fortress and Cathedral, and a collage of various 'sights'. Their presentation recalls the sort of illustrations that were appearing at this time in such publications as *The Illustrated London News* (founded 1842) and *The Graphic* (1869), which proved a more valuable, entertaining and up-to-date source than most books. The *Illustrated London News*'s 'special artist' produced, for instance, a lively sketch entitled 'Taking Water from the Neva at St. Petersburg' in the issue for 7 February 1874. On the same page there was a historically very interesting and probably unique sketch, signed 'FW' (the special artist or another?), showing 'The British Embassy at St. Petersburg Illuminated for the Duke of Edinburgh's Marriage'.

By the beginning of the twentieth century photographs had become the staple form of illustration and the quality and variety improved significantly. Henry Norman's *All the Russias* (1902) was well illustrated 'mainly from the author's photographs', although, once again, only a handful were of St Petersburg. It was, nonetheless, a reminder that we have entered the period of the postcard and there was a proliferation of series of 'types', of scenes from throughout Russia, its provincial cities and towns, but also of the capital and its environs, all the monuments, old and recent, but also a great variety of street scenes, forms of transport, festivities, and mostly coloured. Many were copied in Germany, a few in England, but tourists and residents sent them to Britain in their hundreds. Two books from these years, well illustrated, and wholly devoted to the capital, are worthy of particular attention, not least for their texts, both written for once by men who really knew the city and had lived there for many years.

William Barnes Steveni's *Petrograd Past and Present* (1915), as its title indicates, dates from the period when, for patriotic reasons, the city's name was changed, while George Dobson's *Petersburg* dates from a few years earlier (1910). Steveni accompanies his narrative, which is part history, part contemporary guide, with thirty illustrations, which demonstrate the uses to which photograph was put: photographs of works of arts (an area in which Carrick had, incidentally, been a pioneer), including portraits of personalities as well as of eighteenth-century scenes, alongside photographs of scenes, 'types' and events. It is up-to-date, in that its frontispiece is the Church of the Resurrection of Christ on the Catherine Canal, built on the spot where Alexander II had been assassinated. Dobson describes his various encounters with the late Charles Heath, who had been tutor to Nicholas II, and mentions that he, as well as his wife and daughter, were accomplished watercolourists and that his paintings 'still fetch high prices'. I am unaware of the present whereabouts of any example of his work, as I am of the original watercolours that were reproduced for Dobson's *Petersburg*. It would, however, be more correct to say that Dobson's text was subordinate to the paintings of F. de Haenen, of which there are thirty-two, sixteen in colour and sixteen in black and white, and all full-page. It is an arrangement reminiscent of the early nineteenth century, of the work of Atkinson and Walker and of Mornay and Balston.

F. de Haenen is almost as mysterious and obscure a figure as Mornay. He was either French or Belgian and he was working for the French magazine *L'Illustration* and contributing to the *Illustrated London News* towards the end of the nineteenth century but in 1902 he was sent to South Africa as war artist for *The Graphic*. He must have gone to Russia around the time of the Anglo-Russian Entente of 1907 and the watercolours he made there appeared in *Petersburg* and its companion volumes *Moscow* (1912) and *Provincial Russia* (1913). Two watercolours not used in his books, 'Ice Slide, St Petersburg' and 'Bell Ringers', were, however, recently offered for sale by an American dealer. His published paintings of St Petersburg make a substantial and original contribution to a subject that was much in need of renewal and revival. In many respects they recall the watercolours of Vickers, but add much that was new. There are almost no architectural set-pieces, although the Winter Palace, the Bronze Horseman, the Peter and Paul fortress and other buildings inevitably figure in the background of many paintings, but the emphasis is on scenes and ceremonies and the people are not mere puppets and stage decoration. The 'eternal' Petersburg types – yardman, coachman, wet nurse – all appear, traditional, but individualised, like the old guardsman in front of the Winter Palace. There are additions to the gallery: a trio of students walking down a street, a man and wife drinking tea by their samovar, colourfully attired members of the Duma, drozhki drivers crowding round a tea-stall. The St Petersburg portrayed is demonstrably the city at the turn of the century, Nicholas II's city, in which he is shown with his wife at a famous historical costume ball, reviewing his troops, and taking part in the blessing of the waters.

Photographs of Petrograd in Revolution, of Petrograd/Leningrad under the Soviets appeared in many contemporary books, journals and newspapers, although two watercolours entitled 'Attack on the Winter Palace' and 'Burials of Victims of the Revolution', dated Petrograd 1916, by E. Barnard Lintott were photographed for the second volume of Ambassador Buchanan's memoirs (1923). The originals are now in the Imperial War Museum. It was, however, only to be in the art books of the 1970s and subsequently that St Petersburg became alive again both in impressive reproductions of old paintings, engravings, and photographs and in new colour photography of a quality that was far more impressive than that of the accompanying text. Eric Baschet's *Russia 1904–1924: The Revolutionary Years: A History in Documentary Photographs* (1989) is an impressive collection, while Earl Beasley and Garry Gibbons produced colour photography of often quite breathtaking beauty for the large-sized *Imperial Splendour: Palaces and Monasteries of Old Russia* (1991). The palaces of the capital and its environs figure prominently in that volume, but provide the whole subject for *The Romanov Legacy: The Palaces of St Petersburg* (1994), in which Leonid Bogdanov's camera explores the interiors of some nine palaces, some of which have never been previously revealed. St Petersburg reborn, restored, rebuilt, renovated in the years up to and including the tercentenary, continues to inspire painters as well as photographers. In October 2002 John James, felicitously named but no distant relation of the Oxford man who produced his watercolours in Alexander I's reign, exhibited in London thirty oils he had painted during visits in the summer and winter of the previous year and spoke of discovering a 'sleeping beauty'. What he sought to capture was not the riverscapes and panoramas beloved of so many eighteenth-century artists and visitors, more the little corners by canals and in courtyards and at the ends of streets, parts of houses, rather than the whole, lit by sun, water, or snow, a St Petersburg colour-washed rather than dark and drear, emphasizing the intimacy of a Venice rather than the limitless expanses of sky and square and waterfront.

LIST OF SOURCES, ARRANGED
BY CHAPTER AND ORDERED
BY FIRST QUOTATION

Chapter 1: First Reports of Peter's City

[Defoe, Daniel] *The Consolidator: Or, Memoirs of Sundry Transactions from the World in the Moon.* Translated from the Lunar Language by the True-born English Man (London, 1705)

[Defoe, Daniel], *The History of the Wars of His Present Majesty Charles XII King of Sweden; from His First Landing in Denmark, to His Return from Turkey to Pomerania,* by a Scots Gentleman in the Sweedish [*sic*] Service (London: Bell, Varnam at alii, 1715).

[Defoe, Daniel], *An Impartial History of the Life and Actions of Peter Alexowitz, the Present Czar of Muscovy* . . . written by a British Officer in the Service of the Czar (London: Chetwood, Stagg *et alii*, 1723)

Perry, John, *The State of Russia, under the Present Czar* (London: Tooke, 1716; reprint: London: Cass, 1967)

Whitworth, Charles, *An Account of Russia as it was in the Year 1710* (Strawberry Hill, 1758)

Whitworth, Charles, 'Dispatches', in *Sbornik Imperatorskogo Russkogo istoricheskogo obshchestva [Almanac of the Imperial Russian Historical Society], vol.* 61 (Spb., 1888)

[Weber, F.C.], *The Present State of Russia,* vol. 1 (London: Taylor, Innys and Osborn, 1723; reprint: London: Cass, 1968)

Bruce, Peter Henry, *Memoirs of Peter Henry Bruce, Esq., a Military Officer, in the Services of Prussia, Russia, and Great Britain* . . . (Dublin: Sheppard *et alii*, 1783; reprint: London: Cass, 1970)

Jefferies, James, 'Dispatches', in *SIRIO [Almanac of the Imperial Russian Historical Society]*, vol. 61 (Spb., 1888)

Motraye, A. de la, *The Voyages and Travels in Several Provinces and Places of the Kingdoms and Dukedoms of Prussia, Russia, Poland &c.,* vol. 3 (London: Symon, Newton *et alii*, 1732)

Chapter 2: The City of the First Empresses, 1725–61

[Ward/Rondeau/Vigor, Jane], *Letters from a Lady, Who Resided Some Years in Russia, to Her Friend in England* (2nd ed., London: Dodsley, 1777)

Claudius Rondeau, 'Dispatches, 1728–33', in *SIRIO [Almanac of the Imperial Russian Historical Society]*, vol. 66 (Spb., 1889)

John Cook, M.D., *Voyages and Travels through the Russian Empire, Tartary, and Part of the Kingdom of Persia*, vol. 1 (Edinburgh: for the Author, 1770)

Justice, Elizabeth, *Voyage to Russia* (London: for the author, 1739)

Dashwood, Sir Francis, 'Diary of a Visit to St Petersburg in 1733', edited by Betty Kemp, *Slavonic and East European Review*, vol. 38 (1959), 194–222.

Algarotti, Francesco, *Letters from Count Algarotti to Lord Hervey and the Marquis Scipio Maffei, containing the State of the Trade, Marine, Revenues, and Forces of the Russian Empire*, vol. 1 (London: Johnson and Payne, 1769)

Charles Cottrell, 'Letter from Basel, August 1741', in Igor Vinogradoff, 'Russian Missions to London, 1711–1789: Further Extracts from the Cottrell Papers', *Oxford Slavonic Papers*, New Series vol. 15 (1982)

Finch, Edward, 'Letter from St Petersburg, 2/13 June 1741', in *SIRIO [Almanac of the Imperial Russian Historical Society]*, vol. 85 (1893)

Hanway, Jonas, *An Historical Account of the British Trade over the Caspian Sea*, vol. 1 (2nd ed., London: Dodsley, 1754)

Dumaresq, Daniel, 'Letter', British Library, Add. Mss 32,420, f. 159v.

Chapter 3: Catherine the Great's City and the Northern Tour

Wraxall, Nathaniel, *A Tour through Some of the Northern Parts of Europe, Particularly Copenhagen, Stockholm, and Petersburgh. In a Series of Letters* (2nd ed. corrected, London: Cadell, 1775) [First edition entitled *Cursory Remarks Made in a Tour through Some of the Northern Parts of Europe* (London: Cadell, 1775)]

Coxe, William, *Travels in Poland, Russia, Sweden, and Denmark* (5th edition, London: Cadell and Davies, 1802)

Dimsdale, Elizabeth, *An English Lady at the Court of Catherine the Great: The Journal of Baroness Elizabeth Dimsdale*, edited by A.G. Cross (Cambridge: Crest, 1989)

Norman, George, 'Letter to his stepmother Eleonora Norman from St Petersburg 10 August 1784', Kent Archives Office, Maidstone, U310 c3

Brogden, James, 'Letters', in James Cracraft, 'James Brogden in Russia, 1787–1788', *SEER*, vol. 47 (1969), 219–44

Swinton, Andrew, *Travels into Norway, Denmark, and Russia, in the Years 1788, 1789, 1790, and 1791* (London: Robinson, 1792)

[Colmore, Lionel], *Letters from the Continent: Describing the Manners and Customs of Germany, Poland, Russia, and Switzerland, in the Years 1790, 1791, and 1792: to a Friend Residing in England* (London, 1812)

Parkinson, John, *A Tour of Russia, Siberia and the Crimea 1792–1794* (London: Cass, 1971)

Cathcart, Lady Jane, 'Letter to Mrs Catherine Walkinshaw of 8/19 February 1769', in E. Maxtone Graham, *The Beautiful Mrs. Graham and the Cathcart Circle* (London: Nisbet, 1927), pp. 8–14

Richardson, William, *Anecdotes of the Russian Empire* (London: Strahan and Cadell, 1784; reprint: London: Cass, 1968)

Howard, John, *The State of Prisons* (3rd ed., London, 1784; reprint: London: Dent, 1929)

Newberry, Thomas, 'Letter from St Petersburg, 26 August (OS) 1766 to Charles Dingley of Lamb Abbey', British Library, Add. Mss. 34,713

Henniker, John, 'A Northern Tour in the Years 1775 and 1776 through Copenhagen and Petersburgh to the River Swir joining the Lakes of Onega and Ladoga in a Series of Letters', University Library, Cambridge, Add. Mss. 8720.

Howard, John, *An Account of the Principal Lazarettos in Europe; with Various Papers Relative to the Plague: Together with further Observations on Some Foreign Prisons and Hospitals* . . . (2nd ed., London, 1791)

Harris, Katherine, 'Diary 1777–83', Public Record Office, Kew, Ms. 30/43

Elliot, Sir Hugh, *Life and Letters of Sir Gilbert Elliot*, edited by the Countess of Minto, vol. 1 (London, 1874)

Craven, Lady Elizabeth, *A Journey through the Crimea to Constantinople* (London, 1789)

Storch, Henry, *The Picture of Petersburg* (London: Longman and Rees), 1801 (addition by the translator, the Rev. William Tooke)

Meader, James, 'Letter book', St Peterburgskoe Otdelenie Arkhiva RAN [Petersburg Division of the Russian Academy of Sciences Archive], Razriad IV, op. 1, d. 999

'A Description of the City of Petersburgh', *The Times* (15–17 November 1786)

Chapter 4: Alexander I's Imperial City

Clarke, Edward Daniel, *Travels in Various Countries of Europe Asia and Africa: Part the First: Russia Tahtary and Turkey*, vol. 1 (4th ed., London, 1816)

Carr, John, *A Northern Summer; Or, Travels round the Baltic: through Denmark, Sweden, Russia, Prussia, and Part of Germany, in the Year 1804* (London: Philipps, 1805)

Porter, Robert Ker, *Travelling Sketches in Russia and Sweden during the Years 1805, 1806, 1807, 1808*, 2 vols. (London: Stockdale, 1813)

Freemantle, Captain Thomas, 'Diary and Letters', *The Wynne Diaries*, vol.3 (Oxford: Oxford University Press, 1940)

Bloomfield, Lord Benjamin, *Memoir of Benjamin Lord Bloomfield G.C.B., G.C.H.*, edited by Georgiana, Lady Bloomfield, 2 vols.(London: Chapman and Hall, 1884)

Wilmot, Martha and Catherine, *The Russian Journals of Martha and Catherine Wilmot [. . .] 1803–1808*, edited by the Marchioness of Londonderry and H.M. Hyde (London: Macmillan, 1934)

Storch, Henry, *The Picture of Petersburg*, translated by William Tooke (London: Longman and Rees, 1801)

Heber, Richard, *The Life of Reginald Heber, D.D. Lord Bishop of Calcutta*, by his Widow, vol. 1 (London: Murray, 1830)

James, J.T., *Journal of a Tour in Germany, Sweden, Russia, Poland during the Years 1813 and 1814* (London: Murray, 1816)

Johnston, Robert, *Travels through Part of the Russian Empire and the Country of Poland* (London: Stockdale, 1815)

'A Surgeon in the British Navy', *A Voyage to St. Petersburg in 1814, with Remarks on the Imperial Russian Navy* (London: Phillips, 1822)

Jones, George Matthew, *Travels in Norway, Sweden, Finland, Russia, and Turkey; also along the Coasts of the Sea of Azof and of the Black Sea*, 2 vols. (London: Murray, 1827)

Lytellton, Lady Sarah, *Correspondence of Sarah Spenser Lady Lytellton 1787–1870* (London: Murray, 1912)

Lee, Robert, *The Last Days of Alexander, and the First Days of Nicholas* (London: Bentley, 1854)

Chapter 5: The City under Nicholas I, 1825–55

[Disbrowe, Lady Charlotte], *Old Days in Diplomacy: Recollections of a Closed Century* (London: Jarrold and Sons, 1903)

Granville, A.B., *St. Petersburgh. A Journal of Travels to and from That Capital; through Flanders, the Rhenish Provinces, Prussia, Russia, Poland, Silesia, Saxony, the Federated States of Germany, and France*, 2 vols. (London: Colburn, 1828)

Coghlan, Francis, *A Guide to St. Petersburg & Moscow* (London: Prout, for the author, 1836)

Ritchie, Leitch, *A Journey to St. Petersburg and Moscow through Courland and Livonia* (London: Longman, 1836)

[W., T.D.], *A Hand-Book for Travellers in Denmark, Norway, Sweden, and Russia, being a guide to the Principal Routes in those countries, with a minute description of Copenhagen, Stockholm, St. Petersburg, and Moscow* (London: Murray, 1839)

Thompson, Edward P., *Life in Russia: Or, The Discipline of Despotism* (London: Smith, Elder, 1848)

Cobden, Richard, 'Diary', British Library, Add. Mss. 43674, vol 38 D & E; and 'Letters', *ibid.* Add. Mss. 50749.

Bourke, Richard Southwell, *St. Petersburg and Moscow: A Visit to the Court of the Czar, 2 vols.* (London: Colburn, 1846)

Marchioness of Westminster, *Diary of a Tour in Sweden, Norway and Russia, in 1827. With Letters* (London:Hurst and Blackett, 1879)

[Kinglake, William], 'A Summer in Russia', *New Monthly Magazine*, Parts 2–3 (1846)

Rigby, Elizabeth (Lady Eastlake), *Letters from the Shores of the Baltic* (2nd ed., London: Murray, 1842)

Morton, Edward, *Travels in Russia, and a Residence at St. Petersburg and Odessa, in the Years 1827–1829; intended to give some account of Russia as it is, and not as it is represented to be, &c. &c.* (London: Longman, Rees, Orme, Brown, and Green, 1830)

Raikes, Thomas, *Visit to St. Petersburg, in the Winter of 1829–30* (London: Bentley, 1839)

Londonderry, Lady Frances, *Russian Journal of Lady Londonderry 1836–37*, edited by W.A.L. Seaman and J.R. Sewell (London: Murray, 1973)

Stephens, J.L., *Incidents of Travel in Greece Turkey Russia and Poland* (Edinburgh: Chambers, 1839)

'A Lady Ten Years' Resident in that Country' [McCoy, Rebecca], *The Englishwoman in Russia; Impressions of the Society and Manners of the Russians at Home* (London: Murray, 1855)

Chapter 6: The Reigns of Alexander II and Alexander III, 1855–94

Mahony, J., *Book of the Baltic, Being the North of Europe Steam Company's Route to Denmark, Sweden and Russia, Norway, Prussia and the Hanseatic Ports* (London: Effingham Wilson, 1857)

Weir, Rev. Archibald, 'St. Petersburg and Moscow', in Francis Galton (ed.), *Vacation Tourists and Notes of Travel in 1861* (Cambridge and London, 1862), pp. 1–50

Smyth, C. Piazzi, *Three Cities in Russia*, 2 vols. (London: Lovell, Reeve, 1862)

Liddon, Henry, from John Octavius Liddon, *Life and Letters of Henry Parry Liddon [. . .]* (London: Longmans, Green, 1904)

Dodgson, Rev. C.L. (Lewis Carroll), 'Journal of a Tour in Russia in 1867', *The Works of Lewis Carroll* (Feltham: Spring Books, 1965)

Stanley, A.P., *The Life and Correspondence of Arthur Penrhyn Stanley, D.D., Late Dean of Westminster*, edited by Rowland E. Prothero, vol. 2 (London, 1893)

Laurie, W.F.B., *Northern Europe, (Denmark, Sweden, Russia,) Local, Social, and Political, in 1861* (London: Saunders & Otley, 1862)

Atkinson, J. Beavington, *An Art Tour to Northern Capitals of Europe* (London: Macmillan, 1873; reprinted as *An Art Tour to Russia* (London: Waterstone, 1986))

Sala, George Augustus, *The Life and Adventures of George Augustus Sala*, 2 vols. (London: Cassell, 1895)

Wellesley, F.A., *With the Russians in Peace and War: Recollections of a Military Attaché* (London: Nash, 1905)

Baddeley, John F., *Russia in the 'Eighties': Sport and Politics* (London: Longmans, Green, 1921

Whishaw, Fred J., *Out of Doors in Tsarland: A Record of the Seeings and Doings of a Wanderer in Russia* (London: Longman, Green, 1893)

Anon, *Half Hours in the Far North: Life amid Snow and Ice* (London: Daldy, Isbister, & Co, 1877)

Lyall, Sir Alfred, *The Life of the Marquis of Dufferin and Ava*, 2 vols. (London: Nelson, 1905)

Michell, Thomas, *Russian Pictures Drawn with Pen and Pencil* (London: Religious Tract Society, 1889)

Chapter 7: Straddling the Centuries, the Reign of Nicholas II, 1894–1917

Dobson, G., *St. Petersburg* (London: Black, 1910)

Williams, Harold Whitmore, *Russia of the Russians* (London: Pitman, 1914)

Walpole, Hugh, *The Secret City* (London: Macmillan, 1919)

Scott, A MacCallum, *Through Finland to St. Petersburg* (London: Grant Richards, 1908)

Close, Etta, *Excursions and Some Adventures* (London: Constable, 1926)

Maugham, W. Somerset, *A Writer's Notebook* (London: Heinemann, 1949)

Reynolds, Rothay, *My Russian Year* (London: Mills & Boon, 1913)

Reynolds, Rothay, *My Slav Friends* (London: Mills & Boon, 1916)

Pares, Bernard, *My Russian Memoirs* (London: Cape, 1931)

Bruce, H.J., *Silken Dalliance* (London: Constable: 1946)

Bechhofer, C.E., *A Wanderer's Log, Being Some Memories of Travel in India, the Far East, Russia, the Mediterraneum & Elsewhere* (London: Mills & Boon, 1922)

Baedeker, Karl, *Russia with Teheran, Port Arthur, and Peking* (Leipzig: Baedeker and London: Allen & Unwin, 1914)

Leigh, Maxwell S. (ed.), *The Memoirs of James Whishaw* (London: Methuen, 1935)

Fleming, Andrew M. and Geoffrey Jefferson, *The Work of the Anglo-Russian Hospital (from September, 1915, to June, 1917)* (London, 1917)

Swann, Herbert, *Home on the Neva* (London: Gollancz, 1968)

Steveni, William Barnes, *Petrograd, Past and Present* (London: Grant Richards, 1915)

Stead, Jennifer, 'A Bradford Mill in St. Petersburg', *Old West Riding*, vol. 2 (Winter 1982), pp. 13–20

Meakin, Annette M.B., *Russia: Travels and Studies* (London: Hugh and Blackett, 1906)

Elizabeth Hill, *In the Mind's Eye* (Lewis: Book Guild, 1999)

Jones, Stinton, *Russia in Revolution, Being the Experiences of an Englishman in Petrograd during the Revolution* (London: Jenkins, 1919)
Buchanan, Meriel, *The Dissolution of an Empire* (London: Murray, 1932)

Chapter 8: The City from Revolution to Closure, 1917–38
Wells, H.G., *Russia in the Shadows* (London: Hodder and Stoughton, 1921)
Conway, Sir Martin, *Art Treasures in Soviet Russia* (London: Arnold, 1924)
Preston, Thomas, *Before the Curtain* (London: Murray, 1950)
Lawton, Lancelot, *The Russian Revolution (1917–1926)* (London: Macmillan, 1927)
Bullard, Reader, *Inside Stalin's Russia: The Diaries of Reader Bullard 1930–1934*, edited by Julian and Margaret Bullard (Charlbury: Day Books, 2000)
Paget, Lady Muriel, 'Some Pictures of Soviet Russia: VI Leningrad', *The Daily Telegraph* (7 February 1927)
Monkhouse, Allan, *Moscow, 1911–1933* (London: Gollancz, 1933)
Byron, Robert, *First Russia, Then Tibet* (London: Macmillan, 1933)
Ashmead-Bartlett, E., *The Riddle of Russia* (London: Cassell, 1929)
Stucley, Peter, *Russian Spring* (London: Selwyn & Blount, 1937)
Pope-Hennessy, Una, *The Closed City: Impressions of a Visit to Leningrad* (London: Hutchinson, 1938)
Buchanan, Meriel, 'The Story of an Englishwoman', in her *Victorian Gallery* (London: Cassell, 1956)
Paget Collection, Leeds Russian Archive, University of Leeds, Ms. 1405, Distressed British Subjects in Russia Box
'Home for Needy Britons in Russia: Woman Who Works for Their Comfort in a Forest Glade', *Daily Sketch* (12 October 1936)

Chapter 9: From Leningrad under Siege to St Petersburg Reborn, 1938 to the present
Werth, Alexander, *Leningrad* (London: Hamish Hamilton, 1944)
Berlin, Isaiah, 'A Visit to Leningrad: Encounters with an Impoverished but Unquenched Intelligentsia after the Siege', *Times Literary Supplement* (23 March 2001)
Parker, John, *Forty-Two Days in the Soviet Union* (London: Wells Gardner, Darton & Co, 1946)
Priestley, J.B., *Russian Journey* (London: Society for Cultural Relations, 1946)
Chappelow, Allan, *Russian Holiday* (London: Harrap, 1955)
Edmonds, Richard, *Russian Vistas* (London: Phene Press, 1958)
Newman, Bernard, *Visa to Russia* (London: Herbert Jenkins, 1959)
Wilson, Colin, 'An Outsider in Leningrad' – I: 'Journey to Squalor', II: 'The Great Myth' *Sunday Times* (1960)

Hayter, Sir William, 'Style in Leningrad', *The Observer* (25 December 1960)

Hingley, Ronald, *Under Soviet Skins: An Untourist's Report* (London: Hamish Hamilton, 1961)

Sillitoe, Alan, *Road to Volgograd* (London: Macmillan, 1964)

Thubron, Colin, *Among the Russians* (London: Heinemann, 1983)

Fallowell, Duncan, *One Hot Summer in St. Petersburg* (London: Cape, 1994; new ed. London: Vintage, 1995)

Hogan, Desmond, 'White Nights, Winter Magic', *The Times* (Saturday 9 September 1989)

Wistrich, Robert S., 'Letter from St Petersburg', *Times Literary Supplement* (22 March 2002)

Mooney, Bel, 'The Town that Peter Built', *The Times* (Saturday 15 July 2006)

Chapter 10: Images of St Petersburg

[Walker, James], *Paramythia, Or, Mental Pastimes: being original anecdotes, historical, descriptive, humourous, and witty collected chiefly during a long residence at the court of Russia by the author* (London: Lawler and Quick, 1821)

[Atkinson, J.A. and Walker, James], *A Picturesque Representation of the Manners, Customs, and Amusements of the Russians in one hundred plates* (London: Bulmer, 1803–4)

Robinson, Thomas Philip, 3rd Baron Grantham, *The Grand Tour 1801–1803, being Letters from Lord Grantham to his Mother, from Prussia, Saxony, Russia, Austria, Switzerland, Italy & France* (Penzance: Triton Press, 1979)

Porter, Robert Ker, *Travelling Sketches in Russia and Sweden during the Years 1805, 1806, 1807, 1808*, 2 vols. (London: Stockdale, 1813)

Edinburgh Review, vol. 14 (1809), pp. 170–87

James, J.T., *Views in Russia, Sweden, Poland and Germany* (London: Murray, 1826)

Ritchie, Leitch, *A Journey to St. Petersburgh and Moscow through Courland and Livonia* (London: Longman, 1836)

Smyth, C. Piazzi, *Three Cities in Russia*, 2 vols. (London: Lovell, Reeve, 1862)

Ralston, W.R.S., 'A Few Russian Photographers', *Good Words* (October 1870)

INDEX OF NAMES

Chudleigh, Elizabeth, Duchess of
    Kingston 71
Clark, J. 310
Clarke, Edward Daniel 108–9
Close, Etta 209–10
Cobden, Richard 147–8
Coghlan, Frances 144, 163
Colmore, Lionel 58, 67–8, 86
Constantine, Grand Duke 127, 128, 142
Conway, Sir Martin 249–51
Cook, Dr John 33, 40, 45–7, 49, 54, 55,
    99, 311
Cook, John 311
Cook, Thomas viii
Cottrell, Charles 50
Coxe, James 71
Coxe, Rev. William ix, xi, 56, 59, 60, 65,
    66, 69, 73, 77, 80, 83, 84, 89, 91, 93, 98,
    99, 126, 132
Craven, Lady Elizabeth 96, 128
Cromie, Capt. F.N.A. 238
Cunningham, Edward Francis 303
Custine, Marquis de 146

Dashkova, Princess Ekaterina 114
Dashwood, Sir Francis 34–9, 45, 47, 99,
    127, 301
Daunt, Dorothea 266, 267
Dawe, George 153
Defoe, Daniel xiii, 1–4
Dickens, Charles 164, 189
Dimsdale, Elizabeth 57, 60, 63–4, 72,
    73–4, 77, 80, 93–4, 103–5
Dimsdale, Dr Thomas 57, 74, 103
Disbrowe, Charlotte 142–3, 162
Disbrowe, Sir Edward 142, 162
Dmitrii Pavlovich, Grand Duke 225, 252,
    254
Dobson, George 200–3, 205–6, 216,
    317–18
Dodgson, Rev. C.L. (Lewis Carroll) 172–4
Dostoevskii, F.M. vii, 146, 211–12, 223,
    245, 285, 286
Dufferin, Lord Frederick 189, 190–1
Dunmore, Helen 271

Edinburgh, Alfred, Duke of 175
Edmonds, Richard 283–4
Eliseev Brothers 202, 203, 213, 273, 282
Elizabeth (Elizaveta Petrovna) 37, 38, 51,
    59, 104, 110, 293, 302
Elizabeth (Elizaveta Alekseevna) 135–6
Elizabeth II, HM the Queen 299
Erskine, Dr Robert 13
Eltsyn, Boris 295, 298
Evans, Hill 25, 28, 34

Falconet, Etienne-Maurice 66, 75–7,
    114, 302–3
Falconet, Pierre 303
Fallowell, Duncan 294, 296–7
Fel'ten, Iurii 61, 72, 115
Finch, Edward 50–1
Fontana, Giovanni 16
Fox, Charles James 106–7
Frederick the Great 48, 123
Freemantle, Capt. Thomas 112
Froom, Violet 264

Gardner, James 32
Gibbons, Gary 319
Glinka, Mikhail 155–6, 175
Gogol', N.V. 223, 286, 296
Gorbachev, Mikhail 295
Gordon, Admiral Thomas 35
Gor'kii, Maksim 248
Gould, William 68–9, 112–13
Granville, Dr A.B. ix, 144, 161–2, 312
Green, George 144
Gumilev, Nikolai 220

Haenen, F. de 200, 318–19
Hanway, Jonas 51–3, 59
Harris, Sir James 89, 95
Harris, Katherine 95
Hastie, William 308
Hawkins, Capt. James 67, 85
Hayter, Sir William 288–9, 301
Healey, Rose 270
Hearn, Joseph xiv, 303–4, 305, 307
Heath, Charles 318

SUBJECT INDEX

ACKNOWLEDGEMENTS

I am grateful to the following authors and editors for their gracious permission to include extracts from their works: Lady Margaret Bullard, *Inside Stalin's Russia*; Mr Duncan Fallowell, *One Hot Summer in St Petersburg*; Ms Bel Mooney, 'The Town that Peter Built'; Mr Alan Sillitoe, *The Road to Volgograd*; Mrs Jean Stafford Smith, *In the Mind's Eye*; Mr Colin Thubron, *Among the Russians*.

I acknowledge permission from the Curtis Brown Group Ltd on behalf of the Isaiah Berlin Literary Trust to include passages from Sir Isaiah's 'A Visit to Leningrad'; and from Mr Richard Davies and the University of Leeds for permission to use unpublished papers and photographs in the Leeds Russian Archive.

Most of the illustrations have come from plate books and engravings in my own collection and in that of my friend Mr Robert Dimsdale, but I am also truly grateful to Miss Felicity Ashbee for the photographs taken by her ancestor William Carrick; to Mr Christopher Kingzett and Agnew's of Bond Street for the unpublished watercolours of A.G. Vickers, and to John James for his paintings.